HISTORIC ARMIES AND NAVIES

The Army of Maria Theresa

(*Frontispiece*) *The Empress-Queen Maria Theresa* (The Mansell Collection)

HISTORIC ARMIES AND NAVIES

The Army of Maria Theresa

The Armed Forces of Imperial Austria, 1740–1780

CHRISTOPHER DUFFY

DAVID & CHARLES
NORTH POMFRET (VT) VANCOUVER · LONDON

In memory of James Duffy,
first lieutenant in the regiment of Marschall,
killed at Meissen 21 September 1759

ISBN 0 7153 7387 0

Set in 11 on 13 Baskerville
and printed in Great Britain
by Redwood Burn Limited, Trowbridge & Esher
for David & Charles (Publishers) Limited
Brunel House Newton Abbot Devon

Published in Canada
by Douglas David & Charles Limited
1875 Welch Street North Vancouver BC

Contents

Introduction and Acknowledgements 6

1 The Theresian State 8

2 The Supreme Direction of the Armed Forces 18

3 The Officers 24

4 The Men 47

5 The Infantry of the Line 63

6 The 'Croats' 82

7 The Cavalry 91

8 The Artillery 105

9 The Technicians 118

10 Financiers, Commissaries, Doctors and Priests 123

11 The Control of the Army 135

12 Military Operations 139

13 Maria Theresa's Army and the Test of War 145

Notes 215

Appendix: List of Regiments 221

Bibliography 247

Index 253

Introduction and Acknowledgements

This is a story from the diverse and colourful Habsburg Austrian monarchy in the middle of the eighteenth century, which was perhaps the most creative period of its existence. At the centre of the stage stands the admirable and gracious Empress-Queen Maria Theresa, the mother-figure of Central Europe. The Theresian epoch rivals the Elizabethan Age in its excitement, and the reign of Victoria in its solid achievement, with the telling difference that its presiding genius was a much more agreeable kind of person than the two formidable ladies evoked in our comparison. At once heroic and human, Maria Theresa devoted much of her energy to enhancing both the fighting efficiency and the welfare of her armed forces, which was the one branch of her state for which she harboured 'a real personal interest'. It is one of the objects of the present work to do justice to the magnitude of this creative achievement. Measured by her standard, the activity of her rival Frederick of Prussia appears merely destructive, in the sense that he left an army that was in a worse state than the force he had inherited.

The Army of Maria Theresa also sets out to show that the Austrian army was not called into being 'just to give the Italians somebody they could beat'. On the contrary, Maria Theresa's troops were engaged almost from the outset of her reign in a battle of survival against the greater part of Europe, including the Prussia of Frederick the Great, the most dangerous of all possible enemies. After a bad start, the Austrians not only learnt to deal out at least as much punishment as they received, but evolved a style of warfare which ultimately put Old Fritz at a distinct disadvantage. In the use of its light infantry, and above all in the employment of its mighty artillery, the Theresian army foreshadowed some important aspects of Napoleonic warfare. We ought to set the record straight, now that eighteenth-century military history is attracting an increasingly wide and well-informed public.

It is also timely to recall the high reputation of the Irish who worked and fought for eighteenth-century Austria. Among their ranks were numbered types as varied as Captain MacBrady, the berserker of Schweidnitz, and Field-Marshal Lacy, who was the meticulous manager of the military machine and a leader of society in Mozart's Vienna. They had their counterparts in every monarchy of Catholic Europe, a fact which has escaped so many people who generalise about the Irish character and achievement.

I cannot conceal that my own interest in our theme remains primarily romantic. The period and the place have been invested with a magic for me ever since I began to hear and read about history. A particularly strong impression was made by an illustration in an encyclopaedia, showing Maria Theresa and the infant Joseph before the Hungarian magnates, and I still recall with pleasure a representation of Frederick the Great at Hochkirch, standing outside a tent while his grenadiers streamed past in disorder. I thank Providence that the inspiration is as fresh as ever. There is a peculiar thrill to be had in turning over the pages of a manuscript still encrusted with the sand that was scattered over the ink two hundred or more years ago, and even now one can scarcely visit the field of Kolin without being impressed by the grand scale of the horizon, and the almost tangible atmosphere that reverberates from the events of 18 June 1757. I shall have failed in my chief ambition, if I do not communicate something of these enthusiasms to the reader.

I should like to express my gratitude to the many people who have helped me in various ways, in particular Dr J. C. v. Allmayer-Beck (Director of the Army Museum, Vienna), Dr H. Bleckwenn, Professor J. Kunisch, Dr M. Messerschmidt, and Mr John Edgcumbe. I am much indebted to the officials of the Kriegsarchiv, Vienna, and especially Dr K. Peball, Dr P. Broucek, Dr O. Winter, Dr L. Moser, Herr J. Lippitsch and the ubiquitous Paul Pešek. They run a friendly and truly helpful institution. A nearby establishment, the Café Siller, also did a good deal to maintain morale.

All maps are by the author.

C.D

1

The Theresian State

The Domains of the Empress-Queen

The 'Austria' of the Habsburg dynasty was a whole little universe, an entity which retains the power to stir the imagination in all sorts of ways. The sentimentalist will be inclined to linger in a kind of confectioner's Vienna, inhabited by memories of the waltz kings and the homely *Biedermeier* comforts of Schubert's time. The passing tourist will be persuaded to associate the traditional Austria with tiresomely cheerful Tyroleans who wear leather shorts and have brushes stuck in their hats.

A more representative picture of the old world can be created simply by wandering through the courts and narrow streets which extend to the north of Vienna's Graben Square and St Stephen's Cathedral. Nowhere, perhaps, does the atmosphere of eighteenth-century officialdom hang more heavily than around the building of the old Bohemian Chancellery and the little Judenplatz outside. We may people the palaces and squares by betaking ourselves to the Kunsthistorisches Museum, and absorbing the visions of Vienna which were recorded by the painter Bernado Bellotto in the hot summer of 1759, while Austria's armies were sweating far away on the plains beside the Oder.

However, we must travel much further afield if we are to gain some inkling of the extent and the sheer strangeness of the old empire. Where books and museums fail, it is still possible to recreate the past in an odd corner of the vanished realm like the Bánát of Temesvár, which is nowadays shared between Rumania and Yugoslavia. The terrain is an eerie landscape of thinly-turfed sandhills, which were reclaimed by German colonists after Prince Eugene conquered the region in 1716. Here and there the site of a village is betrayed by a slender white church tower, crowned by an onion dome in best baroque style. Wolves still lurk in the Transylvanian Alps, which rise like green hummocks to the east, while herds of pigs rush down to cool themselves in the grey waters of the half-mile-wide Danube, as it pushes its way towards the Iron Gates. The heat, the vegetation, and the vast horizon are a world removed from Western Europe.

As they existed in the middle of the eighteenth century, the Habsburg domains comprised the area of modern Austria, together with much of present-day Czechoslovakia, Poland, Hungary, Yugoslavia, Rumania, northern Italy and Belgium. How did it all come together?

The lands of the Hungarian and Bohemian crowns signed themselves over to the Habsburgs as a measure of desperation in 1527, after the old independent monarchy of Hungary had been crushed by the Turks. Still further to the east, the principality of Transylvania was won from the Turks in the later seventeenth century, and held in direct subjection to the Vienna administration. Thus the archduchy of Austria was buttressed to the north and east by an arc of territory extending some two thousand miles from Silesia, Bohemia and Moravia by way of Transylvania and Slavonia to the wilds of the Adriatic coastlands.

Southwards across the Alps generations of Maria Theresa's ancestors had campaigned in northern Italy against the hostile French dynasty of Bourbon. The Emperor Charles VI tried to establish a claim to Spain as well, but the Spanish Bourbons threw him out in 1714. He never got over the loss, and he made sure that Austrian court etiquette and ways of doing business were heavily influenced by the gloomy formality of old Spain. It was some consolation that his British and Dutch allies helped Charles to salvage a couple of prizes from the wreck of the empire of the defunct Spanish Habsburgs, to wit the Milanese, and the provinces of the southern Netherlands which were marooned far away in the green and damp lowlands of north-western Europe.

The Empire survived until the end of World War I, when its destruction left a rent in the political and social fabric of Europe which has still to be mended. It is strange to reflect that the old order endured so long largely through the achievement of a long-dead woman, the Empress-Queen Maria Theresa. She took charge of the Habsburg dominions in 1740, at the age of twenty-three, and though she lacked any training in government she preserved her state through a desperate military crisis and went on to rule it for the next forty years according to principles which most people today would still acclaim as models of humanity and reason. Maria Theresa's warmth and spontaneity appeal to us at the present time as strongly as they did to her subjects, and evoke a sympathy which we cannot feel for her tough, calculating or merely obscure royal contemporaries. Here at least the historian and the sentimentalist are in full agreement.

Before we look more closely at the woman and her work, it is useful to take stock of the component parts of the Habsburg dominions.

THE GERMAN HEARTLANDS

At the centre of the Habsburg empire resided the Austrian core, namely present-day Upper and Lower Austria, with the Tyrol and the Vorarlberg, the southern duchies of Styria, Carinthia and Carniola, and the 'Austrian littoral' of Istria, Trieste and Fiume. Across southern Germany there were scattered the enclaves of Vorder-Österreich, of which the most important was the Breisgau with the city of Freiburg.

Leaving the Netherlands and Austrian Italy out of account, it was probably in these 'German' lands that Maria Theresa's subjects were at their happiest. The Tyroleans were poor but free, and most of the remaining Austrian countryfolk lived under a degree of feudal subjection that was irksome rather than intolerable, and certainly preferable to the bondage which obtained in Bohemia, Moravia and Hungary. The Habsburg capital of Vienna was already an important centre of commerce, and elsewhere in Austria there were assets like the Styrian and Carinthian iron, or the salt of the Salzkammergut, which gave rise to a degree of local prosperity.

However, the specifically 'Austrian' contribution to the Habsburg army was surprisingly small. In Maria Theresa's time the Tyroleans shunned army life as an affront to their inborn freedom, while it would have been unthinkable to have formed regiments from folk as unmilitary as the Viennese.

Fortunately the German-speaking element in the army was kept up by invoking the moral authority invested in the office of Emperor of Germany, which the Habsburgs had enjoyed with hardly a break since 1273. Some of the independent 'Electors' and the scores of princes, dukes and municipalities which ruled 'Germany'

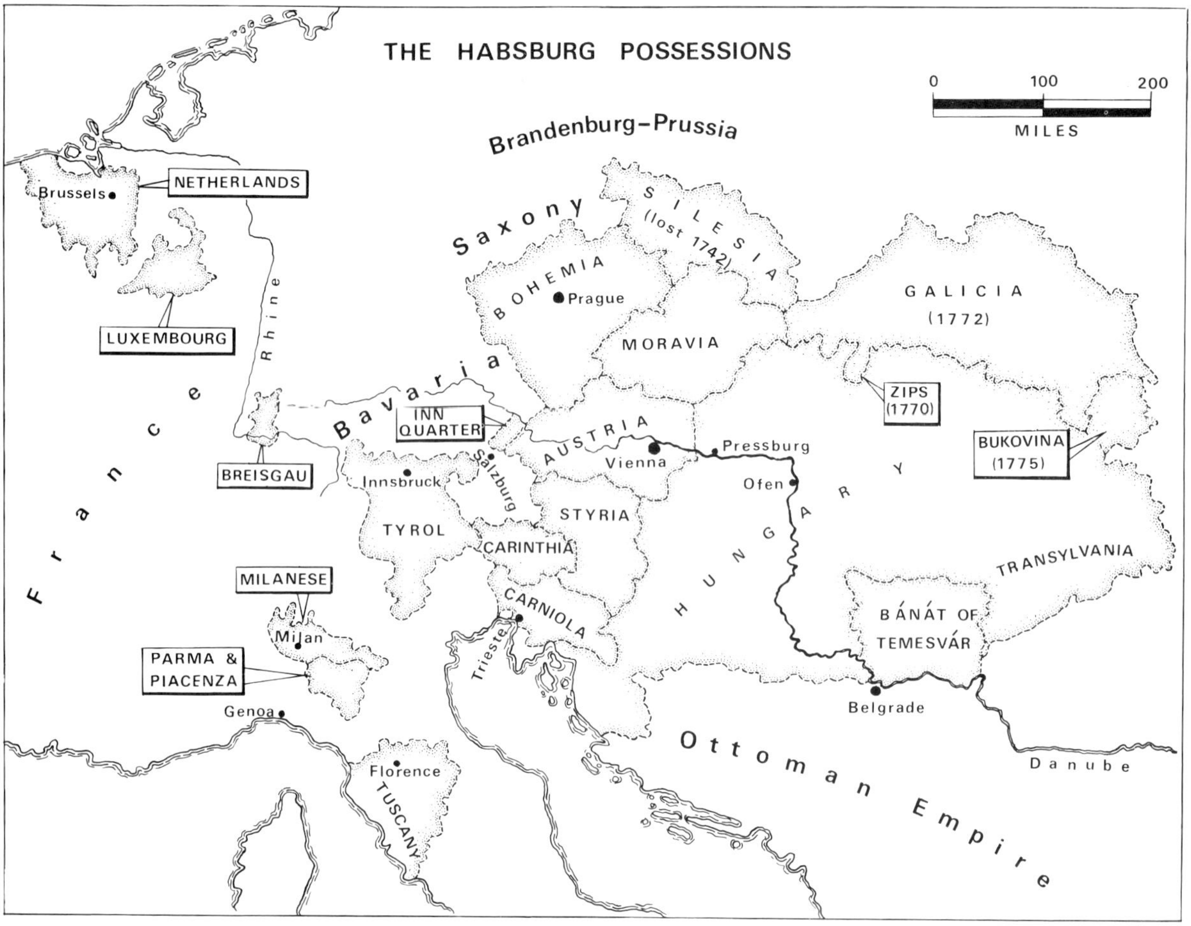

might incline at one time to the French party, or later on to the Prussian, but the majority were pricked in their consciences (if not actually stirred into action) when they heard a rallying call from the Emperor, who was the historic defender of Germany against the Bourbons, Swedes and Turks. Even in time of peace the Imperial agents were constantly at work, fixing up deals with the sovereigns and the cities. Thus the Austrian regiments were able to recruit heavily in the Empire, and fill their ranks with excellent raw material. Prince Charles Joseph de Ligne testified that 'the Empire will always provide us with generals, officers and soldiers of an heroic cast. It is in Germany more than anywhere else that you will find education, honour, and that kind of courage which proceeds from temperament and which is the best of all'.[1]

BOHEMIA AND MORAVIA

The word 'exploitation' is the one which springs most readily to mind when we travel northwards to Bohemia and Moravia (part of present-day Czechoslovakia). Though they were counted as part of the German Hereditary Lands, and were heavily populated by Germans around the fringes, these provinces remained predominantly a region of stocky, broad-faced Slavs, who were bound to the soil in subjection to their feudal masters. At once oppressive and spineless, the majority of the Bohemian gentry had been settled in their estates by the Habsburgs, after the native Protestant nobility was deposed in 1620. While they drove their peasants mercilessly, the new Bohemian nobles proved oddly amenable to direction from above – they submitted to the Elector of Bavaria, when he got himself crowned Emperor in 1742, and, after a period of obstruction, they acquiesced in the very high financial demands made by the Vienna government in 1748.

In the Seven Years War (1756–63) Bohemia actually contributed more than four times as much money as all the lands of the Hungarian crown, and between 20 and 40 per cent more than the Austrian Netherlands, which were the next most productive source of revenue. Together with the physical devastation caused by the war, this weight of taxation precipitated a collapse of the economy, and caused actual starvation in Bohemia and Moravia in the 1770s. Prague, the capital of Bohemia, was a pleasant place which was frequented mostly by such nobles as could not afford the prices in Vienna.

Otherwise the lands of the old Bohemian kingdom ought to have emerged as the most prosperous of Maria Theresa's dominions, taking into account the mines, forests and vineyards of the mountain rim, the excellent beer, the clothing industry of the Bohemian-Moravian borders, and the extensive cultivation of flax in Moravia, 'which gives a pretty aspect to the countryside, when it is in flower'.[2]

Poverty has always been the most eloquent recruiting sergeant of all, so it is hardly surprising that Bohemians and Moravians formed the backbone of many of Maria Theresa's 'German' regiments. However, the Bohemians entered the Austrian artillery with positive enthusiasm, since they inherited a proud gunner tradition from the militant Hussite heretics of the fifteenth century.

THE LANDS OF THE HUNGARIAN CROWN

Nowhere was the power of the nobility more extravagantly and irresponsibly displayed than in the lands of the Hungarian crown, and more particularly in the hills and plains of Hungary proper, which swept from within a few miles of Vienna to the edge of the sandy wastes of the Bánát of Temesvár.

Though the Hungarian lands (excluding Transylvania) accounted for more than one-third of the population and area of Maria Theresa's dominions, the Hungarian contribution to the Habsburg war machine remained disproportionately small – in money terms perhaps less than one-tenth of the total revenues. The trouble was that the Hungarian church and gentry and the almost inconceivably rich noble dynasties like those of Esterházy, Pálffy and Batthyány contrived to unload the burden of taxation upon their wretched serfs, while voting only the most grudging support to the central government. Reforms of nearly every kind were resisted with obstinacy and success, which was why Hungary was left as the most socially backward of the Habsburg lands.

Maria Theresa showed the utmost regard for the prickly Hungarian sensibilities. She displayed herself in all the historic trappings of the 'Queen of Hungary' to the noble assemblies of 1741, 1751 and 1764, she flattered and feasted the great magnates, she left the ancient Hungarian constitutions intact, and she founded the Order of St Stephen as a counterpart to the Golden Fleece. The effort produced some tangible rewards. The Hungarian nobility became powerfully attracted by the kind of distinction which service to the Habsburg state had to offer. More important still, the Hungarians put into the field some properly-organised regiments in place of the feudal contingents of the ancient 'Noble Insurrection'. The Hungarian hussars were admitted to be the finest light cavalry of Europe, while the regiments of Hungarian infantry were worthy of a race that was 'full of courage and intelligence'.[3] All the same, there were times when Maria Theresa would have preferred the hard cash of the Hungarians instead of their sabre-swinging enthusiasm.

Thus the relations between Habsburgs and Hungarians bore the character of an uneasy truce between equals. The 'German' and Hungarian troops were at daggers drawn, and each hated to be placed under the orders of a commander of the other nation.

To the north-east of the Hungarian plain extended the mountains and basins of the principality of Transylvania (*Siebenbürgen*). A melting-pot of Wallachians, Hungarians, Germans and gipsies, it was administered directly from Vienna, but furnished only a few troops to the army, and then only towards the end of Maria Theresa's reign. In contrast, Hungary was closed off to the south by the 'military borders' of Slavonia and Croatia, which were populated by the most warlike folk of the Habsburg dominions. We shall get to know these 'Croats' more intimately in a later chapter.

AUSTRIAN LOMBARDY

Direct Austrian rule in northern Italy extended over the archduchy of Milan and the little duchies of Mantua, Parma and Piacenza. In addition the grand duchy of Tuscany came to the house of Habsburg–Lorraine by treaty in 1738.

The region was as remote in character as it is possible to imagine from the barbarities of Hungary, and Maria Theresa wisely devolved the administration upon a succession of able Italian-born ministers. The Italians had the happy trait of attributing all the benefits of Habsburg rule directly to Maria Theresa, and writing down all the inconveniences to her ministers or to bad advice. Thus the Austrians could rely upon a residue of popular support, when the region happened to be overrun by hostile armies, and Lombardy furnished a couple of more than passable regiments.

THE NETHERLANDS

The Austrian Netherlands covered an area corresponding to present-day Belgium and Luxembourg, exclusive of the area around Liège. An industrious, prosperous and advanced people like the Lombards, the Netherlanders earned the right of being governed by their own élite, or at least by some of the best administrators that Maria Theresa could provide. Maria Theresa's brother-in-law Prince Charles of Lorraine ensconced himself in viceregal state in Brussels, and the capital's intellectual life entered a period of prosperity. The Royal Academy was one of many institutions that were founded under the Austrian rule.

In the provinces the Flemings sung the praises of *de goede Keiserin*, though they feared even a whisper of reform. Harbouring fewer reservations, the French-speaking Walloons of the south and east embraced the Habsburg cause with remarkable enthusiasm, and made up a large part of the contingent of between 12,000 and 17,000 troops which the Netherlands contributed to the army in the Seven Years War. These men combined 'the patience of the Germans with the sense of honour of the French, and their gaiety in the hottest fire'.[4] A regiment of Walloon dragoons dealt the decisive blow at the battle of Kolin (1757), which was the proudest memory of the Theresian army.

In the first critical years of Maria Theresa's reign, her nobility and some of her ministers considered themselves less as parties in a fight for survival than as stockholders in some old and ramshackle concern which had passed under inexperienced management. It seemed only common prudence for the magnates to look first to their own interests, and take steps, if necessary, to place their investment elsewhere. There was one Bohemian noble who at least had the politeness to write to Maria Theresa and ask her not to take it too much amiss if he gave his allegiance to the Elector of Bavaria.

Whereas in Prussia and most of Western Europe the monarchs had long since broken the political power of the nobility, in the Habsburg lands the nobles not only maintained the authority of their *Stände* (provincial assemblies) intact, but carried their separatist tendencies into the very heart of the government.

Likewise the individual organs of administration were inclined to function without reference to the whole. Quarantine regulations were permitted to retard the march of reinforcements to the theatre of war in the dangerous year of 1740 and again in the winter of 1756–7, and it was most unwillingly that the authorities allowed the provisions for the army to cross internal boundaries without having to pay excise.

We should also bear in mind that in this period governments and societies were as yet undisciplined by the Industrial Revolution and the clock, and that underlings were in the habit of regarding a prescription from above as an expression of intent rather than a mandate for action. Experienced administrators came to expect little else. Thus in 1753 the *Hofkriegsrath* (War Council) expressed pained surprise upon learning that Colonel Valenziani had taken a new dress regulation at face value and rushed to have his regiment outfitted in the new uniforms. The *Hofkriegsrath* felt that the precipitate colonel ought to have waited until (as almost invariably happened) the government had had time to change its mind.

The extraordinary diversity of the Habsburg dominions served to compound the normal inefficiencies of the time. In particular there were difficulties of language which threatened to prove disastrous in military affairs. No other army of the time could have produced a column of regiments chattering variously in German, Czech, French, Flemish, Raeto-Romance, Italian, Magyar and Serbo-Croatian, and all passing in review under the eyes of a general who was cursing to himself in Gaelic. This Babel of tongues gave rise to a 'singular confusion'.[5]

Of all these languages German was the most widely known throughout the army, and officers of any ambition could hardly get along without it. 'We have what is called "army German", which sounds well in the mouths of real generals and officers. It must be spoken in an inspiring and abrupt manner, and the soldiers (who are always good judges of such things) often assess the merit of their superiors accordingly.'[6]

In sheer numbers of native speakers, however, the predominant language-group probably remained the Slavonic, as represented by the Czech of the Bohemian troops and the Serbo-Croat of the borderers. French was of course essential for managing the Walloons, and as the polite tongue of eighteenth-century Europe it held the field in most headquarters. Only a few generals, like Loudon, felt really uncomfortable in it.

The Hungarian rank and file, ever aware of their national identity, could be approached effectively only through Magyar. 'Hungarian curses are at once the mightiest and the most peculiar you can find in any language. What is singular about them is that they are susceptible of an infinite variety of nuances, according to the nature of the provocation.'[7] However, it was worth a scholarly officer's while to try some Latin, which was the official language of Hungarian government and law. This was spoken in a tripping and harmonious style which resembled 'the galloping of their horses'.[8]

The regulations and drill books which began to appear in the late 1740s sought to impose German as a uniform *Dienstsprache* in the army, and care was taken in the 'German' regiments to assign non-German-speaking recruits to veterans who could instruct them in the language. In time many even of the 'Croats' learnt German, which they spoke in a characteristically pedantic and guttural style – the source of the esoteric brand of humour called *Grenzwitze* (lit. 'border jokes').

All the same there is a good deal of evidence to suggest that the difficulties of communication remained formidable. There were all too few officers who, like General Siskovics, could command German, Hungarian, Walloon and Italian troops with equal facility. Imagine the embarrassment of General Andreas Panovsky, who on 16 August 1762 found himself in the position of having to get an uncomprehending regiment of Walloon dragoons to charge at a critical stage of the action at Reichenbach. After staring mutely at the men he was seized by a fit of inspiration and burst out with '*Allons foutre, sacredieu!*' The delighted troopers responded with a cry of '*voilà un brave bougre!*', and they tore into the Prussian squadrons like madmen.[9]

At other times it was difficult to tell whether the message had got through at all. An officer once went to report some suspicious movements on the part of the Prussians to Field-Marshal Serbelloni, who was notoriously bad at German. He found the field-marshal

> sitting on his bed, with a cup of chocolate to one side, and holding a book in which he seemed to be totally engrossed. The officer concluded that his entrance had passed unnoticed, and so he repeated his reports concerning the movements of Prince Henry, using a very loud voice. The field-marshal inclined slightly to the right, and then to the left, without stirring from the spot, and finally he stared woodenly at the officer. With his broken German, in which he always used the infinitive ending, he dismissed him with a curt: 'Serbelloni, he move too'.[10]

The forces of unity

So far we have considered only the forces which threatened to pull the loosely-textured Habsburg dominions apart. All the same there were some strong countervailing influences, and chief among these were the character and achievement of Maria Theresa herself.

The only heir of the Emperor Charles VI, Maria Theresa spent the years before her accession in harmless amusements and in learning to be a good wife to the handsome, heavy and more than slightly fatuous Francis Stephen of Lorraine, whom she married in 1736 and loved to distraction. The old Emperor died in October 1740, and for the next two years Maria Theresa and a knot of devoted ministers and generals fought to save her inheritance from dissolution. The Elector of Bavaria impudently had himself made King of Bohemia and Emperor in 1742, but the Austrians proved themselves to be more than a match for the Bavarians and their French allies in the subsequent campaigns in Bohemia and south-western Germany. Finally in 1745 Maria Theresa had the satisfaction of seeing her own beloved Francis Stephen crowned Emperor at Frankfurt.

A much more formidable enemy was Frederick II ('Frederick the Great') of Prussia, who invaded the rich northern province of Silesia in 1740. The Prussians beat Maria Theresa's whitecoats whenever they met in open battle, and in 1745 Maria Theresa had to buy peace at the price of signing away Silesia. She and her ministers appreciated that only a thoroughgoing reform would enable the Habsburg state to survive in proximity to a dangerous neighbour like this.

From 1748 a number of devices added greatly to the power of the Vienna administration. The central government was concentrated in a single *Directorium*, and by entering into a number of long-term agreements the ministers relieved themselves of the burden of having to call on the noble *Stände* at every turn for cash, supplies and recruits. The nobles did not at first recognise how much of their independence they were losing in the process.

The reformed Habsburg army fought with credit in the Seven Years War (1756–63), even if Frederick escaped the retribution which had been prepared for him by Maria Theresa and her French and Russian allies. After this ordeal she resumed the work of remaking the Habsburg dominions, this time in the company of her son Joseph II, who became co-regent after Francis Stephen died in 1765. Maria Theresa did what she could to ameliorate the wretched life of the serfs, beginning with the Crown estates in Bohemia. She introduced new though severe codes of justice, and she laid the foundations of a system of universal elementary education. Trade, industry and agriculture began to flourish, except in war-ravaged Bohemia, and the population of the Habsburg states doubled in the course of the reign – Maria Theresa contributing more than her share in the form of her sixteen little archdukes and archduchesses.

By the time of Maria Theresa's death in 1780 the sum of the Habsburg dominions was of more consequence than the component parts, which had manifestly not been the case forty years earlier. In fact the Empress-Queen had fashioned an Austrian state that was recognisably the same creature which survived until 1918.

Item for item, much the same kind of reform was going ahead in contemporary Prussia and Russia. What imprinted a unique character on Maria Theresa's achievement was the wonderful integrity of her life – her refusal to concede that public affairs should be conducted with any less morality and feeling than her private life. Hence her instinctive abhorrence of Frederick of Prussia, the enemy of her dynasty and subjects, a 'bad man', a 'wicked neighbour', a 'monster', whom she once wanted to call out for a duel with pistols. Hence her leaning towards moderation, even when carrying out necessary reforms, an instinct variously interpreted by her biographers as a finely-attuned sense of political wisdom, or a motherly concern for the happiness of her subjects. Hence, finally, her agony of mind when Chancellor Kaunitz and her own son Joseph II began to carry Austria into the harsh world of *Realpolitik*.

To know Maria Theresa in the setting of her daily family life is therefore to know her as the statesman. Pretty, in a plump kind of way, she presided like a mother hen over her sizeable Imperial brood, with whom she loved to snatch a few hours in some modest chambers tucked away in all the splendours of the Schönbrunn or the Hofburg. The French officer de Guibert was once received in audience, and records his disappointment when he discovered that Maria Theresa was quite alone, without glittering guards or liveried footmen. 'I found only a good bourgeoise, when in my imagination I was searching for a great sovereign.'[11] He did not appreciate that in Maria Theresa the two characters were the same.

Maria Theresa's religion gave her strength in time of test, and reinforced her Viennese *Hausfrau*'s disinclination towards everything that was abstract, doctrinaire or dehumanising. She could never have desired to match her great rival Frederick in his adventurous independence of mind, or the ruthless impersonality of his conduct. By the same token Maria Theresa's subjects responded with a warmth that had little in common with the appalled admiration which Frederick evoked in his own peoples and armies.

Political philosophy knows no terms adequate to describe the tendencies which gradually marshalled all classes of Habsburg society behind the Theresian state. For some time now the great nobles had been engaged in a direly expensive competition in building palaces in Vienna, whether the spacious residences planted around the outer rim of the fortifications, or the flat-sided blocks with absurdly over-proportioned gateways which lined the narrow streets of the Inner City. The court spent the winter in the Hofburg Palace, a complex of buildings on the south side of the Inner City, and in summer the whole apparatus moved out three miles into the country to the impressive new pile of the Schönbrunn. Such was the setting for the crowded and gossipy society of Vienna, which enticed more and more of the nobility from their provincial retreats.

All classes enjoyed strolling along the old ramparts of Vienna, or promenading through the Prater and other royal gardens which were opened to the public after the Seven Years War. Behind the pompous façades of the noble palaces many of the rooms were let out to poor families, while anyone in passable dress and with a couple of florins to spare could gain entry to one of the carnival balls. Maria Theresa herself remained eminently approachable, and until 1753 (when a nobleman went berserk in the Schönbrunn) any individual could turn up unannounced at the public audiences.

Thus in Theresian Vienna the element of physical proximity ensured that the Empress-Queen, her ministers and generals were known as individuals to a wide popular audience. Governmental circles were all too aware that *das Publicum* was capable of expressing its opinion in a variety of ways. Sarcastic verses were frequently posted on the gates of palaces and churches. The wife of the slow-moving Field-Marshal Daun was greeted with a barrage of sleeping caps, and for other targets the ammunition was uncomfortably harder or unpleasantly squashier. All the while a stream of broadsheets and doggerel poems kept the people informed and excited.

Hundreds of miles distant from Vienna, Maria Theresa's subjects and soldiers could share certain fundamental sentiments. Maria Theresa's religion was not different in kind from that of a Bohemian peasant, and town and country throughout the Habsburg dominions were adorned with calvaries and statues of saints, each with its train of kneeling and mumbling devotees.

The sense of everybody-in-the-boat-together was reinforced when Maria Theresa's armies were fighting the heretical Prussians and their godless King Frederick. 'All those who have served Catholic states are aware of an element of religious fanatacism which supervenes when they are at war with Protestant powers.'[12]
 Thus General Loudon could report from Moravia in 1758 that 'all the peasants are

ready to take up arms and go out to fight the enemy. They demand only to be led. This could well bring on a peasant war, which is scarcely desirable, but we must do what we can to sustain these good people in their zeal'.[13]

In popular usage the Habsburg troops were already called simply 'Austrians', and the army was awakened to its specifically national (as opposed to Imperial) identity during the short but interesting period from 1742 to 1745, when the office of Emperor was held by a hostile Bavarian.

The predominant heraldry of the army was the red-white-red which had come from the Norman kingdom of Naples in the twelfth century. Red cuffs and lapels were sported by most of the line regiments until the later 1760s, and the white coat of the 'German' infantry and cavalry was worn with pride for a century to come. 'White is our colour, and so it must remain for ever.'[14]

As for modes of conduct and thought, Maria Theresa liked to think that the Austrians went about affairs with a certain *Milde* and *Munificenz*. The army in its turn took a pride in affecting a certain battle-tested casualness, which was contrasted with the faddish artificiality of Frederick and his troops – those 'beings of Euclid'.[15]

Some at least of the 'Austrians' were aware of influences which overcame all divergences of racial origin. If Joseph Sonnenfels regretted that he could find nobody in eighteenth-century Austria who felt a compulsion like that of Classical patriotism,[16] the Prince de Ligne (who was a Walloon) just as stoutly proclaimed the validity of a concept of 'fatherland' which evoked the ties which attached the members of society to each other, and thus to the head from whom they all derived their welfare. He held that in the Austrian service an important ingredient of this brand of patriotism was its power to absorb and transmute foreigners.[17] Likewise Field-Marshal Khevenhüller maintained that one of the attractions of the Imperial army was that it could show many living examples of foreign soldiers of fortune who had won their way to rank and influence, while others, 'even if not so lucky, may spend their old age eating the Emperor's bread in peace'.[18] Not only the officers, but the entire class of bureaucrats and court nobility had a stake in promoting a recognisable state feeling.

What Maria Theresa demanded (like Franz Josef after her) was a sense of loyalty to the person of the sovereign. The man's place of birth was a very minor consideration. Indeed it was not until 1905 that Vienna did away with the custom by which foreign officers could serve in the Austrian forces while retaining their native citizenship.

By itself a diversity of race and language does nothing to sap a sense of corporate identity in an armed force. Otherwise the army of the later Napoleonic empire would not have given such a good account of itself, or General Alexander have driven the Germans up Italy in 1944 with a host of twenty-six nationalities ranging from Poles to Brazilians.

This body of evidence lends support to the Prince de Ligne's bold assertion that in the Europe of his day the Austrian army was the 'sole national army, although made up of several nations'.[19]

2

The Supreme Direction of the Armed Forces

'Mater Castrorum'. Maria Theresa as head of the army

Maria Theresa held the ultimate responsibility of supreme command of her troops until her dying day, and there was never any danger that, as a woman, she might have proved indifferent to the affairs of her army. In the crisis of 1741 she wrote to Francis Stephen that she was well aware that her salvation and that of her house depended, after God, on the army, and she went on to express her determination to care for the army more as a mother than as a sovereign. Many years later she testified that 'this branch of the state administration was the only one for which I harboured a real personal interest'.[1]

The industrious and inquisitive Empress-Queen attained a breadth and precision of military expertise which put most of her generals to shame. She followed or initiated the progress of every reform in discipline, tactics, dress and weapons, and she was competent to give an immediate and informed opinion on many a matter that was puzzling her 'advisers'. It is significant that in the grand manoeuvres in Bohemia in 1754, while Emperor Francis Stephen went off hunting, Maria Theresa was busy inspecting the magazines and field bakeries.

An excellent horsewoman in her younger days, Maria Theresa was able to ride around the army camps of the 1740s and early 1750s, and follow some of the movements in person. Back in Vienna the Prussian envoy Podewils reported in 1747 that 'she goes to some pains to win over the soldiers to her through her generosity. She frequently distributes money among them, and seldom passes her bodyguards without throwing them some ducats. Her troops accordingly love her deeply, and their regard is strengthened by the steadfastness she displayed under the cruellest blows of fate'.[2]

According to another Prussian, 'she was usually present in person whenever columns marched through Vienna on their way to the army. She encouraged the soldiers with the most gracious expressions, calling them "my children", and smiling with approval when the word "mother" ran like a feu-de-joie through the ranks'.[3] An English volunteer testified from his own experience in the Seven Years War that the Austrian soldiers refrained from deserting because they were 'well paid, well dressed and well fed. Moreover the troops are aware that the Empress is concerned for their welfare, and this consideration binds them to her service for her own sake'.[4]

Maria Theresa liked to establish a personal bond with her generals, and she enquired closely into their welfare and that of their families. Once, when she heard that General Loudon had fallen dangerously ill, she characteristically sent him her doctor and ordered him to get well.

The Empress set a taxing pace in the conduct of public affairs. Her working day commonly lasted from about seven in the morning until seven in the evening. Once a week, or thereabouts, a company of varying size assembled in Maria Theresa's presence for one of the conferences of state. The large and slow-moving *Grosse Con-*

ferenz of the last reign gradually fell out of favour, owing to the increased urgency of public business and the separation of foreign and domestic affairs. By the time of the Seven Years War it had been replaced by the more handy and compact conferences *in mixtis* and by meetings of an *ad hoc* military commission. Many of the most important decisions were taken on a still less formal basis, when Maria Theresa and the chancellor Kaunitz acted on information they received directly from commanders at the theatre of war. According to the court master of ceremonies, Khevenhüller-Metsch, the new cabal system received a significant impetus in the emergency of May 1757.

As the war progressed Maria Theresa and Kaunitz willy-nilly became accustomed to determining campaigns in some detail, because Field-Marshal Daun, who was the nominal commander of the field army, abdicated so much of his responsibilities. The year 1761 saw the foundation of the *Staatsconferenz* of half a dozen ministers of state. Here too the impetus came from Kaunitz, who was less concerned with giving the ministers back their talking-platform than with setting up a machine that would keep the whole body of public administration under his control.

Maria Theresa never allowed the domestic disasters which beset her large family to divert her attention from state affairs. All the same, her sex imposed some important limitations upon her efficiency as director of the military machine. She had to revolve the day-to-day direction of operations upon the generals, and like the rest of the court she had to wait in almost hysterical anticipation for tidings of the wars.

Both circumstance and character held Maria Theresa back from exercising another vital function of supreme command – that of disciplining and pruning the corps of senior officers. Not only did the distance from the theatre of war deprive her of the opportunity of keeping her generals constantly up to the mark, but she was a sweet-tempered person who laboured under a continuing sense of obligation to any person who had once earned her gratitude. Rather than dismiss the octogenarian Joseph Harrach from the presidency of the *Hofkriegsrath* she placed the septuagenarian Field-Marshal Neipperg at his side, and kept the latter gentleman at work until his faculties too began to fail. Thus for most of the Seven Years War the machinery of military administration was encrusted with two layers of senile incompetence. In 1762 a new president was finally appointed in the person of Field-Marshal Daun, who himself had only four more years to live. Daun was succeeded by his protégé, General Lacy, who was the youngest man to hold the office for generations, and in order to cushion the senior functionaries from this appalling shock Maria Theresa had to allow the chief commissary Chotek to retire on full pay, and give Field-Marshal Colloredo the direction of the military academies.

Like all sovereigns, Maria Theresa was to some extent guided by the experience of her experts. Understandably she depended most completely on her ministers in the first couple of years of her reign, and she harboured a lifelong gratitude to men like Bartenstein, Kinsky and Field-Marshal Khevenhüller who gave her their support in that testing period. After weathering the first crisis Maria Theresa began to commission individuals to carry out specific works of reform, always favouring enthusiastic people who approached her with a well-thought-out scheme. In the military field we encounter folk like Prince Liechtenstein, with his plan for remaking the artillery, or Prince Sachsen-Hildburghausen, who had long meditated how to reform the military borders.

The influence of Kaunitz was something else again. Appointed Chancellor in

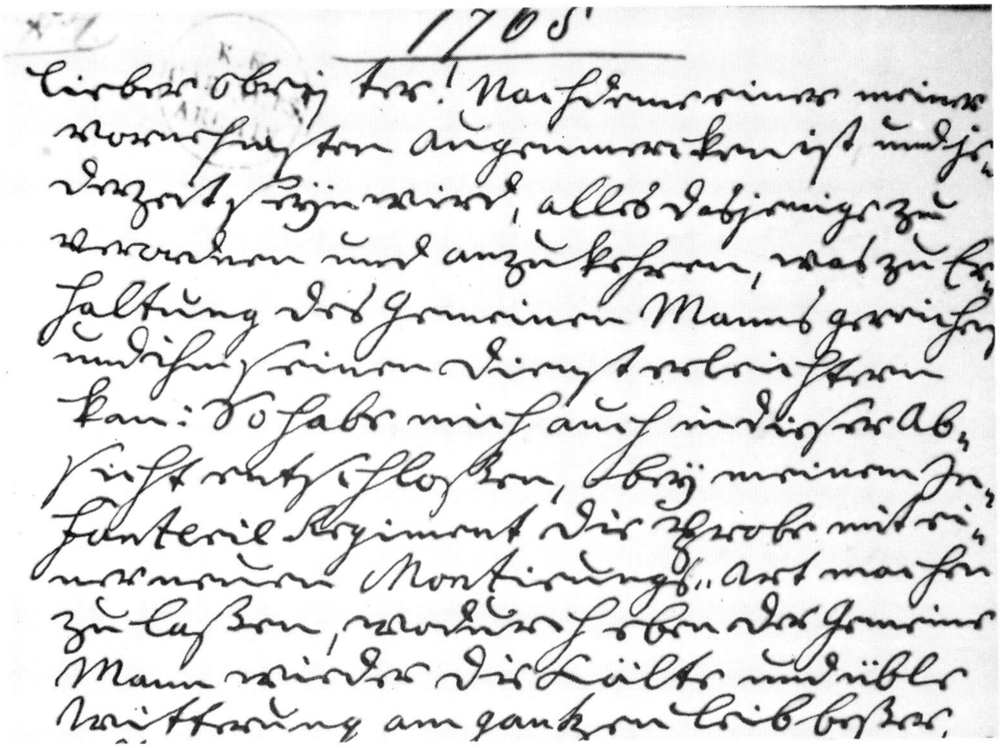

*Characteristic note from Maria Theresa (**see p. 71**). 'Dear Colonel, One of my main ambitions is, and always shall be, to make such regulations and arrangements, as will promote the upkeep of the private soldier and alleviate his duties. With this in mind I have decided to try out a new kind of uniform among my infantry regiments, which will give the ordinary soldier's body better protection against cold and wet, and yet be no heavier to wear. . . .'* (Kriegsarchiv)

1753, he enjoyed the closest confidence of the Imperial family for the next forty years. One of his biographers goes so far as to talk about the 'power like that of a demonic seducer, which Kaunitz won over her soul'.[5] Maria Theresa was too level-headed and (by this time) too experienced to have been led astray quite so completely as that. Kauntiz, however, knew better than all the other 'men around Maria Theresa' how to awaken some of the Empress-Queen's deepest instincts, and how to direct them towards the goals he selected for the Habsburg state.

In all of this we have heard significantly little of Francis Stephen, the consort of Maria Theresa and (since 1745) the Emperor of Germany. For all his imposing bulk and titles, within the Habsburg dominions he took second place of precedence to his wife as Archduchess of Austria and Queen of Hungary and Bohemia. In any case our heavy Emperor needed little enough prompting to turn his mind from official business. Two passions only – hunting and the pursuit of women – were powerful enough to claim his undivided attention. The splendour and duration of Francis Stephen's hunting excursions became famous even in a society devoted to the chase, and the Emperor was displeased at the way his pleasures were interrupted when the Prussians were inconsiderate enough to open hostilities in September 1756, and again when they went over to the attack in April 1758.

The ladies of Vienna were eager to accompany the Emperor on his hunting parties, and when Francis Stephen went to war it was reported to be 'dangerous for a woman of honour and beauty to remain alone in his company'.[6] He was one of the few men who could afford the expensive tastes of the famous Wilhelmine Auersperg, the daughter of his former tutor Field-Marshal Neipperg. His other women tended to be rather long in the tooth, and it is also significant for our military story that he harboured an inclination towards Countess Fuchs, who happened to be the mother-in-law of Field-Marshal Daun.

Otherwise life for the Emperor was one long struggle against boredom. He collected coins, medals, jewels, strange machines and exotic plants and animals, and the courtiers became skilled in laying on all kinds of little diversions for his amusement. Like some people of otherwise limited intellect, he possessed a certain skill with cards and money, and the people of Vienna were grateful for his reassuring presence at the more spectacular of their fires, though perhaps they would have preferred the fire-brigade.

The last words are with Frederick of Prussia. 'The Emperor gives the impression of a good bluff innkeeper who leaves all his affairs to his wife.'[7]

The Hofkriegsrath

The most notorious and least understood of the Habsburg military institutions, the *Hofkriegsrath* (Court Council of War), saw to the routine administration of the army. The *Hofkriegsrath* was founded by the Emperor Ferdinand I in 1556, and its functions were last defined by instructions of 1650 and 1668.

The *Hofkriegsrath* proper hived off specialised works of administration to organs like its *Obrist-Land-und-Haus Zeugamt* (for ordnance and the arsenals), the *Fortifications-Bau-Zahl-Amt* (for fortresses and other military construction), and the *General-Feld-Kriegs-Auditoriat-Amt* (for military justice). There were even branches of foreign affairs which had come under the management of the *Hofkriegsrath*, and so this unlikely organisation was responsible for relations with Russia (until 1742) and with Turkey (until 1753).

There existed much debatable ground which was disputed by powerful and independent organisations. Chief of these rival outfits was the *General-Kriegs-Commissariat* (of which more anon) which won free of the *Hofkriegsrath* at the end of 1746 and spread its activity into all kinds of matters relating to pay, recruiting, head-counting, rations and supply. A third party with interests in the same field was the *Obrist-Proviantamt*, which was a department of the civil financial administration.

The *Hofkriegsrath* had more than enough troubles within its own organisation. At the outset of the reign the institution was composed of one president (old Joseph Harrach), one vice-president, and thirty-six counsellors of whom the only ones of any consequence were the four *geheime Referendare*. A staff of more than a hundred clerks, archivists and doormen completed the establishment. The military were fond of complaining of the quality of the administration, and if we believe the soldiers the personnel was made up of inexperienced clerks and failed commissaries, 'whose ability extended no further than working out a contract or some other procedure of military finance'.[8] Out of sheer frustration Field-Marshal Khevenhüller once boxed the ears of the first *Referendar* Augustin Wöber in front of several witnesses.

In their turn the counsellors might have asked what kind of performance the army could expect, when they were left unpaid for the first two years of the reign, and when they were disposed in so many buildings around Vienna that 'the *Hof-*

kriegsrath was scattered all over the place and separated . . . not just from its subordinate departments, but from its offices and records as well'.[9]

In theory all the incoming documents ought to have been made the subject of a paper called a *Referat*, which detailed the contents and the arguments advanced by the counsellors, and ended with the *Hofkriegsrath*'s decision. Since, however, it was physically difficult for the counsellors to gather in a single place, the president, vice-president and *Referendare* got into the habit of opening the incoming correspondence themselves and sending out instructions on their own authority. Little attempt was made to observe proper paths of communication, with the result that even the regimental commanders were left in the dark as to whether their ensigns and NCOs were carrying their grievances direct to the *Hofkriegsrath*.

Above all there was that mass of documentation which reflected what Andrew Wheatcroft has called 'the Habsburg passion to get everything down on paper'. Colonel Hiller posed the question 'How is it possible to ensure a proper management of military affairs from a *Hofkriegsrath* which consists . . . of civilian officials who are skilled only in devoting the most enormous correspondence to the most insignificant items, as the one means they have of making themselves indispensable?'.[10] By 1771 every company of Croats had to maintain seventy-two separate files, and send in two weekly reports, ten monthly reports, two quarterly reports, and a consolidated return every six months.

Oddly enough, the *Hofkriegsrath* in Maria Theresa's reign was entirely innocent of the one charge which is usually laid to its account – that it bound the operational freedom of commanders in the field. Reduced as it was to an organ of administration, the *Hofkriegsrath* had neither the will nor the capacity to determine plans of campaign. It lost much of its significance even as a postbox, for in the Seven Years War the army commanders were expected to correspond on all important matters direct with Maria Theresa or Francis Stephen. If the dispatches were debated at all, it was in one of Maria Theresa's 'conferences', and in any event the replies were written out by Kaunitz's chancellery. With absolute consistency Maria Theresa encouraged the generals in the field to make up their own minds and act on their own account. She sent binding and detailed instructions only when the field commander was unwilling to shoulder the responsibility for direct action.

Some of the *Hofkriegsrath*'s worst abuses were eliminated as a consequence of an *Instruction* of 23 March 1745, which seems to have been penned by Maria Theresa's cabinet secretary Ignaz Koch, who had once been a counsellor himself. The personnel were drastically reduced in number (the *Referendare* to three, and the other counsellors to eleven), although the survivors were given handsome salaries from the proceeds of the Hungarian contribution and the taxes which the officers had to pay upon their promotions. The whole conduct of affairs was regulated and streamlined, and the colonels and generals were given the very needful control of the stream of correspondence from the army.

So as to relieve the *Hofkriegsrath* of some of its burdens, the administration of military justice was entrusted in 1753 to a separate *Justizkolleg*. Less happily the *General-Kriegs-Commissariat* took flight in 1746 and entrenched itself in opposition to the *Hofkriegsrath*.

Otherwise nobody put forward any constructive ideas until after the Seven Years War. The 72-year-old Field-Marshal Neipperg was installed in 1755 as vice-president to Joseph Harrach, whom Maria Theresa did not dare to remove from office, on account of his past services and powerful family connections. Neipperg himself was 'old, enfeebled in health, and by character a father of difficulties'.[11] He pursued a vendetta against Augustin Wöber, but his own management of affairs was painfully complicated, and he retained a measure of influence only by keeping up a secret correspondence with his old pupil Francis Stephen.

On 30 January 1762 Field-Marshal Daun began a short but fruitful term as president. He regained a good degree of control over the *General-Kriegs-Commissariat*, and he brought a number of generals into the *Hofkriegsrath*, which helped to restore its credit among the military men. It was a pity that he was not afforded the time he needed to carry out his longer-term ambitions of using the *Hofkriegsrath* as a means of lending technical support support to the generals in the field, and of encouraging a spirit of professionalism among the officers.

General Lacy, Daun's chosen successor, followed his old chief in the post in 1766. Lacy found that affairs were still badly muddled, and he made it his business to bring all the departments and dependencies of the *Hofkriegsrath* under unified control. It was under his reign that the work of reincorporating the *Commissariat* was completed. He rounded off his work by moving many of the scattered offices to a large building on the square Am Hof, which was vacated by the Jesuits when they were expelled from the Austrian dominions in 1773.

By now Lacy was worn out by the day-to-day drudgery of the president's job, and in 1774 he gave way in favour of the fat and jolly Field-Marshal Andreas Hadik, who had recently managed the occupation of Galicia with great efficiency. The new president put forward a paper urging that the administration would actually be speeded up if the running of the *Hofkriegsrath* became less centralised. However, Lacy and Joseph II continued to exercise a very tight control of military affairs from outside the council, and in 1780 an anonymous memorandum commented that 'nowadays the Austrian *Hofkriegsrath* exists as an empty form. The Emperor directs everything, and he does with the army exactly what he likes'.[12]

The commanding generals and inspector generals

The local peacetime command of the army devolved upon senior 'commanding generals', each of whom was made responsible for the affairs of one of the non-Austrian provinces or kingdoms (the Netherlands, Bohemia, Moravia, Hungary, Transylvania, Slavonia and the generalcies of Carlstadt and Warasdin).

In no other continental army was it quite so difficult to establish uniformity as the Austrian, with its troops of myriad races, scattered in little garrisons over thousands of miles. At one extremity the clouds over the Netherlands coastline could be seen from the cliffs of Kent. At the other end of the empire the noise of Austrian saluting cannon could be heard over the marshes of the Black Sea littoral.

In 1765, therefore, Field-Marshal Daun adopted a Prussian practice and appointed three 'inspector generals', each of whom would see that uniformity of standards was maintained in one of the branches of the service (General Lacy for the infantry, Lieutenant-General d'Ayasasa for the cavalry, and Lieutenant-General Beck for the military borders). On top of this the inspector generals acted as a channel of communication – they informed the local commanders of all the changes that were decreed by Vienna, and they drew on their own experience to send suggestions for reform to the *Hofkriegsrath*.

3

The Officers

Social origins

It is no exaggeration to claim that every aspect of the life and institutions of Maria Theresa's 'Austria' represents an order of complexity about five times more confused than in the Prussia of Frederick the Great. This heartening statement certainly applies in full force to the origins of the Theresian officer corps, a body of gentlemen of very diverse social and national provenance.

Whereas the bulk of the Prussian officers were drawn from a remarkably homogeneous class of small-time landowners, the Habsburg officer corps was distinguished by a fundamental social imbalance. As the Prince de Ligne put it: 'In our service you descend at once from the *grands seigneurs* to the parvenus'.[1]

At the top of the scale we encounter the great magnates who astonished foreign visitors with their magnificent style of life. People like these maintained one or more palaces in Vienna, and ruled as virtual sovereigns over thousands of serfs out in the country. Among the higher generals in Maria Theresa's reign appear no less than five princes Esterházy, four princes Lobkowitz and six counts Colloredo. As for the Harrachs, there was no getting away from them. They had a large palace on the Freyung in Vienna, as well as extensive estates nearby on the Hungarian border, and in the earlier part of the reign they owned one brother (Friedrich) who was Chancellor and another (Joseph) who was President of the *Hofkriegsrath*.

As individuals, if not as a class, the *grands seigneurs* were capable of considerable generosity. The Esterházys and Pálffys raised or maintained entire regiments out of their own pockets, while Prince Liechtenstein contributed ten million florins of his personal fortune to the work of reforming the artillery.

Below the level of the *grands seigneurs* the Austrian army lacked the stabilising influence that came from any class which could be compared with the Junker squirearchy of Prussia. The Prussian staff officer Hans v. Winterfeldt shrewdly observed that it was of fundamental importance for the Austrians to persuade the nobility to make a military career. 'They will never get anything done . . . unless they can compel the Bohemian counts to serve as free corporals or ensigns.'[2]

One of the radical problems came from the fact that most of the sons of the nobility attended the new provincial *Ritterakademien* or were sent to Halle, Leyden or other foreign universities, and only rarely took a path that would lead them into the state service. Maria Theresa was acutely aware of what was needed, and in the 1750s she gave every encouragement to the poor but respectable nobility to enter the new state-initiated foundations like the Theresianum, the Wiener Neustadt military academy and the reorganised engineer academy. In almost every case she evoked little enthusiasm.

The social gap was filled by a parvenu nobility of state and army service, which was demarcated at the upper end fairly sharply from the world of the *grands seigneurs*.

 The courtier Khevenhüller-Metsch wrote that the 1753 promotion of the Knights of the Golden Fleece caused displeasure to people of discrimination in such matters, who noted that it embraced a creature like the chief commissary Salburg, who was not of ancient or illustrious birth.

At the lower end the Habsburg nobility of service and indeed the officer corps as a whole was remarkably easy to enter. Field-Marshal Khevenhüller taught his cavalry officers that in the Austrian army there was no 'pre-eminence of the nobility',[3] and even the mighty Prince Joseph Esterházy was moved to agree:

> Subordination consists of obedience, submission to orders, respect, courtesy, and the observance of a difference between junior and senior . . . the nobility enjoys no preference in this regard whatever, for all the things are determined by rank. The higher a man's rank, the more it is up to him to distinguish himself and win merit.[4]

Cognazzo explained:

> It is a great virtue of the Austrian service that promotion is the unfailing reward of good service . . . by his courage, military experience and intelligence the lowliest soldier may win his way step by step from the musket to the sash of an order, from the society of his tent companions to that of the *Hofkriegsrath*.[5]

In this respect it is worth mentioning that in Maria Theresa's reign almost one-third of the holders of the Knight's Cross of the Military Order were of non-noble origin. Cognazzo himself was well acquainted with the career of an individual 'who began as a clerk to a regimental commander . . . then became a regimental auditor with the rank of lieutenant. A stroke of good fortune brought him to the full rank of captain, and in the Seven Years War the natural course of things made him colonel commandant of a regiment of hussars'.[6]

In any event it was quite easy for a persistent officer to make his way into the nobility of service. Maria Theresa was liberal in handing out the *Nobilitätsdiplom*, which implied no actual grant of land, and in April 1757 she decreed that she would bestow this document upon all officers who had served for thirty years with unblemished conduct. Thus was formed the most loyally Habsburg of all classes – the landless nobility of the new creation which owed everything to the dynasty.

National origins

Alongside the native Khevenhüllers, Trauns and Dauns of Maria Theresa's army we encounter such a quantity of foreign officers that it almost seemed as if the Austrian soil was incapable of producing good stock[7] – such was the combined effect of the diversity of the dominions, the unique opportunities for advancement, and the Habsburg tradition of prizing loyalty to the person of the sovereign above national origin. Out of the 177 recipients of the Knight's Cross of the Military Order of Maria Theresa in the Seven Years War, 72 had German names, 22 Irish or Scots, 21 French, 20 Italian, 18 Slavonic, 11 Magyar, 11 Flemish or Scandinavian, and 2 Spanish.

Some of the liveliest and most enterprising of Maria Theresa's commanders hailed from Hungary. Foremost was the brave and selfless General Nádasti. 'Not just the Hungarian cavalry, but the whole mounted arm without exception was devoted to him. Even the infantry held him in . . . generally high esteem.'[8]

The hussars and regiments of Hungarian infantry were officered principally by native Hungarians, to whom Maria Theresa awarded complete parity of status with the officers in the German regiments.

A high proportion of Maria Theresa's officers was furnished by the Empire, and Prince Albert of Saxony wrote approvingly of the armies of Austria as forces 'in which the first houses of Germany considered it an honour to serve'.[9] Dignitaries like the lords of Baden-Durlach, Baden-Baden, Brandenburg-Bayreuth, Zweibrücken-Birkenfeld, Anhalt-Zerbst, Sachsen-Gotha and Mecklenburg-Strelitz made a signal contribution to the service, for they usually kept their regiments in splendid condition, and filled them with prime recruits from their own lands. The other German officers came from all quarters of the Empire — Bavarians like Preysing, Saxons or Thuringians like Römer, Marschall and Jahnus, Hanoverians like Schulenburg-Oyenhausen, Rhinelanders like zum Jungen, Elmendorf and Nesselrode, and folk of Brandenburg-Prussian or Pomeranian stock like Brunyan, Buccow, Damnitz, Dönnhoff, Normann, Kalckreuth and Schröder.

The many Lutherans and Calvinists among the officers from the Empire were allowed to exercise their religion in private. In some cases it was diplomatically useful for the Austrians to have some Protestant officers at hand, as was proved after the capture of the heretical city of Breslau in 1757, when the Calvinist Lieutenant-General Sprecher was cunningly installed as governor, with the Lutheran Major-General Wulffersdorff as his commandant.

Whole regiments were officered almost entirely by Protestants, and at least one of Maria Theresa's ministers feared the outcome if Frederick tried to represent his quarrel with Austria as one of religion. The dreaded exodus never took place, despite Frederick's energetic propaganda. In any case there were some of the heretics (notably Schulenburg, Brettlach and Burghausen) who saw the error of their ways and embraced the True Faith of their own accord.

Italian officers owned a generally high reputation in the eighteenth century, and both Austrian Lombardy and the other Italian states produced commanders who did credit to 'that country where they have always known how to combine good manners with subtlety, courage and military talents'.[10] Piedmont was the native land of General Guasco, the hero of Schweidnitz, and the Colonel Caramelli who performed so well in command of the grenadiers at Kunersdorf. From the Lombard aristocracy came Visconti, Clerici, and the cold, slow-moving Serbelloni whose temperament stood in such contrast to that of southerners like Lucchese d'Averna, a hot-blooded Sicilian who was bred up in Spain. Pallavicini and Botta were born to the old aristocracy of Genoa, while the Piccolominis belonged to a family of papal nobility which had given generations of service to the Habsburgs.

A further distinctive Latin contribution to the army was rendered by the Spanish families of Cifuentes, Cordova, Montoja, Puebla and Vasquez. Their names recalled the Spanish ambitions of the old Emperor Charles VI, who showed extravagant generosity to the Spaniards who had declared themselves in his name.

Moving northwards, we meet another reminder of Charles VI's lost causes, in this case the duchy of Lorraine, which had been ceded by the Empire to the French in 1738. This part of the world blessed the Habsburgs with the gifts of Francis Stephen and his brother Charles and (more usefully, perhaps) those of the commanders Sincère, Dombasle, Ville and Ruttant.

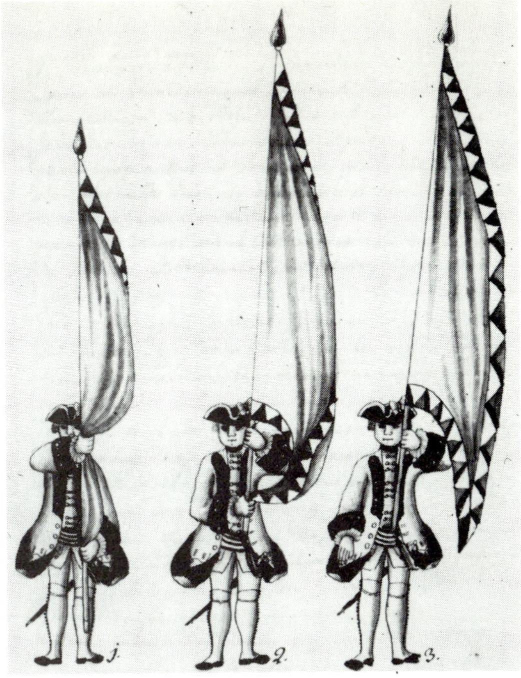

The officer in society (*Mansfeld, from Stephanie's* Die abgedankten Officiers, *1770*)
Ensigns (*Manuscript of 1749 Infantry Regulations*, Kriegsarchiv)

The Netherlandish tribute was remarkable for the high military and artistic gifts of Prince Charles Joseph de Ligne and Duke Karl Leopold of Arenberg. Another distinguished Netherlander, François-Sébastien de Clerfayt, began his career in the later part of the reign and went on to command Austrian armies in the 1790s.

The story of the Habsburg Irish is probably the most bizarre and revealing of all. Altogether the Irish gave the army of Imperial Austria some thirteen field-marshals, two presidents of the *Hofkriegsrath* and dozens of other generals. At the latest count the number of junior officers ran well into the hundreds. The Irish military men were themselves just one wing of an entire society which was uprooted from its homeland by religious discrimination. Irish civilians by the score were active in the Habsburg dominions as doctors, teachers, financiers, scholars and administrators.

The Irish soldiers arrived in Austria like creatures from outer space. It was soon evident that most of them were good fighters, and the Imperial heralds were suitably impressed when the Irish summoned up their long memories (and sometimes also their powerful imaginations) to compose long and impressive pedigrees. The Brownes boldly claimed descent from Hengist and Horsa, while the O'Donnells did not shrink from tracing their line back to the Dark Ages. Irishmen of all kinds liked to shroud themselves in an aura of mysterious aristocracy by adding the prefix *de* or *von* to the name of their native village or county. Thus the Irish could match every Karst von Karstenwerth and every Radetzky von Radetz with a Macquire von Inniskillin or a Kavanagh von Ballybrack. Some of the gentlemen acquiesced in the ways in which their names were mangled by their German neighbours, and so the historian can become familiar with names like 'Neulau' and 'Ottowart' without realising that he is looking at the honest Irishmen Nolan and O'Dowd.

The Irishmen liked to hang together, as Field-Marshal Daun noted in 1760, and the Hibernians came to hold an established position in eighteenth-century Austria. St Patrick's Day was the occasion of sentimental reunions, and a Vienna newspaper of 1765 records that the Spanish ambassador (whose name, by the way, was O'Mahony) celebrated 17 March by holding a banquet for a large number of Irish military men, and that the entire Court wore Irish crosses in honour of the occasion.

Prague had a powerful attraction for the newly-arrived Irish nobility. It was a beautiful city with a lively social and cultural life, and not nearly so expensive to live in as Vienna. It stood within convenient reach of the estates of the Brownes and other families, and practically every Irishman in the Imperial Army must have known his way to the House of the Irish Franciscans in the 'Street of the Irish' opposite the Powder Tower. These friars acted as a kind of clerical Mafia, and helped to keep up links between Irishmen in Central Europe, as well as passing on messages and enquiries to their native land. Prague was also the home of scores of Irish doctors, which enabled the Hibernians to find care for the body as well as for the soul. Further south Irishmen likewise congregated at Graz, and also across the Alps at Parma, where many of their sons were educated at the Noble College.

It was for a different kind of Irishman that Mozart wrote the part of Don Basilio in *The Marriage of Figaro*. This was Michael Kelly, who was the son of the Master of Ceremonies at Dublin Castle and famed for his fine tenor voice and polished manners. This gave rise to an embarrassing incident in 1787, when Kelly gained an audience with Joseph II. Kelly went to the Schönbrunn, and found Joseph chatting with a group of generals, among whom were numbered the old war horses Dalton, Dillon and Kavanagh. The Emperor was delighted at this encounter between Kelly, who was the epitome of the elegance of Georgian Dublin, and these representatives of an older and rougher Ireland. Gaelic has always been a mystery to Dubliners, and so Kelly was at a loss when Kavanagh made some remark to him in that language. Joseph turned around at once. 'What, Kelly,' he said, 'don't you know the language of your own country?' Without thinking, Kelly replied 'Please, Your Majesty, none but the lower orders of the Irish people speak Irish.' Joseph laughed aloud, and poor Kelly could have bitten his tongue off, but luckily the elderly generals were too polite, or possibly too deaf, to take him up on his rude remark.[11]

Adventurous and well-affected folk of all nations could serve in the army as 'volunteers', without entering the officer corps proper. In the Seven Years War the authorities gave a ready welcome to scions of princely houses like Dom João de Bragança and Prince Louis of Württemberg, as well as to accredited officers from the French, Russian and Saxon courts. Khevenhüller-Metsch retails the edifying story of the French general Montazet, who wore a blue coat, like the Prussians, and was mistakenly hacked about by the Austrian cavalry at Hochkirch. The drastic operation actually improved his looks, 'for his nose used to be somewhat crooked, but has now healed perfectly straight'.[12]

The fledgling officer

A large number of Maria Theresa's officers, and certainly nearly all the generals, entered the service in their boyhood or teens. Recruiting officers were instructed to try to obtain young noblemen as cadets for the regiment . . . these must be well built, of pleasant countenance and intelligent, for they are going to be trained as officers. The recruiting officer may be assured that nobody in the regiment will thank him for bringing in unsuitable cadets, be they of the most eminent families.[13]

Regimental proprietors were permitted to admit *Regiments-Cadeten* on this footing throughout the reign, but Maria Theresa felt that there was something haphazard about the system of rounding up cadets at random and leaving their instruction to the regiments. On 14 December 1751 she accordingly announced that she had decided to set up a proper military academy. Her ideas on the subject were probably influenced by her chief financial adviser, Count Haugwitz, who had travelled through Carinthia and Carniola in 1747, and seen how the young nobles were wasting their time hunting and fishing. The chosen creator was General Leopold Daun, and the site was the old Imperial *Burg* at Wiener Neustadt, a small town twenty-five miles south of Vienna. On 17 July 1752 Daun and Francis Stephen drove out to see the work, and one of the courtiers had to admit that 'a wonderful amount has been done in a short time'.[14] The place opened on 11 November with a complement of 191 cadets.

The Academy comprised two corps of a nominal 100 cadets each – one made up of the sons of the nobility of the Hereditary Lands, and the other of the sons of deserving officers or civilian officials. The cadets entered the Academy in their early teens, or sometimes younger still, and followed a course of from two to four years.

The cadet's day began when he was roused at five in the morning. He attended chapel at six, then drank a measure of soup to fortify himself against the strenuous morning of inspections and drill. Lunch was followed by an afternoon devoted to the study of fortification, artillery, mathematics, and the French, Italian and Czech languages, and the day was rounded off by a three-course supper. Time was also found in the syllabus for instruction in riding and in the polite accomplishments of dancing and fencing. A strict discipline was imposed on the younger cadets, but their older brethren were allowed a looser rein and some of the best among them were selected for the cadet government of corporals.

Maria Theresa followed the progress of the Academy with the closest attention, and she found it convenient to drop in on the place from the Imperial hunting lodge of Laxenburg. She was delighted at what Daun was doing, and she instructed the regiments to set aside places for the products of Wiener Neustadt, the first twelve of whom completed their courses in 1754.

The Wiener Neustadt cadets were fed and educated free. At the same time she established the Vienna *Theresianum* as a free finishing school for 100 sons of poor nobles and officers, and (just in case the nobility remained ignorant of what was going on) she sent descriptions of the *Theresianum*, the Wiener Neustadt Academy and the reformed *Ingenieuracademie* to the Austrian and Bohemian *Stände* for circulation among the noble families. Among the higher nobility the response was disappointingly small, and Maria Theresa exclaimed 'it is quite unbelievable that nobody is willing to take advantage of these favours'.[15]

Daun used to rule the officer academies 'on a military footing, in other words in an arbitrary and almost despotic manner'.[16] Towards the end of the reign, however, some officers began to feel that the training was elementary and unrealistic, and Maria Theresa accordingly sent General Franz Joseph Kinsky to have a look at several foreign military academies, notably the establishment at Stuttgart in Württemberg. It was largely on the Stuttgart model that Kinsky set about reforming Wiener Neustadt when he became *Lokaldirektor* in 1779. He replaced the NCOs by increasing the number of officer instructors, he persuaded Maria Theresa to present the Academy with a colour of its own, and he put affairs in general on a more military establishment. In later years Kinsky's former pupils looked back on him as 'a most well informed and estimable man, a loyal servant of the state and a true father to the pupils'.[17]

Regimental officers

The officer aspirants were variously admitted to the regiments as *Volontäre*, *Ordinari Cadeten* (the sons of serving officers), *Regiments Cadeten* or the senior *Fahnen Cadeten*. From there they advanced to the rank of ensign (*Fähndrich* in the infantry, *Cornet* in the cavalry). Already in 1752 the *Inhabers* were instructed to put aside every third vacancy for the future products of Wiener Neustadt. The ensign derived his name from his original function in life, which was to carry his unit's colour or standard on parade and in battle. He worked closely with the NCOs, and he had the special responsibility of seeing to the welfare of the sick and wounded. In return the elder officers of all ranks bore a responsibility towards the ensigns, and 'when a young man comes among them straight from his mother or a Jesuit college to begin his service, nobody must be permitted (as happens only too often) to amuse himself by leading him astray by various subterfuges. This kind of conduct does you no credit. After all, the young man is still your comrade, and he will be serving alongside you'.[18]

In 1748 the number of ensigns was reduced to eight to the regiment, and finally in 1759 the ranks of ensign and cornet were abolished altogether and the young men were made second lieutenants (*Unter-Leutenants*) instead. The actual responsibility of carrying the colours or standards was entrusted to reliable NCOs or men who bore the new rank of *Führer*.

With the appearance of the second lieutenant in 1759, the former lieutenant was renamed the first lieutenant (*Ober-Leutenant*). As before, he functioned as the captain's right-hand man in the running of the company.

The lot of the Austrian subalterns (ie the ensigns, cornets and lieutenants) was not a particularly enviable one. The Prussian commentator Berenhorst claims that the tribe was mostly recruited

> from NCOs who happen to be good at writing, from the Viennese court nobility, from sons of the lowest classes of Imperial functionaries, and from officers of fortune, the household officials of princes and counts and other lowly people of the non-labouring classes. To these must be added many Netherlanders and Italians of similar provenance. In other words they are all people who, except for the sons of officers and the products of Wiener Neustadt, are devoid of praiseworthy principles and warlike pride, and have never known what it was to sit at a father's knee and learn tales of ancestral deeds – it hardly matters whether they were fables or not.[19]

Thus (according to Berenhorst) was created a kind of officer proletariat, from which few men could hope to rise to a captaincy.

The picture was somewhat overdrawn, for Berenhorst came from a service where officer rank was regarded as a preserve of the nobility. All the same, Maria Theresa's army owned many lieutenants who had decades of ill-rewarded service behind them, and again and again the Austrian subaltern was reminded that he crouched at the very bottom of a great hierarchy of rank. Some of the colonels tyrannised their young officers mercilessly, and decorum between the ranks was maintained by a strict and (by Prussian standards)[20] very uncomradely code of etiquette. In the earlier part of the reign compliments were paid by raising the hat and bending the knee, a procedure which Maria Theresa regarded as 'totally unmilitary',[21] and as late as 1769 the regulations stipulated that on encountering a staff officer or general the junior officer must remove his hat, stand still and be ready to pay further respects when the potentate came close. In the off-duty hours the Austrian custom decreed that a junior officer must stand until his senior was seated, a rite which was enforced even between first and second lieutenants. Not surprisingly, the use of the familiar second person singular (*Du*) was not current in the officer corps until the nineteenth century.

The captain was the head of the company or squadron (he was called *Hauptmann* in the infantry and dragoons, and *Rittmeister* in the cuirassiers and hussars). He disciplined and administered the officers and men under his command, and answered directly to the regimental major. Otherwise he owned little of the authority of his counterparts in the Prussian army, for most of the company economy was managed by his regimental seniors and the officials of the *Commissariat*.

Senior officers were entitled to retain captaincies in their regiments, which gave rise in 1748 to the new rank of *Capitain-Leutenant*, an unfortunate class of person who did all the work for the nominal captains but collected none of the perquisites.

In 1769 each squadron of cavalry was assigned two captains, one of whom, the *Erster Rittmeister*, commanded the squadron as a whole and directed one of the two component 'wings', while the other, the *Rittmeister en second*, was responsible only for the second 'wing'.

Some of the best captains were detached to command the grenadier companies or élite squadrons of cavalry. As well as being a first-class officer, the grenadier captain was supposed to present the image of a 'highly civilised man, since he stands general watch in field and garrison and comes more to the notice of the generals than do the other officers, a circumstance which he can turn to his great advantage'.[22]

The major (*Obrist-Wachtmeister*, then *Major* from about 1757) was a stern-minded person who implemented the orders of the regimental commander. He inspected the troops daily, kept the captains and subalterns up to the mark, and rode before the troops with drawn sword whenever the regiment paraded or marched. As a man whose fundamental task was to enforce standards, he was expected to 'lay aside all familiarity and friendliness in affairs pertaining to the service, and to inspire great fear and respect whenever he appears with the regiment'.[23]

New officers were powerless to take up their duties before they were 'presented' to the regiment by the major. For this onerous work he was entitled to demand a present from the new officer – usually a brace of pistols or the equivalent in cash.

A position of second major was introduced in the Seven Years War and was made permanent in 1769, which facilitated tactical command now that the battalion was assuming greater importance as a fighting unit. In the sphere of administration the second major received reports and returns from the regimental adjutant who commanded the NCOs and who collated the muster lists from the companies.

The lieutenant-colonel (*Obrist-Leutenant*) was supposed to be present in person whenever the regiment appeared as a body. Otherwise he left the detailed management of drill to hard men like the major. His own sphere extended over the administration and welfare of the regiment in general, and he was expected to ensure that humanity was not forgotten in the running of affairs. He played a central part in some of the regimental ceremonies, giving the current password (*Parole*) to the officers, and presenting the daily and weekly reports to the colonel commandant.

In the absence of the colonel proprietor, that vitally important personage, the colonel commandant (*Titular Obrist*) carried on all the regiment's business. He guarded the privileges of the regiment, promoted officers and NCOs, directed the administration, and received and signed the reports and rolls. In view of the extent of his responsibilities, it is surprising that the colonel commandant had to be satisfied with a lieutenant-colonel's pay until 1755, when he was at last given a salary appropriate to his rank.

An important stage in the evolution of European standing armies was reached when the colonel proprietor (*Obrist-Inhaber*, *würklicher Obrister* or *Obrister*) was transmuted from the virtually untrammelled owner of his regiment into a military functionary, subject to direction by the state. In Austria this process made considerable strides in the Theresian period.

At the outset of the reign the *Inhaber* was in undisputed possession of the rights which Maximilian I had ceded to his colonels in 1508, in recognition of their generosity in raising regiments on his behalf. Except in the regiments of cuirassiers the *Inhaber* exercised an independent judicial authority (the *Jus gladii et aggratiandi*) which gave him the power of life and death over the men of the regiment. He advanced the officers and NCOs (though in practice the work was often devolved upon the commandant), and he did not hesitate to appoint officers from other regiments over the heads of officers of his own who might be senior or more deserving.

No officer, NCO or man could marry without the *Inhaber*'s permission, and this potentate's power even extended beyond the grave, for he could claim a *douceur* of a horse or 400 florins from the estate of every dead officer, and grab all the possessions of such officers as died intestate. As the supreme manager of the regiment's economy, the *Inhaber* could tap many further sources of wealth. With any contrivance he could divert some of the bounty money from the recruits, impose stoppages on his men, and keep back some of the *Verpflegs-Geldern* which were supposed to buy uniforms and equipment. On top of his colonel's pay he drew the income of captain of the *Leib-Compagnie*, but he was able to draw his general's salary only when he took the field or assumed command of a fortress.

Tactics, drill and words of command were left very much to the whim of the *Inhaber*, and he selected the colours of cuffs and lapels according to his taste.

The *Inhaber*'s freedom was systematically exploited by a number of bad men like General Samuel Schmettau, who deliberately left their regiments under strength while drawing money for the full establishment. Conversely a good *Inhaber* was willing to take on all kinds of unofficial obligations. He helped the women and children, he paid the debts of his officers, and he attended to the embellishment of his regiment 'by engaging fine-looking soldiers through better conditions or pay, by cultivating plenty of style, finery, panache and elegance, by building up a splendid and numerous corps of musicians, and other things of that kind'.[24] The

Prince de Ligne claimed that his campaigns in the Austrian service cost him over 800,000 florins, of which he devoted more than 200,000 to the welfare of his regiment and the other units under his command. Other conscientious *Inhabers*, like Joseph Esterházy or Leopold Daun, drew up excellent regulations which inspired the official codes of later years.

Whether they were misused or not, the *Inhaber*'s privileges took a hammering once Maria Theresa began to remake the army. In 1748 the *Inhaber*'s power to impose corporal punishment was restricted, and in the following year the new infantry regulations inaugurated the series of official codes which laid down set rules for tactics and the management of regimental affairs. In 1765 the *Hofkriegsrath* assumed the right to appoint all officers above the rank of captain, and two years later the colours of the uniform facings were allocated by lottery. In 1769, an important year, many of the strange regimental financial customs were abolished, the regiments were given a designation by number (instead of the *Inhaber*'s name) and the colonel commandant was given enhanced prestige as the mainspring which set all the other parts of the mechanism in motion.

The generals

The hierarchy of senior officers ran in the following ascending order:

> Major-General (*General-Feldwachtmeister*, or G.-FWM) Lieutenant-General (*Feldmarschall-Leutenant*, or FML) Full General (*Feldzeugmeister*, or FZM in the infantry; *General der Cavallerie*, or GdC, in the cavalry) Field-Marshal (*Feldmarschall*, or FM).

The rank of major-general was regarded as 'one of the most onerous functions which can exist, whether in field or garrison. It demands men of great liveliness, experience and skill'.[25] Essentially an executive instrument, the major-general commanded a brigade of two, three or more regiments.

The lieutenant-general managed a division or *Department* of two or three brigades.

Full general and General der Cavallerie, *Seven Years War period* (Ottenfeld)

Next in command came the full general, who exercised authority over an entire wing of infantry or cavalry, or (in the absence of other full generals) over wings of both arms.

The Austrian army was burdened with a grotesquely large corps of field-marshals. The Emperor Charles VI owned an excessively generous disposition, and the recipients of his bounty survived so long that Austria entered the war in 1740 with more than thirty field-marshals, hardly any of whom were fit to take active command of an army. Maria Theresa and Francis Stephen did nothing to redress the imbalance. Far too many of their field-marshals owed their exalted rank to a variety of bad reasons – because Maria Theresa wished to soothe their ruffled feelings, because the corps of generals needed to be cheered up, or (as happened in 1754) simply because the treasury desired to gather in money by way of fees.

Promotion and pay

Promotion in the Theresian army was at once expensive and unpredictable. The *Hofkriegsrath* exacted a set fee upon every advance in rank, and on 2 April 1745 a new scale of fees demanded greatly increased contributions from newly promoted officers, ranging from 50 florins from the new lieutenant to 2,000 from the new field-marshal. The formalities were arranged by agents in Vienna, who required a sweetener for their trouble, and, as we have seen, the ensigns, lieutenants and captains were required to give presents to the regimental major. The newly appointed *Inhaber* had to pay 400 florins to the commissary who 'presented' him to the regiment, while upon further promotion the senior officer yielded up a riding horse with full accoutrements to the general in authority over him.

In theory promotion proceeded from seniority or outstanding service, as determined for subalterns and captains by the *Inhaber*, and for senior officers by the *Hofkriegsrath*. The system, however, was subject to a number of almost irresistible pressures.

A hard-up or greedy *Inhaber* would be inclined to favour candidates who were willing to back up their enthusiasm with plenty of cash. People of this generous disposition could be speeded up the rungs of promotion, or, if they came from outside, could be inserted in the regiment by the process of *Aggregation*, which had originally been instituted as a means of finding places for officers from disbanded regiments. In 1748 Maria Theresa declared that *Aggregation* would have to end, 'so as not to cut off deserving officers from the path of promotion'.[26]

The advancement of able or lucky officers was greatly accelerated in wartime. The superb drillmaster Siskovics was rushed out of turn from grenadier captain to major, and a couple of days later he became colonel commandant of the regiment of Haller – a progress which so disgusted the lieutenant-colonel that this gentleman went off and joined the Prussian army. Beck was a major-general at twenty-seven, while the energetic Loudon took only four years to pass from major to full general. Maria Theresa was convinced that generals ought to be promoted on the strength of talent rather than seniority, and she regarded the career of Field-Marshal Lacy as a convincing proof of the importance of promoting a good man out of turn.

We find prohibitions or at least strong disapproval of the sale of commissions in Prince Eugene's edict of 1703, in General George Browne's private *Kriegs-Exercitium* of 1716, in various decrees of Charles VI and Maria Theresa, and finally and definitively in an outright ban in 1848. For the most part, however, the authorities seemed to have been resigned to keeping the habit under a modicum of restraint. No officer was supposed to buy his promotion by more than one rung at a time, or to injure the rights of others during his ascent.

The middle-aged officer looked upon his captaincy as an investment in money and labour, much as we nowadays regard a medical or legal practice, and he knew that when he came to retire he could realise something like 10,000 florins on the sale. All this gave a valuable element of flexibility:

> By this means the invalid officer, or one who is approaching that state, may be replaced by one who is younger and more active.
>
> Mediocre or bad officers can be purged from the regiment, making way for others who are more suitable.
>
> Wealthy men, who are always useful to a regiment, are encouraged by this prospect to opt for the military life.[27]

The officers' income was calculated on a complicated scale which comprised a money salary and a series of rations – 'mouth portions', bread rations, fodder rations, and *servis* (the allowance for firewood and light). At the top of the scale in the 1750s the field-marshal drew an annual 10,000–10,800 florins cash, with 150 'mouth portions', 45 bread rations, 54 fodder rations and 150 florins in *servis*. The ensign had to content himself with 228 florins in pay, 4 'mouth portions', 2 bread rations, 1 fodder ration and 4 florins in *servis*.

The monthly cash equivalent of a 'mouth portion' was 4 florins, and of a fodder ration 3 florins. As a general rule the 'portions' and rations could be made over in money or kind, though in theory an officer could draw the fodder ration only in kind and according to the actual number of his horses. All officers above second lieutenant always drew their *servis* in cash.

The French officer G. A. de Guibert concluded that Austrian generals were not particularly wealthy, as compared with their counterparts in France, but he added that they at least had the advantage of being paid at set rates. At the regimental level the subalterns seem to have had little opportunity or inclination to put much money aside, which placed them in some embarrassment when they had to fit themselves out for campaign.

The Austrian officer could retire with the minimum of formality. He merely had to send the request to the *Hofkriegsrath*, and serve on in his regiment until the consent arrived, which usually did not take very long. However, there was a real deterrent to leaving the service in the smallness of the pensions, which amounted to an annual 100 florins for an ensign, 150 for a lieutenant and 200 for a captain. On 2 April 1772 an official memorandum drew attention to the host of worn-out officers who could not be put up in the invalid houses, and made the comment that 'there are many of those gentlemen who are unable to exist on such pittances, and consequently have fallen into the utmost penury or other circumstances which bring the rank of officer into discredit'.[28] The facilities for the officers in the houses were therefore extended.

A number of the orphaned sons of officers were brought up in the Wiener Neustadt Academy, while others were admitted to the *Militär-Knaben Stiftung*, which was set up at Petau in 1768. It was decreed that in the Petau foundation 'the whole education and sustenance of the officers' children must correspond to the nature of their profession, and fit them to stand up to a life of hardship and fatigue'.[29] However, the young gentlemen at Petau were educated and accommodated separately from the sons of the NCOs and men, and they were placed directly in the regiments as cadets on reaching the age of seventeen or eighteen.

Uniforms and equipment

The impressive individuality of the eighteenth-century Austrian officers was at its most blatant in the matter of military dress. As Joseph Esterházy remarked to his regiment, there were some officers who were inclined to wear a proper uniform 'only as if they were doing a favour to their colonel'.[30] An observant Frenchman was struck by the

> difference in dress and manners which obtains between the Austrian and Prussian officers. The Austrians are entirely French in style, what with their coloured waistcoats and the great variety in the ways they wear their uniforms . . . from officer to private soldier the Austrians are distinguished from the Prussians by their bearing, by their dress, and, if I may say so, by their cast of features. I could almost have believed I was in a French garrison.[31]

When we have a description of the appearance of a specific officer, his garb is liable to show some remarkable variations from the regulation norm. There is the testimony of a Prussian lieutenant who was stricken in the bottom at the battle of Prague, and abandoned with the rest of the wounded when the Prussians retreated several weeks later. The Austrians took over the care of the unfortunates, and our Prussian records how

> amongst others Prince Kinsky came up to see us. He was wearing a blue coat with narrow silver braid, and I took him for a regimental surgeon. I begged him earnestly to take just one look at my wound, and showed him my naked behind. But he just laughed and said 'I don't know anything about that. I'm Prince Kinsky'.[32]

From the regulations we gain some inkling both of the determination of the authorities to enforce uniformity, and of the extent of the irregularities they were trying to correct. The infantry regulations of 1749 sought to impose a norm for officers' dress, and the edition of 1769 went on to stipulate, with some elaboration:

> All officers without exception must wear their sashes, as also gaiters of the same pattern as worn by the NCOs from *Feldwäbel* upwards. This applies on all appearances and parades of the regiment, and on every kind of service except ordinary drills and church parades (when they do not have to wear the sash), or in the field, where they may be permitted to put on boots. In no circumstances may they appear on duty with cloaks, button-up cloaks [*Roquelaures*], or furs, or wearing winter- or nightcaps under their hats. If they are allowed to put on a greatcoat in wet weather, this must be white and of the uniform style. Off duty, they dispense with the sash, and may appear according to circumstances in boots, gaiters or stockings. However, they must always have their hair

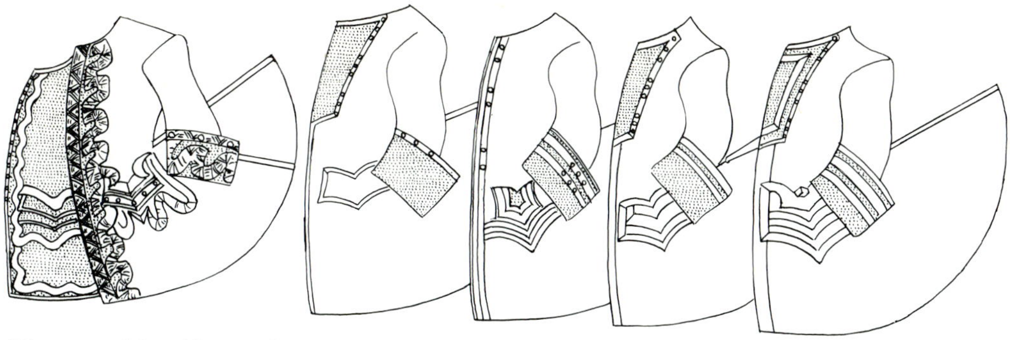

The generals' uniforms of 1751. From left to right, field-marshal (Feldmarschall), *full general of infantry* (Feldzeugmeister), *full general of cavalry* (General der Cavallerie), *lieutenant-general* (Feldmarschall-Leutenant) *and major-general* (General-Feldwachtmeister)

dressed in a pigtail, and wear the regimental uniform complete with sword, as perpetual signs of their officer status.[33]

Except for the better quality of the cloth, and certain items to be specified shortly, the regulation uniform of the Austrian officer was almost identical for most of the reign with that of the private soldier.

The hair was curled into locks at the side, and at the back it was drawn into the long military pigtail. The locks and crown were powdered, and the three-cornered hat was jammed on top of the whole confection.

The officers of both infantry and cavalry wore a sash wound about their middles immediately over the waistcoat. The colours were the Imperial black and yellow, and the materials and cost were laid down in some detail in a regulation of 18 December 1748. Only the generals were permitted to wear sashes of cloth of gold, and the rest had to content themselves with silk or wool.

At the beginning of Maria Theresa's reign the most evident sign of the German officer's authority was his partisan – a kind of short, broad-bladed pike. The weapon was about six feet long, including the blade and the shaft of polished black wood. The decoration of the head was meticulously determined by the rank of the wearer, from the gilded and tasselled blade of the colonel to the simple polished metal of the lieutenant (the NCOs carried a plain half-pike called the *Kurzgewehr*). The partisan went out of use in the late 1750s or early 1760s.

The stick was a further token of office. Everybody who laid claim to any kind of authority was proud to own one of these objects – whether the field-marshal with his decorated and jewelled baton, the corporal with his hazel stick, or the auditors, clerks and surgeons with their 'Spanish tubes'. A number of sayings were associated with the little wand that was carried by the ensign – 'nobody can lean on the *Herr* ensign's stick' or, more curiously still, 'it ought to bend when you lift up a girl's apron'.

The sword was worn with many small variations in form throughout the reign, though it seems to have been left to the individual whether to sport a sword knot as well.

The generals retained their regimental uniforms until, in November 1751, the *Hofkriegsrath* sent out instructions and drawings which gave details of a range of special generals' uniforms. The breeches, waistcoat and cuffs were of a light reddish brown. The coat was white, with gold buttons, and it was decorated with zigzag or wavy borders of gold braid according to the general's rank.

The eighteenth-century aristocrat surrounded himself on campaign with many of the comforts that he enjoyed at home. The English volunteer Horace St Paul took the field with the Austrians in the Seven Years War and brought along with him a tent complete with mobile kitchen, bed and chairs. His *petit portmanteau* was kept in perpetual readiness, and it contained a morocco-leather writing stand, six shirts, six cravats, eight handkerchiefs, six towels, four pairs of stockings, a pair of breeches, three waistcoats, two pairs of gaiters, bed linen with a kidskin coverlet, two night-caps and two sleeping hoods, a mirror with razor, brush and shaving soap, hair powder and pomade with combs and dressing gown, slippers, clothes brushes and boot scrapers, riding coat, candles with brass candlesticks, a box of drawing instruments, and maps and books.[34] Baggage like this was difficult to rescue in time of disaster, and (since the Austrians were beaten rather often in the 1740s) some officers lost their goods several times over in the course of a war.

The better-off subalterns and the captains and majors went to war with one private waggon each, as the regulations permitted. The colonel had two waggons, the general from two to four, and the field-marshal was allowed five, which was rather few by the standards of foreign armies. Various ordinances forbade the officers to attach their carts to the transport train, or to commandeer army horses and vehicles for their own purposes – which suggests that these convenient customs were commonplace.

The officer was permitted to detach only a couple of soldiers from his company as *Fourierschützen*, or batmen, but there was in practice no limit on the number of invalids or other people who could be hired as private servants.

The officers were quartered on private houses, when they did not camp with their regiments or dwell in one of the few barrack buildings. Here, too, every officer's entitlement was laid down in the regulations which came out in the later 1740s and the 1750s. The subalterns were each allotted two rooms and a kitchen, while the field-marshal enjoyed a full suite of ten rooms and a kitchen. On campaign the generals had their quarters selected for them by the staff quartermaster.

The pay and the rations were quite inadequate to sustain the poorer officers in the field. Field-Marshal Daun informed Maria Theresa on 14 May 1757 that if he did not hold open table many officers would 'get little or nothing to eat'. Maria Theresa offered to defray the cost of a free table for thirty or forty subalterns, but Daun had to reply that this arrangement would still be of little use to the young officers who found themselves at any distance from headquarters. The subalterns had to spare their horses, and rather than make the long journey they would content themselves with 'a spoon of soup'.[35]

On the cramped and murderous battlefields of the eighteenth century officers of all ranks stood in the same acute danger. The Prince de Ligne tells how he won large sums of money in a gambling session with five officers on the eve of the battle of Breslau, and how every one of his debtors was killed on the next day without having paid up.[36] Elsewhere he has a rather nasty story about a rich young Walloon officer who died of wounds:

> His father wanted to have the body. But where on earth were we to find it among the 'salt pots' [grave pits] where the corpses had been thrown in thou-

sands at a time? The father was four hundred leagues away, and we knew of his wish two months after the event. Luckily the army was encamped near the battlefield, and the officer who was entrusted with this task took the first body he lighted upon. This happened to be the corpse of a Prussian soldier. The body was sent to Namur, where a thousand masses were offered uselessly for its benefit. I have seen the tomb, which was a fine affair of marble.[37]

Generally speaking, the Austrian officer corps was careful to observe the code of honour which used to ameliorate some of the acerbities of war in the eighteenth century. At Rossbach in 1757 the Duke of Voghera, leading the cuirassier regiment of Brettlach, saluted and received the salute of the nearest Prussian general, then launched his men into the charge. The incident was typical of the spirit of the times. Most gracious of all, perhaps, was the gesture of Joseph II, who during some manoeuvres near Prague in 1776 formed a square of six grenadier battalions around the spot where the Prussian field-marshal Schwerin had died nineteen years before, and fired three salvoes of muskets and cannon in his memory. Frederick the Great wrote to his brother Prince Henry: 'Past centuries can show nothing to compare with such magnanimity. This is better than the deed of Achilles, who is praised to the skies by Homer, yet who had the body of Hector dragged from his chariot around the walls of Troy.'[38]

The Austrian officers seem to have fared reasonably well in Prussian captivity. The custom of the eighteenth century gave the officer prisoner the status of a guest until such time as the belligerent governments got around to arranging a cartel – an agreement which specified the going rates of exchange for every rank of prisoner. A field-marshal, for instance, was returned to his friends for something like 3,000 rank and file soldiers or 15,000 florins, while a colonel merited a mere 130 men or 650 florins. The price of a private was set at around 5 florins.

Meanwhile the officer prisoner made himself as comfortable as he could. Some of the Austrian generals (and even some of their wives) became part of Berlin society, and more particularly the circles which revolved round the Queen of Prussia and Prince Henry's wife Wilhelmine. General Thürheim provoked frissons of delicious horror among the ladies, by showing the silver plate which filled an old wound in his head, while General Beck made a particularly good impression on the queen's master of ceremonies, who talks of him as 'a small man with finely-drawn features and a penetrating gaze'.[39]

An impression of the lot of the junior officers comes from the young Captain Johann Franz Khevenhüller-Metsch, who was captured while looking after a party of sick at the time of the battle of Leuthen. After a hard march and an uncomfortable night he was brought before King Frederick, who told him in a scornful way that he had missed nothing by not being present at such an uninstructive battle. The captain replied with spirit that he 'had been present at four other actions in the same year which had been instructive enough, to wit Kolin, Görlitz, the bombardment of Liegnitz, and most recently the battle of Breslau'. Frederick promptly changed the subject of conversation. Khevenhüller-Metsch was thereupon detained with about seventy other officers at Neisse. The conditions were pleasant enough, and a few months later he was released by way of exchange, and returned to his parents 'burnt brown like a gipsy, but otherwise healthy and looking well'.[40]

The Austrians made some considerable hauls of Prussian prisoners, capturing almost one-tenth of Frederick's entire corps of officers on the single day of Maxen

(21 November 1759). Enemy private soldiers were usually sent to the southern provinces of Austria. A Prussian author wrote in 1778 that 'twenty years ago the common sort of people in Carinthia and the Tyrol still regarded Protestants as not quite human. However, the affair of Maxen had the effect of disabusing a good ten thousand folk of these and many other superstitious delusions'.[41] Most of the junior officers ended up at Hainburg and Bruck-an-der-Leitha on the Austro-Hungarian borders, or at Krems, which was a very pleasant town in the Wachau. Once they had given their parole the Prussians were free to wander as they pleased:

> The town of Krems was in a romantic situation, with the wide Danube flowing on the one side, and terraced vineyards rising to the crests of the hills on the other. As further attractions there were the beautiful tree-lined avenues which followed that majestic river to the monastery and town of Stein and the market town of Mautern. All of this offered us plenty of agreeable walks, and we took advantage of them in perfect safety.[42]

Nearly all the generals, and some of the other officers, were accommodated in some style as the personal 'house prisoners' of Maria Theresa in Vienna. At the end of the Seven Years War 250 of these gentlemen held a farewell dinner, at which General Finck proposed a toast to the Empress-Queen. The fanatical General Fouqué presented the Austrians with their only really awkward guest. He protested that the Prussian officer prisoners were being paid in low-value Dutch coinage, and made himself such a nuisance that in September 1761 he was consigned to Carlstadt in Croatia. In retaliation Frederick had the Austrian lieutenant-generals turned out of their quarters in Magdeburg and sent to the citadel: 'A number of the generals did not like the idea of exchanging their comfortable quarters in the town for a fortress chamber, and it became necessary to evict them by force.'[43]

What was the peacetime life of the Austrian officer? At first sight this gentleman does not seem to be renowned for his sense of grinding devotion to duty. In theory at least he could gain private leave at a fee of four florins per month, and we hear an official complaint to the effect that 'the officers are often away from their regiments or posts for a year at a time, leaving others to carry out their duties'.[44] If the reprobates claimed most of the attention, we must still bear in mind that a large body of poor or conscientious officers lived a severely constricted life. The existence of the officers of the Croats could be bleak, even terrible, while their cousins among the hussars had not yet acquired the later reputation of the light cavalry for carefree extravagance. Thus in 1762 the French envoy in Vienna successfully discouraged one of his young countrymen from entering the Austrian service as an officer of hussars. He explained that affairs were not on the same footing as in France, where an officer need do only four months' duty in the year, leaving himself free to pass the whole winter in Paris and perhaps make the acquaintance of a wealthy heiress:

> Here, on the contrary, you are liable to be stationed in peacetime in some ghastly Bohemian or Hungarian village. You can get leave at the very most only once every two years, so as to spend the Carnival season in Vienna. And you won't do yourself much good if you renew your application too often.[45]

Officers of all arms knew one of the nuisances of the Austrian service, where regiments were shuttled from one station to another every two or three years. For the officer this was 'more troublesome and inconvenient than if he was placed in one permanent quarter. Then at least, when a war ended, he would know in what country and under what roof he could lay his head'.[46] Such was the case in Prussia.

In the earlier reign the less well-off subaltern had precious few places where he could spend his off-duty hours in an agreeable manner. Cafés became prominent only in later decades, and meanwhile the inns offered the only escape from the regimental guardroom, where the officers congregated to eat, drink, gossip and gamble.

All this encouraged an unsophisticated kind of entertainment, and the Prince de Ligne looked back with regret to the lively young officers of the 1750s, who

> created all sorts of commotions. While we were spending a winter in quarters in Dresden, for example, we walked around in chains, played at ghosts, changed the shop signs about, and danced quadrilles with the sedan chairs when we came across people who were being carried away from some grand dinner. Amongst other amusements, we used to cry out fire alarms and squirt water over the citizens who appeared at the windows, or go to the camp and cause the tents to collapse. On one occasion, when I was enjoying myself in this manner, I heard a pistol fired by an officer who was not particularly fond of jokes.[47]

While a modicum of horseplay was tolerated, all sorts of pressure could be brought to bear on young officers who threatened to get above themselves:

> Just see them at Minkendorf or Prague, when the Emperor [Joseph], Lacy, Hadik or Loudon commands the army! The day before the subalterns might have ordered a village about in a high-handed fashion, but now they shrink before the splendour of heroes of this kind . . . Garrison life in Vienna also does much for the education of these young gentlemen. They are valued for their own worth, if they happen to be intelligent and modest, and know how to live. If, however, they hope to impress other people by their pushing and boastful behaviour, they are left to stew in their barracks.[48]

The prosperous senior officer naturally had a much wider world at his disposal – the comedy and ballet, the royal apartments, the ante-rooms of the noble palaces, and (even in wartime) a restorative excursion to take 'the cure' at Karlsbad or other resorts. Lacy was especially fond of the ambience of Spa in the Ardennes, and after the Seven Years War he begged Count Nugent, the Austrian envoy to Berlin, to meet him there so as 'to live, to eat, to drink, and let ourselves go a little . . . In Spa we can admire great rocks, the peculiar beasts of the mountains and all sorts of other things which are well worth seeing'.[49]

Lacy and his like were valued in polite society on account of their varied experiences and their knowledge of mankind. Again the respect was accorded to the man rather than to his uniform, which was the reverse of the priorities obtaining in Prussia.

Gambling was the first recourse of most of the officers who craved stronger sensations. On occasion the stakes were ruinously high, and it was not unknown for a captaincy or a colonelcy to change hands on the fall of a single card. The authorities were willing to acquiesce in a little play for small stakes, but gambling on credit was always regarded with severe disfavour. Finally on 2 June 1753 the order went out forbidding any officer, without the written permission of his regimental commander, to fall more than 100 florins in debt.

A whole string of edicts testify to the inability of the authorities to keep down the Austrian officers' love of hunting on campaign – which was one of the many traits which they shared with their English counterparts. We have a characteristic specimen from the field service regulations of 1749, which proclaimed that offenders were going to be punished regardless of rank. 'At the same time hunting dogs and indeed all other kinds of dogs are to be banished from the army or shot.'[50]

The duel flourished almost everywhere in eighteenth-century Europe, but in the Austrian service it was crushed by an astonishingly draconian edict of 1752. The challenger, the challenged and the seconds – all were to be beheaded, even if the duel turned out to be a bloodless affair; if one of the participants fled, his property was to be administered by the state, and restored to his heirs only after the offender had died in exile.

Next to the French, the Austrian officers enjoyed probably the best selection of wines of any European army, and above all the splendours of Tokay and the other Hungarian vintages. All the same the Austrians do not seem to have been great drunkards, judging by the little which the regulations have to say on this head.

Blatant sexual immorality was rare and somewhat dangerous in Theresian Austria, but the statuesque and empty-headed ladies of Viennese society considered themselves out of fashion if they did not have a cavalier of some kind to tow in their wakes. Many a young officer-about-town acquired his knowledge of worldly manners from a high-born inamorata perhaps as much as a dozen years his senior – the kind of arrangement which inspired the *Rosenkavalier* of Richard Strauss. Princess Wilhelmine Auersperg (1738–75) probably took first place as the educator of young officers and the consoler of the older ones. 'She was of the medium size, her complexion of clear brown, her eyes grey, her hair chestnut, luxuriant and glossy.'[51]

Two at least of the senior commanders were assisted by feminine influence. As the father of the devastating Wilhelmine Auersperg, Field-Marshal Neipperg had a strong claim to consideration from her circle of admirers, among whom was numbered Emperor Francis Stephen himself. Then there was the complicated case of General (later Field-Marshal) Daun, who married Josepha Nostitz in 1745. The lady was a grieving widow, and the match aroused all the more speculation since 'both the newly-married partners have passed the age when love is spiced by mystery'.[52] What was more important was the fact that Josepha was the daughter of Countess Fuchs, who in turn was Maria Theresa's nanny and yet another of the objects of the Emperor's affections. Thus when Daun was on campaign the *Feldmarschallin* was able to safeguard his flank at court, rather like Marlborough's Duchess Sarah in the London of Queen Anne.

The Austrian officer was rarely discouraged from marrying, if he found a suitable woman, though the artillery regulations of 1757 cold-heartedly stipulate that no gunner officer was to marry unless he could show that his spouse would have enough to live on if she became widowed. The mobilisation of the summer of 1756 revealed that the wives of the poor officers of all arms were living under very hard conditions.

Many of the wives of the more wealthy officers wished to accompany their husbands into the field, and they were severely disappointed when (as usually happened) they were ordered to stay at home. General Hadik was made slightly ridiculous by the way his spouse trailed about with him almost everywhere he went, while the *Feldmarschallin* Königsegg almost died of chagrin when her husband set off to take command in the Netherlands in 1745.

When a wife was not present to exercise her authority, the regimental provost stepped in to take her place:

> He must make due report to the regimental chaplain when he discovers that an officer is keeping a woman under the pretence of a cook, a cleaner, a laundress or the like. The other whores are usually to be found plying for their living among the sutlers, and the provost is to expel them from the regiment without further ado. Should they come back, he is to have them flogged and cast out by his assistant. If they return yet again, he is to shave their eyebrows, cut off the hair from their heads, and have them whipped on their way once more.[53]

Once placed under arrest for any reason, an officer was bound to go meekly and silently to his place of confinement. Any representations had to be left to his comrades, who were supposed to enter their pleas within twenty-four hours.

Maria Theresa was very fond of intervening on the side of respectability. She had all sorts of devices for the reform of erring young officers, which was why the Prince de Ligne used to go about in terror of her, much to the amusement of the court. In 1779 she consigned Lieutenant Carl Montoja to correction in the monastery at Beraun, in the wilds of Bohemia. Next year the chastened young man wrote to her to explain that his confinement had entered the second year,

> and all the time I feel as if I am being buried among rocks. Now my eyes are opened. Now I see the magnitude of my faults. Often and deeply have I regretted them.[54]

Morale and proficiency

Nowhere are Maria Theresa's imaginative and creative instincts more evident than in her ambition to build up a sense of pride and cohesion in her corps of officers. As early as 1747 the Prussian envoy reported:

> She seeks to grant distinctions to the military men, who certainly stand in higher esteem than they did under the late Emperor. She has frequently stated that it is only through the sword that one may make one's fortune under her rule. When officers are on duty with her she invites them to dine at her table, regardless of their rank. This habit gives great displeasure to the high nobility . . .[55]

She was in full agreement with Daun when he pointed out that they could not hope to attract the nobles and wealthy magnates to the profession of arms,

> unless we can do everything we can to make the military class an object of emulation. This consideration gains all the more importance from the fact that the treasury cannot possibly give higher pay to the considerable armed forces which Your Majesty is compelled to maintain.[56]

It was 'out of special grace and favour for the military'[57] that Maria Theresa decided that officers would be allowed access to the apartments wearing uniform beneath their Spanish court dress. The only etiquette that the officers had to know was to bend the knee three times on approaching and leaving the Imperial presence. The appropriate decrees went out on 25 February 1751. In later years Joseph II characteristically drove things to an extreme. He seldom ventured forth except in uniform (like his rival Frederick the Great) and he relieved his officers altogether from the obligation of wearing the Spanish *Mantelkleid.*

In 1757 Maria Theresa gave veteran officers of good repute an automatic entitlement to nobility. Ten years later she awarded senior officers the 'permission to hunt large and small game on the Crown estates in the German and Hungarian Hereditary Lands',[58] and in 1771 she enlarged the *Elisabeth-Stiftung* for hard-up old generals.

Most of all, the Austrian army prized the white crosses and the red and white ribbons of the Military Order of Maria Theresa. The day of Kolin (18 June 1757) was declared the birthday of the institution. The Order consisted initially of two grades, those of Grand Cross and Knight's Cross. An intermediate grade, that of Commander, was introduced in 1765. Emperor Francis Stephen became Grand Master of a specially-appointed chapter, which was to be convened at intervals to sift through likely candidates. This body was under instructions (by statute no 3) to look for specific deeds of gallantry, and ignore claims based upon 'high birth, long service, wounds sustained in action, or past merit, let alone simple favour or second-hand recommendations'.[59]

Disappointingly enough, the first batch of crosses went on 7 March 1758 to grand personages like Daun, Nádasti and Prince Charles of Lorraine. The later promotions were, however, much more inspired, and by the end of the war the 177 knights numbered in their ranks heroes like the sixteen-year-old Second Lieutenant Baron Mylius, who took part in the storming of Glatz in 1760.

Frederick the Great wrote in the War of the Bavarian Succession that Austrian generals were willing to take unjustifiable risks, just to gain the Order. The award retained its peculiar magic until the very end of the Habsburg Empire, and was bestowed sparingly even in the great bloodletting of World War I.

Maria Theresa and her fellow reformers were determined that the officers must earn their enhanced status through hard work and professionalism. Daun stressed that

> intelligence is the distinguishing feature of the body of officers, just as courage is that of the soldiers . . . Experience by itself is incapable of enabling one to acquire military knowledge in a systematic way. A foundation of theory is necessary, if you want to equip yourself to carry out important military functions. It is not enough for a commander to master weapons. He must also be conversant with books, maps and topographical sketches. He must own a precise understanding of the fundamental principles of military knowledge.[60]

Some of the more ambitious younger officers began to despise their happy-go-lucky seniors. The Prince de Ligne had no time for the kind of general who used to say 'in the old days we didn't bother about drill. We gave the soldiers something to do, and some of the officers spent all day dancing with Tyrolean girls, while others went to headquarters and eventually returned to their tents drunk or ruined by gambling. . . . In the old times we were happy, scruffy, and . . .' here the Prince de Ligne used to step in with a tart '. . . and you got beaten'.[61]

If the years brought a gradual improvement in technical efficiency, there were still too many ways in which the reputation of the Austrian officer corps remained frankly bad. A Prussian observer accused the Austrians of lacking a sense of tactical initiative, and he claims that throughout the Seven Years War

> they thought only of parrying the blows which were directed at them. Every commander remained just where fate had placed him at the beginning of the action, without bothering about what was happening in the other parts of the field. All too often they seemed to be almost indifferent to the outcome of a battle.[62]

Browne's generals let him down badly at Lobositz. So did most of Daun's at Hochkirch, and after this last battle Daun remarked sagely that there had been many operations which 'could not be executed as they could and would be, if we had more generals who showed a trace of ability or enterprise'.[63] Later in the war, when it was a question of ransoming some of the captured Austrian generals, Daun commented that it would be better to leave these 'heroes' in the hands of the enemy. Maria Theresa was well aware of the problem. Indeed it is likely that statutes nos 3 and 21 of her Military Order were deliberately drafted so as to galvanise her sluggish commanders into displaying some kind of initiative.

There is also a distinct impression of a lack of mental activity, at least concerning the problems of the service. As the French volunteer Champeaux remarked, 'in general they do not get down to hard work. They look upon study as a tacit avowal of incapacity'.[64] The Austrian army certainly had its quota of highbrows – men like the essayist and freethinker Prince Charles Joseph de Ligne, his fellow Netherlander Field-Marshal Arenberg, who was a friend and correspondent of Voltaire, the keyboard virtuoso and composer Major Ignaz Beecke, Lieutenant-Colonel Ayrenhoff the playwright, and the engineer general Phillip Harsch, who was a skilful flautist and a patron of artists and musicians. However, we look in vain for any body of literature to compare with the memoirs of the contemporary Prussian officers, who were a lively and critical body of men. Even in professional matters very little ever got written down. When an unusually inquisitive officer tried in 1756 to assess the evolution of the Austrian cavalry in recent decades, he was forced to rely largely upon hearsay, for there were so few men in the Imperial service 'who give themselves the trouble of putting together observations or useful descriptions of campaigns'.[65]

The physical and intellectual idleness of some of the officers was compounded by a feeble sense of corporate responsibility. At the outset of the reign the crisis of 1740–1 provoked a rash of desertions, most notably that of Field-Marshal Seckendorff, who went over to the Bavarians. In later years the Prussian spymaster Hans v. Winterfeldt was able to entice a number of Austrian officers into the Prussian service, and he found little difficulty in persuading several more to send him reports and plans.

Even commanders of irreproachable loyalty were fond of feuding among themselves in a most destructive way. During the mobilisation of 1756 the generals were notably slow to betake themselves to the field – some because they disliked the commanders, and others because they wanted to fix themselves up with the baggage appropriate to their rank. Serbelloni eventually turned up at Piccolomini's headquarters in September and declared that 'the Empress should not be under the misapprehension that she can order about a general of cavalry like a major'.[66] In the subsequent campaigns the army divided itself up into the parties of the *Nádastianer*, the *Daunianer*, the *Lacyianer*, the *Loudonianer* and the like, and it is not going too far to suggest that the rift between Loudon and the Lacy–Daun connection may have cost Maria Theresa the war.

We must conclude that many of Maria Theresa's officers failed to respond to her efforts to train them up and imbue them with a sense of pride. At the lower level the explanation was largely one of figures. As Kaunitz pointed out in 1757, 'the lack of officers is one of the principal defects of the Imperial army'.[67] There were just three or four officers to run the large infantry company of 200 men, and five or six to direct the squadron of cavalry. These numbers were frequently reduced by half, according as officers became unfit for service or were sent away to command detachments. 'In these circumstances,' wrote Prince Charles of Lorraine, 'we have to leave the private soldiers to their own devices, even though the men are of use only when there are officers to lead them.'[68]

The lack of corporate pride and communal purpose was a more complicated malady, which derived perhaps from the cosmopolitan background of the officer corps, and its lack of class unity. It is important to bear in mind that Maria Theresa inherited her army at a time when a spirit of faction had already set in among her officers. In the last years of Charles VI the Prince of Sachsen-Hildburghausen detected a passion for place-hunting, which he attributed to the way in which seniority and merit were overlooked when officers were promoted. Field-Marshal Khevenhüller preferred to look to a more fundamental cause – to a breakdown in the spirit of order, which had once been maintained at root by a corps of able NCOs.

As a woman Maria Theresa could do little to curb the natural instinct of some military men to devote more energy to worsting their domestic rivals than to beating the common enemy. The Austrian service owned no figure to compare with Frederick of Prussia, who was at once the active director of the field army, the focus of loyalty and the source of all distinction.

4

The Men

Recruiting

For most of its existence the Theresian army resorted to a crop of ill-assorted expedients to harvest a crop of more or less willing recruits, and only at the end did it think of basing itself on a 'modern' system of conscription. The wonder is that the quality of the rank and file remained fundamentally good.

The primary obligation of recruiting lay on the individual regiments, which armed themselves with the appropriate authority from Vienna and sent out officers to gather in volunteers. The recruiting parties for the 'German' regiments ranged through the German Hereditary Lands and the *Reichsunmittelbare* areas of the Empire, though elsewhere in Germany they needed the permission of the city or the reigning prince. The negotiations with the German sovereigns were considered a 'branch of foreign affairs',[1] and were managed by the Chancellor, the *Reichshofkanzlei* and the President of the *Hofkriegsrath*. In 1766, to avoid confusion, each regiment was assigned a fixed recruiting district (*Rayon*) within the Empire. The ordinary regimental recruiting brought in a notoriously high proportion of shady characters, but some of the very best human material in the army came by way of those princes of the Empire who raised and maintained regiments for Maria Theresa largely at their own cost.

The proportion of foreigners among the rank and file varied considerably from time to time. It was very high at the outset of the reign, but the war with Bavaria and Saxony closed off much of the Empire to Austrian recruiting, and so in 1744, out of a total of 52,391 recruits, only 19.4 per cent were drawn from outside the Habsburg dominions.[2]

While every 'German' regiment had its own flavour, it was also 'an aggregate of men of all the Hereditary Lands. Together with the recruits from the Empire they formed a compound in which troops of the various nations were certainly intermingled, yet never so closely bound as to provoke undesirable consequences'.[3]

In principle the non-German 'national' regiments were supposed to recruit only from their own countrymen, but on 12 September 1756 the Netherlands and Italian regiments were allowed to recruit in the Empire, and on 3 January 1758 the Hungarian regiments were given authority to enlist deserters and foreigners of all nations.

The appallingly severe discipline which obtained in Frederick's army encouraged a mass of men to desert from the Prussian service. These fugitives were given a ready welcome by the Austrians, whether they intended to enlist in the army or not, and bounties were paid to men who were enterprising enough to bring over their muskets, pistols or horses. The Prince de Ligne claimed that enemy deserters were a useful acquisition for the army, being skilful, brave and determined people.[4] This striking observation did not entirely accord with his own experience. One day,

General Lacy wanted news of the enemy. He called out to a Prussian hussar on outpost duty 'Ten ducats for you if you desert!' He really had no hope of success, but the hussar galloped up to us, braving a carbine shot from his neighbour on the way. He told us what he knew and Lacy duly paid up, even though the information was of little value. Now we had to decide what to do with him. General Lacy proposed that I should take him into my service. He proved incorrigible, stealing everything he could lay his hands on and lashing out with his sabre in all directions. He was such a dangerous character that whenever I returned to camp at night-time I made him walk in front of me, and kept a hand on my pistol. It was all my fault – I have never been able to send anyone away. Luckily he killed a sutler. He deserted once more and relieved me of my embarrassment.[5]

The mechanisms of 'voluntary' recruiting are not without their interest. The infantry recruiting officers went on their rounds accompanied by a little train of clerks, medical orderlies, musicians, and NCOs and private soldiers chosen from 'the most senior, the best and the finest-looking men of the regiment'.[6] The playwright Gottlob Stephanie knew the realities of the army from his service with the Austrians as a *Feldwäbel*, and in his play *The Recruiting Officers* (*Die Werber*, Vienna, 1763) he presents us with the ideal of a responsible and humane recruiter in the person of the dragoon captain Werten, who maintained that you did not need confidence tricks to attract men into the service, as long as you could offer the recruit a real prospect of advancement. 'Provided he is an able man, and is confident that he can make his way thereby, he will cheerfully shoulder his musket, being assured that he will not have to carry it for long.'[7]

The Prince de Ligne, who was less scrupulous, tells us that canny recruiting officers found good hunting grounds at the country fairs. It was a good idea for them to make no positive attempt to catch any men until two or three days had passed. This gave the peasants time to run out of money and get into fights, and they were then only too keen to escape justice by enlisting in the army.[8] Cognazzo adds some enlightening details as to how the trap was baited: 'There are a number of attractive tricks which work almost irresistibly on the minds of the mob – a ringing handbell, the persuasive patter of a recruiting officer who is up to all the dodges of the charlatan's trade, seductive music, and a beaker which is kept full of sparkling wine.'[9] An attractive uniform was by no means the least of the inducements, which was why Prince Fürstenberg specified in 1770 that his regiment must be allowed to sport facings of yellow.

The financial inducement was offered by a bounty ranging from twenty-five florins for the infantryman to fifty or more for the cuirassier and dragoon. Eighteen or more florins might be deducted as stoppages for pay for uniform and side arms, which indicates that the bounty alone could have played little part in winning men over.

Cognazzo claims that once the 'volunteer' appreciated his fate, it was no better than a pressed man's.

We should not allow ourselves to be blinded by delusions about 'love of country' or 'inclination towards military service'. If we take the trouble to investigate the most important impulses which bring the lads to the free recruiting table, we shall find that they are things like drunkenness, a frenzy of passions, love of

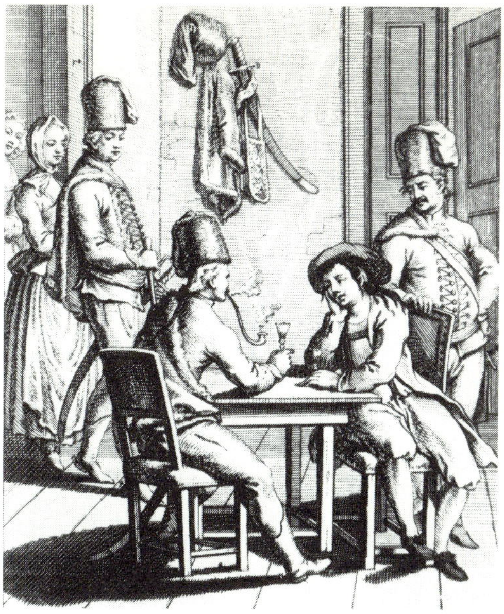

The recruiting table (Mansfeld, from Stephanie's Die Werber, *1763)*

> idleness, a horror of any useful trade, a wish to escape from parental discipline, inclination towards debauchery, an imaginary hope of untrammelled freedom, sheer desperation, the fear of punishment after some sordid crime, or however else you care to define the motives of worthless people like these.[10]

Outright compulsion was, however, very rarely employed in regimental recruiting. There were very few cases like that of the young haberdasher's apprentice of Vienna, who in 1744 was forcibly enlisted at the instance of his prospective father-in-law. On joining the transport of recruits to Italy he found that he was the only individual out of three hundred men who was not a volunteer. The officers of his regiment were sorry to hear of his fate, but said that they were powerless to do anything about it. Our unwilling recruit therefore solved his problems by deserting.[11]

In general the recruiting officers shunned Frenchmen, Jews, Turks and gipsies. The preferred ages were between eighteen and thirty, and officers were unwilling to accept recruits of less than 5ft 5in in height.

Because cavalry service was inherently so attractive, the recruiting officers of this arm were forced to go about their business with some circumspection, so as not to divert recruits from the unglamorous infantry. The mounted regiments were on the lookout for men who had been brought up with horses and were used to hard work – people like blacksmiths, ploughmen, carters and cattle drovers. Recruits were taken from the ages of eighteen to forty, and the minimum height was fixed at 5ft 4in.

The second main source of recruits in the older period was the conscripts furnished by the *Stände* of Austria and Bohemia. The process was costly and haphazard, for the *Stände* gained a rebate on taxation of anything between twelve and twenty-four florins for every conscript delivered up, and each year the government had to negotiate the agreements afresh. Considered as groups, the Austrian and Bohemian *Stände* each furnished the recruits in annual batches of between three and eight thousand. The selection of the conscripts was largely the business of the feudal lords, who rounded up vagabonds and peasants' sons willy-nilly. No workable alternative was found to this horrible system before the last decade of the reign.

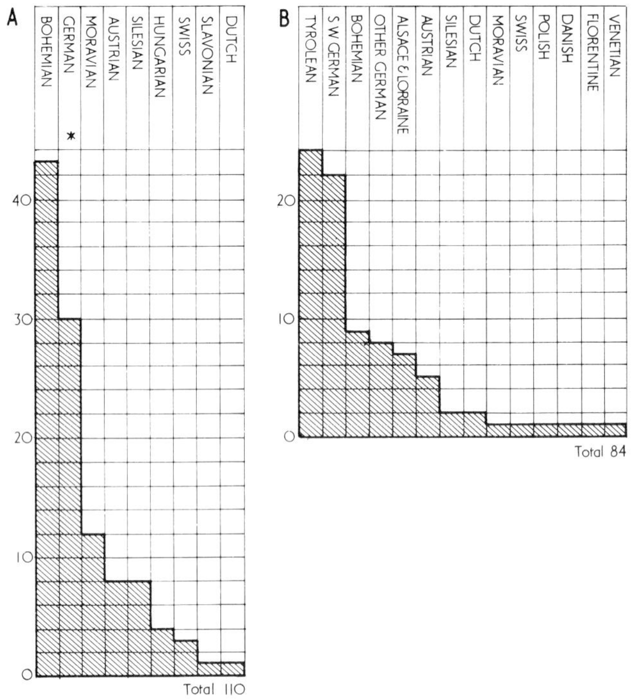

Origins of Recruits: (left) *The Company of Lodron in the regiment of Marschall (IR NO 18) 29 November 1756 (rank and file). There were seven Lutherans and five Calvinists. All the rest were Catholics, including all the Austrians, Bohemians, Moravians and Silesians. Twenty-one of the soldiers had civilian trades, of whom five were shoemakers, five carpenters, three millers, two textile workers, two masons, one a tailor, one a coppersmith, one a law student and one other;*
(right) *The grenadier company of Hamilton in the regiment of Macquire (Tyroler Land-und-Feld Regiment IR NO 46) 24 May 1759 (rank and file). Only six of the total were Protestants, and all of these were Lutherans. Twenty-four of the grenadiers had civilian trades, namely five shoemakers, three carpenters, two tailors, two textile workers, two smiths, two nailsmiths, one locksmith, one miller, one tanner, one gardener, one student and three others.*

Lifelong service was decreed for all men from corporal downwards. The first important exception was made on 12 May 1757, when a military conference decided to offer contracts of limited service to 'capitulants' – men who were willing to sign up for six years or the duration of the war. Daun hoped that 'in time they may be promoted to NCOs or even further, according to their aptitude for the service and other talents'.[12] The evidence of the muster lists shows that a good many men took up the offer. The six-year capitulants remained an important resource of the army for the rest of the reign. Field-Marshal Philip v. Moltke stated in 1768 that the capitulants made up 'almost the third part of the whole army', and that in his own regiment they were the source of the best NCOs.[13]

Whatever his motives, the poor recruit was never in greater need of encouragement than just after he had been processed, packaged and forwarded to his regiment:

> The newly-recruited soldier is usually sad and downcast, having been snatched from his parents all at once and carried away from his birthplace. Agricultural

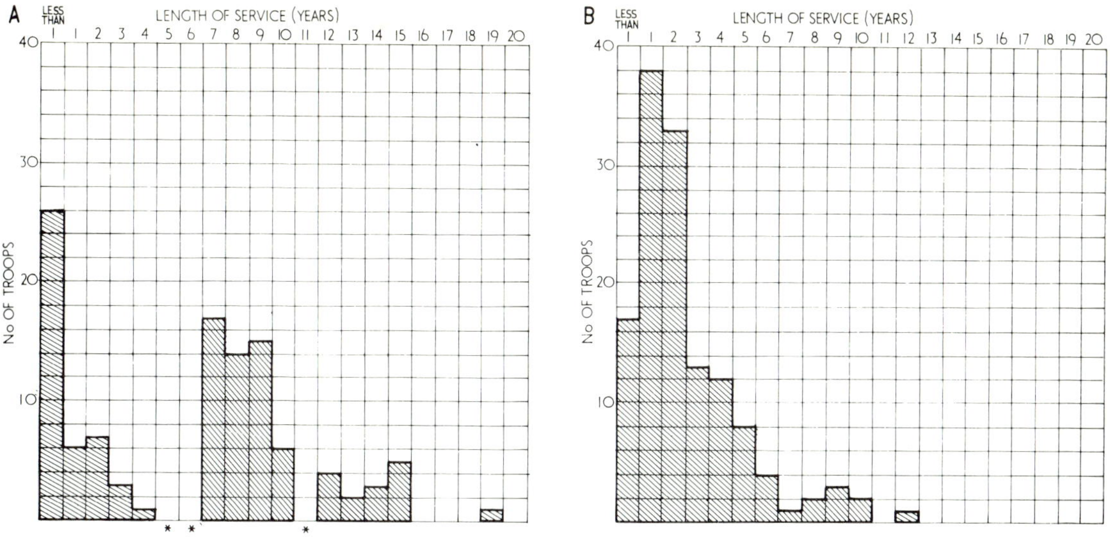

Patterns of Service: (left) *Regiment of Marschall* (*IR NO 18*), *Company of Lodron 29 November 1756. This chart shows the service pattern of a company which has just embarked on war after several years of peace. There is a clearly recognisable group of veterans who were recruited in the middle or late years of the War of the Austrian Succession. Recruiting fell off sharply immediately after the peace, but it has been resumed with great urgency upon the approach of the Seven Years War;*
(right) *Regiment of Los Rios* (*IR NO 9*), Inhaber's *Company, 17 January 1760. The ravages of war are only too evident in this chart, which indicates that the veteran troops have been wiped out and the gaps filled by recruits*

> work may be hard in its own way, but the recruit is in no condition to stand up to the duties and toils of the soldier's life. Hence it is a good idea to accustom him to his new conditions gradually.
>
> You cannot do better than to cheer these people up in one way or another.[14]

The thousands of muster lists still preserved in the War Archives in Vienna give us an indication of the kind of people who were caught up by the older recruiting systems. In time of peace the great majority of men enlisted in their early or middle twenties, and we find a preponderance of soldiers with seven or more years of service. In wartime, however, recruits began to appear in their late teens, and after a number of bloody campaigns most regiments carried on their books a large number of soldiers whose service was reckoned in months or at the most a couple of years. The number of men who had served a civilian trade varied considerably from regiment to regiment, though shoemakers, textile workers and tailors were most prominently represented. Except among the *Stände* recruits, married men accounted for a tiny fraction (often 3 per cent or less) of the total.

The most obvious shortcoming of the older method was that it failed to produce enough bodies. The infantry was roughly 9 per cent (about 12,000) short of establishment at both the beginning and end of the Seven Years War. Between times the regiments were so badly depleted by the campaigns that some of the ensigns had to make contracts with the Jews of Prague, Metz and Strasbourg, who undertook to furnish recruits upon commission.

In contrast the Prussian regiments were virtually immortal, for they were constantly replenished by reservists (*Cantonists*) from specially earmarked tracts of territory. General Creutz therefore urged that a system of cantonal conscription would not only enable the Austrian army to be brought up to strength in a four-week mobilisation, but would create

> a close bond between the peasant and the soldier. Since every district would have its own regiment, this unit would become a second homeland and family for the peasants. When they leave their native villages, it would be to enter a regiment that was composed in the main of their friends, relatives and acquaintances.[15]

After the Seven Years War Lacy argued that the fundamental tie of military service ought to oblige for life, like any other vocation. He enlisted the support of Joseph II, and in 1765 and again in 1766 he put forward positive proposals for a cantonal system. Maria Theresa hesitated, for Kaunitz urged that a sound economy was a source of greater strength than an inflated military establishment, but Lacy and Joseph won the day. The enrolling of the males of the German Hereditary Lands was begun in 1770. An appropriate law was published in 1777, and finally the actual *System* was put into full operation in 1781. The new arrangement co-existed with a scaled-down version of the old regimental recruiting and the enlistment of capitulants.

The liability to cantonal conscription extended to males aged between twenty and forty and measuring 5ft or more. Exemption was accorded to nobles and to only sons who were due to follow their fathers in a trade, and the conscription did not extend to Italy, the Netherlands, or (until 1784) Hungary or the Tyrol. The artillery carried on its own recruiting as before, as did the regiments from the exempted provinces, but all the conscripts were put through a two-year course of basic infantry training, after which the men suitable for the cavalry were selected according to physique. The trained soldier was recalled to the colours for only six weeks a year, leaving him free to carry on with his civilian calling for the rest of the time. As a matter of principle, leaving was 'never to be refused to men whom anyone calls to a proper employment'.[16]

It is by no means easy to assess the social impact of conscription. There were undoubtedly many nobles who feared that their serfs were going to be spirited away. Likewise among the people all the unpleasant apparatus of lists, passes and painted house numbers awakened a dread of lifelong military servitude. The Prussian commentator Berenhorst makes the point that when Lacy released the soldiers on leave he forgot an essential feature of the Habsburg lands, where (unlike Prussia) 'the family of the agricultural labourer has its domicile only by virtue of the arbitrary will of the feudal lord, and possesses no establishment of its own, to which the soldier can return whenever he is released'.[17]

On the other side Field-Marshal Wallis argued that 'the system of releasing soldiers on leave gives the peasant and the farmer the helpers they must have in order to be able to carry on trade and the rural economy'.[18] Lacy himself claimed that the cantonal principle not only enabled a larger army to be put on foot at smaller cost, but respected the 'natural freedom'[19] of the men and encouraged them to be docile. There were at least some patriotic souls who appreciated the flexibility of the new arrangements:

 In 1780 an officer happened to enter the house of a prosperous townsman in the course of inspecting the conscription rolls of his district. The householder approached him with his three sons and said 'Here are my three sons. Look at them, and see if they will be suitable for you. The eldest is sixteen, the middle one is fourteen and the youngest is thirteen. I am only too glad to deliver them up to a master who will use them for our common good. When I become old and infirm, he will send one of them back to me. And when he does not need them, I know that he will restore all three'.[20]

The soldier's life

Nowadays armies claim to value drill for its 'spiritual' worth, but in the eighteenth century its purpose was to turn the soldiers into automata, capable of performing a number of machine-like functions in the close-order tactics of those times. The recruit was initiated gradually into the wonders of the science, learning first how to stand and march without weapons, then acquiring the rudiments of musket drill, and finally building up the speed of all his movements.

> A new man should be encouraged to acquire inclination and love for the service, and not be dismayed and made timorous right at the beginning. He is to be instructed through well-meaning representations, not through reprimands or abuse. The new man ought not to be made to feel the impact of drill all at once, let alone be greeted with blows or other ill-treatment, especially if he happens to be simple in the head or have no command of German.[21]

The regulations enjoined the soldier to remain 'as silent as a mouse'[22] on the field of battle, and 'if any soldier seeks to demoralise the others through faint-hearted talk, or look around him preparatory to taking flight and therefore lose his

A study in physiognomy. One of the curious illustrations from the manuscript of the 1749 Infantry Regulations (Kriegsarchiv)

Bishop Felbiger, the pioneering educationalist

place in the ranks, such offender or offenders are to be run through by the sword of the nearest officer or NCO'.[23] This kindly sentiment reflected the influence of Prussian discipline.

The soldier of the eighteenth century might find himself out of actual combat for weeks or months at a time, but when the rival commanders did get around to staging a battle, the consequences were murderous in the extreme. Prince Charles Joseph de Ligne remembered that after the bloody campaign of 1757 his company went to winter quarters so depleted that the chaplain was left with nobody to say the responses at mass.

Once taken prisoner by a civilised enemy like the French or Spanish, the Austrian private soldier was usually marched off to captivity in some fortress or castle. If he fell into the grip of the Prussians, however, he was more than likely to be forcibly enlisted in the ranks of Frederick's bluecoats. The Austrians retrieved some of their lost brethren by cartel, and offered bounties to encourage the rest of the men to make their escape.

In peacetime the regiments of infantry were scattered all over the Habsburg domains. Every three years or so they marched to a new station in some distant province, apparently to obviate the risk of an 'all too great familiarity' with the local townsmen and peasants. In contrast the majority of the cavalry regiments rarely strayed from Hungary, 'for no subsistence in the world is to be obtained as cheaply as in this kingdom. The entire horse ration for a month amounts to a mere three florins, and consequently no more than thirty-six florins in the course of the year'.[24]

One of the fundamental objectives of the 1748 political and economic reforms was to bring about a physical separation between the civilians and the military. Some of the troops were therefore lodged in purpose-built barracks. These remained few and bad. A French officer describes the accommodation in the Austrian barracks as 'immense halls where an entire company of 160 men sleeps, lives, and does its cooking. The windows are low and narrow, and the stench is horrible'.[25] The connecting stairways were narrow and dirty, and it was pathetic to see how the grey-faced soldiers' brats had to labour up the steps.

Since the treasury could not meet the expense of wholesale barrack-building, most of the soldiers were still lodged in the towns and villages, whether individually among the householders, or in small *Cameradschaften* in improvised 'semi-barracks' (*Quasi-Kasernen*) where they came under a modicum of supervision.

The system of accommodation remained no less vicious in the later part of the reign. Joseph II wrote in 1776:

> The majority of the barracks and semi-barracks were badly built, and the health of the inmates suffered in consequence – we began to set up more barracks immediately after the Seven Years War, but for these reasons we had to abandon them once more. Then we took another pernicious course. We scattered the troops much too widely among the peasants in the villages, which was a considerable burden on the countrypeople, as well as being detrimental to the training of the soldiers. We finally settled on the single well-tried remedy, namely the practice of assigning the soldiers to the towns and settling them among the citizens in the so-called 'military rooms', by which the townsman enjoyed a rent from his house without any direct vexation from the soldiers, while the troops were kept healthy and under close supervision.[26]

Six hundred thousand florins were actually assigned for setting up the 'military rooms' in Bohemia alone, but most of this sum was diverted to the work of converting the former Jesuit houses into barracks, which left far too little to bring the 'military rooms' up to an acceptable standard.

The regulations decreed that in accommodation of all kinds, 'the muskets are to be arranged in a uniform fashion on the racks, with the cartridge pouches and side-arms hanging alongside. The same goes for the uniforms and knapsacks and for the caps, which are to be arranged in a neat fashion on further racks on top'.[27] The beds were wide, thick, dirty things to which the soldiers were assigned by pairs, on the 'hot bunk' system, one man taking his rest while the other went abroad.

The men were given free allowances of firewood and candles of good beef tallow. In terms of pay the private was entitled to between 5 and $6\frac{1}{2}$ kreutzer per day (at 60 kreutzer to the florin), which he collected every five days in his captain's tent. The bread ration came to a daily $1\frac{3}{4}$–2lb, though meat and all other extras had to be bought by the soldier out of his own pocket.

Pay was all too often in arrears in the earlier part of Maria Theresa's reign, which greatly provoked desertion. It was a different story after the finances were put on a sound footing in 1748. Cognazzo testifies that he 'served through the Seven Years War from beginning to end, in various corps and in all kinds of situations, but I never knew of an instance when an officer went short of his monthly salary, or the soldier did not have his pay dispensed meticulously on the appointed day'.[28] After the war some of the provinces actually asked for soldiers to be billeted on them, on account of the stimulus of trade.

From the evidence of the regulations the soldier would appear to be a meek and browbeaten creature, who received orders with bared head, and who in public was forbidden to eat, drink, smoke, shout or run. In practice he enjoyed considerable liberty, especially when he lived in one of the scattered little billets. The kinds of satisfaction open to an intelligent private soldier are revealed by the case of Josephus Wiener (afterwards the famous man of letters 'Joseph v. Sonnenfels'), who enlisted as a penniless and ill-educated youth in the regiment of Deutschmeister in 1749. He rapidly rose to the rank of corporal, and became known as the best drillmaster and recruiter among the NCOs. Serving in Styria, Carinthia, Hungary and Bohemia he came to know conditions over a wide area of the monarchy:

> I learnt the French language from the deserters who came over to us as recruits. I acquired Italian from deserters who reached the regiment from Italy. I picked up Czech from the girls at Sobotka and Jung-Bunzlau. I read whatever I could get my hands on, and formed a literary style in imitation of the authors.[29]

He obtained his release in 1754, but he recalled the names of his captain and colonel with gratitude, and until the end of his days he was proud to show his old soldier's coat to his highbrow friends.

Military justice harboured a horrifying range of punishments for the less well-disposed soldier. The corporal punishments culminated in running the gauntlet – an arrangement by which the offender had to run as much as ten times up and down a double rank of up to three hundred of his comrades, who were belabouring him all the time with sticks or straps. This barbarity did not reach the same peak of sadistic perfection as in Prussia, but it was capable of causing the death of the victim.

If an outright death penalty was decreed, the favoured methods were hanging or shooting. By a nice old custom the ensign of the condemned man was expected to ask the colonel for remission, and he waited by his horse booted and spurred, ready to gallop off to the place of execution with any last-minute reprieve. Maria Theresa herself was known to have intervened on behalf of a deserter, the news of whose death-sentence reached her while she was playing cards. She hastened to a writing table and dashed off a note to the vice-president of the *Hofkriegsrath*, telling him that desertion by itself did not merit a hanging.

Maria Theresa's instincts accorded with the opinion of good old commanders like Khevenhüller, who maintained that 'subordination is no slavery'. Maria Theresa and Daun imposed some important limitations on the freedom of disciplinary action in the late 1740s and early 1750s, and it now became an offence for an officer or NCO to kick a man, or beat him with a stick over the head, in the face or on the feet.

The relatively humane discipline of the Theresian army made a good impression on the British general Burgoyne, who toured the Continent after the Seven Years War and expressed a decided preference for the tone prevailing in the Austrian army over that of the Prussian:

> They are not yet arrived at the extraordinary steadiness of the latter under arms, but cannot fail of soon attaining it, with the advantage of seeing their ends compassed with good will and little severity . . . zeal, emulation and honour, with equal subordination, will outgo any diligence arising from dread of punishment or other slavish principles.[30]

The day-to-day enforcement of discipline was the business of the provost (*Profoss*) and his assistants. The *Hofkriegsrath* received many requests from veteran NCOs to be appointed to this responsible and profitable post, and the Prussian ex-soldier Laukhard remarked enviously that

> the Imperial provost is a man of consideration, whom the officers and men address as their '*Herr Vater*'. He has good pay and a pleasing uniform. The Prussian provost, on the other hand, is usually an ill-paid old invalid, who wears a grey livery with green braid. He has no junior assistants to confine the prisoners or to cut the sticks and switches for him . . .[31]

The Austrian soldier did not feel quite the same compulsion to desert as his Prussian counterpart, who was subject to a very harsh discipline. Desertion, when it did occur, was most liable to set in among recruits from the Empire, or in the army generally after a disastrous defeat like the one at Prague in 1757. Severe punishments were decreed for deserters and those who harboured them, but Maria Theresa wisely abrogated the old death-sentence for desertion, calculating that people would now be more inclined to deliver the fugitives up. General pardons periodically wiped the slate clean and invited the deserters to return, and in any case the Austrian articles of war established a useful distinction between the *Deserteur*, who simply ran off, and the treacherous *Ueberläufer* who actually went over to the enemy.

The married soldiers were the ones who were the least likely to make themselves scarce. Many companies owned between three and five men of this kind, who had been given the colonel's permission to marry suitable girls. Strong and healthy farmers' daughters were usually considered a good choice. The wives contributed a good deal to the regiment – they washed the laundry, kept the barracks and billets clean, and helped to tend the sick and wounded on campaign.

In the 1740s a regiment on the march still had something of a horde of the *Völkerwanderung*, with all the attendant women and children, but already in 1749 we note an attempt to restrict the old freedoms:

> In future none of the wives of the infantry shall be permitted to march alongside the regiments except such as are childless, and then only in order to serve the soldiers with spirits . . . All wives who have children, or who find difficulty in walking on account of age, shall be kept . . . with the rest of the regimental baggage behind the stragglers at the tail of each column.[32]

The process was hastened by the coming of the Seven Years War. The *Stände* recruits exceeded the normal limitation of one married man in every ten, and on 28 November 1756 a military conference decided that their wives and children must be left at home and entrusted to the care of their feudal lords. Finally in 1775 the general rule was established that no wives were to follow the regiments into the field.

The story of the army's children is associated with one of the most remarkable enterprises in the history of education. Somewhat to the amusement of Frederick of Prussia, Maria Theresa approached him after the Seven Years War and 'borrowed' the gifted Ignaz v. Felbiger, who was the Catholic bishop of Sagan in Silesia and a pioneer of the principle of universal elementary education. On Felbiger's initiative a *Schulkommission* was set up in every province of the Hereditary Lands on 6 December 1774, and over the following years a network of three grades of school (the village *Trivialschule*, the district *Hauptschule* and the model provincial *Normalschule*) began the daunting task of providing a primary education for all children between the ages of six and twelve.

The military responded with extraordinary enthusiasm. Up to now the education of the children of the regiment had been the responsibility of the chaplain, who, according to the infantry regulations of 1769, was empowered to seek out a soldier to help him in his work. With the introduction of the Felbiger system, however, a large number of officers put their influence behind the new educational drive, for they appreciated how schooling would prove useful in all sorts of ways – it would prevent the soldiers' children from running wild, would provide the army with a fund of literate NCOs, and would benefit the soldiers and the community at large by producing a body of educated and employable veterans.

In Bohemia the regiments of Hessen-Darmstadt and Arenberg taught both the army brats and local children in their regimental schools, while on the military borders Major-General Schilling set up no less than twenty-two schools for the children of the 'Croats'. Major-General Franz Kinsky felt inspired to write about education at large, and Colonel Braun of the regiment of Stein conceived the idea of encouraging the progress of his soldiers by prizes. The Prussian Berenhorst wrote scornfully about

> decrees relating to the greatest possible enlightenment of the junior NCOs and the men, and their instruction in reading, writing and arithmetic. Only learned men were now to be promoted. Enthusiasm begat exaggeration. In order to draw attention to themselves, various commanders made their pupils learn plays by heart – and actually perform them.[33]

Perhaps most significant of all, First Lieutenant Arond of the regiment of Wallis came to Vienna with a plan for training up a body of soldier-teachers in the *Hauptnormalschule* of St Anna. The first batch of thirty-one NCOs and men were given a grounding in reading, writing, arithmetic and methods of instruction, and they were told to

> inculcate their pupils with principles that are calculated to make them think and act . . . as good Christians, upright members of human society, civilised beings and future defenders of the fatherland. We must remember that most of them have already devoted themselves as children to the way of life of their fathers.[34]

Maria Theresa accompanied Joseph to a public examination of these student-teachers on 3 August 1780. She had consistently supported Felbiger's ideals, and in this year, the last of her life, she dismissed the *Hofkriegsrath*'s objections as *verbiage*, and declared that the project of setting up military schools throughout the army was at once 'necessary, useful and practicable'.[35]

The military life inevitably produced a number of teak-hard veterans who were prepared to soldier on from one generation to the next. In the middle 1730s the Emperor Charles VI happened to inspect the regiment of Alt-Daun as it marched through Vienna from the Rhine to the new war against the Turks, and he discovered two old soldiers – the drum major with fifty years' service, and a private with fifty-three – who were looking forward to the fresh campaign. Likewise the muster lists of Maria Theresa's reign reveal many a company with a sprinkling of soldiers in their fifties.

Such men as could not stand the course were supposed to be removed from active service as 'invalids'. Provision was made for the Austrian and German veterans in the Vienna *Armenhaus*, for the Bohemians and Moravians in the great house at Prague, for the Hungarians and foreigners in the invalid house at Pest, and for the Netherlanders in the invalid free company at Limburg. These places were maintained partly from state funds and partly from stoppages from military pay, and the inmates received small pensions as well as free accommodation, bread and *servis*. Wives and children were also accommodated, though they had to leave the house upon the death of the father of the family. By 1750 the *Invalidenhofkommission* was responsible for the welfare of a total of 6,000 invalids, some of whom were put up in the houses, while the rest lived outside with assistance.

The more active invalids were encouraged to set themselves up in trade, or establish themselves as colonists along the military borders. In the Seven Years War a number of the aged gentlemen helped to garrison the fortresses and escort prisoners. An important sorting-out process was initiated by Field-Marshal Lacy in 1771. While the authorities now excluded the half-invalids from pensions or accommodation altogether, they were also aware that

> there are men who have declined to have themselves taken in care as invalids, whether because they harbour groundless prejudice and abhorrence towards the invalid houses, or simply because they are ignorant of the benefits . . . Such aged invalids are incapable of earning their keep, and the burden of their maintenance consequently falls upon the state. When a long-serving soldier ends his life in this miserable way, it can only provoke among the other citizens an ineradicable horror of military service.[36]

The proud old veterans were now told that they were still at liberty to enter an invalid house, and that they were prefectly free to leave again if their circumstances improved.

The company NCOs

As visible signs of his authority, the NCO was distinguished by the broad braid on his hat, his red and yellow sword knot, his stick and (until 1759) the infantry *Kurzgewehr*.

The *Gefreyter* (lance-corporal) was the man in authority who stood nearest to the soldiers. A reliable but limited veteran of at least a dozen years' service, he was 'freed' from strenuous duties (hence his German title) and he supervised the basic military family of the six- or seven-man tent *Cameradschaft*.

The company was divided for administrative purposes into four, five or six *Corporalschaften*, each of which was entrusted to a corporal. This post was admitted to be one of the most difficult and tiring in the company, 'and for that reason it must be held by men who are good, healthy and not too old'.[37]

The *Feldwäbel*, *Führer* and *Fourier* collectively comprised the company's *kleine Prima Plana*, so called because their names appeared at the bottom of the first page of the muster list.

The *Fourier*, or company clerk, was responsible both to the *Führer* (colour sergeant) for keeping up the records, and to the regimental quartermaster for distributing billets and pitching the company's tents.

The *Führer* occupied an intermediate rank. He acted as the deputy of the *Feldwäbel*, and frequently carried the colour or standard for the ensign or cornet – a responsibility which he took on permanently when the ensigns and cornets became 'second lieutenants' in 1748. With all this he was also responsible, with the assistance of the *Fourier*, for keeping up the company muster lists, records and accounts, as well as helping to look after the sick – for which reason a married *Führer* was at an advantage.

The *Feldwäbel* (sergeant-major) stood on the next rung of command and was an important man in every respect. Under the authority of the captain and lieutenants he was responsible for all the detailed running of the company – training the recruits, inspecting the soldiers and their billets and tents, calling the roll, distributing rations, and preserving the alignment and order of the company on the march.

Oddly enough, the *Feldwäbel* received less pay than the company clerk, a circumstance which perhaps reflected the Austrian army's order of priorities. 'What can be the justification', asked Field-Marshal v. Moltke, 'of putting the *Fourier* on a par with the *Feldwäbel*? After all the *Fourier* rarely smells powder smoke, and in the winter he can do his work behind a comfortable stove'.[38]

After the *Feldwäbel*, we leave the hierarchy of the company NCOs. As individuals the Austrian NCOs were probably every bit as proficient as their famous counterparts in the Prussian army, and from the places they were assigned in the line of battle we can see that they were expected to lead the men into action, and not just push them forward with their half-pikes. The pity was that the Austrian NCOs were so badly overworked, for the miserly establishment allowed half a dozen or less to the company, and about seventeen *Feldwäbels* to the full regiment.

The regimental staff

The colonel commandant, the lieutenant-colonel and the major had a number of skilled people who helped them to run the regiment.

Immediately at the colonel's side stood the *Auditor*, a canny individual, well-versed in legal affairs, who administered summary military justice (*Standrecht*) and often acted as the colonel's private secretary.

The *Quartiermeister* had a rank equivalent to the most senior lieutenant. As the direct employer of the company clerks he managed the regiment's accounts and muster lists, and he also had the responsibility of assigning billets and staking out the regiment's camps. The regimental *Proviantmeister* acted as his deputy, and saw that the regiment was supplied with bread and fodder in wartime.

One of the peculiarities of the Austrian army was that the vital function of *Adjutant* (or *Wachtmeister-Leutenant*) was exercised not by an officer, but by an NCO who was the equivalent in rank only of the most senior *Feldwäbel*. He was expected 'to behave courteously towards all the officers, and not presume to establish friendly relations with them'.[39] None of this could have been very good for regimental discipline.

The *Regiments-Feldscher* (*Regiments-Chirurg* from 1752) was responsible for the medical services of the regiment, and he directed the ten ordinary *Feldscher*, or orderlies, who were distributed among the companies. We shall see more of his work later.

In wartime a suitable NCO took on the self-explanatory work of the regimental *Wagenmeister*. He went to the issuing of the *Parole* (password) every evening, so that he knew how to arrange the regimental transport on the following day. Until 1769 he owned the privilege of acting as sutler to the regimental staff.

The very considerable powers of the *Profoss* have been discussed already. Another formidable gentleman was the *Regiments-Tambour* (drum-major), who commanded the drummers and pipers of the infantry, and the trumpeters and kettle-drummers of the cavalry. In camp he assembled all the drums in a pyramid at the *Feldwache*, where also were kept the partisans of the colonel and lieutenant-colonel.

 He was master of the nineteen Austrian regulation drum beats, from reveille to

NCOs with half-pikes. Note the stick hanging from the right-hand lapel (1749 Infantry Regulations)

tattoo. He was also expected to be acquainted with the foreign drum beats, and 'since it often happens that the *Regiments-Tambour* is sent to parley with the enemy, it is very useful for him to have the command of several languages'.[40] The cavalry kettle-drums were supposed to have been suppressed in the 1760s – the dragoon drums first, followed by the drums of the cuirassiers and dragoons – though cavalry drums are still given specific treatment in the cavalry *Reglement* of 1769.

Every regiment had its own *Büchsenmacher*, or armourer, to keep the weapons in good order, a sensible arrangement which did not obtain in all foreign armies. The repair of souls was entrusted to the *Caplan* or *Regiments-Pater*, whose activities will be investigated later.

The honour of the Theresian soldier

The Theresian period witnessed a determined and on the whole a very successful effort to enhance the standing of the private soldier. Some fairly brutal abuses had certainly been uncovered by the inspections that were carried out before the Seven Years War. Indeed everything that was forced and artificial in the eighteenth century seems to be summed up in the policy of Count Kálnocky, commandant of the Hungarian infantry regiment of Gyulay, who ordered his men to buy false moustaches, and then had them beaten when they failed to pay up. Likewise the Field Service Regulations of 1749 had to direct a condemnation at the commanders who

> seem to be ashamed of speaking in an affable way with the private soldiers. Some of them actually labour under the delusion that it detracts from their officers' status to approach the private man other than through blows, threats

> and curses. Nothing could be more harmful to our service, and nothing could be more shameful.[41]

By the middle 1750s the worst malpractices had been identified and outlawed by regulation. Not just the authorities in Vienna, but at least a large minority of generals and officers were informed by the conviction that the private soldier was a human being, with a brain, a heart and a soul that were capable of grasping the concept of honour. In contrast the bruised and browbeaten *Kerl* of the Prussian army was allowed at the most to share only in the collective honour of his regiment.

Soldiers of any age would have been willing to recognise commanders like Khevenhüller, Browne, Nádasti, Daun and Loudon as first-class leaders of men. Even among the intellectuals Joseph Sonnenfels proclaimed his pride in the fact 'that I have carried a musket and spent my time in a guardroom . . . I should be neglecting an essential duty, if I failed to avow my esteem for a condition of life to which I owe so much'.[42]

Slightly odder in our eyes is the power which Maria Theresa and her generals attributed to cash rewards. We are inclined to forget that in the eighteenth century many of the most enlightened spirits liked to give people a solid reason for showing loyalty – whether through the florins that were showered on the Austrian soldiers, or the beer that was dispensed for English electors.

When money ran out, the general could still resort to an old-fashioned style of exhortation. Major-General Joseph Esterházy told the private soldier of his regiment to bear in mind that

> he has the honour of serving the greatest monarch in the whole world . . . he must therefore incline himself to carry out all reasonable orders with a willing heart, and bear with patience all the hardships which he may endure through heat, cold and rain, comforting himself with the thought of better times ahead. I know that many soldiers are fond of saying 'Why the hell should we put up with all this? It's all right for the generals and officers. They eat and drink as much as they like, and they've got their horses', and so forth. Yes, but the officer frequently has to endure the same hardships as you, and remember that most of them would never have become officers and generals if they had not been through all this in the first place.[43]

Whatever the source of inspiration, the constancy of the Austrian soldier was a force which Maria Theresa's enemies had to reckon with. The English volunteer Lloyd concluded from his service in the Seven Years War that

> The Austrian Army is composed chiefly out of the class of labourers, vassals of the great lords; they are obedient and patient, and bear without a murmur the greatest hardships; and though their religion does not rise to any degree of enthusiasm [i.e. 'fanaticism'], probably from want of being excited by an able leader, yet it keeps them sober, and free from vice: objects must strike hard to make any sensible impression, which once received lasts long, because not easily effaced. By education and temper, proper to form a good soldier, and superior to any other, who are not raised by some species of enthusiasm.[44]

Here was a more lasting resource than the brittle mechanism of the Prussian military machine.

5

The Infantry of the Line

Organisation

Maria Theresa's arch-enemy Frederick of Prussia inherited a remarkably well-managed army, and he kept its basic organisation intact throughout his reign. In contrast the Austrian military institutions were in a state of perpetual but creative ferment. The organisation of the infantry regiments in particular underwent a number of complicated changes, which are best presented in tabular form:

1740: Regiment of three battalions and two grenadier companies; battalions of five companies each.

1748: Regiment of four battalions and two grenadier companies; battalions of four companies each (five in Hungarian regiments).

1756 peace establishment: Regiment of three field battalions, one garrison battalion and two grenadier companies; battalions of four companies each.

1756 war establishment: Regiment of two field battalions, two grenadier companies and one garrison battalion; field battalions of six companies each and garrison battalion of four.

1769 peace establishment: Regiment of three battalions and two grenadier companies; two field battalions of six companies each, and one garrison battalion of four companies and two grenadier companies.

1769 war establishment: As in the peace establishment, except that the third battalion was reinforced by two extra fusilier companies.

The German infantry regiment owned a nominal 2,300 officers and men in 1740, 2,408 in 1748 and on the peace establishment of 1756, 2,693 on the war establishment of 1756, 2,215 on the peace establishment of 1769, and 2,707 on the war establishment of 1769. The size of the fusilier company varied from about 130 to 160 officers and men. The battalion was somewhat weaker than its Prussian counterpart – by as much as 150 men in the War of the Austrian Succession – and in both absolute and proportionate terms it had an inadequate complement of NCOs.

For tactical purposes the battalion was broken into sixteen platoons (*Züge*), each seven or eight files wide and each file on three or four ranks (always three ranks for the grenadiers, and for the fusiliers as well from 1757).

Categories of infantry

Specialist grenadiers were introduced in the Austrian infantry in 1700, as particularly strong and enterprising men who were trained to throw grenades. The grenade as such was a passing fad in warfare, and the Prince de Ligne remarked that 'a single howitzer shell causes more execution than all the bombs of our twenty thou-

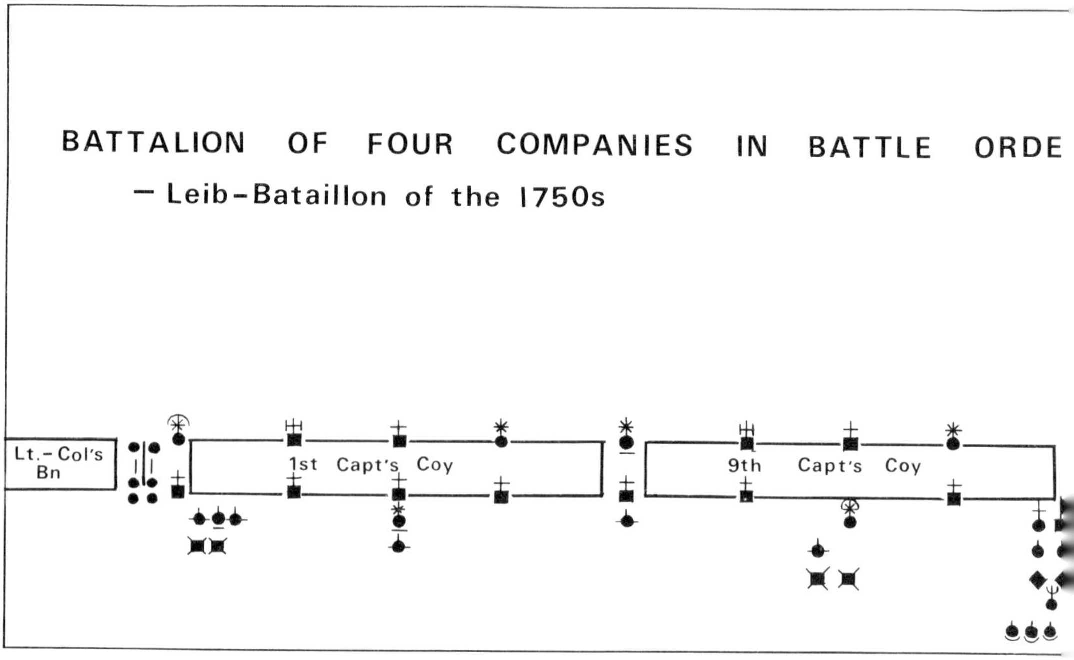

sand grenadiers'.[1] However, these people continued to earn their keep as élite troops in their own right, distinguished by their stature, their haughty bearing, their ferocious moustaches, and above all by their grenadier bearskin caps. Cognazzo observed 'how experience has taught us that in our army it does a man good simply to give him a grenadier bearskin. Just because he is treated with a little distinction he is less inclined to desert, and he fights better'.[2]

At the outset of the reign every regiment of line infantry had its own permanently attached companies of grenadiers, each 110 officers and men strong. In later years the Austrian army, like many others of the time, began to detach the grenadiers from the parent regiments of fusiliers and combine them as masses of élite troops to carry out particularly desperate and dangerous enterprises. Twenty-two companies of grenadiers were used in this way at the battle of Prague in 1757, and again at Breslau later in the same year. In a further development the grenadiers were formed into scratch battalions in the camp of Skalitz before the opening of the 1758 campaign, and they fought as such at Domstadtl and Hochkirch.

The reputation of the parent regiments depended very much upon their grenadiers, and the *Inhabers* were unwilling to see these splendid creatures pass under the command of a strange major or lieutenant-colonel. Finally in 1769 the system was regulated by the device of forming the grenadiers into nineteen permanent battalions of between four and six companies each, which were to be commanded by lieutenant-colonels and appropriate staff appointed directly by the *Hofkriegsrath*. Two further battalions were added to the number in 1770. The grenadiers retained the facings of their parent regiments, which kept alive a useful spirit of competition between the component companies in the massive new battalions.

Besides her solid mass of German infantry (forty-four regiments in 1740) Maria Theresa owned a number of more or less exotic infantry regiments hailing from other provinces or kingdoms of the monarchy. Three regiments of Hungarian infantry stood at her disposal at the beginning of the reign (IRs 19, 34, 51). In the electric atmosphere of the Pressburg *Landtag* of September 1741 the Hungarian magnates talked of raising no less than 21,600 men to form thirteen additional

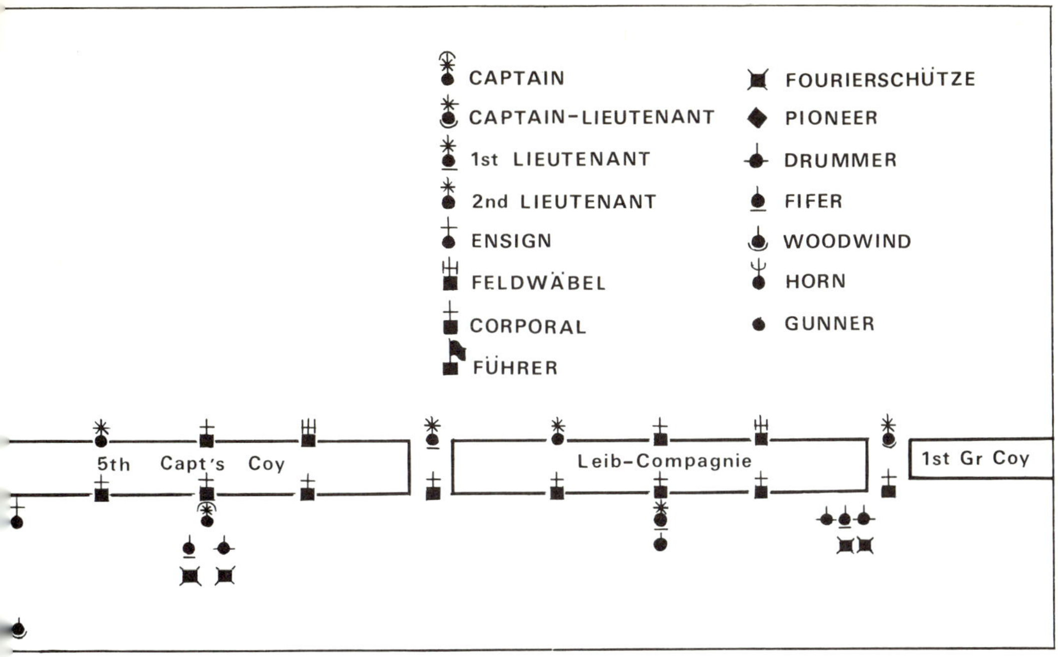

Grenadiers. On the left the regiment of Waldeck – red cuffs, collar, stock and cap badge; gold cap tassel, brass cap frontal and buttons. On the right the regiment of Wurmbrand – red cuffs, lapels, collar and turn-backs; black stock, red cap bag with silver tassel, white buttons (David Morier, c 1748. By gracious permission of HM the Queen)

Hungarian infantry. The regiment of Erherzog Ferdinand (IR NO 2) c 1762. White coat with yellow tasselled Litzen, *cuffs and turn-backs; white shoulder straps; yellow and white barrel sash; dark blue waistcoat with yellow braid, dark blue pants, dark blue sabretache with yellow devices; sabre with iron furniture. The hair is dressed in Hungarian plaits (Lt-col V Gibellini. By courtesy of Belmont-Maitland Ltd, proprietors of* Tradition)

regiments, but the recruiting proved so disappointing that the number was soon reduced to a more realistic six (IRs 2, 31, 32, 33, 37, 52). By November 1742 the number of the new soldiers was put at 14,877 troops actually with the colours – and 3,055 deserters – and many of the recruits received their baptism of fire in bloody riots, like the one which led to a pitched battle between indignant peasants and the regiment of Haller.

The lively Hungarian troops proved their worth convincingly enough, once they got to grips with the common enemy. Both the old and the new regiments were placed on a common establishment in 1744, and five years later the authorities determined on a distinctive uniform that combined elements of Hungarian national dress with the rococo fashions of Western Europe. The hat was the characteristic Western tricorn, but the waistcoat was a Hungarian-style dolman and the belt was covered with a barrel sash. The white coat was decorated with tasselled button-holes, and in place of the gaiters and breeches of the German infantry the Hungarian sported half-boots and tight-fitting hose (*gátyak*) that were decorated down the front with Hungarian knots. By his left-hand side hung the heavy Hungarian sabre – and it was not intended just for display.

The six Netherlandish infantry regiments (IRs 9, 30, 38, 55, 58, vii) wore uniforms of the same cut as those of the German infantry, though the cloth was of Netherlands manufacture and was more durable and expensive than the Moravian material of the rest of the army. Most of the men were drawn from Flanders and Brabant, but considering the relative populations a higher proportion came from the duchies of Luxembourg and Limburg and the Walloon provinces of Hainault, Namur and Tournai. French names predominated in the muster lists, and in general parlance these units were known as 'Walloon' regiments – a term which evoked the prestige of the famous Walloon regiments in the service of Spain.

The Italian 'national regiments' were uniformed and drilled on the same footing as the German and Netherlandish. The army owned one Italian regiment (IR 48) at the beginning of the reign, and in 1744 Marquis Giorgio Clerici spirited up 2,300 vagabonds and ruffians in a remarkably short time in order to raise a regiment of his own (IR 44).

Whatever their record as fighters in the nineteenth century, the Tyroleans showed a marked aversion to any kind of military service in the reign of Maria Theresa. In 1745 the small and useless *Tyroler Land-Bataillon* was reconstructed into an eleven-company-strong *Tyroler Land-und-Feld Regiment* (IR 46), which was put on the establishment of a German regiment three years later. As its name implied, the new regiment was intended to serve both in Tyrol and in the field. Enlistment was on an attractive system of five- or six-year 'capitulations', but so few natives were willing to come forward that about half the rank and file were recruited from outside the province – chiefly men from southern and western Germany, with a sprinkling of Bohemians, Alsatians and Lorrainers. It proved just as difficult to recruit native officers, and in March 1758 the *Hofkriegsrath* decided that an approach on this head must be made to the Tyrolean authorities, 'for the said regiment is overcrowded with so many strange foreign cadets'.[3]

In 1766 all the native troops of the regiment were scraped together and formed into a third battalion, which was given the old name of the *Tyroler Land-Bataillon* and destined only for local duties. The device seems to have made the contribution of the Tyrol to national defence appear more inadequate than ever, and in 1771 the government prevailed on the Tyrol *Stände* to raise the establishment of the regiment to a total of 6,000 men, of whom 4,000 were to be available for duties outside the Tyrol.

An Alpine regiment of much higher repute was the short-lived *Graubündtner Regiment Sprecher* (IR viii), which was raised by Salomon Sprecher v. Bernegg in 1743. Recruited in Germany and the Swiss canton of Grisons (Graubündten), its justice and administration were managed according to ancient Swiss codes. The complement of 2,600 men was divided into two companies of grenadiers and twenty of fusiliers. After performing good service in the later campaigns of the War of the Austrian Succession the regiment was disbanded in 1749, on the grounds of economy.

The *Deutsches Feld-Jäger Corps* was another excellent but ephemeral unit. Many armies of the time appreciated the advantage of using forest gamekeepers (*Jäger*) as light infantry, for the natural field craft of these people and their mastery of rifled weapons gave them a decided advantage in broken country over the infantry of the line, who moved in mass formations and were armed with the smooth-bore musket. General Lacy raised 400 of such *Jäger* in 1758. By 1760 their number had risen to 1,000, and they were now given an establishment of ten companies and attached to the *Pionier-Corps*. The *Jäger* won free again in 1761, and they enjoyed a last glorious taste of independence before they were disbanded in 1763. The corps was revived in the War of the Bavarian Succession, but abolished just as quickly as before when peace returned. The *Jäger* wore a leather helmet and a serviceable coat of that bluish grey that went by the name of *Hechtgrau* (pike grey).

The Theresian army never arrived at a really satisfactory means of reinforcing regiments that became battered and depleted in the course of the campaigns. The cantonal system was prepared only in the last years of the reign, and meanwhile the device of 'garrison battalions' offered an inadequate substitute. Such garrison battalions were first designated in 1756, when the term was applied to the third battalions of the field regiments, which were composed of the less fit officers and men and destined to act as trained reserves. In the event the battalions were sucked into the field in the course of the following year, even though their complements were decidedly feeble. As some kind of substitute, *Depositorien* of up to 200 officers and men were set up for every regiment during the winter of 1757–8.

After the Seven Years War the third battalions were usually employed for garrison duty, separately from the two field battalions. In 1769 the name *Garnisons-Bataillon* was replaced by the more glamorous-sounding *Obristleutenants-Bataillon*. However, the dreary function remained the same, and many of these 'lieutenant-colonels' battalions' were sent to occupy Galicia when the Austrians took over the province in 1772.

In the interests of economy the government also sought to make some use of those invalids and half-invalids who had been mustered out of the field army altogether. At the beginning of the Seven Years War a four-battalion *Invalidencorps* was raised in the Hereditary Lands, and another of seven companies in the Netherlands. A fully-fledged *Oesterreichisches Garnisons-Regiment* came into existence in 1760. It was disbanded at the end of the war, but the principle of the thing appealed to the calculating Field Marshal Lacy, and in 1766 he founded an *Erstes Garnisons-Regiment* from the half-invalids of the Prague house. A *Zweites Garnisons-Regiment* was established in 1767. The nucleus of a third was raised in the Netherlands in 1772, and four years later it duly became the *Drittes Garnisons-Regiment*.

In contrast to the servile respectability of the garrison regiments, the free corps and free companies offered the nearest military equivalent to the licensed piracy of the naval privateers. Men of all nations flocked to these units in the hope of adventure and plunder, since the free companies acted on the fringes of the regular armies and were capable of taking off on all kinds of exciting forays. Companies of this kind were commanded by individuals who raised their outfits on a business basis and solely for the duration of the war. A typical deal was arranged by one Colonel Otto in 1778, when he contracted to raise a free corps of 800 infantry and 200 cavalry, and undertook 'not only to clothe and arm his corps himself but to command it in person. He is forbidden to enlist Imperial subjects, let alone any Imperial deserters'.[4] In return Otto was to receive forty florins for every man whom he produced properly clothed and armed at Eger, the assembly station in north-west Bohemia.

Free corps sprang up in profusion in every one of Maria Theresa's wars. Most notorious of all was the *Panduren-Corps von der Trenck*, which began its disreputable life in 1741. After a career of pillage and rapine, as well as some daring *coups de main*, the corps was taken over by the relatively respectable Major Johann Daniel Menzel. One of the major's admirers wrote that it was important to draw a distinction between lawless freebooters of the type of Trenck and a true partisan leader like Menzel (even if it was not easy for the ignorant to appreciate the difference):

> The only kind of person suitable for this profession is one who belongs to no regiment, and who has a natural bent for such forays. This activity can offer him a path to fame and fortune. Yet, despite every precaution, it is also a means by which you may occasionally incur some odium.[5]

Most of the free companies sported coats of darkish green, particularly in the later wars, but the Trenck freebooters managed to distinguish themselves even in the matter of dress. Trenck himself admitted that they 'struck people as being particularly frightful, because their heads had been shaved, leaving only a scalp lock'.[6]

One of the notable features of the Austrian service was the absence of privileged regiments of guards – 'no Mamelukes, no Praetorians, no Janissaries'.[7] The ordinary marching regiments did garrison service in Vienna by rotation, and ceremonial lifeguard duties were entrusted to the non-combatant units of the *Trabanten-Garde* and the mounted *Arcieren-Garde*, which owned only about 100 officers and men each. By custom every member of the guards was paid sixty florins annual *Zapfengeld* by the city of Vienna, as recompense for waiving his ancient privilege of trading in wine and beer. The small Tuscan Swiss Guard was taken into the Austrian service in 1745, and in deference to Magyar sensibilities a noble Hungarian *Leibgarde* was created in 1760. Three years later the noble *Arcieren-Garde* was renamed the German *Leibgarde*, so as to make clear the distinction from the Hungarian guards.

In 1769 numbers were issued to every regiment of infantry, cavalry and hussars, which further reinforced the impression of uniformity. The numbers were awarded in the first instance according to the seniority of the *Inhaber* of the time. The infantry regiments retained the identical numbers until the dissolution of the monarchy in 1918, but the cavalry and hussars had a complicated arrangement by which their numbers changed according to the relative seniority of each new *Inhaber*.

Seeking to marshal all possible manpower against the King of Prussia, Maria Theresa took several foreign regiments into her pay for the duration of the Seven Years War. Three regiments of infantry and one of cavalry were hired from Modena in 1757 and placed in garrison in Lombardy, thus freeing the infantry regiments of Pallavicini and Mercy to march to the theatre of war in the north. Another Italian unit, the Tuscan infantry regiment, was taken over in 1757, and saw active service in Loudon's army three years later.

On 16 September 1757 the Bishop of Würzburg signed over the infantry regiments of Roth-Würzburg and Blau-Würzburg. This acquisition was doubly important, since Würzburg was the most influential state of the Franconian Circle of the Empire, and because the Würzburg troops were excellent fighters, as they were going to prove in the defence of Leuthen village. The contingent of the German *Soldtruppen* was reinforced by the infantry regiment of Lambert, which was hired from the bishop of Mainz on 27 September 1756.

Uniforms and equipment

Three quotations sum up the Austrian philosophy of military dress:

> There can be no doubt that a soldier who has a poorish or stained uniform, yet is cheerful and healthy, is likely to fight better than a soldier who owns a splendid uniform but has nothing to live on. (memorandum of 1740)[8]

> It is my intention that an equality should be observed in the matter of uniforms, and that all useless display should be abandoned.
> (Maria Theresa, 1748)[9]

> I can think of no other troops who have a greater uniformity of dress than the Austrian soldiers. (Guibert, 1773)[10]

In the middle of the eighteenth century, one of the most elegant ages in the history of costume, the Austrian infantry wore what was possibly the most simple, tasteful and pleasing uniform of any European service. It was not so lumpish as the British uniforms, and it was less skimpy and less loaded with senseless detail than the Prussian.

The effect was not achieved without some effort. The War of the Austrian Succession brought a measure of uniformity (thanks largely to the practice of issuing uniforms centrally through the Vienna *Hauptmagazin*), and on 16 March 1754 the *Hofkriegsrath* instructed the regiments in great detail as to the norms of every item of military dress. Certain regiments still affected tight 'Prussian' coats, while others (notably in Bohemia) had their muskets lacquered and sent their coats to be decorated by the Jews, but by October 1757 it could be said with confidence that the whole of the German infantry was 'equipped with identical items of clothing and with white coats'.[11]

During this period the full infantry uniform comprised a coat, a waistcoat, a hat, a pair of gaiters, a pair of breeches, two stocks, two shirts, two pairs of stockings, a pair of shoes, a cartridge pouch, an oil flask, a water flask, a priming needle, brushes, musket, bayonet and knapsack.

The hat of the earlier part of the reign was a black felt tricorn. The edges were trimmed with plain braid, though in some regiments the design was scalloped. There was a cockade on the left turned-up side of the hat, and small bobs at the two rearward corners. A sprig of oak leaves was frequently worn on the hat in the War of the Austrian Succession, as a ready means of distinguishing the Austrian infantry from the French and Spanish troops, most of whom also wore a white uniform.

The grenadier cap was a black bearskin, which had a long tasselled cloth flap hanging down the side or back. The hair at the side of the grenadiers' heads was kept short, 'since the custom is to seat the cap well down over the eyes'.[12] The grenadier cap was calculated to inspire terror in the enemy, but otherwise it was a useless encumbrance, giving no protection against the sun, and absorbing a considerable weight of rainwater. The general effect was decidedly odd when it was worn by men with small heads or faces. Except on important occasions like parades or battles, the grenadier kept his cap in a linen bag and wore a common tricorn instead.

Off duty both the infantry and cavalry wore a comfortable forage cap (*Holtz-Kappen* or *Holtz-Mütze*) which was made from the cloth of old coats. In cold weather it was frequently kept under the hat or cap for the sake of warmth.

The hair was dressed into double locks at the side and a long, unpowdered whip-like military pigtail at the back. Both locks and pigtail were kept in place by papers (*Papilotten*) when the men were off duty, and Maria Theresa was outraged by the 'blasphemy' when soldiers dared to appear in this condition in church. Military beauty could be further enhanced by the wearing of moustaches (false in some regiments).

The head was jammed in place by a stock – a neck-cloth of stiff fabric. Red stocks became the regulation wear in 1754, though most of the regiments seem to have retained their black stocks as well.

According to the circular of 1754, the lower edge of the coat was to extend to within an inch or so of the ground, when the man was in a kneeling position. In cold weather the lapels were buttoned across the chest, and the three-buttoned 'round' Austrian cuffs were pulled down over the fingers. The coat was cut in generous style, and 'caused the soldiers considerable inconvenience during their exercise of arms. In more than one action our brave grenadiers threw off their huge sack-like coats in which they were clothed, so as to be able to load more briskly'.[13]

The body of the coat was delivered by the manufacturers in the *Perlgrau* of the undyed wool, but the soldier soon brought it to an immaculate white by the liberal application of pipeclay. The Habsburg white was regarded as an eminently practical hue at a time when the infantry of the line wore its uniforms for display rather than camouflage.

> This colour is by far the best and most handsome for military wear. The white coat always looks good, whether it is new or old. It is so easy to restore the appearance of an old coat by applying pipeclay. After a little wear, blue coats become whitish, pike grey coats turn a dirty ashen colour, and green coats go yellowish. Repairs to a white coat hardly show up at all, whereas they look terrible on a dyed coat.[14]

The units were distinguished by the colour and shade of the cuffs and lapels, the design of the shoulder strap and the clasps at the coat tails, and the letters of the *Inhaber*'s monogram which adorned the cartridge pouches of some regiments. The turn-back skirts were originally of the same colour as the cuffs and lapels, but in the 1750s they assumed the white of the rest of the coat.

Beneath the coat the soldier wore a waistcoat (*Camisol*), which in the German regiments was of the same white cloth as the coat and breeches. It reached down as far as the middle joints of the fingers, when the hand was resting naturally by the side.[15]

From 1754 black gaiters (*Gamaschen*) were stipulated for field conditions, and their white counterparts were reserved for parades. This was in accordance with the Prussian practice. The gaiters constricted the leg rather badly, and they proved to be particularly inconvenient in wet weather, which was why it was decided on 3 October 1756 that 'the soldiers should help themselves out instead with their woollen socks'.[16]

A medical textbook of 1758 urged that the shoes should be made of thick and strong leather, which was to be stitched with waxed thread and smeared with wax, 'so that it is quite impossible for water to penetrate inside'.[17] Half boots were worn by the Hungarians, and by the infantry generally from the later 1760s.

A radically new uniform was introduced in 1767. The impulse almost certainly came direct from Maria Theresa, who had long been dissatisfied with the old uniform and wrote in 1765:

One of my main ambitions is, and always shall be, to make such regulations

(left) *The new infantry uniform of 1767. Showing the characteristic leather cap; buttoned-up coat with coloured cuffs, collar and turn-backs; exterior belt, and sword with 'mameluke' hilt* (Ottenfeld)
(right) *Grenadier. Showing the positions of cartridge pouch, water bottle and calfskin knapsack. The tricorn hat was for everyday wear* (Ottenfeld)

> and arrangements, as will promote the upkeep of the private soldier and alleviate his duties. With this in mind I have decided to try out a new kind of uniform, among my infantry regiments, which will give the ordinary soldier's body better protection against cold and wet than before, and yet be no heavier to wear.[18]

The general appearance of the new uniform was well described by an Englishman. He observed that the troops made

> a fine appearance, and the army in general are more judiciously clothed than any other I have seen.
>
> Instead of coats with long skirts, their uniform is a short jacket of white cloth, with waistcoat and breeches of the same, and each soldier has a surtout [greatcoat] of coarse grey cloth, which he wears in cold or rainy weather. This he rolls up in a very small bulk when the weather is good, and it is little or no incumbrance on the march. They have short boots for shoes; and, in place of hats, they wear caps of very stout leather.[19]

The cap in question was a round, flat-topped affair, with a heavy leather flap standing up in the front. This new headgear was introduced as an experiment in the regiment of Lacy (IR 22) and it became an important feature of the uniform of 1767. The Austrian cap, or *Casquet*, exercised a significant influence on European military fashion for several decades afterwards, and it may well have provided the inspiration for the famous 'Waterloo shako' of the British infantry in 1815. The Austrian grenadiers continued to wear their bearskins.

In their new coat Maria Theresa and Lacy sought to combine the advantages of the Prussian and the old Austrian uniforms. It was shorter and tighter than the earlier version, and it was fastened down the front with a single row of buttons. Collars were now made universal, and together with the narrow lapels and the little turn-backs they gave the coat a neat, buttoned-up appearance, but deprived the uniform of much of the elegance of the 1740s and 1750s. The distinguishing colours of the collar, lapels and turn-backs were allocated among the regiments by lottery, though the *Inhabers* were usually able to arrange a swap if they were particularly attached to the regiment's old colour. The greatcoat was universally admitted to be an excellent inspiration, and it was 'usually the last item of clothing which the deserters like to sell off'.[20]

The soldier stuffed his bread ration, spare clothing and personal gear into a commodious knapsack, which was worn low down on the back and hung from a strap passing over the left shoulder. The material in the earlier part of the reign was usually ticking, though unshaved calfskin began to gain the upper hand from about 1755. At Chotusitz and Leuthen the victorious Prussians found Austrian knapsacks piled in neat rows on the ground, which indicates that the knapsack was usually discarded before an action.

The grenadiers and the Hungarian infantry wore long curved sabres throughout the reign, a circumstance which (because the grenadiers were ferocious and the Hungarians were excitable) provides us with some of the very few authenticated instances of the use of cold steel weapons in the open field in the eighteenth century. Cognazzo claims that swords came in very useful whenever muskets were broken or unserviceable, and 'I have often seen fusiliers standing about defenceless, or at the most clutching bayonets like kitchen knives, and all because there were no spare muskets at hand'.[21] There is the well-attested case of the Hungarian regiment of Haller, which ran out of ammunition in the battle of Kolin and proceeded to carve up the Prussians with its sabres.

An ordinary *Fusiliersäbel* was issued to all the remaining infantry of the line in 1765. The single-edged blade was 21½in long and slightly curved, and the strange-looking 'mameluke' hilt lacked any knuckle guard.

The musket ammunition came in the form of cylinders of thin, stiff cartridge paper, each containing a leaden ball and a charge of powder. The soldier carried his personal stock of up to forty cartridges in a pouch of thick black leather which hung by his right hip from a white leather strap. Among the peculiarities of the Austrian service was the fact that six of the cartridges were of buckshot, at three or four little bullets to the round. Elsewhere in Europe the priming pan was usually filled with coarse powder direct from the cartridge. However, the Austrian infantry regulations of 1749 describe the use of a powder horn, which enabled the pan to be primed with fine powder in the antique style, without diminishing the powder in the cartridge.

The Austrian infantry went to war at the beginning of the reign armed with the Model 1722 *ordinäre Flinte*, a muzzle-loading smooth-bore musket patterned largely on the Model 1717 French musket. At 18.3mm the calibre was smaller than that of the Prussian musket, and so the wounds inflicted by the enemy weapon were 'more considerable and dangerous'.[22] The large priming pan was set above a 'round' lock plate, and the frizzen was protected against damp by a leather cover (*Futteral*) which hung from the sling. The length of the barrel was 43in, and the musket weighed rather more than 11lb. The bayonet was 18in long, and it had the usual triangular-sectioned blade of the time.

The ramrod was made of beech, and it was very liable to snap in the heat of action. On 8 December 1744 the authorities therefore decided to introduce a stout

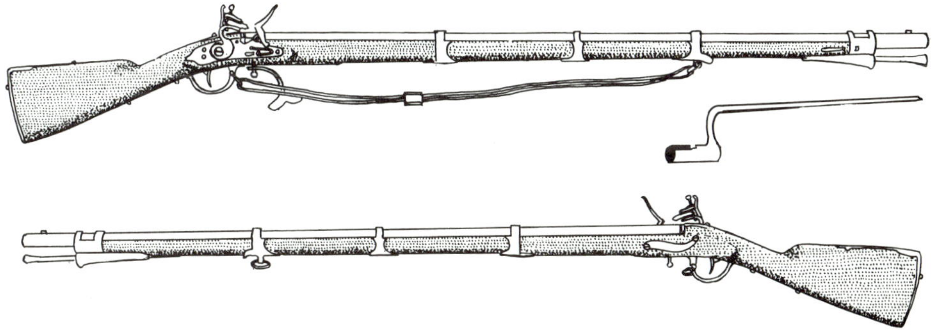

The Commissflinte *of 1754*

iron ramrod in the Prussian style. Further changes followed apace. In 1748 the order went out to rearm six regiments with a musket to the design of Johann Schmied, who was a military clerk with an inventive turn of mind. The new weapon was light, but unfortunately somewhat fragile, and in 1754 Prince Liechtenstein summoned a commission of officers and technicians to compare the Schmied musket with specimens of three different models which were supplied by the Penzeneter works. Features of all four weapons were incorporated in the *Commissflinte* of 1754, the weapon which was going to see the army through the rest of the century.

The *Commissflinte* was of the same calibre as the Model 1722 musket, though the barrel was a little shorter (at 39¾in) and it was secured to the woodwork by three stout bands, instead of the under-barrel pins of the Model 1722. The barrel was of good-quality iron, carefully drilled out in a single operation, and the 'flat' lock plate and all the lock parts were made of wrought steel. The butt plate and the mounts were of iron, and the stock was made either of beechwood stained black (in the fusilier companies) or of polished walnut (for the grenadiers). The musket was equipped with a sling and *Futteral* of white leather, and the whole weapon weighed about 9lb exclusive of the bayonet. In dirty weather the butt and the lock were encased in a fabric bag.

The shortlived *Feld Jäger Corps* was armed with a 15mm rifle. This was a typical military adaptation of the contemporary German hunting rifle, with eight exterior facets to the barrel and six interior grooves. In 1768 the new units of the *Grenzscharfschützen* were issued with a curious weapon with two superimposed barrels – the upper being rifled for accurate long-range work, and the lower a smooth-bore tube for rapid fire at closer ranges. Neither of these rifles mounted a bayonet, though the 1768 model came with a long spear with three lugs, upon which the sharpshooter could rest the barrel according to his convenience.

Hand grenade throwing continued to feature in the drill books of Maria Theresa's reign, though the actual bomb had passed out of use before her time, largely because people were not strong enough or brave enough to use it effectively. When the grenade was eventually reintroduced it was in the form of a projectile to be shot from hand-artillery. After some trials in actual combat, several grenadiers in every squadron of mounted grenadiers were issued in 1761 with *Gewehrhaubitzen* – carbines with short, wide barrels which could propel the grenades well beyond throwing distance. Eight years later a number of similar weapons were distributed among the infantry.

In 1747 Major-General Joseph Esterházy was already most specific concerning the way in which the uniforms and equipment were to be maintained. He told the soldiers of his regiment of Hungarian infantry that they must

> cultivate cleanliness, and keep themselves free from vermin in the head and clothes. They are to wash and comb themselves frequently. Twice a week they must have themselves shaved and put on a cleanly-laundered shirt. Hats are always to be kept clean and neatly turned up. Likewise the grenadiers must cultivate the habit of hanging their bearskin caps in the sun and air, and beating them out so as to prevent the fur from getting matted; they keep their tricorns tied behind them to the strap of the cartridge pouch. The hair is to be kept neatly combed and curled, so that it does not hang in the eyes, and the pigtail is to be neatly braided and it is to reach down to the waist. The stock is to be wound tidily around the neck above the shirt. The coat, dolman and breeches are all to be put on carefully and neatly, and the pockets in the coat and dolman are not to be filled with all kinds of rubbish. At all times the skirts of the coat are to be turned back. The shoes must show no creases, and they are to be neatly laced up. The soldier is always to keep a stock of needles, together with thread and patches in the colour of the uniform, so that he can patch and sew up any tears in the cloth. Shoes are changed around daily, and the soldier must turn out in a white shirt and cleanly dressed on parade and on every Sunday and feast day. He is to obtain whatever brushes are necessary to keep the

uniform and shoes clean. He must also furnish himself with a handkerchief, so that he does not have to wipe his nose on his cuff, or blow through his fingers.[23]

The regulations specified that the musket and all metal parts of the equipment were to be kept 'mirror bright', and some keen regiments got the bad habit of loosening the bands and screws of the musket, so as to make a more resounding clatter when the weapon was slammed about in drill – a custom not unknown in twentieth-century Sandhurst. Altogether the cult of spit and polish took a heavy toll among the small arms. Cognazzo remarks:

> we polished our weapons unceasingly, and in the course of time the musket barrels became so thin that after a few live rounds they were liable to burst and melt, with unfortunate consequences. This was revealed to our astonished eyes in the campaigns of 1756 and 1757. Many regiments got off scarcely eight or ten volleys before we saw a couple of hundred of these beautiful, gleaming muskets lying useless on the ground.[24]

The fetish of smartness actually grew more compelling after the Seven Years War, when the official infantry code of 1769 did not hesitate to tell the men exactly how they were to do up their breeches and gaiters.

Colours

The colours of the regiment served as rallying-points in battle and as the focus of loyalty. At the beginning of the reign every company of fusiliers had its own colour, but in 1748 the number was reduced to two per battalion. The grenadiers owned no colours whatsoever until they were formed into combined battalions in 1769.

The infantry colour of 1740 was a single sheet of silk, adorned with devices in applied silk or embroidery and measuring 6ft by 4ft 6in. The *Leibfahne*, or colour of the *Inhaber*'s company (later battalion) had a field of white silk, decorated on the reverse side with the Imperial double eagle and on the obverse (ie with the staff to the left) with some religious emblem. The colours of the other companies (later battalions) had the double eagle on both sides, and the fields were coloured uniformly within the regiment – whether yellow, green, red or red-white-red. Both the *Leibfahne* and the ordinary colours were edged on three sides with a characteristically lively Habsburg border of flames or triangles. The staff side had no border. The staff itself was wound about with spirals of cloth – black, yellow, red and white.

A new heraldry was decreed in 1743, when the Elector of Bavaria had himself made Emperor. The double eagle was to be replaced by a religious device, and a grass-green field was determined for all save the *Leibfahne*. It is doubtful whether many regiments actually replaced their colours before a circular of 22 December 1745 restored the old designs and standardised the range of colour schemes. The *Leibfahne* retained its white field, but in all the other companies the field was to be of Imperial yellow. The colours for the borders were determined as black, yellow, red and white, in no particular order.

The colours became badly tattered in the course of the Seven Years War (when they were not actually lost), and, as always, they proved uncomfortable to carry on account of the weight of embroidery and appliqué-work. In 1766, therefore, it was determined that the devices were to be painted in oils directly on the silk. The new colours were light to carry, but the oil paint was liable to fade, and if the colour got wet it had to be dried off before it could be rolled up and cased.

The presentation of a new set of colours was a matter of great moment for the regiment, and the occasion was celebrated by feasting and fireworks. There was the interesting episode on 15 May 1748, when the regiment of Kollowrath set up some pavilions for this purpose on the meadows near Schönbrunn. The festivities went ahead according to plan until a wretched captain, who was half deaf and who had perhaps 'imbibed a little too deeply of the wine', took such umbrage at a well-meaning remark of the colonel commandant Franz Aulock 'that he not only knocked the colonel down, but snatched his sword away and would have run him through if the officers on the spot had not prevented him. The unfortunate captain, who had a wife and children, was summoned before a court martial and condemned to be shot, though subsequently he was reprieved'.[25]

Tactics

Maria Theresa proclaimed to the army in 1749 'How it has come to Our notice that Our Imperial infantry possesses neither a uniform drill, nor any uniform observation of military practice. These two shortcomings not only give rise to various disorders, but promote dangerous, harmful and damaging situations both in the field and in garrison.'[26] In the first ten years of the reign the army had certainly gone about the business of fighting in a great variety of ways, which owed something to sets of private and public regulations, but probably rather more to the whim of individual colonels.

In the earlier period Field-Marshal Neipperg commissioned tactical codes for infantry and cavalry, which were completed in July 1741. General Maximilian Browne composed a set of principles of his own and circulated them in his armies in 1746 and again in 1756. This was followed by the notable *Regulament* of Major-General Joseph Esterházy, an informative and influential work which he printed in 1747. Nobody took much notice of an uninspired official infantry *Reglement*, which had been drawn up by a commission of generals and published in 1737.

In the era of the pre-Seven Years War reforms one of the most urgent tasks was therefore to impose an equality of practice upon the army. An important fruit of the deliberations of the Military Reform Commission was the *Regulament und Ordnung des gesammten Kaiserlich-Königlichen Fuss-Volcks*, which was published in 1749. The inspiration came from sources as diverse as the legalistic *Ämterbücher* of the early sixteenth century, various old administrative instructions, private codes of conduct (notably the Esterházy regulations of 1747), the lessons of the recent war and the example of the Prussian army. Maria Theresa herself is said to have contributed information which she gleaned from two interviews with an ex-Prussian captain called Doss. The Prussian ambassador reported to Frederick that

> every regiment is in possession of this book, but the penalty for communicating its contents is nothing less than cashiering with disgrace. For this reason neither I nor any of the other foreign envoys have been able to obtain a copy. In general it is modelled according to the drill of Your Majesty's troops, but several officers have assured me that the Austrians are going about things in such a way that they will never come near, let alone equal, the success of the Prussians.[27]

The *Regulament* treated of every aspect of regimental affairs in almost obsessive detail, and, just in case the reader should remain in any doubt as to what was meant, the manual exercise of arms was illustrated by a lengthy series of engravings. The fundamentals of the 1749 *Regulament* were left unchanged by Field-Marshal Lacy's revised editions of 1769, and they underwent substantial modification only in the code of 1805. Even then the Theresian methods of deployment and the articles of conduct in garrison and the field held sway until the middle of the nineteenth century.

The 1749 *Regulament* laid down that

> the men are to be arrayed in four ranks, each three paces distant from the next, and the files one pace apart. The whole regiment is to be drawn up with the tallest and best-looking men in the first rank, the slightly less tall in the fourth rank, the smaller or middle sized men in the second rank, and the smallest and ugliest in the third. The same principle determines the allocation of the men along the files from the flanks towards the centre'[28]

From 1757 the number of ranks was reduced from four to three, as was already the case with the grenadiers. In battle conditions 'the assigned officers and NCOs are responsible for seeing that the second rank is brought up as closely as possible behind the first, and that the troops push forward when they level their muskets. Since the third rank does not fire, these precautions go far to obviate the possibility of any injury or damage to the men in front or to the side'.[29] Altogether the three-rank battalion took up a frontage of between 240 and 300 paces, including the interval for the cannon. All formations could be thickened up and shortened, if necessary, by doubling up the files.

The battalion was divided into the sixteen tactical blocks of the little Austrian platoon, each seven or eight files wide (ten for the grenadiers). For all evolutions, however, the platoons were combined two-by-two in half divisions (each the rough equivalent of the large Prussian platoon), or in full divisions or companies of four platoons each. When it came to converting a formation of march into line of battle,

Arrangement of a company or full division

—1st CAPT'S COY, EARLIER SEVEN YEAR'S WAR

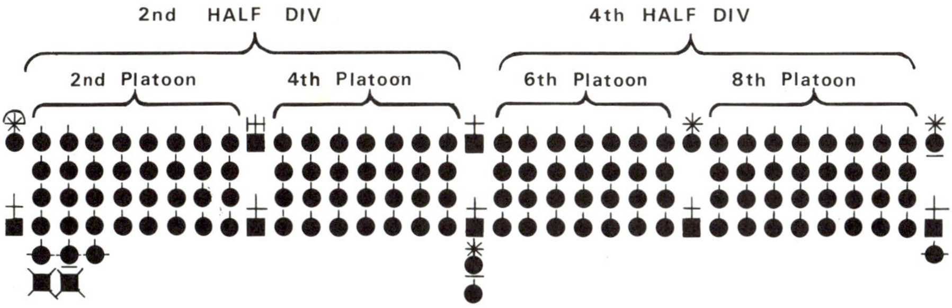

the Austrians seem to have preferred the rather old-fashioned technique of processional deployment by wheeling from open column. Wheeling could be accomplished by platoons, half divisions, battalions or even larger formations, although, as the Prince de Ligne describes, the officers always had to contend with the 'sheep-like instinct' which caused the men to cling together in the columns: 'I cannot recall a single action when we did not see dozens of columns which we had to try to break up – I with the flat of my sword, and my corporals with blows with their sticks.'[30]

In the Seven Years War movements were carried out at the 'ordinary' or 'middle' pace, and rather less frequently at the double. The 'ordinary' and 'middle' paces seem to have corresponded with faster or slower versions of the natural pace. However, the regulations of 1769 emphasised that 'the knees must be kept absolutely stiff while raising and putting down the feet during the step; in every pace the foot must be raised the natural distance from the earth, and put smartly down again without stamping'.[31]

When moving across open country or along broad roads the army marched by preference in closed columns on a divisional frontage. The men marched at their ease, with muskets slung, and the officers were sometimes reminded to ride by the side of the road so as not to cover the troops with mud or dust. On parade or in action, however,

> the men must observe a correct posture while they are marching, with the head and eyes always inclined to the right, and when they pass by an officer they must look him straight in the eye . . . the musket is to be carried in the proper way. The trigger guard must be pressed into the body, so that the musket cannot waver, and the right hand is to hang motionless down the man's right-hand side.[32]

The Austrian army was burdened with fire tactics of truly abominable complexity. As soon as the troops were drawn up in line of battle the officers were expected to make a rapid inspection to see that the muskets were in good condition, with the flints firmly screwed in place, and that the cartridge pouches were full and ready. The leading two ranks were then ordered to fix bayonets, and when the time came to open fire the first rank flopped down on the right knee and crouched forward over its muskets. The second rank closed up and levelled its weapons over the first, while the third remained with shouldered muskets or occasionally pointed its muskets between the files of the second rank. The fourth rank (while it still existed) formed a reserve.

There were instances when the first rank was ordered to fling itself down so sharply that a number of the men suffered ruptures. Once they were on their knees, the men sometimes had to be beaten in order to get them to stand upright again and expose themselves to the enemy fire. Thus the battle of Parma in 1734 ended with a large proportion of the infantry crawling about on the ground.

In theory the fire could be delivered by individual ranks along a platoon or divisional frontage, or by divisions, half divisions or platoons firing as units. Divisions and platoons were also supposed to be capable of blasting away with volleys on the advance.

A special drill was devised for almost every eventuality, beginning with a 'hedge fire' (*Höcken-Feuer*) given by the first rank of each platoon in succession. 'This tactic is employed when the enemy are posted and concealed in hedges or brushwood, and we cannot get at them from the flank or any other side except frontally.'[33]

The files could be spread further apart when it was necessary to hold a length of rampart or trench (*Retrenchment-Feuer*), and the troops were trained to fight back-to-back if they were caught marching along a sunken road or on a track through a thick wood (*Doppeltes Weeg Feuer*). The prescriptions for *Brücken-Feuer* concerned an elaborate manoeuvre which was designed to launch the grenadiers over a bridge in the face of the enemy.

On the subject of *Hohlen Weeg* and *Gassen Feuer* the 1749 regulations explain that 'The first device comes into operation when the enemy is hidden or placed in a sunken road or other defile, and wishes to prevent us from passing through. *Gassen Feuer*, however, is employed in streets on the occasion of a riot or when a fortress is being taken by storm.'[34] Both these evolutions were accomplished by a caracole of column of platoons – each platoon firing in succession, then splitting in two to allow the half platoons to wheel off to the right and left and make way for the next platoon to come up behind.

Buckshot was to be employed against infantry at ranges below a hundred paces. When the troops came under attack by cavalry they were to keep up a sustained fire with the same ammunition, 'but as soon as the cavalry come within ten paces the first two ranks stand fast, and level their bayonets against the necks or heads of the horses, so as to make them frightened and confused, while the third rank is to fire at the riders'.[35]

Orders to the battalion as a whole were transmitted by the drums at the command of the major. Within the sub-units the officers put their men through their motions through shouted orders, the prescribed sequence for fire being *Man wird chargiren!* (load!), *Macht euch fertig!* (make ready!), *Schlagt an!* (present!) and *Feuer!*

In dealing with the tactics of cold steel we enter the field of mythology, and more specifically Classical mythology. Towards the middle of the eighteenth century a number of authorities compared what they had read of ancient military history with what they could see of the inadequacies of the musket, and arrived at the conclusion that an attack without firing must be an irresistible force. This school of thought owned several adherents in Austria, among whom were numbered Field-Marshal Khevenhüller himself, and the General Thüngen who maintained that 'battles are won less by fire than by the actual break-in'.[36]

It was the impressive composure of the advancing infantry, as much as the sharpness of their blades, which was expected to discomfort the enemy. The regulations of 1749 describe the infantry as marching to the attack in silence and with shouldered muskets. A command of *Marsch! Marsch!* set the men off at the double, but even in a bayonet attack only the first rank was supposed to lower its muskets, and it was to deliver a volley just before the physical contact.

One of the tactics of the grenadiers and Hungarian infantry was to send their rearmost ranks around the flanks of the company or battalion so that they could get at the enemy with their sabres, as actually happened in 1757 in the battles of Prague and Kolin.

These and other remarkable occurrences were duly noted by contemporaries, for it was rare for the niceties of the parade ground or textbook to survive the first moments of any action. As regards the tactics of cold steel, the Prince de Ligne encountered only one authenticated case of a bayonet fight in the open field. This was occasioned by a coincidence in the combat at Moys on 7 September 1757, when his regiment and a Prussian force climbed the Jäckelsberg hill from opposite sides and ran into each other at the top.

The difficult tactics of 'fire and retire' were carried out with notable success by the regiment of Jung-Colloredo (IR No 40) at Lobositz, and again by Loudon's grenadiers at Liegnitz. The field of Kolin witnessed some interesting displays of textbook precision in fire tactics, most remarkably by the Hungarian regiment of Ezherzog Carl (IR 2), which delivered volleys just as if it had been on the drill square. 'There were even officers who drove regulation pedantry so far that they made the soldiers hold their muskets at the "Present", so as to correct the aim and make sure of hitting the enemy.'[37] Otherwise the combats almost always resolved themselves into uncontrollable fire fights, which were staged at a range of rather over a hundred paces and endured until one or other of the sides lost its nerve and fled.

The parade-ground rate of fire of five rounds per minute sank to two or less in real combat. All the same, the soldiers were under continual pressure to maintain the rate of fire, and they were liable to adopt a number of more or less pernicious practices. According to the Prussian habit the musket might be held in the left hand and loaded on the slant, without setting the butt on the ground, or the man might omit to ram the charge and bullet home and simply shake them down the barrel by striking the butt on the earth. Many a soldier was shot by his own rearward ranks, and in a very revealing comment Cognazzo states:

> The battle of Kolin in 1757 was the sole instance in my career when I have seen orderly and well-judged volleys delivered by tight and compact ranks. All the same there were many brave lads who fell wounded from behind, without ever having turned their backs on the enemy.[38]

On top of this the musket of the time was inaccurate in the extreme. The Prince de Ligne once issued the 144 men of a company with ten rounds each and ordered them to fire at a long cloth target which he painted to represent the frontage of four enemy platoons. Out of the 1,440 carefully-aimed rounds only 270 hit the cloth. He found that at 100 paces it was necessary to aim at the knees, at 150 at the buckle of the belt, at 200 at the chest, at 250 at the moustache and at 300 at a point one foot above the man's head.

All the best examples of Austrian tactical proficiency come from the period which falls between the great Bohemian exercise camps of the middle 1750s and the last stages of the Seven Years War. Otherwise the standard of Austrian infantry drill remained fairly bad throughout the reign. The French military pundit Guibert saw the regiment of Colloredo go through its paces at Olmütz in 1773, and he remarked that the deployments were invariably badly done, with no proper intervals being observed; the advance in battle order was executed slowly, to the accompaniment of much chatter, and the ranks were out of alignment along all their lengths. Thiébault put his finger on one of the reasons. The Prussians, he wrote, had large garrisons, and customarily manoeuvred in long lines, 'whereas in the Austrian service, though the troops are drilled just as diligently, they are frequently scattered in small garrisons for the sake of economy'.[39]

Mirabeau attributed the failing to the great size of the company, to the paltry establishment of officers and NCOs, and to the lowly status of the subaltern:

> The Austrian army looks splendid under arms. It is well dressed, well equipped

> and well armed. It is composed of tall and active soldiers. Yet with all this it is deficient in co-ordination, uniformity and training. It simply does not know how to move. You cannot see an Austrian line advance three hundred paces without losing its alignment and intervals and fall into grievous disorder – something which would be inconceivable in the Prussian army. An Austrian column cannot march without getting strung out, or form into line without having to extend or close itself up.[40]

In part the confusions derived from the regulations themselves, which betrayed an obsession with forms and ceremonies, and with laying down procedures for every conceivable happening in garrison and in the field. Much space was devoted to the prescribed salutes and evolutions with swords, partisans, muskets and colours on particular occasions and before assorted dignitaries. The 1749 edition of the infantry regulations had a special drill for Good Friday, a 27-page *Exercitium* for the obsolete boar spear (*Schweinsfeder*), and an enumeration of the procedures required of NCOs and privates when they approached to make their reports through doors or tent entrances of various heights:

> If the soldier delivering the report is offered a glass of wine, he is to bring his musket from the 'present' to a position in front of his left foot . . . he removes his hat in the prescribed fashion, but instead of raising his fingers in the salute he must take hold of the glass. Once he has drunk, he replaces the hat and once more presents arms.[41]

While the Prussians gave the recruit a modicum of training in wartime and could feed him into the battle after three weeks, the Austrians wasted time in inculcating mastery of a host of details of the manual exercise of arms. Cognazzo claims:

> I know of regiments which as late in the campaign [of 1758] as the battle of Hochkirch still had between two and three hundred men who could not be incorporated in the line of battle, because they did not know how to load and fire. We had been playing at training these men for the whole summer.[42]

6

The 'Croats'

Historical evolution

The 'Croats' were a force of light infantry, recruited principally from the militarised Slavonic population which had been settled along the eastern borders of the Habsburg empire. They gave the Theresian army a unique character, and presented it with some strong advantages.

> Taking everything into consideration, there are no light troops who are their equals. The House of Austria owes all its military fame to its Croats and hussars. Without them it would have gone under in the War of 1740, and perhaps even in that of 1756. (Mirabeau)[1]

The principle of forming a border of military colonists was a very ancient one, which went back to the soldier-settlers of the later Roman and Byzantine empires, and was represented in later times by the cossacks of the Tsar.

In the Habsburg lands the eastern military border was created as a direct result of the destruction of the Hungarian army and state by the Turks in the battle of Mohács, on 26 August 1526. In 1535 the Archduke of Inner Austria (ie Styria, Carinthia and Carniola) was already giving special privileges to the Slavonic peoples who were fleeing from the advance of the Turks, and seventeen years later the refugees and auxiliaries were placed under military command. Finally in 1578 the work of maintaining the military border was formally devolved upon the Inner-Austrian *Stände*. In the course of time the numbers of the *Grenzer* (lit. 'borderers') was swelled by fresh waves of refugees, notably the Greek Orthodox Serbs who flooded into the Carlstadt and Slavonian generalcies in the 1690s and again in the later 1730s.

Although they were sadly lacking in organisation and discipline, the wild Croats made their presence felt in the campaigns of the War of the Austrian Succession, as well as furnishing 20,000 men to guard the eastern borders. Along the Danube they struck terror into the French and Bavarians (and not a few of their own commanders), and at Hohenfriedberg on 4 June 1745 they created a sensation when they plundered the Prussian war chest and Frederick the Great's tent. Old Fritz told his generals that they had little to fear from the Croats in the open country.

> But it is a different question in the woods and mountains. In that kind of terrain the Croats throw themselves to the ground and hide behind the rocks and trees. This means that you cannot see where they are firing from, and you have no means of repaying them for the casualties they inflict on you.[2]

Meanwhile within the monarchy the Croats had received a much-needed disciplinarian and champion in the person of Prince Joseph Sachsen-Hildburg-

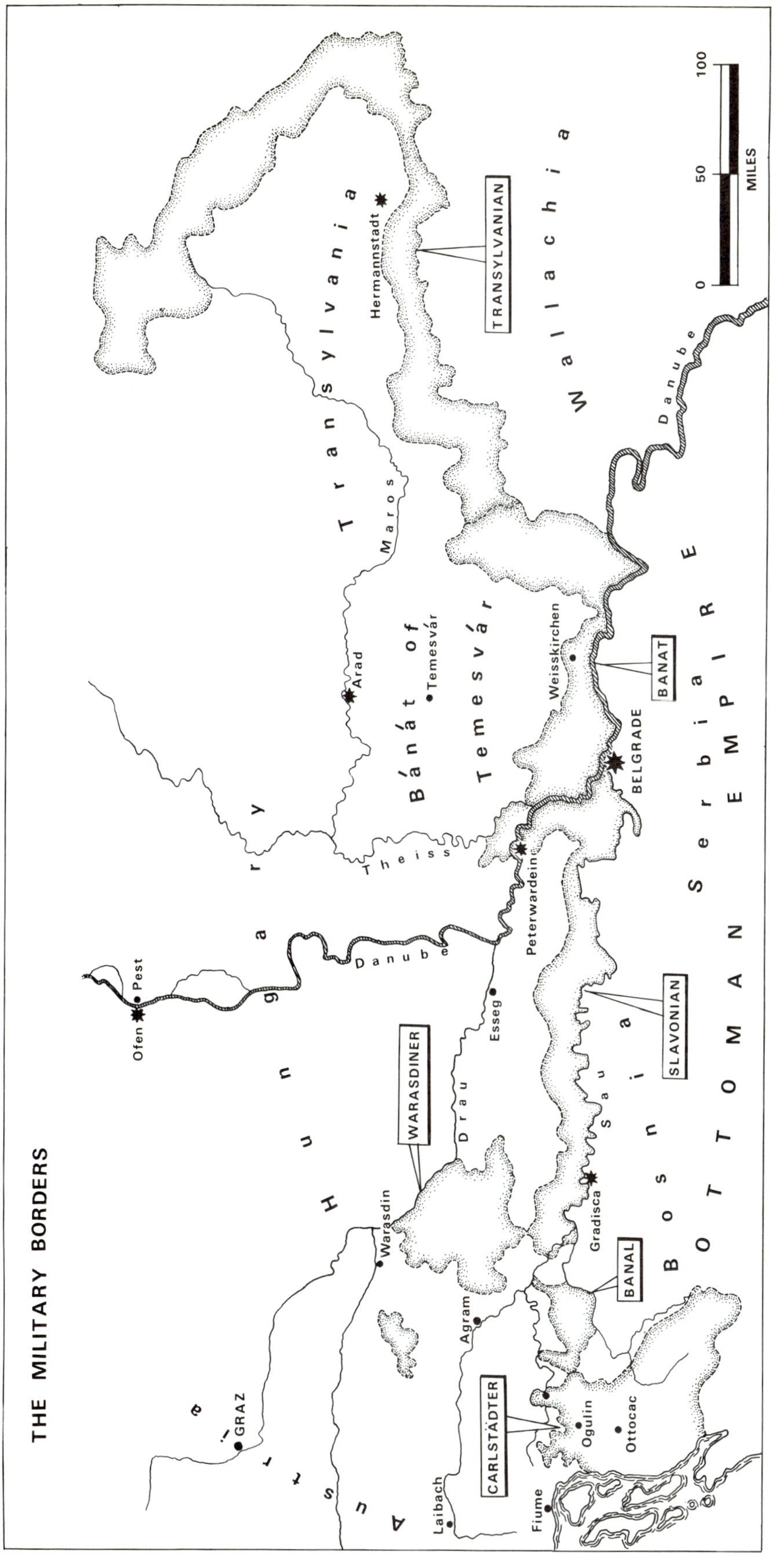

THE MILITARY BORDERS

hausen, who prized the military borders as 'a treasure of the Imperial monarchy, such as could never be bought and paid for in money'.[3] Maria Theresa abolished the Inner-Austrian *Kriegsrath* at Graz in October 1743, and transferred its functions to Hildburghausen, as head of a new *Militär-Directorium* for the borders. Hildburghausen held this office from 1744 to 1749. He imposed a severe military code in 1745, and over the next four years he created powerful units of Croats on fixed establishments – namely two regiments of Warasdiners, four of Carlstädters, three of Slavonians and associated companies of *Grenz-Husaren*. The Croats responded well to most of the changes, and Hildburghausen claimed that 'the Croats train so diligently, that a Croatian regiment learns as much in one week as a German regiment in a whole half year'.[4]

Hildburghausen resigned in 1749. His *Directorium* vanished with him, but the essentials of his work were continued by Field-Marshal Carl Batthyány, who reorganised the Banal borders, where he set on foot two regiments of infantry and one of hussars.

While preserving the Croats' special way of fighting, Maria Theresa resolved that the *Grenzer* 'shall be regarded in every particular as the equal of the other regiments'.[5] This allayed the grievances of many of the Croat officers, who had threatened to resign if their men were still to be regarded as *irregulär*. As a further sign of the enhanced status of the Croats, the government in 1754 issued a new administrative and judicial code for the borders – the *Militär-Granitz-Rechten* – which was milder in tone than the old Hildburghausen version. Originally intended only for the Warasdiner and Carlstädter borders, it was given a wider application after the Seven Years War.

The whole experiment was endangered when, in January 1755, an extensive mutiny broke out in the Kreutzer and St Georger regiments of the Warasdin generalcy. The blame lay partly with the high-handed ways and lack of imagination of some of the Austrian commanders, but partly also with the fact that the new requirements from Vienna coincided with a diminution of the obvious danger from the Turks. In other words, the whole orientation of the institutions of the military borders was undergoing a change.

Maria Theresa dispatched Lieutenant-Colonel Philipp Beck to the seat of the troubles, and this cunning and sympathetic little man was able to persuade the mutineers to lay down their arms and present their grievances in writing. Back in Vienna the chancellor Kaunitz, who was another champion of the Croats, pointed out the value of a region which had the capability of putting a force of 50,000 men into actual service, instead of merely laying out an equivalent contribution in money. He added that the Croats 'contributed greatly to the salvation of the whole monarchy', and that they offered human material 'from which we could fashion infantry of the best and most formidable kind'.[6]

Field-Marshal Neipperg went to Croatia to conduct a thoroughgoing investigation on the spot. Gratifyingly enough, the Warasdiners made no trouble about handing over the ringleaders among the mutineers, and they declared that they wished to remain under military administration. A number of reforms were set in train, now that the air was cleared. On 29 June the government announced that it would furnish the arms and equipment free, and make arrangements for the Warasdiners to buy their uniforms at closely-regulated prices. (It was only in the impoverished Carlstadt generalcy that the state furnished uniforms gratis.) The deal was incorporated in a new *Regulament* of 11 October, which supplemented the code of 1754

Liccaner Croat. He is wearing an earlier form of the Croatian uniform – red jacket with green cuffs and yellow braid; sea green waistcoat with yellow braid; red pants; red and green barrel sash; black cap; sword with iron furniture; white and red Opanken *shoes. (By courtesy of the Albertina Collection)*

and met nearly all the grievances of the Croats.

The misunderstanding with the Warasdiners was sorted out just in time, considering that hostilities were about to break out with Prussia. Strengthened, disciplined and trained, the Croats mustered 34,000 infantry and 6,000 border hussars at the outset of the new war in 1756. Kaunitz expected great things of them. As he pointed out to the Emperor:

> Public opinion does not do justice to the *Grenzers*. Yet these people are the ones who reach the enemy first, who maintain the closest contact with them and keep them in a state of perpetual unrest. The Croats undergo more discomfort and danger than the other troops, without receiving the same care. They have to run rather than march. No hardship is considered too great for them, and their losses are considered almost unworthy of note. But it is thanks to the Croats and the hussars that the army can sleep in peace, that the regular troops are spared, and that our lands are protected from enemy raids.[7]

The chancellor was not going to be disappointed in the performance of his favourites.

Altogether 88,000 Croats saw service in the course of the Seven Years War, making up probably more than a quarter of the army. There were 9,000 Croats engaged in the fighting around Prague in May 1757. It was the Croats who sustained the first shock at Kolin, and 7,000 of them took part in the assault at Hochkirch. They were the first in position at Maxen, and the first to storm into the fortress of Schweidnitz in 1761.

Commanders like Loudon, Beck, Draskowitz, Lusinski, Jahnus, Ried and Brentano made their reputations as leaders of Croats. All the time, however, the Croatian commanders had to contend with the instinct of other generals to split the *Grenzers* up into penny packets:

> No general believed he could exist away from the main army unless he had several hundred or upwards of a thousand of the 'redcloaks' scattered about him to see to his safety. Hence we had some of these brave men almost everywhere, but never had them in a united corps.[8]

Loudon was well aware of the tendency. In 1757 he suggested to Maria Theresa that two battalions of grenadiers should be assigned to the Croats. He indicated that 'although the Croats are essentially an extremely brave people, they have so far been unable to deliver an attack in an orderly formation. Every time we attempt it, they disperse again in their old fashion'.[9] Loudon's project was taken up, and combined forces of Croats and grenadiers or hussars saw action at Kolin, Moys and Maxen.

Inevitably some of these very active troops fell into the hands of the enemy. The Prussian preacher F. E. Boysen came to know many of the allied prisoners who were gathered at Magdeburg in the Seven Years War. In his estimation the Austrians, Russians and Swedes were far more civilised than the French or Germans, and

> among the Austrians I would give pride of place to the 'Pandours', whom the newspapers are so fond of decrying for their wildness and barbarity . . . I can testify to their civilised behaviour. Not only did they conduct themselves in a polite fashion, whenever I had to hold a service in the high school, but their manner towards me was one of courtesy and seemliness, even though their religious beliefs must have led them to regard me as an heretical preacher. Once when I visited the late Dr Damisch, who was their physician, he told me that these men were not without means, and that he was well paid for his medical ministrations.[10]

The work of expanding and consolidating the military borders was resumed immediately after the Seven Years War. In the original Croatian territories the generalcies of Warasdin and Carlstadt were combined in May 1763 under the authority of Philipp Beck, who was now a full general. In the same year the military boatmen of the Danube, Sava and Theiss were united into a battalion of *Tschaikisten*. Beck became the first *General-Grenzinspektor* in 1765. By now the total population of the military borders had reached 350,000, of whom about three-quarters were of Slavonic stock, while the rest were Magyars and the closely-related Széklers. The adherents of the Greek Orthodox faith were in the majority, except in the Warasdin generalcy and the recruiting areas of the Gradiskaner and Broder regiments.

Beck held his post for three creative years. His successor was the polyglot General Joseph Siskovics, who preferred to conduct his business from Vienna – an arrangement which led to the setting up of the *Militärgrenze* department of the *Hofkriegsrath*. Work had already begun on raising two regiments in the sandy Banát, and the creation of a new military border in Transylvania. The cadres of two regiments of in-

Warasdiner Creutzer Croat. In this example the short jacket has evolved into a coat. The coat is white, with light green cuffs, collar, turn-backs and tasselled Litzen; *light green waistcoat with white braid and yellow buttons; white pants; white and yellow barrel sash; sword with iron furniture. The pack is of grey cloth, bound with red cord or straps; the red cloak has been rolled up and tied to the bottom of the pack.* (*By courtesy of the Albertina Collection*)

fantry and one of horse were formed from the Székler peoples of Transylvania in 1764, and a matching set from the Wallachians in 1766. Unfortunately the Széklers objected that they were already doing enough to support the monarchy by paying high taxes, without having to do military service as well, and so the organisation of the Transylvanian borders was not completed until the 1780s.

The military training of the *Grenzers* went on apace. A Frenchman saw three hundred Croats drilling after the Seven Years War and remarked: 'They all perform well under arms. They look splendid, and no other troops in the world can match their warlike air.'[11]

In the War of the Bavarian Succession the Carlstadt and Banal regiments could put only one battalion each into the field, on account of the depressed state of their homelands, while the new Banát and Transylvania borders contributed nobody at all. However, the Warasdiner regiments were present in the shape of two battalions each, and they found plenty of scope for their peculiar talents in the fighting which raged along the hills and forests of north-east Bohemia.

By the end of the reign the military borders formed a tract of territory between 20 and 60 miles deep, and extending no less than 1,000 miles in length, all the way from the arid mountains above the Adriatic and across the plains of the Sava, the Danube and the Theiss to the furthest reaches of the Transylvanian Alps.

Institutions

The establishment of the Croatian regiments was very large indeed, the regiments of Warasdiners and most of the regiments of Carlstädters owning four battalions each, with nominal complements of between 3,860 and 5,000 men. The colossal Liccaner regiment of the Carlstadt generalcy was composed of six battalions with (in 1749) a total of 5,785 officers and men. The individual Croatian battalion comprised sixteen companies of fusiliers and two of grenadiers.

According to custom, only a single *Division* or levy of one-third of the regiment's strength was liable to be called up for wartime service, though by agreement with the Croats the second levies were summoned up on several occasions during the Seven Years War. The serving levies left their homes in the spring, and regardless of the state of the campaign they returned when the stipulated term expired in the late autumn, as though propelled by the same kind of homing instinct which drives herds of pigs and geese along Croatian or Serbian roads today. There was very little the generals could do to stop them. Individual deserters, on the other hand, were rare and they were abominated by their comrades. They were declared perpetual exiles, and their houses were burned down and the sites strewn with salt.

The responsibilities of the Croatian officer appeared endless. Guibert wrote:

> You can scarcely conceive of the kind of life which these people lead. Most of them dwell in isolated little houses which have been built by the government. They enjoy no kind of society for six months of the year – not only are they far distant from one another, but the snow falls early in the season and remains on the ground well into the year . . . I can picture no more wretched condition to which a thinking being could be condemned by a miserable fate.[12]

The captain had to keep up registers of population, cattle and crops, determine which households were to furnish a soldier, and adjudicate in disputes between families – and all this on top of having to lead his fit and active men in the field.

In the earlier part of the reign a large proportion of the officer corps was made up of foreigners – Germans, Dutch, Italians and some French – together with a number of Austrian officers who had been banished from the regiments of the line. Loudon became a lieutenant-colonel attached to the Slavonians early in the Seven Years War, at a time when such a post was 'often the summit of the career of a captain who was superannuated, or otherwise unfit to do service as a major'.[13] When the question of mobilising the second division was mooted in November 1756 it was found that 'there are too few officers with these people, and without officers we cannot hope to make good use of them'.[14]

In the course of the Seven Years War the number of native officers began to increase, as a consequence of the *Regulament* of 11 October 1755, and in any case a number of the best 'German' officers embarked on a career with the Croats – some attracted by the prospect of profit, but others lured by the excitement of the life and the parity of status with the regiments of the line. When Guibert toured the borders in 1773 he found that the officers were of the same calibre as in the rest of the army, and that the Croatians had actually come to prefer the foreign officers, whom they trusted to be less partial than their own countrymen.

The military borders were virtually innocent of commerce or manufactures, and the people supported themselves by working as free tenants on the lands which had been allocated among them by the crown. The conditions of this strange military and social contract were laid down in some detail in the successive codes, of which the edition of 1754 defined the most important clause in the following terms:

> 14. Since they enjoy Imperial privileges, all able-bodied males are bound to render service and are subject to military jurisdiction. The statutes bind them to carry out military training, and they obey willingly whatever directions the officers give them in this respect. Whoever refuses these duties will incur the loss of privileges, and, according to circumstances, physical punishment or the death-penalty.[15]

The land was divided up into parcels, each of which corresponded to the holding of one soldier. In the Carlstadt generalcy the homesteads formed between eight and twelve yokes of land, each yoke consisting of a lot 200 paces long by 50 wide. The sale or subdivision of land was forbidden.

In the relatively fertile Warasdin generalcy the Croats were able to form villages, but in the generalcy of Carlstadt and in Slavonia the population was scattered in small hamlets or isolated homesteads. Here and there could be seen the simple house of an officer, set amid a small garden or a field of corn, but the soldiers lived in draughty cabins of wood. The centre of the cabin floor was reserved for a fire, over which was baked a poor unleavened bread of millet, oats and sometimes the seeds of wild grasses. The enjoyment of wine and meat was almost unknown. If the householder was prosperous enough to own any furniture or domestic utensils, these were heaped up in a corner.

The question of Croatian military dress is a difficult and complicated one, and the cause of grievous vexation to the authorities at the time, and much agony to students of costume ever since. In the early 1750s the *Grenzers* began to appear in uniform and stylised versions of the national dress – namely a fur hat or high felt shako (*Klobuk*), a distinctive red cloak, an embroidered dolman with barrel sash, an hussar-type pelisse or short open jacket, tight and richly-decorated pants (*Schoitasch*), and shoes (*Opanken*) with elaborate strap bindings. In the course of time this colourful garb succumbed to a degree of Western influence. A short coat appeared in the Seven Years War, and this in turn gave way in the 1760s to a full uniform coat in the style of the Hungarian infantry. The shako and the famous red cloak survived almost intact, and in any case the Croat often preferred to wear his home-made 'house uniform' of brown cloth.

Many people were struck by the way in which the Croats' apparently crushing style of life produced the best light infantry in Europe. The Prussian officer Archenholtz commented that

> their territories are characterised by sandy and rather barren soil, many woods which are inhabited by wild beasts, by a chain of mountains and by a climate of extremes. But these are the very conditions which harden the already large and strong frames of the Croats, accustom them to all the hardships that life can offer, and form them into soldiers. In this backward land the people must hunt

in order to live, and this circumstance compels them to brave every danger. Hence their great courage. They display astonishing composure in putting up with hunger and thirst, frost and heat, as well as the most extreme physical pain, even under the hands of the surgeons. Death holds no terror for them. In their love for fatherland and prince no other people surpass them.[16]

With all of this the Croats remained essentially a survival of the later Middle Ages, when military skill was a matter of national speciality – the Swiss producing pikemen, the English archers, and so on. The direction of their military training was questioned by Joseph II, who made a tour of the military borders in 1779 and began to wonder whether the natural bent of the Croats towards open-order fighting was being neglected. Berenhorst went so far as to claim that there was something fundamentally misconceived about the policy of turning the Croat from a 'highwayman' into an imitation of the regular soldier. In any case the Croats lost the monopoly of their old way of fighting in the Napoleonic period, when élite regiments of regular troops throughout Europe were given special training as light infantry.

As a social and economic phenomenon the backward military borders could not be reconciled with the tendencies of the nineteenth century. The grasping hands of the Hungarian politicians reached out to this extensive land, where it seemed to be impossible to maintain the warlike character of the people without holding agriculture and the economy in a state of more than medieval depression. The one enduring value of the Croats to the Habsburgs resided in their loyalty, which contributed so much to the salvation of the dynasty in the revolutions of 1848–9.

The sense of obligation of the Emperor Francis Joseph died with the passage of time. The last of the *Grenzer* regiments was disbanded on 1 October 1873, and the military borders were finally incorporated in the lands of the Hungarian crown on 1 August 1881. Abortive projects to revive the Croatian military institutions were made by Major-General Clam-Martinić on 13 May 1918, and again by the SS Lieutenant-Colonel Meduna in October 1941. The Yugoslav government would like to forget that the military borders ever existed, while the 'liberal' historians of the West have long shown great indulgence towards the wildest excesses of the Magyars and the Serbs, yet regard any manifestation of Croatian nationalism as somehow illegitimate.

It is more pleasant to recall the days of the grateful Empress-Queen Maria Theresa, and the contribution which the 'Croats' made to her cause. 'The honour of the army resides in our 60,000 Croats', wrote the Prince de Ligne. 'They never desert. They are sober, obedient, easy to lead, tireless, and as splendid-looking as they are proficient.'[17]

7

The Cavalry

Eighteenth-century commanders exploited the mobility of mounted troops in a number of ways. They guarded the two open flanks of the army; they swept the enemy horse from the field and overran such enemy infantry as was shaken or already in flight, as at Kolin, Maxen and Kunersdorf; and they did outpost duty and undertook raids and reconnaissances.

The cavalry was subdivided according to the size of its mounts and the nature of its specialised functions. The cuirassiers were biggish men, mounted on heavy horses, and they bore the brunt of the fighting in formal battles. The dragoons were a slightly lighter breed of cavalry, capable of taking their place alongside their heavy brothers in line of battle, but also suitable for more widely-ranging enterprises. From Hungary came the hussars – light and wiry men, perched on swift horses, who excelled in undertakings where dash and speed were at a premium. Finally in 1759 the Austrians established a new kind of horseman, their *Chevauléger* or light dragoon, who was intended to combine the lively virtues of the hussars with the more solid qualities of the 'German' cavalry (ie the cuirassiers and dragoons).

Organisation

The cavalry regiments went to war in 1740 on an establishment of twelve ordinary companies and one élite company. The dragoon regiments owned a complement of about 1,000 officers and men, but the cuirassiers and hussars reached this number only from 1743.

The peace establishment of 1748 reduced the strength of the regiments to 800 officers and men each. The cuirassiers retained almost their full establishment of horses, because these heavy animals were difficult to obtain in a hurry upon mobilisation, but the horse complement of the dragoon regiments was allowed to fall by 200 or more. On the outbreak of the Seven Years War, however, the cavalry regiments were brought to a fully mounted establishment of 1,015 officers and men.

The two-company squadron seems to have been first introduced in 1751. In the Seven Years War this new and powerful entity replaced the company as the main administrative and tactical unit, which produced a regiment made up of six squadrons and one élite company. In 1758 the sixth of these squadrons was set aside as the *Reserve-Escadron* – one of its component companies being designated the *Depositorium* for replacements, while the other, the *Reserve-Compagnie*, did duty in garrison. For tactical purposes the squadrons could be combined two-by-two to form a *Division*, of which every regiment owned three.

In the winter of 1761–2, when the monarchy was very hard up, the establishment of the cuirassier and dragoon regiments was reduced to about 850 officers and men each, and that of the hussar regiments to 1,000. Several regiments were disbanded after the Seven Years War, which enabled the remaining regiments to be placed on an establishment of seven squadrons (including the *Reserve-Escadron*). Thus the individual regiment could put a theoretical 1,439 officers and men into the field in wartime. The establishment of the ordinary company varied considerably in Maria Theresa's reign. It was a paltry 75 officers and men in the Seven Years War, but rose to 174 or even more in the post-war period.

The organisation and employment of the dragoons was not essentially different from that of the cuirassiers, though it was part of the pride of the former gentlemen to cling to usages, names of ranks and items of dress which reminded them of their origins as mounted infantry. The cuirassiers in their turn regarded the dragoons as half-breeds, and the despised hussars as little better than mounted bandits.

In the matter of organisation the hussars differed from their comrades in the 'German' cavalry only in the pronounced difference which obtained between the hussar peacetime and wartime establishments. This led to some hurried searches for men and especially for horses whenever war broke out. The regimental establishment sank to 160 men and 361 horses after the peace of Aix in 1748, but rose to a height of 1,335 men and horses at one stage of the Seven Years War.

The best men and the strongest horses of the cavalry were concentrated in special high-grade units – the carabinier companies of the cuirassiers and the mounted grenadier companies of the dragoons. They owned no standards of their own, but they always took the post of honour in front of the regimental drums. In 1768 these élite companies were combined into two independent Carabiner Regiments, consisting of seven squadrons apiece (eight from 1769). The component companies came over intact from the parent regiments, and in the following years the carabinier regiments lived a parasitical existence, recruiting their officers and men directly from the best material of the other regiments. The men of the former dragoon grenadier companies wore caps instead of hats, otherwise the uniform was almost identical with that of the cuirassiers.

The *Chevaulégers* owed their origin to the general lightening of cavalry which was evident in Austria in the third quarter of the eighteenth century, when some of the cuirassiers were disbanded or made into dragoons, and some of the dragoons were converted into a superior light cavalry. The impulse probably came from the need to make use of the hussar-type remounts which were being purchased in the Ukraine, Moldavia and Wallachia.

The process began as early as 1 February 1758, when six extra companies were established in the dragoon regiment of Löwenstein (DR 14). These *Chevaulégers* acquitted themselves magnificently on 17 June 1758, when they defeated the crack Prussian dragoon regiment of Bayreuth in an action to the east of Olmütz, and made off with the Prussians' silver drums. The combined regiment went on to fight with distinction at Hochkirch, and in March the next year the *Chevauléger* element was increased to ten squadrons and made into a separate regiment under Prince Löwenstein. Five regiments of dragoons were made into *Chevaulégers* in February 1760. All the newcomers were converted back again by 1765, but another dragoon regiment was reconstituted as *Chevaulégers* in the same year, and four more followed in the 1770s. Joseph II in particular was much taken with the new cavalry. He was the *Inhaber* of a regiment of *Chevaulégers* himself, and he was often portrayed in its green coat.

The cuirassier was crowned with a smallish black tricorn hat. The edges of the hats of the officers and NCOs were braided with gold or silver according to rank, though the braid of the rank and file disappeared in 1758. Originally decorated merely with a button and a bow, the hat sprouted a black and yellow plume after the Seven Years War. A protective cap of iron strips was fitted inside the crown in 1757, which was another imitation of a Prussian practice.

The cuirassier regulations of 1751 laid down that 'the hair must always be kept well combed, but it is never to be curled with papers or powdered. Still less must the moustaches be dyed black'. In the cuirassiers that fiendishly uncomfortable device the stock was of a stiff black cloth or horsehair.

The old pearl-grey coat and leather jerkin of the cuirassiers gave way in the middle of the century to a plain white coat with red cuffs and skirt turn-backs. (The regiment of Modena (CR iii) was unique in owning cuffs and skirts of dark blue.) The breastplate was worn immediately over the coat, which was of a more generous cut than the corresponding *Kollet* of the Prussian cuirassiers.

(left) *O'Donnell cuirassier (CR No 14), Seven Years War. Red cuffs, turn-backs and shoulder straps on white coat; white waistcoat, yellow buttons, red breeches, sword with brass furniture. The coat was worn without the cuirass, except in action (By courtesy of the Albertina Collection)*

(right) *Sachsen-Gotha dragoon (DR No 28). Red coat with blue cuffs, lapels, turn-backs and shoulder strap; yellow aiglets; blue waistcoat; yellow buttons; straw breeches; sword with brass furniture (By courtesy of the Albertina Collection)*

The sleeved waistcoat (*Aermelweste*) was usually of white cloth, bordered at the bottom with strips designating the wearer's rank. After the Seven Years War the elegant waistcoat was replaced by a sleeved bodice (*Leibel*), made from the cloth of old coats and dyed the regimental colour.

Off parade the trooper discarded his tricorn and coat in favour of a forage cap and the *Aermelweste*. For stable work and other messy duties he put on a simple smock (*Kittel*). In 1764 a proposal was made to replace the coat and waistcoat by the antique jerkin of buff leather. However, the cavalry reform commission pointed out that the regiments of Anhalt-Zerbst and Anspach had worn this gear in the 1762 campaign, and had suffered severely from the cold and wet.

The burdensome breastplate provided the most distinguishing feature of the cuirassier uniform. It was a shaped slab of wrought iron, lacquered or painted in black. It had a lining of white leather or ticking, and was bordered with a roll of white chamois leather, or, in the case of the officer's cuirass, with a frill of red cloth or velvet. At 32lb the breastplate was too heavy to be worn except when absolutely necessary, and in daytime even the cavalry sentries were permitted to take this object off and lay it on the ground in front of them.

The corresponding *plastron*, or back-piece, was left in store for the eventuality of a Turkish war, when cavalrymen were liable to be cut about by scimitars or shot at with arrows. Antique-style tailed iron helmets were left in reserve for the same purpose, and they were actually worn by the cuirassiers and dragoons in the Turkish campaigns of 1788–9.

The breeches were usually of red or straw-coloured cloth, though for all except the most formal wear both they and the boots were covered by ticking overalls (*Ueberzugshosen*), which were fastened by buttons running down the outer sides. The boots were high and heavy affairs, furnished on the inside with *Faschinen* – stiff leather linings which reached down to the ankle. The *Faschinen*, breastplate and iron-lined hat combined to render the cuirassier almost defenceless, once he was thrown from his horse. On ordinary dismounted duty, the cuirassiers and dragoons were permitted to wear the far more comfortable shoes and stockings.

In wet weather the large *Radmantel* (literally 'wheel cloak') could be stretched forward with the reins, and it provided excellent protection both on horseback and in camp. Unfortunately the *Radmantel* was liable to flap about badly in high winds, and after the Seven Years War it was replaced by the *Roquelaure*, a kind of sleeved cloak which could be done up in the front with buttons. This garment was of white cloth.

The cuirassier's sword hung in slings from a waist belt. The blade was straight and stiff, and its form was prescribed in 1748, and again with more exactitude in 1769. It was supposed to be long enough to enable the trooper to cut down to the navel of a standing infantryman, without having to bend in the saddle – a requirement which made for a length of between thirty-two and thirty-eight inches. There was a broad and shallow central blood channel, and the point, originally aligned centrally, was placed on a line with the back of the blade in the later 1760s. Until about the same time the *Inhaber* was allowed a wide discretion in the matter of the design of hilts and scabbards. The fashion was for basket hilts, though they were rarely so enclosed as the Prussian model, and the material was brass or polished iron (gilded or silvered for the hilts of the officers and NCOs). The scabbards were clad in leather or iron, and decorated according to the taste of the *Inhaber*. Metal cladding was finally made the norm in 1775.

The cuirassier carried his carbine either suspended from a broad white carbine belt of white leather, or fastened down the right-hand side of the saddle with the muzzle resting in a shoe. The two pistols were kept in holsters that were fastened to the front of the saddle and protected by ornamental covers of the same cloth as the saddle cloth. The cartridge pouch was a smaller-capacity version of the infantry pouch, and contained holes for only about fifteen rounds at a time.

It was only in 1750 that authorised patterns of carbines and pistols were issued to the *Inhabers*. The authorities, who were perpetually fascinated with innovations in small-arms, decreed in 1759 that twelve men in every squadron of cuirassiers were to be armed with a *Musketon* (or *Trombon*). This was a carbine with a squashed-down bell muzzle specially designed to fire twelve buckshot at a time in a destructive swathe. Two years later the remarkable *Gewehrhaubitz* made its appearance among the mounted grenadiers (see p 74).

The dragoons were particularly fond of their bayonets, which they retained from the days of their earlier career as mounted infantrymen. The weapon was withdrawn in 1769, but reissued in 1770 in the form of a metal spear which could be folded under the carbine barrel when not in use.

It was also in 1770 that the Milanese clockmaker Giuseppe Crespi put forward a design for a breech-loading carbine. His project was to cut away the last few inches of the breech to make room for a rearward-pivoting tube, which swung upwards to receive the powder and bullet. All the dragoons, carabiniers and *Chevaulégers* were issued with the new weapon in the course of the 1770s. Crespi's design was a good one, but it suffered from defective sealing where the tube met the barrel (as did virtually all breech-loaders before the gas-tight cartridge was invented in the middle of the next century). So many men were burnt in the face and hands in the course of the War of the Bavarian Succession that the Crespi carbine was withdrawn from service in 1779.

Those cross-bred beasts the dragoons retained items of equipment of both infantry and cavalry provenance. Booted and spurred like the cuirassiers, they were nevertheless spared the burden of the breastplate, and they managed to cling to their bayoneted carbines, their infantry-style coats, and the characteristic dragoon aiglets.

Regiment by regiment the dragoons entered the Seven Years War wearing coats of a wide variety of distinctive colours – dark blue, green, red or white. Dark blue coat and breeches were made the norm in 1757, but the new uniform was introduced only gradually, with the result that the de Ligne dragoons made their celebrated charge at Kolin with the veterans wearing their familiar green and only the recruits clad in blue. A red coat was decreed in 1765, though only a few regiments got around to buying it before a final decision was made in favour of a white coat two years later.

The highly-favoured *Chevaulégers* retained their old dark green dragoon coats until 1765, when they received a smart rig-out comprising a grass-green coat with poppy-red cuffs, and breeches of white for the men and of light straw for the officers. The officers retained the dragoon tricorn hat, but the men were issued with a felt hat bearing the Imperial monogram.

Origins, uniform and equipment of the hussars

What the Croats were to the 'German' infantry, the ferocious hussars contributed to Maria Theresa's cavalry by their irrepressible enterprise and dash. Originating on

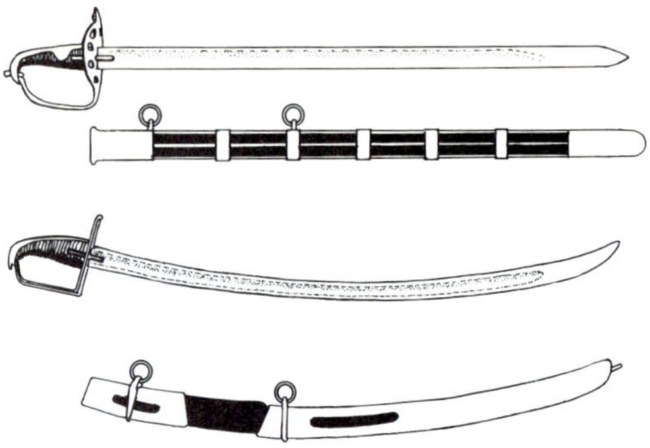

Cuirassier sword and hussar sabre

Palatinal hussar (HR No 36). Kalpak *with red bag; light blue dolman and pelisse with white braid; red and white barrel sash; red pants and yellow boots; sword with iron furniture (By courtesy of the Albertina Collection)*

the Hungarian plains, the hussars were still in the middle of the eighteenth century very much an attribute of the Habsburg army, even though Hungarian renegades and foreign officers like the Prussian Zieten began to train up passable imitations of the *genre*. Mirabeau commented:

> The Hungarian has an inborn spark, and a natural inclination towards stratagems. He lives in a country which abounds in horses. He learns to be a horseman in his childhood, and, having nothing better to do in that half-savage land, he teaches his horse all sorts of tricks, and acquires a peculiar mastery of that kind of equitation. His land is thinly populated and the dwellings are consequently sparse, which means that when he is out riding he must keep a sense of direction, in order to be able to retrace his path. With his kind of upbringing, the Hungarian becomes a perfect light cavalryman without further training.[1]

Maria Theresa had eight regiments of regular hussars standing at her disposal on her accession in 1740. These relatively respectable gentlemen were joined by successive waves of wild men from the East, beginning with 2,100 volunteers from the Jazygier and Kumanier, who were peoples of the Theiss river region. They reached Neipperg's army in Silesia in the summer of 1741. In action they adopted the endearingly simple technique of charging flat-up in disorder until their horses crumpled beneath them. For the rest of the time they plundered and burnt heretical villages and

> attacked all the travellers they found on the road. They presented their pistols and asked their victims whether they were Catholics or Lutherans. If they were

> Catholics, they were merely relieved of their money and otherwise spared. If they happened to be Lutherans, they were robbed, badly beaten up and carried away as prisoners.[2]

Great were the promises of support made by the Hungarian magnates in the historic Pressburg *Landtag* of September 1741. *Insurrections-Husaren* began to flood out to the theatre of war, and over the following year the *Stände* and individual magnates continued to dispatch groups of strangely assorted enthusiasts to take part in the fighting. Thus on 1 July 1743 Vienna was honoured by the passage of an hussar regiment which had been raised by the Transylvanian *Stände* and entrusted to the command of Colonel Kálnoky (HR 17):

> Among the ranks was a private hussar of uncommon strength. Her Majesty at once ordered him to put on a display in her presence. He lifted up a royal chamberlain, the younger Count Wilczeck, with his left arm. This gentleman was pretty corpulent, and must have weighed almost three hundredweight, yet the hussar carried him almost playfully up and down the room as if he had been a child, and showed not the slightest strain.[3]

Not long afterwards the herculean hussar was shot for robbery.

If the number and quality of the volunteer hussars fell somewhat short of expectations, there were still enough good men to fill out three new regiments of regular hussars and make a powerful contribution towards driving the French and Bavarians from Bohemia and up the Danube. The enemy troops retailed a horror-story to the effect that an hussar had been seen to cleave a Frenchman's head in four pieces with a single cut, and 'there were scarcely twenty officers in the whole of the French army who had not lost some of their baggage through the speed and bold courage of the Austrian hussars'.[4] Otherwise the hussars were used on all the tasks suitable for light cavalry, being employed

> for reconnaissance work, or for launching quick attacks in battle and throwing the enemy into confusion. They never attempt to make a stand, especially when they come under heavy fire. They disperse like lightning, but they can reassemble in an instant'.[5]

Nádasti, Baranyay, Fesztetics, Trips, Ghilányi, Berenklau, Hadik – a whole generation of commanders made their names leading hussars in these exciting times.

The hussars were reduced to some kind of order after the War of the Austrian Succession, and it is significant that the code of hussar regulations which came out in 1751 approximated in nearly every respect to the regulations of the 'German' cavalry. All the hussar regiments now received proper pay, which means that hussars should no longer have been under any necessity to live on plunder or whatever *douceurs* their colonels felt inclined to give them.

The first campaigns of the Seven Years War indicated that the old predatory instincts were not to be tamed so easily. The authorities in Vienna resigned themselves to the fact that the hussars were incorrigible robbers, and they put it to Daun that

> it might be a good idea to permit such *Grenzers* and hussars, who have already taken some booty, to send it back to Hungary under reasonably small escort.

> This would not only relieve them of anxiety lest their plunder should change hands again, but spur on their countrymen to take military service.[6]

There was a characteristic episode on 1 August 1759 when a captain and about thirty hussars forced their way into the Prussian town of Halle and split up in search of plunder:

> they had made appropriate preparations for this expedition, and brought along the necessary gear like axes, hatchets and jemmies. When the householders were slow to open their doors of their own accord, the hussars burst them open and presented their sabres at the citizens' throats, threatening to hack them in pieces on the spot if they did not unlock all the doors and chests and yield up their money and treasures.[7]

The design of the hussar uniform was famous for its extravagance and absurdity. The features were derived from the Slovakian national costume, as modified by the Jazygier and Kumanier, and finally interpreted by the Hungarian magnates. The hair was worked into fierce little plaits, and the head was crowned by a fur *Kalpak*, or flat-topped cap. The *Kalpak* was 10½in high, and it owned a long bag (*Ueberzeug*) of coloured cloth which hung from the crown down one of the sides. A tall felt *Csakelhaube* (shako) was worn as an everyday alternative to the *Kalpak*, and after the Seven Years War it replaced its furry brother altogether.

The rest of the outfit consisted of light boots, long tight pants with overalls, a barrel waist sash, a frogged dolman, and a fur-lined pelisse which could be worn either as an ordinary outer jacket, or in a more typically 'hussar' fashion by inserting the left arm in a sleeve, which left the rest of the jacket hanging in an abandoned fashion from a cord which passed across the neck and over the right shoulder. The regulations go into some detail:

> The pelisse must be cut sufficiently well to enable the man to button it up comfortably from top to bottom, and still allow him to reach back to his shoulder with his hand and move about freely. As for the length, the bottom edge should fall one-and-a-half inches short of the seat when the man is sitting. The sleeves should reach to the wrist. They are to be lined only with thin, good-quality ticking, to prevent them being too bulky. The edging of the slit in the sleeve is to reach within two inches of the elbow.
>
> The dolman must be close-fitting, rather than broad, and it should be long enough to permit one inch of the material to appear below the barrel sash.
>
> The pants reach up to the hip, and they are cut in such a way as to enable the man to walk, lie and sit with freedom.[8]

The rig-out was completed by a cloak with a broad collar. The officers' uniforms were richly worked with gold and silver, and their off-duty dress was a strange amalgam of East and West, with the Hungarian boots, pants and dolman clashing rather badly with the rococo white coat and tricorn hat. The officer carried a mace (*Buzogány*) or axe (*Fokos*) as a specific sign of his authority.

The hussar gloves were of white leather, with gauntlets reaching three inches above the wrist. The cartridge pouches and carbine straps were of the same model as worn by the 'German' cavalry, but the straight *Pallasch* of the cuirassiers and dragoons was replaced by a heavy curved sabre which had a blade (according to the regulations of 1751) 32in long and 1½in wide. For most of the reign the choice of hilt and mounts was left to the *Inhaber*, as indeed were the colours and design of the hanging pouch (*Sabretache*), the saddle cloth (*Shabraque*) and the covers of the pistol holsters. Nobody took any notice of an order of 1757, which sought to impose dolmans and pelisses of dark blue (*Franzblau*), and only in the late 1760s did the authorities manage to enforce a new and limited range of colours – red for the *Sabretaches* and *Shabraques*, blues and greens for the dolmans and pelisses, and blue or madder red for the pants.

Hungarian saddles and harness were lightly built. The stirrups were worn very short, by the standards of the time, and the spurs were consequently positioned near the side of the horse's chest, which made both riders and mounts somewhat jittery when they were in closely-packed formations.

Every company (later squadron) of the hussars owned its own *Estandard*. This was a double-sided swallow-tail flag, very much like the standard of the dragoons. Only the cuirassiers carried square standards. Throughout the cavalry the standards were of stiff silken material, heavily embroidered in silk or metal thread. The *Leibstandarte* had a white field, with the double eagle on the obverse side, and an image of Our Lady on the other. The field of the other standards was that of the distinguishing regimental colour, and the emblem of the Madonna was usually replaced by the *Inhaber*'s monogram.

Cavalry tactics

The regiments of horse were divided into half a dozen squadrons apiece, each composed of two companies and three tactical *Züge*. The ordinary squadron owned about fifty files of three men each, which, allowing a frontage of one long pace for every horse, gave the squadron a frontage of about sixty yards.

The regiments marched by preference in a column of four files. Tactical columns could be formed of squadrons, companies or *Züge*, and deployment into line seems to have been most commonly achieved by the processional movement, as with the infantry. In time of battle the cavalry were drawn up in exceptional instances in two ranks, but more frequently in three. In the latter case it was important to have

> good, reliable and well-mounted men positioned in the first rank, the recruits and the less good men in the second rank, the most senior and reliable in the third rank. The most steadfast troopers of all are placed on the flanks of the various ranks.[9]

Intervals of five paces were normally allowed between the ranks, and the files were closed up if possible knee to knee, and in any event tightly enough to prevent an enemy rider from barging through. In battle the first-line squadrons were permitted intervals of eight short paces at the most, but gaps of anything between thirty and fifty paces were permitted for the squadrons in the second line, so as to allow any badly-mauled units from the first line to pass through and rally in the rear.

When action was imminent, the senior captain of the squadron placed himself in the centre of the squadron, or even a short distance in front of the first rank 'so that he may be seen at all times by his squadron'.[10] The *Estandarten-Führer* rode alongside him or immediately behind. The lieutenants were deployed on the flanks, and the second captain either joined them or stationed himself behind the centre of the squadron. The object was to keep the squadron together by physical and moral force. However, the Field Service Regulations of 1749 contain a curious passage to the effect that immediately before the charge was launched, the *Estandarten-Führer*, accompanied by the centre three files and a trumpeter and a drummer, was to fall back 150 paces, with the intention of acting as a reserve and rallying-point in the event of a reverse.

The cavalry was forbidden to receive an attack at the halt. When it came to making a charge of its own, the 1751 regulations stipulated that

> the squadrons must remain well closed up in their ranks and files, and maintain a common frontage with the rest of the regiment. At a distance of about two hundred paces from the enemy they are to break into a trot, and when they come within twenty or thirty paces they are to attack at a full gallop . . . Every cavalry officer must be firmly persuaded that two things are of fundamental importance if you want to beat the enemy: the first is to assail them with the greatest speed and force, and the other is to seek to take them in the flank.[11]

If the cavalry regiments were stationed on the flanks of the army, they were to keep pace with the infantry and break into a sudden gallop when only twenty paces from the enemy. In any case the Austrians rarely gave their horses their heads in a wild *carrière*, like the Prussians in the last stage of their charges, and the Prussian cavalry general Warnery claims that the Austrian horses were not accustomed to a sustained gallop, citing an action on 4 December 1757 when the Prussian hussars easily overhauled General Nostitz and a force of retreating Austrian dragoons.

There is ample evidence to show that rival forces of cavalry seldom met in head-on collision. In the Prince de Ligne's experience the onrushing lines halted as if on the drill field, turned aside and trailed each other on parallel courses for a couple of minutes, then broke off contact altogether. Actual hand-to-hand combat occurred only when a fleeing force was overtaken by the enemy, in which case the victors and vanquished rode alongside exchanging blows, with the worst riders attracting most of the punishment.

The regulations of 1751 forbade the cuirassiers and dragoons to employ their firearms in Western warfare, except in the confusion of a melée. The hussars were, however, permitted to fire by squadrons on the flanks of the battlefield, and in peace-time even the 'German' cavalry trained against the eventuality of a Turkish war by learning to shoot from the saddle. The Turks were dangerous enemies at close range, but they were liable to be upset by fire, and for this reason the regiments stationed in Hungary were trained to hold their carbines high in a threatening manner during the advance.

Despite every admonition, the 'German' cavalry persisted in the bad habit of using fire against the Prussians in the Seven Years War. The cuirassiers are said to have delivered carbine volleys on the fields of Lobositz and Reichenberg, and the Prussian field-marshal Schwerin was particularly struck by the odd conduct of 800 Austrian dragoons in a skirmish near Königgrätz on 22 September 1756:

> Our friends the Austrians are always great ones for shooting, and they certainly lived up to their reputation in the action on the 22nd. Not only did they shoot at our men, but in order to heighten the effect of their threatening display they

fixed their bayonets on the muzzles of their carbines. Thus armed, the first rank advanced against our hussars on horseback. Our hussars, however, were not put out of countenance by this display, and promptly fell on them, wishing nothing better than to try conclusions with cavalrymen who had armed themselves with bayonets in such a frightful way.[12]

Maria Theresa was impelled by a sound instinct when, in 1764, she told the cavalry reform commission not to bother to introduce the cavalry to all the niceties of infantry fire-tactics: 'I do not set much store by firing by cavalry.'[13] The cavalry in general, and more particularly the dragoons, were already expected to be versed in a simplified version of the infantry drill. The regulations of 1751 devoted no less than 54 pages to this subject, together with 17½ on the dismounted drill of the dragoons grenadiers.

Proficiency

The Austrian cavalry was the only branch of the army to decline in relative proficiency in the period of Maria Theresa's great wars. The reasons were investigated by a deeply concerned officer of cavalry who wrote an anonymous essay on this theme in 1756.[14]

Our informant explains that in the Turkish campaigns of 1737–9 the cavalry had needed no persuading to stay together in tight formations, since there was little good plunder to be had from the enemy, and the Turks cut up any individuals who strayed from the ranks. At the outset of Maria Theresa's reign the cavalry did well enough in the battle of Mollwitz,

> though if our courage had been backed up by a modicum of good order, the fight would have been given a better outcome. At Chotusitz we likewise chased the enemy cavalry from the field, and it was all the more regrettable that the victory was snatched from our hands by the fact that our horse fell into pernicious disorder and lusted for plunder in a shameful way . . . in those times the Prussians could neither ride nor fight, and their ignorance of the cavalryman's trade drove them to despair. They did not even know how to tighten their girths properly, so that their saddles were liable to slide and deposit them under their horses.

Nor did the other members of the hostile alliance offer much of a challenge, since 'we were dealing with enemies who were in a state of still greater disorder than us. The French wrote marvellously about cavalry affairs, but they actually performed them very badly'.

Before the Seven Years War, however, the Prussian cavalry was transformed by General Seydlitz, who was probably the first horseman of his time. Thus by 1756 the Prussian cavalry could ride 'like the wind', and manoeuvre and attack in compact formations. In Austria, on the other hand, 'we do not bother very much about the art of riding . . . and in this respect as in many others the enemy have become our superiors'. Some officers of fortune gave themselves airs as riding instructors, when they could not master their own horses, 'and most of them are capable of doing no more than hacking around on an old broken-down English horse'. In the same period a 'spirit of contradiction' set in among many of the cavalry officers, who not only uttered loud complaints about the new and admittedly complicated foot drill, but opposed necessary reforms of all kinds. Not even the events of 1756 could bring the officers to a better way of thinking:

> In the last campaign you heard no sentiment more frequently expressed than 'I haven't bothered to read the regulations. I don't need them, and I don't want them!' . . . unconsidered remarks like these are frequently spoken in front of the private troopers, and they are hardly calculated to inspire them with confidence.

This analysis received some support from the later episodes of the Seven Years War. The Austrian cavalrymen did best when they launched limited counter-attacks at some particularly desperate stages of an action (as at Hochkirch or Torgau), or when they helped to push over an enemy who was very badly battered already (as at Kolin and Kunersdorf). However, the Austrians seem to have been incapable of putting into the field a battle-winning battering ram to compare with the cavalry of Seydlitz. Warnery observes that

> the Austrian troopers hold the bridle in both hands without being able to stop their horses . . . their cavalry is so heavy that it cannot exploit whatever advantages it gains. Thus it is certainly capable of driving back the enemy, but can never do them much damage. Large-scale evolutions remain unknown to the Austrians, and their drill book is full of things which are useless in combat.[15]

Already fighting for its reputation, the Austrian cavalry was dealt a severe blow by the drastic economies of the winter of 1761–2, which struck two squadrons from the establishment of every regiment of cuirassiers and dragoons. Hence in the decisive campaign of 1762 the command of the open field passed to the Prussians.

Over the same period the Prussian hussars had responded very well to their training at the hands of the generals Zieten and Winterfeldt, and Maria Theresa had to complain on 28 May 1757 that it seemed as if the Prussians were better at light cavalry work than the Hungarians. Warnery claimed:

> In placing the hussars on the footing of the 'German' cavalry, the Austrians turned them into amphibians – or perhaps it just seemed to me to be so because our hussars had become so much better. We hardly heard of the Austrian hussars in the later campaigns, and after the battle of Prague they never awaited the shock or fought hand to hand.[16]

This was slightly exaggerated, for the Prussian hussars fought more like dragoons than proper hussars, and they were careful to ensure themselves against defeat in open combat. Not only was the individual Prussian regiment larger than the Hungarian by five squadrons, but the Prussians appeared in huge corps of several regiments at a time, making a mass of thousands of men, flanked by artillery. On the attack their favourite tactic was a wheel in mass formation.

The revival of the Theresian cavalry dates from the mid-1760s. Field-Marshal Lynden set up a reform commission at the end of 1764, and called in for consultation such luminaries as the cavalry generals Lowenstein, O'Donnell, Althann and Albert of Saxony. Likewise General Hadik and Lieutenant-General Nauendorff addressed themselves to the reform of the hussars in 1765.

The fruits of their labours were found in a new set of hussar regulations and the revised 'German' cavalry regulations of 1769 and 1772. Squadrons and files were thickened up, the evolutions improved, and signals entirely ousted in favour of simplified verbal orders. A greater uniformity was meanwhile imposed upon clothing and equipment, and much attention was focused upon creating an effective medium cavalry of dragoons and *Chevaulégers*. The effect of the reforms was cumulative. General Mack wrote:

> As late as 1769 our cavalry did not know how to ride. It could neither direct nor master its horses, and there was not a single squadron which was capable of holding to its course . . . there was no question of breaking and reforming in an orderly fashion. By 1773, however, order was restored.[17]

The scrappy fighting of the War of the Bavarian Succession emphasised the value of the lighter cavalry. The hussars did well, but the cavalry as a whole

> had to cover the long chain of border mountains, which extended from Eger to Bielitz. There were no fortresses or defensible places, and it very soon became evident that our horse was incapable of withstanding the united cavalry of the Prussians and Saxons.[18]

In the winter of 1778–9 all the field squadrons of dragoons and hussars were accordingly reinforced to 180 men each.

Remounts

There was seldom any lack of recruits for the exciting but not particularly dangerous life of a cavalryman. In contrast, the authorities never arrived at a really satisfactory system of providing enough horses for the eager troopers to ride. In part the difficulty arose from the divergence that obtained between the peacetime and wartime establishments of horses, which was compounded by the fact that the regiments (especially the hussars) were slow to respond to calls to make up the difference when hostilities threatened.

Another source of trouble arose from the failure of Hungary and Transylvania, the horse-breeding areas of the monarchy, to supply anything like the required quantity of cavalry horses. The hussars had to be mounted principally on the light 'Polish' horses from the Ukraine, Moldavia and Wallachia, while the dragoons and more especially the cuirassiers needed the heavy animals of Holstein and Hanover. Not only were these cuirassier horses very expensive, but they were difficult to transport across Germany in time of crisis. Thus three regiments of cuirassiers were disbanded in 1769 and another four in 1775, as opposed to only a single regiment of dragoons.

The stock of horses was replenished by a variety of means. The hussars sometimes made up their numbers by direct purchase, while the *Stände* occasionally furnished animals in return for cash or the remission of taxes. However, by far the greater proportion of remounts came by way of contracts which the state placed with expert dealers – men like Pazelt of Prague, Norbert Kolinsky of Iglau, Johann Georg Nägerele of Klagenfurt, Nathan Moyses Goldschmidt of Cologne, or the Johann

Heinrich Altvatter who provided the 2,002 cuirassier and dragoon horses for the first 'augmentation' in the Seven Years War. The largest horse fairs were held in Württemberg, Ansbach and Bavaria.

That famous connoisseur of horses, Lieutenant-General de la Reintrie, was made director of remounts in 1760 and put forward the idea of buying as many horses as possible within the confines of the monarchy. The argument was elaborated in an anonymous memorandum after the Seven Years War. The author pointed out that it was a matter of national security, and not just the millions of florins which were being lost to the monarchy. In the late war it had proved difficult enough to ensure the supply of the north-west German horses, even though the transports passed through lands that were mostly occupied by the French or other friendly powers:

> Just think of what would happen if we were faced with a similar situation, and did not have these circumstances acting in our favour. If we relied exclusively on foreign sources of remounts, it is easy to see that the Austrian cavalry, that vital part of our army, would presently be destroyed.[19]

For these reasons the peasants were now encouraged to breed horses for purchase by the contractors, and the state established a number of breeding-stations in Bohemia and Moravia, which, according to General Burgoyne, were

> furnished with stallions and mares from all countries at the Emperor's expense in order to breed horses for the army. These studs are carefully superintended, the different breeds and crosses are tried, and those will be multiplied which appear best adapted to the climate and soil, and to the use they are intended for.[20]

The studs were in active operation by 1770. However, the scheme of peasant horse-breeding broke down, because it was so difficult to supervise so many small establishments. In the War of the Bavarian Succession the government was therefore forced to look once more to the *Stände* and the contractors. The Jewish dealer Julius made some particularly useful purchases in Holstein, and by himself he managed to provide 2,842 horses for the cuirassiers and 1,153 for the dragoons. Finally, between the years 1779 and 1781 the government prepared the way for a kind of equine conscription by having all the horses of the peasants enrolled and inspected.

The preferred cavalry horse was a dark-coated mare or gelding aged between four and seven years, and standing sixteen hands high for the cuirassiers, fifteen for the dragoons and fourteen for the hussars. The prices rose phenomenally in the course of the reign. In terms of florins an acceptable cuirassier horse came in the 80s in the War of the Austrian Succession, in the 90s in the Seven Years War, and in the 160s in the War of the Bavarian Succession.

In the earlier part of the reign the veterinary care of these expensive animals was the responsibility of the regimental smiths (*Fahnenschmiede*), who were of variable quality. A *Thier-Arzneischule* was, however, established in 1766, in imitation of the French and Swedish veterinary schools, and in 1769 a qualified *Ober-Schmied* was placed on the establishment of every cavalry regiment.

8

The Artillery

The great power of the Theresian artillery not only swung the military balance in favour of Austria in the last period of the reign, but through its influence gave new force to the gunnery arm in general and laid an essential foundation for the warfare of the Napoleonic period. Here lies eighteenth-century Austria's major contribution to the art of war.

Development

The growing proficiency of the Austrian artillery was associated above all with the name of Prince Joseph Wenzel Liechtenstein. Born in Prague in 1696 and educated at the Carolinum, he became the *Inhaber* of a dragoon regiment in 1725 and a Knight of the Golden Fleece in 1740. Liechtenstein's distinguished military and diplomatic career almost came to an end when he was cut down at the battle of Chotusitz in 1742. What impressed him most painfully in this action, however, was the effect of the eighty-two well-served Prussian cannon, which presented a striking contrast to the antiquated Austrian guns.

Liechtenstein worked out a comprehensive plan for reforming the artillery, and Maria Theresa was so impressed that she made him *Generaldirector* of the whole artillery arm in 1744. Liechtenstein had scarcely begun to get his schemes under way before he was whisked off again to the wars. He commanded the Austrian army in north Italy in 1746, but before the war was over he was back with his beloved guns, and in 1748 the premature death of Prince Johann Karl delivered to him the fabulous Liechtenstein family fortunes, which people said were founded upon the secret of the philosopher's stone. Over the following years he poured out his money without stint to finance experiments and support the gunners' orphans and widows and all the other needs of the corps.

As a master of what we would now call 'public relations', Liechtenstein was renowned for the lavish and ingenious way in which he laid on entertainments at his house near the cannon works at Ebergassing, south-east of Vienna, and later at Pressburg after he was appointed commanding general of Hungary in 1753. However, Liechtenstein established the home of the artillery in his native Bohemia, and his working life was concentrated in the corps headquarters at Budweis and the exercise and experimental grounds to the north at Moldauthein. Here he built laboratories and a 'polygon' of fortification, and oversaw experiments in ballistics, cartridges, rapid fire, mines and mortar bombs. He published editions of the French technical authors Belidor and Deidier, and he was generous in rewarding people who came to him with well-thought-out projects for inventions, even if the devices ultimately did not work.

Prince Joseph Wenzel Liechtenstein
Butt used in Liechtenstein's experiments at Moldauthein (Kriegsarchiv)

A most curious assortment of folk aided Liechtenstein in his labours. From an old Austrian family came Andreas Feuerstein and his famous brother Anton, who was ennobled for his services in 1757. Johann Schröder hailed from Prussia, the *Feuerteufel* Theodor Rouvroy from Luxembourg by way of Saxony, and Nikolaus Alfson from Norway. Most striking of all was the example of the Swiss carpenter Jacquet, an illiterate mechanical genius who installed a new range of horizontal drilling machines in the cannon works at Ebergassing. The whole team was inspired by the conviction that artillery was the 'soul of an army'.[1]

The main achievements of the Liechtenstein period of artillery reform may be itemised as the introduction of a new range of artillery in 1753, the expansion and militarisation of the personnel, the creation of the artillery fusiliers, and the publication of the artillery *Reglement* in 1757.

The new power of the artillery was evident from the first engagements of the Seven Years War, and the Prussian general Warnery frankly avowed that 'the Austrian artillery was far superior to ours, both in number and quality'.[2] Altogether seven crosses of the Military Order of Maria Theresa were awarded to artillery officers in the course of the war. Liechtenstein himself was active in forwarding ammunition and ordnance of all kinds to the armies in the field, though he was unfortunate enough to lose his temper at a conference on 28 May 1757, and thereby forfeited his place in the innermost counsels of the monarchy.

Within his own realm Liechtenstein's position remained unassailable, and after the war he was awarded the almost unique distinguishing title of *Hoheit* (Highness). He died in 1772 at the age of seventy-six. 'Never has the loss of a patriot been so unanimously and generally regretted as that of this truly great and unforgettable man. He was a benefactor of his fatherland, and a father to many thousands of its subjects.'[3]

Liechtenstein's place as *Generaldirector* was taken by the able General Franz Ulrich Kinsky, and Joseph II took the opportunity to insist that the artillery corps should be conducted less as a private empire than as a department of the army, subject like the other organs to the *Hofkriegsrath*. Kinsky carried through a drastic reorganisation of the corps, and he abolished many of the picturesque anomalies which had survived since the days of the medieval trade guilds. Kinsky retired at the beginning of 1778. The new *Generaldirector*, Lieutenant-General Joseph Colloredo, enjoyed the full support of the Emperor in establishing a new cannon foundry and in the work of tidying-up after the War of the Bavarian Succession.

A significant increase in the quantity of ordnance was noticeable throughout the period of the reforms. The army in Bohemia in 1745 was equipped with a feeble complement of 94 field pieces, and of these 35 were lost at the battle of Hohenfriedberg. The army went to war in 1756 with a much more respectable total of 203 field pieces, and the train reached a wartime peak four years later with 458. The establishment of field pieces attained 648 in 1768, 666 in 1772 and no less than 1,060 by the end of the reign. In the last period the heavy 6-pounders and 12-pounders accounted for more than half the total.

Organisation

The *Deutsches-Feldartilleriecorps* comprised the miners (of whom more anon), and the officers, NCOs and *Büchsenmeister* (private gunners) of the artillery. Before the Seven Years War, Liechtenstein reorganised the inchoate mass of gunners into three brigades of eight companies each. In 1757, under the pressure of the war, he set up the *Artillerie-Füselier Regiment* to assist the gunners to handle the pieces, and in 1758 he increased the brigade establishment to ten companies apiece, making thirty companies in all.

From Spanish times the Austrians inherited the separate corps of the *Niederländisches National-Artillerie* and the *Lombardisches National-Artillerie*. The Netherlandish artillery owned an establishment of eight companies and about 600 men, and of these between 100 and 300 served with the field army at any given time in the Seven Years War.

Liechtenstein gave the supporting organisations a fixed hierarchy of rank and pay, but otherwise left their antiquated structures intact. These consisted of the *Ross-Partei* (the transport organisation), the *Feld-Zeugamt* (which maintained the artillery of the field armies), and the more permanent and static *Haus-Artillerie* (which kept up the ordnance in the arsenals and fortresses). In peacetime the *Ross-Partei* and the *Feld-Zeugamt* existed only in cadre. Thus, while Liechtenstein brought about a transformation in ordnance and tactics, 'the same did not apply to the administration'.[4]

On 1 May 1772 the new *Generaldirector* Kinsky imposed a thoroughgoing reform on the whole apparatus. The three brigades of the German field artillery were remade into three *Feld-Artillerie Regimenter* of four battalions each. Every battalion was composed of four companies, which produced a total of forty-eight companies. A separate *Garnisons-Artillerie* took over the fortress artillery, and the old *Feld-Zeugamt* and the *Haus-Artillerie* became two departments of an all-embracing *Zeugwesen* (ordnance department). Kinsky signed over the *Ross-Partei* to the emergent state military transport organisation, and he abolished the artillery fusiliers altogether. This last move was a very bad one, since the gunners now had to resume the old practice of borrowing infantrymen when they went on campaign. These conscripted assistants served 'unskilfully, unwillingly and negligently'.[5]

Not the least of Liechtenstein's achievements was to set in train a badly-needed expansion of the corps of *Büchsenmeister*. The establishment of the German gunners rose from a wholly inadequate 800 in 1746 to 1,000 in 1749, 2,000 in 1755, 3,126 in 1760 (the highest number in the Seven Years War), and nearly 5,000 in 1769.

For most of the reign the gunners gloried in a proliferation of antique-sounding ranks. Every group of four of Liechtenstein's companies was directed by an *Ober-Stückhauptmann* (major). The plain *Stückhauptmann*, or captain, was in charge of the individual company, and under his authority the *Stückjunker* (first lieutenant) commanded an infantry regiment's-worth of field artillery, in other words between four and six guns. So as to keep control of what was going on, the artillery officers usually went into action on horseback.

The remaining ranks descended from *Alt-Feuerwerker* (second lieutenant) by way of *Jung-Feuerwerker* (*Feldwäbel*) and *Corporal* to the plain *Büchsenmeister*. Kinsky renamed the *Büchsenmeister* as '*Kanonier*' ('*Bombardier*' for the howitzers), and in his unsentimental way he substituted the normal military titles for the old ranks.

The corps had no need of open recruiting. Instead the advantages of the gunner's life attracted volunteers in plenty from the other arms of the service, as well as educated civilians like hard-up students or unlucky tradesmen. The requirement was for a man who was well-built, stood over 5ft 5in tall, and could read and write in German. No foreigner was accepted into the artillery, on account of the secret nature of its lore, and in any case the majority of the gunners hailed from Bohemia, which was the spiritual and physical home of the Habsburg artillery.

The recruit was assigned to a *Corporalschaft* for his first training. In their turn the *Büchsenmeister* and NCOs attended brigade schools to learn how to calculate ranges, elevations and charges, how to build batteries, and how to serve the cannon, howitzers and mortars. Examinations were held in the spring under the authority of the chief technician of the corps, the *Oberfeuerwerksmeister*, and every summer from the early 1750s the gunners assembled for joint training in the exercise camps.

Promotion to officer rank almost always proceeded from within the corps. Candidates had first to qualify at the central school which Liechtenstein established in 1744 at the artillery depot at Bergstadl near Budweis. Here the aspirants were inducted by experienced officers and NCOs into the principles of the design and service of the pieces, as well as the mysteries of arithmetic, geometry, trigonometry, mechanics, hydraulics, optics, ballistics, military building and fortification.

Except, perhaps, for the incorrigible madmen who found fulfilment as hussars, none of Maria Theresa's soldiers were happier than her gunners. The tone of the discipline was set by the introduction to the *Reglement* of 1757, which proclaimed that 'we must seek in the artillery to encourage the men in their duties more through love of honour, and good treatment, than through brutality, untimely blows and beatings'.[6] One of the most dreadful fates which could befall a gunner was to be transferred to the infantry, and if the poor man wished to make his way back again he had to go through the ordeal of standing inside a circle of his former comrades and pleading his cause three times over.

Safe in the bosom of the corps, the gunners enjoyed rates of pay that were one-third greater than in the infantry. They owned ancient rights to the church bells of captured towns, as well as the power to exact a levy from any non-gunner officer who wished to attach his baggage to the artillery train. On top of this the gleeful gunners levied tolls and excise on folk who passed through their barracks, and until 1757 they were entitled to claim quotas of wood, straw, hay, cattle tongues and calves' heads from the local fairs. Morale was further enhanced by the homogeneity of class and national origin. As stout Bohemians the gunners were renowned as connoisseurs of beer and dumplings, and they were willing to hire civilian musicians at considerable expense in order to maintain their reputation for good music. St Barbara's Day (4 December) was an occasion of great festivity, as was the promotion of any of the officers.

The corps took pride in looking after its widows and dependents, which was one of the many traits which it inherited from its past as a trade guild. There was a sad increase in these unfortunates in the Seven Years War, which was one of the reasons why the gunners went on to found their *Witwen-und-Waisen-Confraternität* in 1774.

The gunners and artillery fusiliers wore infantry-type coats of fawn (*Rehbraun*). The facings were orange-red, but only the Netherlandish gunners owned lapels as well as cuffs. Both kinds of artilleryman had little black leather boxes which were worn frontally on a belt passing around the waist, as well as a vent pricker (*Besteck*) which was mounted on a black-yellow cord slung over the left shoulder. Boots and leather breeches were worn as optional foul-weather gear by the ordinary gunners, and as a matter of routine by most of the officers. The hair at the back of the head was sometimes dressed into a short, clubbed pigtail called the *Canone*, which seems to have been unique to the artillery.

The gunner's hunting knife (*Hirschfänger*) was replaced in 1758 by a grenadier sabre. The ordinary fusilier sabre was substituted in 1772, and this in turn gave way to a more 'agricultural' artillery sword two years later.

The ordnance

KINDS OF ARTILLERY

The mainstays of eighteenth-century artillery were the long-barrelled cannon which fired solid shot or canister. These were grouped as field guns (such as 3-pounders, 6-pounders and light 12-pounders) which gave close fire-support to the infantry, and as the heavier and longer-ranged battery guns (like heavy 12-pounders, 18-pounders and 24-pounders) which were assembled in larger batteries or employed in siege work.

In contrast the howitzers and mortars had short and stubby barrels, specially designed to throw explosive shells without shattering the brittle cast-iron casings. The howitzers were mobile field pieces, mounted on stocky versions of the ordinary cannon carriages, while the mortars were specialised weapons for static siege warfare and sat on massive wooden beds.

Maria Theresa inherited a range of artillery which was at once cumbersome and feeble. The 3-pounder on the model of 1718, for instance, fired a shot of about the size of a tennis ball from a barrel which was thirty calibres long and weighed more than 1,000lb. Many creatures like this were lost at Mollwitz in 1742, and more at Chotusitz in 1742 and Hohenfriedberg in 1745. The Austrians filled out their depleted artillery trains with some new pieces of lighter construction, about which we know little. However, the revival of the ordnance was essentially the work of Major-General Anton Feuerstein, the chief of the *Feld-Artillerie-Corps*, who came to Liechtenstein with a project for a completely new system of artillery. He sought above all to pare weight to a minimum by shortening and lightening the barrels, and introducing lighter and more efficient gun carriages.

Feuerstein's 'system' underwent extensive testing from 1745. It was given official approval in 1750, and the new guns were introduced in 1753. The sequence ran as follows:

Name	*Calibre*	*Length of barrel*	*Weight of barrel*
3-pounder field piece	75mm	115cm	530lb
6-pounder field piece	96mm	152cm	912lb
12-pounder field piece	120mm	190cm	1,790lb

The barrels of all these field pieces were sixteen calibres long. Not only were they cheaper to make and easier to transport than the old long barrels, but they heated up less badly during rapid fire, and sustained less damage to the interior while they were being loaded. The vents were drilled with a forward slant, so that the tube of the empty fuse was thrown clear of the crew when the piece was fired.

The Feuerstein battery pieces comprised short and long versions of 12-pounders, 18-pounders and 24-pounders. They were much longer and heavier in proportion than the field pieces, and medium versions were not introduced until 1764.

Feuerstein's system owned only two calibres of howitzer. These were the 7-pounder (150mm calibre) which weighed 617lb, and the 10-pounder, which weighed 1,676lb.

There were four shell-firing mortars (10-pounder, 30-pounder, 60-pounder and 100-pounder), and one pierrier, or thin-walled mortar which discharged showers of stones.

The barrels of all the pieces were cast from a durable bronze, and a generous windage (the equivalent of one-ninth of the bore) made sure that the shot or shell did not stick in the bore. Four 6-pounders fired between 4,000 and 7,000 rounds each in an experiment in 1777, and after this severe test the bores were found to be enlarged by only nine sixty-fourths of an inch.

In 1757 the Croats were issued with some ultra-light pieces – a 1-pounder cannon, and 2-pounder, 2½-pounder and 4-pounder howitzers. This ordnance was very ineffective, and it soon passed out of use.

In the Seven Years War the Prussians devised a number of batteries of fast-moving horse artillery, based on their light 6-pounder cannon. Some of the guns fell into the hands of the Austrians, when Finck's corps capitulated at Maxen in 1759, and Field-Marshal Daun commissioned Anton Feuerstein to set up a mobile battery in imitation. By 1760 Feuerstein was able to put into the field twelve 3-pounders, which were drawn by teams of four horses each (instead of the usual two) and accompanied into action by mounted gunners. In the following year the Russians helped Loudon's corps to set up a further horse artillery battery of four 6-pounders.

In 1762 Colonel Rouvroy projected a system of purpose-built horse artillery, which was designed to accommodate four of the gun detachment on the trail of the carriage, which was to be lengthened and upholstered with a 'sausage' seat. Some of the ordnance was actually built, but Rouvroy's scheme appears to have come into general use only towards the end of the century.

Horse artillery of a more conventional kind enjoyed a revival when, on 5 March 1778, Joseph II assigned mounted crews to twenty-four 6-pounder cannon and eight 7-pounder howitzers. The new artillery performed remarkably well in the first cam-

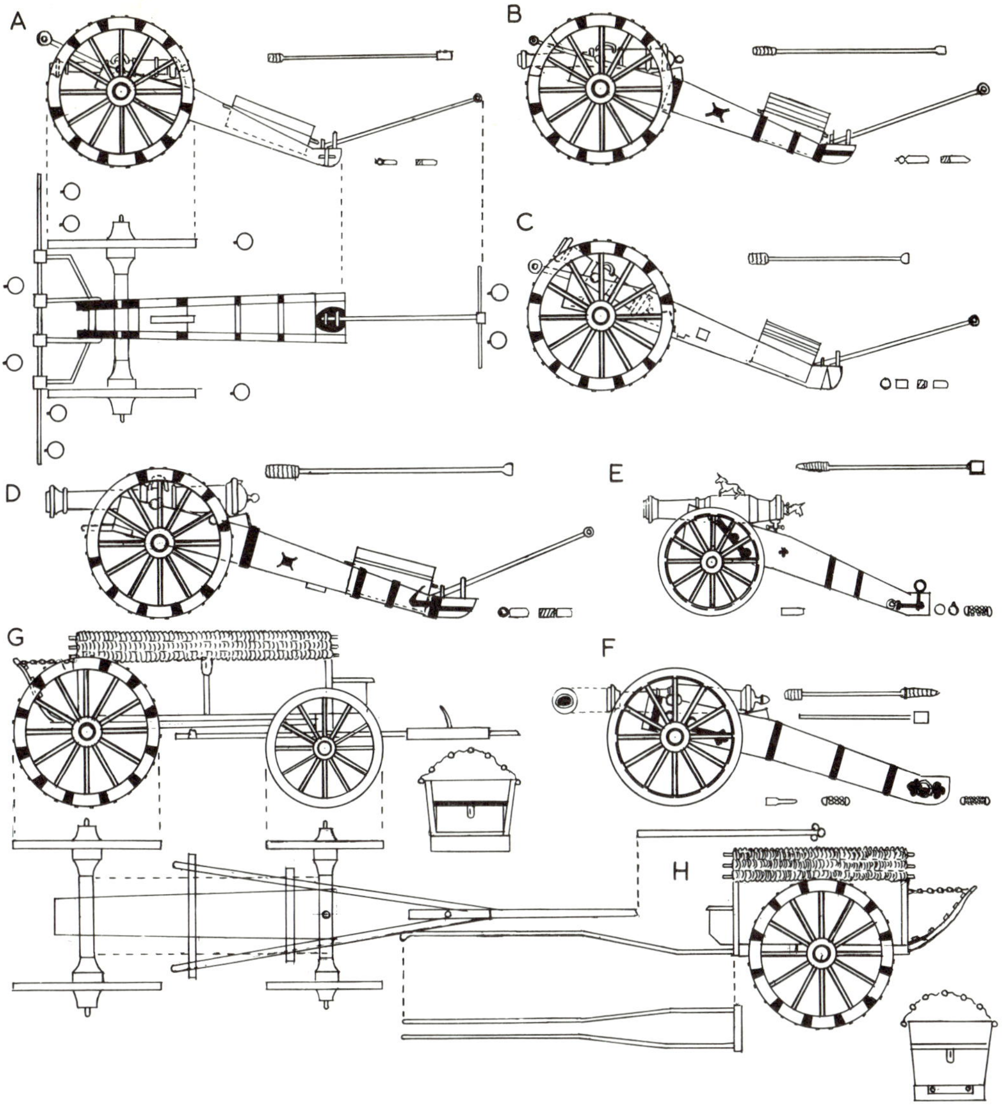

The ordnance of the Theresian army:
A 3-pounder cannon (1753), showing the draw- and pushing-bars in position, and the locations of the gun detachment while the piece is in motion
B 6-pounder cannon (1753)
C 7-pounder howitzer (1753)
D 12-pounder cannon (1753)
E Russian 12-pounder unicorn howitzer
F Russian 12-pounder oval-bore grape howitzer
G large ammunition cart
H small ammunition cart

paign of the War of the Bavarian Succession, and by the spring of 1779 the horse artillery comprised one-twelfth (84 out of 1,060 pieces) of the complement of field artillery.

During the Seven Years War the Russians tried to saddle the Austrians with a range of eccentric artillery which had been introduced by their master general of the ordnance, Piotr Shuvalov. These were a canister-firing howitzer with an oval bore, and a long-barrelled shell-firing howitzer called the 'unicorn'. Liechtenstein had little confidence in the new weapons. In the autumn of 1759 he forwarded four canister howitzers and two unicorns to Daun's army 'from political considerations and out of special regard for the Russian court',[7] but in February of the next year the pieces and their bombardiers undertook the long trek back to Russia.

CARRIAGES, AMMUNITION, CAISSONS, TRANSPORT AND STORAGE

The fresh and rational approach of Liechtenstein and his partners was very evident in the design of the gun carriages. These were both light and strong – the cheeks being only one calibre thick, but firmly braced with bands of iron. Special attention was given to the problem of adjusting the weight of the gun over the axle. The cheeks of the carriage were now pushed further forward over the centre of gravity, which rendered the trail easy to lift on field service. To facilitate road transport, however, an additional rearward pair of trunnion holes was cut in the cheeks of the 12-pounders: the barrel was lifted back on to them on the march, 'so as to obviate the forward preponderance of weight, which used to cause the long barrel to shake, and also to distribute the weight more equally among the four wheels'[8] – ie the two wheels of the gun carriage and the two wheels of the limber which received the trail of the carriage on the march. This arrangement proved far more satisfactory than the bad old compromise of having a single set of trunnion holes, and it was widely copied by other armies.

Liechtenstein established a common axle and just two types of wheel for the whole range of field artillery and supporting vehicles. He thereby ensured that spares were always at hand in the event of a breakdown. The 36-inch diameter wheel served for the front wheels of the large ammunition cart, and the 51-inch wheel for the field guns and howitzers, for the small two-wheeled ammunition cart and the rear wheels of the large four-wheeled ammunition cart. He laid down that

> The gun carriages and the wheels are to be painted all over in oil colours – the wood in dark yellow, and the ironwork in black. This practice is eminently serviceable as well as economical: It gives much better protection than before against damp and other climatic conditions, and so the greater durability of the wood repays the cost many times over.[9]

The barrels were elevated and depressed by a wedge, which from 1748 was driven by a screw. The mop-cum-rammer and the traversing bars were carried on the carriage itself, and like all the other items of equipment they were marked with the number of the gun. This was an expression of the proprietorial pride of the teams of Austrian artillerymen, who were assigned to the individual pieces for a whole campaign at a time – 'both officers and men feel their honour is engaged in taking a close interest in the upkeep of their equipment and ammunition. Thus the whole ordnance is most carefully maintained'.[10]

The classic round of the artillery was the solid iron roundshot, which in Austria was usually cast in the normal way, but then reheated and forged over so as to render the surface tough and smooth. For short-range work, however, canister was the favoured round. This consisted of large quantities of small balls (usually 3oz), which were crammed into a cylinder of sheet iron. The top of the cylinder was closed with an iron lid, and the bottom with a one-inch-thick sabot of wrought iron, and the intervals between the balls were filled with sawdust. There were 30 such shot in the 3-pounder round, 60 in the 6-pounder, and 120 in the 12-pounder cannon and the

7-pounder howitzer. Lead canister (and sometimes even two superimposed cylinders of the same) were employed at short ranges. Iron canister was preferred at longer ranges, for the shot did not become distorted under the impact of discharge, and their greater elasticity added considerably to the ricochet effect.

The charges were of coarse-grained black powder, and were usually calculated at about one-quarter or one-third of the weight of the roundshot, and rather more than one-third of the weight of the canister. The 7-pounder howitzer had to fire over a wide range of elevation, and consequently had charges of 43 oz, 30 oz, 24 oz and 16 oz.

Austrian gunpowder was renowned for its strength, and the effect was enhanced when Liechtenstein had the charges packed in linen cartridges, which were bound together with a sabot and the shot or canister, and rammed down the barrel intact. The linen surface of the cartridge was covered in a protective paste devised in 1755 by *Stückhauptmann* Johann Hasewander, and painted in white oil paint. Hence the powder was held firmly and neatly together, and preserved against spillage and damp. The fuze was a narrow and carefully-made tube of sheet metal, filled with an explosive composition. The lower end of the tube terminated in a sharp copper cone, which, when the fuze was ignited, was driven by the priming through the fabric casing of the cartridge, thus ensuring that the main charge took fire.

The allowance of ammunition was reckoned at 150 shot and 70 canister for the 3-pounder, between 160 and 180 shot and 50 canister for the 6-pounder, between 120 and 160 shot and 30 canister for the 12-pounder, and between 120 and 140 shells and 20 canister for the 7-pounder howitzer.

For most of the reign the pieces had a small stock of ready ammunition stored in a little chest which fitted between the brackets of the trail of the carriage. In 1774 the ammunition was transferred to a larger chest which was set in the Prussian style on top of the limber.

The main reserve of ammunition was carried in separate ammunition carts, which Liechtenstein assigned on the basis of one small cart (two horses and two wheels) to every 3-pounder cannon and 7-pounder howitzer, and three small carts to every two 6-pounders or 12-pounders. From 1759 the 7-pounder howitzer and the 6- and 12-pounder cannon were allotted the more capacious four-wheeled ammunition cart, which was drawn by four horses. The cartridges were carried from the vehicles to the pieces in leather bags.

The ammunition carts were light and well-designed, and the cartridges were arranged upright along the six or eight compartments into which the chests were subdivided. 'The gunners watch over their ammunition solicitously, and so it is kept in very good condition throughout the longest campaigns'.[11]

The carts accompanied the pieces into action, and as they were exhausted so they were replenished from the *Artillerie-Reserve*, a mass of extra 2-, 4- and 6-horse ammunition carts which were positioned behind the second line of the army in battle. Between 200 and 400 gunners were assigned to the reserve, so as to prepare the ammunition and act as replacements for casualties among the first-line gunners. A second reserve was created in 1757, and it was stationed further still to the rear.

The guns were drawn along the roads by strong and rather expensive horses. Two animals were assigned to the 3-pounder, three to the 7-pounder howitzer, four to the 6-pounder cannon and six to the 12-pounder. The artillery transport was the business of the *Ross-Partei* (literally 'horse party'). This organisation owned only a tiny cadre in peacetime, but it was expanded dramatically in the event of hostilities,

Netherlandish Büchsenmeister. *Fawn coat, waistcoat and breeches; orange red cuffs, lapels and turn-backs; yellow buttons; yellow cord and tassel; sword with brass furniture; hat with yellow braid. The uniform of the German artillery was identical, save for the absence of the lapels and coloured turn-backs* (*By courtesy of the Albertina Collection*)

Three-pounder in action. No 2 is standing by the muzzle with his rammer, while the Vormesiter *is inserting the fuze into the vent* (Ottenfeld)

when drivers were recruited *en masse* and the horses were bought or hired in their thousands. In the last three campaigns of the Seven Years War the *Ross-Partei* attained a strength of 1,177 carts, 5,257 horses and more than 3,000 personnel, in addition to 166 hired carts and their complement of drivers and horses.

In 1757 the wartime *Ross-Partei* was divided into *Trupps* of 100 horses and 50 drivers each. There were sixty such *Trupps* on foot in 1762, but at the end of the war the entire personnel of the *Ross-Partei* was slashed to 96 men. A new kind of arrangement was essayed in the War of the Bavarian Succession, by which time the artillery transport formed part of the larger military transport organisation. Lieutenant-General Rouvroy was distressed to see how the system sank into chaos in the first campaign. The muddle derived partly from the ignorance of the artillery officers and NCOs, 'who had no knowledge of horses and teams, but principally because of the way the transport was organised into companies and divisions, which fell into complete disorder because the artillery was dispersed so widely'.[12]

The lighter pieces marched with the regiments, but the train of heavier artillery was usually inserted between the columns of the army, which led to a lot of complicated sorting-out when the Austrians had to put themselves in order of battle. The Prussians, in contrast, used to march their heavy guns along the side of the army nearest the enemy, so that they merely had to wheel the guns round and open fire.

Guns, equipment, muskets and ammunition of all kinds were held in a great number of depots. The chief depositories were at Vienna, Prague, Olmütz, Budweis and Bergstadl, but there were additional stores in countless small towns, villages and castles. Upon mobilisation most of the 3-pounders were sent direct to the regiments, while the rest of the pieces were assembled as the army's artillery reserve. In 1772 Kinsky abolished the old ordnance department, the *Haus-Artillerie*, and replaced it by a new arrangement of twelve regional departments, which stood under the authority of an overall *Zeugwesen*. Except in Vienna, the new organisation was staffed by invalid or otherwise decrepit officers and men of the artillery – a thoroughly bad arrangement which lasted until the middle of the nineteenth century.

The artillery in battle

The men who served the guns fell into two categories – the professional gunners (*Büchsenmeister*) who did all the skilled work of loading and aiming, and the *Handlanger*, the artillery fusiliers or borrowed infantrymen who provided the brute force needed for traversing and moving the gun.

In action the no 1 gunner inserted the charge and shot into the muzzle of the piece, whereupon no 2 rammed the round firmly home. The chief gunner was the *Vormeister*, or no 3, who pushed the fuze into the vent and directed no 5 and the *Handlanger* in elevating and traversing the piece. When everything was arranged to his satisfaction, the *Vormeister* commanded no 4 to touch off the fuze. The responsibility of no 6 was to convey the ammunition from the trail box or the ammunition cart which was positioned about twelve paces behind the piece.

The number of *Handlanger* varied according to the calibre of the piece – six for a 3-pounder, eight for a 6-pounder, twelve for a 12-pounder and eight for a 7-pounder howitzer. When the *Vormeister* desired the gun to be traversed, one or more of the *Handlanger* heaved upon the traversing spike and swung the trail to right or left as the *Vormeister* signalled. The heaviest work of the *Handlanger* came when they had to push and pull the gun forward, for the piece was unhitched from the horse-drawn limber as much as 500 paces from the line of battle, and thereafter it had to be moved by main force. The trail was lifted off the ground by a wooden bar, which passed transversely through an eye in the traversing spike, and the piece was hauled muzzle first by lines which passed from hooks on the carriage and axles to belts around the remaining *Handlangers*' waists. Additional traction could be applied to the 3- and 6-pounder cannon and the 7-pounder howitzer by passing a bar through four short cylinders that were set on prongs projecting from the cheeks of the carriage on either side of the muzzle.

A strong fresh team of *Handlanger* could heave a field piece forward at greater speed than marching infantry, and the regulations recommended:

> Whether advancing or retiring, you should first make a fairly long bound, then get off several rounds from the same spot and finally move a fair distance in the same way as before. This will enable you to maintain a much higher rate of fire than if you move after every shot.[13]

The 3-pounder's roundshot carried 500 paces point-blank (ie the range of near-horizontal flight), and at 800 paces it could penetrate nearly 5ft of well-rammed earth. However the calibre was too small for a really destructive effect, and the proportion of 3-pounders in the artillery was drastically reduced in the later reign. The piece was very easy to move on the battlefield, but only two horses were provided for road transport, which meant that the gun became immobilised as soon as one of the beasts was incapacitated.

The 6-pounder was a more impressive performer, with its point-blank range of 600 paces and penetration of 7ft, and it proved to be a useful weapon for showering enemy infantry with canister. Feuerstein's masterpiece was, however, the light 12-pounder (800 paces and 7½ft), which greatly heartened the Austrian troops by hitting the enemy at long range. This was the first time that a piece of such heavy calibre had been made into a truly mobile and effective field gun, and it soon came to be recognised that a light but hard-hitting 12-pounder of this type represented the optimum combination of firepower and mobility. The Feuerstein 12-pounder became father to the 'Austrian' 12-pounder of Frederick the Great's army, grandfather of the massed batteries of Napoleon's army, and great-grandfather of the 'Napoleon' gun of the American Civil War. Thus the Feuerstein system of artillery brought smooth-bore ordnance close to its final perfection.

In the campaigns of 1760 and 1761 the gunners were ordered to take into the field a number of captured Prussian 24-pounders. These were thoroughly bad guns, being heavy, short-ranged and inaccurate, and the artillery was saddled with these monsters only 'through the clamour of the people who admired Prussian artifacts'.[14]

At the other extreme the Feuerstein 7-pounder howitzer seemed to the Austrians to be a most economical and versatile 'area' weapon. It was drawn by only three horses, yet it carried up to 2,000 paces with shell and 800 with canister.

Details of all these weapons were duly noted by the French gunner Jean-Baptiste de Gribeauval, who was borrowed by Maria Theresa in the Seven Years War and rose to the rank of lieutenant-general in the Austrian service. Gribeauval sent a detailed report on the Imperial ordnance to the French war minister on 3 March 1762, and the example of the Austrian artillery probably became Gribeauval's chief inspiration when he remade the French artillery in the 1770s.

The Austrian gunners practised twice a week with special 1-pounder training pieces, and in the field they could deliver four rounds per minute without difficulty. The accuracy with roundshot was acceptable out to 1,000 paces, where the field artillery could score 40–70 per cent hits on a target the size of a company, but thereafter the effect fell off markedly, and sank to hits of only 15 per cent at 1,500 paces. The 7-pounder howitzer scored 20–30 per cent hits at 1,000 paces, but only 2 per cent at the longer range.

The artillery officers were told to make certain that the *Büchsenmeister* did not aim too high, and likewise to

> take the utmost care to prevent the gunners and assistants from running away as soon as the enemy open their musket fire. On the contrary they must direct a heavy fire of canister at the enemy, which will silence their musketry soon enough.[15]

Liechtenstein worked out a rational and effective deployment of artillery in the field. The greater part of the 3-pounders were told off in fours or sixes at a time to the individual infantry regiments, where they came under the command of a *Stückjunker*. Every third battalion in the first line of battle, however, was assigned a pair of 7-pounder howitzers instead. Liechtenstein confirmed an old Austrian practice, according to which,

> when the enemy is standing in battle formation, a platoon of infantry is positioned in front of every couple of pieces in the first line, so as to conceal them from enemy reconnaissance . . . the platoon remains there till the time comes for the artillery to open fire, when it breaks off to right and left.[16]

The remaining howitzers and 3-pounder cannon, together with the 6- and 12-pounders, were placed at the disposal of the army as a whole. The 3-pounders and the 6-pounders were usually disposed in small batteries of up to four pieces, but it was found advantageous to concentrate the 12-pounders in a single central battery, and (together with the 7-pounder howitzers) in two flanking batteries whence they could strike at the hostile cavalry. A proportion of pieces of all calibres was held in reserve behind the second line in three or more groups.

The guns were assigned to their tasks on the battlefield by the chief of the field artillery, who stood at the right hand of the commander of the army – a position which indicated the power and prestige of the Theresian artillery.

9

The Technicians

The Engineers

As the term was understood in the eighteenth century, the military engineer was an officer who was primarily concerned with building, defending and attacking fortresses. To begin with, Maria Theresa was very badly off for these vital experts. She found that they had a proper organisation only in the distant Netherlands, where two 'brigades' of seven officers each had been set up in 1732. The seventy-two remaining engineers were 'scattered and virtually concealed in an anonymous fashion all over the place, and none of them believed that he needed to refer to any of the others'.[1]

The qualifications of the engineers were of the most diverse kind. Prince Eugene had experienced an appalling lack of native engineers in the War of the Spanish Succession, and in 1718 he had founded engineer academies in Vienna and Brussels so as to supply the deficiency. Unfortunately with the passage of time the Brussels institution became an unspecialised military academy, while the one in Vienna lost its vocational military connections almost entirely, like the future French *Polytechnique*.

In these circumstances a valuable contribution was made to the stock of native engineers by the unfortunately-named 'Chaotic Foundation' (*Chaotische Stift*), which was established as an orphanage from the legacy of Baron Chaos in 1663. The Chaotic Foundation grew steadily in prestige, and it began to attract young folk who had a bent towards military engineering, notably the future Theresian engineers Harsch, Rochepine and Giannini. However, the director urged in 1743 that it was important to provide the place with better technical facilities, 'so as to separate the officers from the other scholars, who are bad and young'.[2]

The parlous state of military engineering in the earlier part of the reign was revealed by the way the Austrians mismanaged their siege of the powerful French garrison in Prague in the summer of 1742. The technical side of the operation was entrusted to General Ferdinand Philipp Harsch (a product of the Chaotic Foundation), who drew up a list of siege requisites and

> admitted that he took as his model one of the memoranda reproduced by Saint-Rémy (*Mémoires d'Artillerie*, 1702) for a siege of one of the most important fortresses of Europe. Unfortunately our director found therein all sorts of terms which were unknown to him, and he had to look up the meanings in a dictionary, which did not always explain the sense particularly clearly.[3]

In 1747 Maria Theresa commissioned Colonel Paul Ferdinand Bohn to reduce engineering affairs to some kind of order. He was made *Prodirector* of a new corps of engineers, though (because things were done in that way in Austria) Prince Charles of Lorraine was placed in nominal command over his head as *General-Genie-Director*.

Zimmerleute, *with their distinctive caps, aprons and axes* (*Manuscript of 1749 Infantry Regulations*, Kriegsarchiv)

Sappers (Ottenfeld)

Bohn retained the existing Netherlandish brigade of engineers, and reorganised the remaining officers into the various brigades of the German Hereditary Lands, Hungary and Italy, making a grand total of ninety-eight officers. Each of the four brigades was placed under a colonel, who was responsible for keeping up the fortresses in his district. Meanwhile Bohn as *Prodirector* was busy examining officer candidates, touring the fortresses in the spring, and evaluating projects for military construction in the winter. The structure of the corps and the duties of the officers were detailed in a *Regulament* which was published on 20 July 1747.

As overall director of military education, Field-Marshal Daun tried to ensure the supply of future generations of native engineers. In 1754 he renovated and embellished the buildings of the Chaotic Foundation in the western suburbs of

Vienna, and united it as an *Institut* with the Vienna engineering academy. Six years later the school came under the authority of the *Prodirector* of the corps.

The performance of the new corps fell somewhat below expectations. In the defence of Prague in 1757 the only Austrian engineers present were a colonel and a major, both of whom were comprehensively ignorant of everything that had to do with engineering. Later in the year, when the Austrians were besieging Schweidnitz, the Saxon officer Callenberg, who was strongly pro-Austrian, was angry to discover that, after all the money that had been spent on the corps, the management of the siege was taken over by the French brigadier-general Riverson and seven of his countrymen. Likewise in the brilliant defence of Schweidnitz by the Austrians in 1762 the technical side of affairs was left largely in the hands of Gribeauval. After the war the French officers continued to make a major contribution to Austrian engineering affairs, and they did a great deal to set up the new system of fortress defence in Bohemia against the Prussians.

In 1761 the original white coat of the engineers was replaced by one of more serviceable blue. In siege conditions, however, the officers allowed themselves considerable latitude as to their appearance.

The sappers

One of the principal causes of the dismal performance of the Austrians in siegework was the gap that yawned between the engineer officers on the one hand, and the unskilled soldier-labourers on the other. Thus in the attack on Schweidnitz in 1757 the Austrians were careful to make use of the men of the Walloon regiments, who had some experience in digging trenches from their service in foreign armies. It was left to Gribeauval to suggest that the Austrians ought to create a proper corps of sappers, who would provide a nucleus of skilled labour for siege warfare.

The *Sapeur-Corps* was duly set on foot in April 1760, with an establishment of three companies of a nominal eighty-five officers and men each. The officers were interchangeable with those of the engineers, while the men were made over in contingents of four from every regiment of infantry. All the men were to be strong and able-bodied, and one in every four was expected to be able to read and write.

The new corps earned its keep very soon indeed. In July 1760 the corps commander Major Bechard helped to plan and carry out Loudon's spectacular *coup de main* on the fortress of Glatz, and he was chosen to bear the thirty-three captured colours in triumph to Vienna. In 1762 twenty-four of the sappers made an heroic contribution to the defence of Schweidnitz. No less than ten of the number were killed and eleven wounded, and three of the officers were awarded the Military Order of Maria Theresa, which must have been a record for a unit of this size.

The original sappers came to the corps in 1760 clad in the tattered uniforms of their parent infantry regiments. Before long they were rigged out in a new corps uniform of leather breeches, leather cap, and a *Hechtgrau* coat with turn-back skirts and cuffs of carmine red.

The pioneers

Every infantry regiment held on its establishment a handful of pioneers (*Zimmerleute*), who helped to clear away obstacles on the march and to make minor works of field fortification. They sported aprons and grenadier-type fur caps, and carried axes as the specific sign of their function.

Early in the Seven Years War General Lacy urged that it would be most advantageous to have a combined corps of such people standing at the immediate disposal of the commanding general, who could send them ahead with the advance guard to widen and repair roads and set up light timber bridges. Daun replied that a single battalion of pioneers would be adequate, and so in January 1758 Maria Theresa approved the setting-up of a pioneer battalion of four companies of 111 officers and men each. The companies were assigned a number of bridging waggons, which bore 32ft-long beams and 10ft-high uprights. The pioneers proved to be so useful that in 1759 the corps was augmented by more than 600 officers and men.

Most inadvisedly, the corps was disbanded as part of the drastic economies that were carried through in the winter of 1761–2, and after the war Lacy argued in vain that the army should retain at least a cadre of the pioneers.

During their short existence the pioneers wore the leather cap and *Hechtgrau* coat of the *Jägers* and sappers, but with cuffs and collar of grass green.

The Pontoniers

The eclipse of the pioneers threw their rivals, the *Pontoniers*, into all the greater prominence. The bridging trains of the War of the Austrian Succession had been essentially improvised affairs. It was easy enough to bring the heavy pontoons of sheet metal or wood up the Danube to serve in the campaigns against the Bavarians and French, and the personnel could be filled out by enlisting the *Tschaikisten* – the Danubian boatmen who had originally been raised for military service against the Turks. But it proved much more difficult to assemble an adequate bridging train on the northern theatre, for the Bohemian and Moravian watersheds separated the régime of the Danube from those of the Elbe and Oder, and the heavy pontoons were very difficult to transport overland.

In 1749 the business of crossing rivers was reduced to some kind of order, with the setting up of an *Obrist-Schiffamt* (which administered the bridges) and two military *Pontons-Compagnien* of thirty-four officers and men apiece. The old pontoons were replaced by twelve pontoons of wood, and eighty of tin or copper which were destined for the northern rivers, while the former two-wheeled transport carts were replaced by more substantial four-wheelers. With the demise of the pioneers towards the end of the Seven Years War the pontoniers took over the light *Laufbrücke* as well.

In the field the pontoon train usually marched behind the advance guard. When a crossing was to be effected in the presence of the enemy, the infantry of the advance guard made the first passage on wooden pontoons and whatever boats could be obtained from the locality. Once the bridgehead was secure the pontoniers threw across one or more bridges, using the flimsy sheet metal pontoons and the remainder of the wooden pontoons. Smaller rivers were crossed by building bridges of local timber or the beams of the *Laufbrücke*.

The *Pontoniers* wore infantry-type coats of a distinctive light blue, with cuffs and waistcoat of red.

Austria entered the third year of the War of the Austrian Succession almost devoid of artificial defences. There was no stronghold on the upper Danube to stay the progress of the French and Bavarians. In the north, all the fortresses of Silesia had been lost to the Prussians, leaving Bohemia and Moravia uncovered; the only places of any account were Prague, with its decaying ramparts, and the Moravian strongholds of Brünn and Olmütz.

There were ways in which the virtual absence of fortresses actually served Austrian interests. Frederick commented that 'in Bohemia and Moravia you are often embarrassed to find secure places [for the magazines], since there is hardly a single town which is defensible'.[4] By the same token, however, the Austrians had nowhere to assemble their own stores in safety when invasion threatened. This was why they lost great quantities of supplies when the Prussians poured into Bohemia in April 1757. Olmütz was the only place on the theatre which was put into a reasonable state of defence, and it performed magnificently when the Prussians took the path through Moravia in 1758.

After the Seven Years War the Austrians for the first time had the leisure to think about setting up a coherent network of fortresses. On the Turkish borders the fortresses of Gradisca, Esseg and Peterwardein were considerably strengthened, and a completely new fortress was founded at Arad so as to secure the communications between Hungary and the Banát.

As for the defence of the border with Prussia, General Lacy drew Daun's attention in 1764 to the line of the upper Elbe, which curled so conveniently round the foot of the mountains on the Austrian side. Lacy's inclination was to establish a fortress by the river at Pless, where there was a spacious site which commanded the main entry from Silesia and dominated the interesting area of the confluence of the Elbe, the Aupa and the Metau. This view coincided with that of five French engineers who were called in for consultations, but that bird of ill-omen General Harsch (Bohn's successor as *Prodirector*) urged instead that they ought to fortify the town of Königgrätz, which stood on a cramped site a dozen miles downstream. Prince Charles of Lorraine came down in favour of Harsch, and work on the Königgrätz site began in 1766.

The war of the Bavarian Succession emphasised how important it was to lend every conceivable reinforcement to the line of the upper Elbe. Joseph accordingly made an extensive tour of the Bohemian border, and concluded that the Pless site still deserved a fortress of its own.

The foundation stone of the new fortress of Josephstadt at Pless was laid in 1780, and the work on the vast brick ramparts was completed in thirteen years according to the designs of Joseph's argumentative French protégé General Querlonde. Away to the west the course of the lower Elbe as it flowed towards Saxony was secured by a town fortress at Kopist, which was renamed 'Theresienstadt' and fortified to the designs of Pellegrini.

Königgrätz and the two newer fortresses were actually put in a state of defence in 1795, in a period of tension with Prussia, but they played no active part in either the Napoleonic wars or the disastrous events of 1866. In World War II the proud name of Theresienstadt was defiled by the Nazis, who made the place a transit camp for their Jewish victims, while Josephstadt is now a Soviet garrison.

10

Financiers, Commissaries, Doctors and Priests

The finances

The welfare of the Theresian army and the survival of the Austrian state hung from year to year upon the ability of the Viennese government to pay its way. The resources of the monarchy were potentially vast but virtually unrealisable, since the greater part of the wealth was retained by the nobles and the clergy. Hence nothing short of a fundamental reorganisation of the state was capable of tapping some of these riches.

In 1740 the annual income of the state was reckoned at just 20,000,000 florins, and the debts at a crippling 101,000,000. Without the English and Dutch subsidies the monarchy could scarcely have survived the decade. As it was, the pay of the officers and men sank far in arrears (by as much as eight months for the army in Italy in 1746), and there were regiments which were supported only by the generosity of some of the wealthier commanders.

After the War of the Austrian Succession Maria Theresa set herself the task of raising the state revenues to an annual 40,000,000 florins, of which 14,000,000 were to be devoted to maintaining an army of 108,000 men. A vital part in the operation was played by the Silesian refugee Count Friedrich Wilhelm Haugwitz, who in 1748 established the principle of the 'ten year recess', by which the provincial *Stände* would be freed from their obligations of supplying accommodation and provisions for the army, in return for making over direct contributions in cash. The all-embracing *Directorium in Publicis et Cameralibus* was set up in the following year and took over the hitherto separate Austrian and Bohemian chancelleries, which simplified the administration of the system.

The provinces undertook to raise the money by levying taxes on rents and fixed property, but the actual size and duration of the contributions became a matter of much debate. Bohemia was the most generous, contracting to raise 5,270,488 florins per annum for ten years. At the other extreme Carinthia had to be forced into paying anything at all, while Hungary exacted large political concessions and yielded up only a miserly pittance in return.

By 1754 Maria Theresa had attained her objective of 40,000,000 florins. Seventeen million came from the provinces by way of contributions in cash. The balance was made up by taxes, fees, and the proceeds of various state enterprises – including the system of tobacco monopoly which continues to produce a vile weed in Austria today.

In 1753 a useful currency convention fixed the silver content of the florin (at 23.39 grammes), and rated the worth at one-half of a Reichsthaler. The same year saw the first minting of the two-florin *Maria-Theresien Thaler*, a coin which has remained in high demand ever since on account of its intrinsic worth and artistic value. The spectacular décolleté of the portrait was particularly well received in the Levant.

While the doubling of the state revenue was sufficient to keep the newly-expanded army of 108,000 men on foot as a going concern, there was nothing to spare for assembling provision magazines, preparing for mobilisation, or building new fortresses or the barracks which would have enabled the troops to have been kept together in larger bodies.

Kaunitz reckoned that the extra cost of a new war would amount to something like 10–12,000,000 florins per annum. In the event, the cost of the single campaign of 1760 reached 44,000,000 florins, while the extraordinary costs of the war as a whole amounted to no less than 260,000,000. The existing financial structures were incapable of bearing the burden. Kaunitz put the blame on Haugwitz and his centralising tendencies, and in 1761 he took a much more direct hand in internal affairs and broke up the mighty *Directorium*. This was more than a little unfair, because the financial system of 1748 was essentially a peacetime measure, designed to keep an unmobilised army in existence on an adequate footing. The wonder is that the 1748 system survived as well as it did.

Since Maria Theresa shunned the kind of extortion and fraud by which Frederick kept the Prussian military machine in operation, she had to make fresh appeals to the public spirit of the *Stände*, and imposed a variety of ill-assorted taxes. As usual, Austria and Bohemia bore the heaviest burden. On top of this 147,000,000 florins and 18,000,000 florins-worth of natural produce were raised by credit – namely 90,000,000 from the German Hereditary Lands, 32,000,000 from the Vienna Stadtbanco, 26,000,000 from the Netherlands, 11,000,000 from private loans, and a paltry 7,000,000 from Hungary. By 1761 the service of the loans amounted to more than 4,000,000 florins, and in the following year the shortage of cash induced the Stadtbanco to issue notes (*Coupons*) to the value of 12,000,000, which were backed by the credit of the Habsburg lands and represented the first introduction of paper currency to Central Europe.

Throughout the war the soldiers were paid promptly and in undebased coinage, which was a fair achievement in itself. In the winter of 1761–2, however, the army in Silesia was reinforced by a corps of Russians, and the government seized the opportunity to carry through a number of drastic economies. All officers from major upwards were told to content themselves with paper money, which was redeemable only after the war, and two companies were struck from the establishment of every regiment of infantry, cuirassiers and hussars and from the staff dragoon regiment. The officers and men were redistributed, but the paltry savings in administration were made at the price of a diminution in the effectiveness of the regiments: 'The disadvantageous effects of this reduction on the following campaign . . . must be known to everyone who served in Silesia in that year'.[1] General Lacy complained that Maria Theresa ought simply to have explained her embarrassment to the army, for the officers and soldiers would have gladly served on half pay.

The end of the Seven Years War brought precious little relief to the Austrian economy, thanks to the inflation in prices, the obligation to serve the 165,000,000 florins worth of debts contracted during the war, and the great size of the army, which eventually reached a wartime strength of more than 200,000 men. The legacy of Emperor Francis Stephen amounted to more than 30,000,000 florins, but this sum was consumed by the state after 1765 with no apparent relief to the economy. Bohemia sank into stagnation and ruin in the 1770s, and the cost of the War of the Bavarian Succession brought the whole of the Habsburg economy to the verge of collapse.

 Bearing these gloomy facts in mind, it is legitimate to question whether Austrian ambitions after 1750 continued to correspond with the realisable resources of the monarchy.

War industry

The deficiency in cash was all the more regrettable since, in material terms, almost all the needs of the army could be met from within the Habsburg dominions.

Flax was cultivated on a large scale in Moravia, and the manufacture of woollen cloth became a speciality of the little towns along the Bohemian–Moravian border, and more particularly of Iglau, which could produce a white uniform at a cost of a little over six florins. By 1757 the cost of the infantryman's entire uniform and equipment was brought down to fifteen florins, or twenty florins with the musket. His total expense in uniforms, equipment, pay and rations was defined in 1749 as an annual forty-seven florins eleven kreutzer.

Small arms were manufactured principally from native ores, notably the iron of Styria, which was reputed to be more finely grained than the Swedish. Almost all the sword blades were forged by the Pottensteiner Factory or by Moosbrugger and his companion swordsmiths at Waitz. The blades were expected to prove their temper by cleaving a nail in two without denting the edge.

The muskets, carbines and pistols were supplied to the Imperial arsenals mainly by the privileged *Armaturs-Gesellschaft* at Wiener Neustadt, and by the Steyr firm of Schöffler and Haager and their local rivals the Penzeneters. Small quantities of rather bad weapons were manufactured from 1749 in the factories at Weipert, Prossnitz and Karlsbad in Bohemia and Moravia, and in the crisis of the Seven Years War inferior muskets were bought in thousands at a time from the gunsmiths in the Netherlands. After the Seven Years War, however, Anton Penzeneter the younger was able to overcome nearly all his competitors and carry on a flourishing business based on his workshops at Steyr, Hainfeld and Vienna.

Good bronze artillery was cast at Vienna and at the Netherlandish foundry at Malines, and in smaller quantities at Prague, Innsbruck, Graz, Ofen in Hungary and Hermannstadt in Transylvania. After the Seven Years War the French brothers Poitevin took charge of the arsenal at Vienna, and set new standards in the economy, skill and uniformity with which the pieces were manufactured.

The production of gunpowder was a monopoly exercised by the artillery. This was a large-scale and profitable business, thanks to the passion of the nobility for game shooting, and when de Guibert visited the mills in 1773 he was struck by the cheapness and strength of the military gunpowder, which he reckoned to be as good as the sporting powder used in France.[2]

The Kriegs-Commissariat

One of the most extraordinary features of the Austrian service was the all-pervading influence of the commissary branch. The essential function of its officials was determined in 1749 to consist 'of supervising the military establishment, economy and discipline for the common good'.[3] In detail the commissaries held musters in the spring and autumn to see that men, horses and equipment were present in the official numbers and state; they issued uniforms, equipment and weapons, supplied the army with victuals, accepted recruits and remounts into the regiments, compiled the company muster lists, shared in the administration of the regimental pay, rations and accommodation, and even helped the *Profoss* and chaplain to maintain standards of discipline, morals and religious observance.

The outfit was commanded by a *General-Kriegs-Commissarius*. Under his authority functioned a hierarchy of officials – the *Ober-Kriegs-Commissäre*, the *Kriegs-Commissäre* and the *Amts-Officiere*. Their numbers were considerably expanded in wartime (in 1746, for example, there were eighty-three of them), but whenever peace returned many of the officials left the service altogether, and the rest were kept on half-pay or retainers.

The commissaries were unpopular with military and civilian alike. The Emperor Francis Stephen remarked in 1751 that timber would become scarce if a gallows had to be built to hang every dishonest official of the commissariat, and in popular speech it was the custom to cap a string of insults with the exclamation – 'and you're a commissary as well!' In Cognazzo's experience the worst specimens had risen from the ranks of the clerks and lackeys.[4] This is confirmed by the story of a certain Koschinna, a former lackey in the Kaunitz household, who acquired some expertise in financial matters and was able to buy himself the title of 'Baron Koschinna v. Freudenthal'. In the Seven Years War the new baron embarked on a career as a commissary:

> In his manners he was wild, crude and gross, and gave no indication of ever having been in service with an eminent gentleman. He was cruel, even tyrannical, when he had the power to torment people who refused to fall in with his ideas. At the sight of the slightest danger, however, he was overcome with that crawling fear and timidity which commonly plagues men of dictatorial mentality.[5]

All this helps to account for the cringing tone of the regulations of 1749, which advised the commissaries to

> cultivate a courteous and modest manner. When you compose your letters you should employ rather too many compliments than too few, as a sign of the special regard which is due to the military. The job of the commissary had attracted a good deal of prejudice, and you must do everything you can to render our work less hateful in the sight of others.[6]

The most 'glorious' years of the commissariat were associated with the name of the veteran official Count Franz Ludwig Salburg, who embarked on his reign as *General-Kriegs-Commissarius* in 1746. On 28 December of that year Salburg won for the commissariat the status of a department of state (*Hofstelle*) completely independent of the *Hofkriegsrath*. In the Seven Years War Salburg resolved to soldier on regardless of mounting criticism and a horrible disease which was eating away his nose, but in the middle of the campaign of 1757 he was removed from office and the commissariat department was annexed by the Haugwitz *Directorium*. This measure caused 'great confusion in the supply system, to the prejudice and hindrance of military operations'.[7] The muddle in supplies served to immobilise the Austrians after they captured Breslau, and allowed the Prussians to seize the initiative in the series of events which culminated in the disastrous battle of Leuthen on 5 December.

In 1761, after the fall of the *Directorium*, the commissariat was reconstituted on more rational lines. It was made answerable to the *Hofkriegsrath* for questions of military supply, and to the three new departments of civil finance for its contracts and accounting.

Systems of military economy

The means of keeping the Austrian army supplied with victuals and fodder were of a complexity which almost defies description, and which was given to engendering handy terms like the 39-letter *Generalfeldproviantverpflegsadmodiazion*. Broadly speaking, these necessities came at various times from three sources – provincial authorities, private contractors, or a state-administered *Regie*.

In the earlier part of the reign the provinces were under the obligation to provide the army with provisions and fodder in peacetime, and with winter quarters in time of war. The details were worked out between the officials of the *Stände* on the one hand, and the army commissaries on the other. The great financial and administrative reforms of 1748–9 effected an important change of emphasis. The fundamental objective was to secure an enduring peace, and with this in view it was essential 'to keep on foot a sufficient armed force in both wartime and peacetime'.[8] The old hand-to-mouth expedients were now plainly inadequate. The provinces were therefore relieved of their old obligations, and sizeable contributions in cash were substituted. Here the government had two ambitions in mind – 'to stop the soldiers oppressing the civilians who give them quarters',[9] and 'to have a reliable sum by way of contributions paid over correctly and at a proper time'.[10] As many troops as possible were now lodged in barracks or 'semi-barracks', and the regiments drew their rations from new state magazines which were established throughout the provinces.

The outbreak of the Seven Years War interrupted the operation of the new scheme, and only after 1763 was it possible to ascertain how well the army would get along without the direct assistance of the *Stände*. Immediate purchase by the state was found to be a reliable though expensive means of keeping the army supplied. The alternative system of provisioning was by way of contractors, who usually worked several at a time in an *Admodiazion*, or combine. They in turn employed a host of sub-contractors, who were 'mostly townsmen of a settled and prosperous kind'. The contractors promised to deliver supplies at their personal risk and cost, and it was said to be in their own best interests to 'deliver everything in the proper quality and quantity, and by accurate volume and weight, out of fear of provoking any dissatisfaction'.[11]

Where the difficulty arose was in stipulating a satisfactory price. If the contractors stood to make excessively high profits in time of stable prices, they were just as liable to bankrupt themselves in time of inflation and leave the state to pick up the pieces. Immediately after the Seven Years War the supply of the army was turned over entirely to the merchants. The Jew Lazar Österreicher took on the important contract for the troops in Austria and Bohemia, but he proved unequal to the task, 'having insufficient knowledge of the job, and owning inadequate private means to carry on an undertaking which was on so large a scale and which extended over several provinces'.[12] In 1765 the deal was cancelled and the contract taken on by the merchant syndicate called the *Grechtlerische General-Admodiazion*. The Grechtler concern itself lost 1,192,236 florins, owing to the rising cost in cereals, and the state resumed the management of affairs when the contract ran out on 1 November 1770. The expenses continued to rise, and by February 1774 the state had assigned 7,400,000 florins to keep the supply machine in operation.

At the regimental level the colonel had to perform a balancing act between the monies he received from the central Military Chest (*Kriegs-Cassa*), and the cost of the supplies, uniforms and equipment he drew from the stores. Most regiments consequently lost their bearings in a blizzard of paperwork, especially after the reforms in military economy in 1748 involved the regiments in making returns for literally thousands of items. This proliferation of business led commandants to 'devote themselves more to regimental economy and accounts than to real military service'.[13] Attempts were made in 1755 and 1757 to reduce affairs to some kind of order, but by 1761 many regiments had run deeply into debt, the total deficit amounting to 727,409 florins for supplies and 751,016 for uniforms and equipment. The complexities were in no way abated after Lacy took over the management of things in 1766. This ingenious Irishman required the colonels to forward accurate information as to their needs, based on their monthly returns, but deprived them of the authority to draw the necessary supplies and goods from the stores. These were now furnished directly by the state. Lacy thereby

> lost the love of the officers, for he robbed them of the power to deceive their sovereign. Hitherto the captains supplied the needs of their companies, and they had become accustomed to making at least twice as much as their entitlement on the cost of cloth, hats, shoes and the like. The senior officers were usually in a conspiracy with the paymasters to appropriate part of the military chests for themselves. All this has now ceased. Everything that the soldier needs is supplied from huge magazines at the Imperial expense. The Austrian soldier receives his full pay on the minute, he is better dressed than any soldier in Europe, and he is maintained in a way that is most beneficial to his health and bodily strength. The great field-marshal has been rewarded for this masterly arrangement by scorn and contempt.[14]

Supply in the field

In the field the daily allowance of bread stood at $1\frac{3}{4}$–2lb. The loaves were prepared by baking companies, which were equipped with mobile and efficient ovens that were the envy of foreign powers.

Whereas the bread ration was issued free, the soldier had to buy his meat from the regimental butcher – a civilian tradesman who was subject to the same kind of supervision as the sutlers (see below). Although the state did not take a direct part in the retail side of the business, the authorities made sure that sufficient cattle were sent to the theatre of war to keep the army supplied at reasonable rates. The animals were usually herded along behind the baggage.

Wine, beer and other comforts were purveyed by the regimental sutlers – fairly disreputable folk who were grudgingly licensed by the staff auditor of the army, and kept under supervision by the regimental *Profoss*:

> Every now and again the regiments ought to send some trustworthy men to go to the tents of the coffee-purveyors, Jews and butchers, and likewise to mix with

the tradesmen at headquarters, so as to see and hear if there are any folk there who are inciting the men to desert.[15]

Bohemian beer was well worth buying from the sutlers, but their wine was all too often a horrid concoction of red fruit juice laced with raw spirits, which gave the soldiers bad stomach cramps.

The weight and composition of the horse rations varied considerably according to the locality and the season of the year. In the summer months raw green fodder might account for one-third of the weight of the ration, and in time of hardship (as in 1757) a proportion of barley was mixed with the oats and hay which made up the dry feed.

In the mass the men and beasts consumed food at a frightening rate. The rise in demand during the reign is best shown in diagrammatic form:

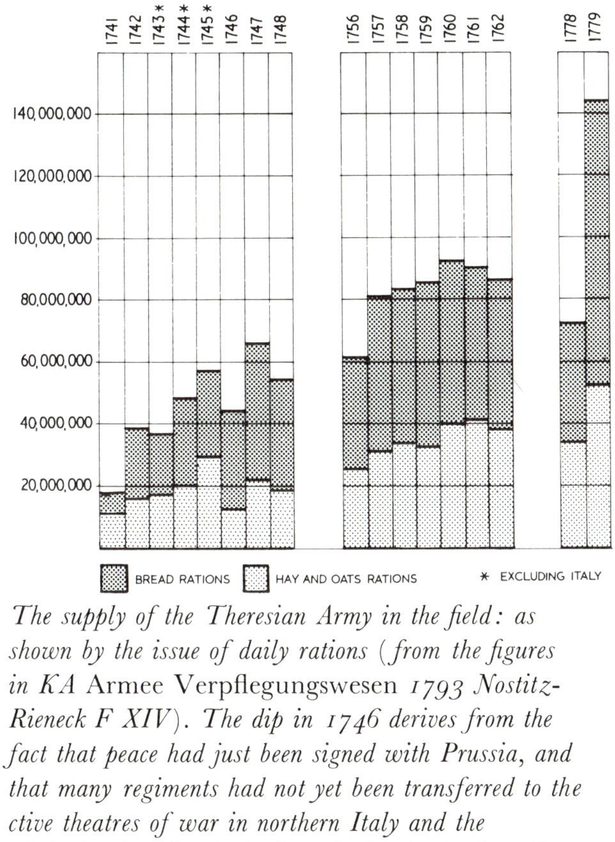

The supply of the Theresian Army in the field: as shown by the issue of daily rations (from the figures in KA Armee Verpflegungswesen *1793 Nostitz-Rieneck F XIV). The dip in 1746 derives from the fact that peace had just been signed with Prussia, and that many regiments had not yet been transferred to the ctive theatres of war in northern Italy and the Netherlands. The slackening of effort in the later Seven Years War is small but significant. The huge scale of the issues in 1778–79 was clearly a great burden on the Austrian economy.*

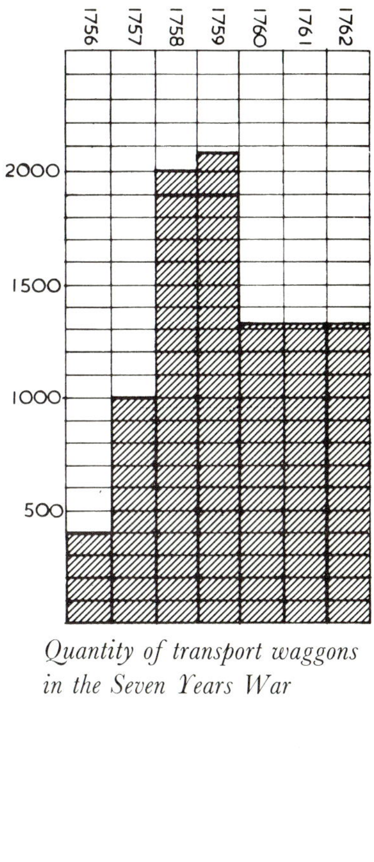

Quantity of transport waggons in the Seven Years War

This pattern indicates a seven-fold increase in rations for the troops and a five-fold increase for the horses.

In the War of the Austrian Succession the normal way of obtaining supplies was by direct purchase by the state, though there were a number of important exceptions: in the northern theatre in 1741 the army was maintained by the Bohemian and Moravian *Stände*; in the Netherlands from 1745 to 1748 the army looked to contractors; contractors actually supplied the armies in Italy with fodder throughout the war, and from 1746 with bread as well.

In the Seven Years War state purchase and contract are found in association. Resort was also made on occasion to the *Stände*, even though the provinces had been relieved in 1749 of the obligation of keeping the army supplied in peacetime. The whole process was supervised by the specialised staff of the *Feld-Proviant Amt*, which had the responsibility of keeping the army fed in wartime, and was answerable both to the Treasury and to the *Kriegs-Commissariat*.

In addition the armies did a good deal of foraging on their own account, and the ability to keep their own animals fed – while starving the enemy's – was an important attribute of celebrated commanders like Browne. The business of mowing or confiscating the fodder was more especially the work of the cavalry, and great care had to be taken not to weaken the operational strength of this arm by detaching too many troopers at a time, as actually occurred before the battle of Prague. Whenever an expedition returned to base, the regimental officers were to 'watch the fodder being delivered, and see if any goods have been taken from our subjects and packed up in the bales or elsewhere'.[16] The army was by no means so particular when it was a question of exacting fodder or 'contributions' in cash in enemy territory.

When opportunity offered, the stocks of flour, salt, oats, peas and other provisions were piled in large magazines in or near the theatre of war. Fortresses and castles were considered the best sites.

For mass transport of supplies the army was thrown for the greater part of the reign entirely upon private enterprise. The department known as the *Feld-Proviant-Fuhrwesen* was simply an organising body, which owned no permanent establishment of vehicles or animals, and no permanent transport personnel except three veteran overseers (*Verwalter*) who were kept on after the Seven Years War. When hostilities broke out, the government simply hired everything it needed from the civilian coaching and carting concerns.

The 'system' worked rather better than might have been expected: 'From supervisor down to ordinary waggoner, the personnel knew all about the driving and horses. There was no expensive corps staff, and no posts for military officers which the state had the burden of maintaining in peacetime.[17] As an example of the flexibility of the apparatus we may cite the first chaotic weeks of the Seven Years War, when the Austrian contractor Dietrich got the first vital stocks of ammunition and artillery requisites from Vienna to Prague and Pardubitz within fourteen days of signing his contract.

The later statistics from the Seven Years War confirm the impression that the Austrian effort reached its peak in the third or fourth campaigns of that struggle. From a mere 400 waggons in 1756 the complement of the transport train reached 2,070 in 1759, then sank to 1,340 in 1760 and remained at that figure until the end of the war. The highest number attained by the personnel was 3,990 and by the horses 8,280.

There was still the problem of organising the carts in a passably 'military' fashion after they had reached the theatre of war. Someone complained in 1758 that

> the waggon trains are often so long that you are unable to see from one end to the other. But what causes the most trouble is that the trains are kept in no proper order and that no satisfactory escorts can be provided. Hence part of the

> baggage arrives, early, and part comes up late. Nobody bothers about keeping any station. All they want to do is to get ahead of the others.[18]

Finally in 1760 the mass of drivers and vehicles was divided into four *Verwalterschaften* or six *Officierschaften* apiece, each *Officierschaft* consisting of fifty or more waggons.

After the Seven Years War the machine was broken up in the usual fashion. In July 1771, however, we detect the first beginnings of a state *Fuhrwesens-Corps* when preparations were being made to occupy Galicia. The organisation reached a strength of four companies during the actual operation in 1772. The greater part was disbanded over the following years, but in 1776 Lacy used the survivors as the foundation upon which to build up a properly organised state transport corps of 821 men and 448 horses. These in turn formed a small professional nucleus for the huge expansion of the Austrian transport in the War of the Bavarian Succession, in which the men and animals reached grand totals of 21,388 and 37,797 respectively, of which 10,967 drivers and 16,188 horses were destined to haul the artillery.[19]

An entirely different dispensation provided for the more immediate needs of the regiments. These owned a complement of vehicles, drivers and animals which they retained from one campaign to the next. The size of this 'regimental' transport varied considerably in the War of the Austrian Succession, as the army hired more or less transport in the mass – the larger the army transport the less the regimental transport, and so on. In the Seven Years War, however, most of the infantry regiments owned a vehicle for the regimental chest, a cart for the field smithy, between six and nine supply waggons for the bread and dry fodder, and three carts (or from 1758 thirty-one mules) for carrying the tents. Every regiment of cavalry owned between three and four supply waggons, but bore all the rest of their needs on their horses. These facilities provided about four days' food for the troops, and five days' fodder for the horses. In addition the individual soldier carried four days' bread in his knapsack, and the cavalryman packed three days' fodder into a bag which he fixed behind his saddle.

The characteristic cart of the time was a covered vehicle in 'Wild West' style, which came in light and heavy versions, both drawn by teams of four horses, or occasionally by teams of six oxen. Mules were employed for lighter transport in the mountain campaigns of the War of the Austrian Succession, and again for carrying tents in the Seven Years War. It is odd that the Austrians did not think of using their own excellent Hafflinger ponies.

In theory, rivers offered 'at once the easiest, cheapest and most satisfactory form of transport'.[20] The Danube certainly offered an easy path into Bavaria, but the Austrians owned no equivalent avenue in the northern theatre, if we except the navigable reach of the Elbe below Melnik in Bohemia. Frederick of Prussia was much better placed, for the Oder and the lower Elbe enabled him to bring his heavy supplies all the way from his rearward magazines to the theatre of war.

Medical services

In most lands the story of the medical care of the eighteenth-century soldier is a grisly and unhappy one. If the Theresian army offers a little relief it is principally due to the efforts of two men – the Irish *Protomedicus* Dr Brady, and the medical dictator Gerhard Van Swieten, who was a Dutchman.

As chief doctor of the army Brady lodged a formidable indictment on 29 January 1744 concerning the disorganisation and indiscipline prevailing in the medical services. He described how the *Kriegs-Commissariat* refused to allow him to inspect the hospitals or control the issue of medicaments, how its bureaucrats appointed and moved doctors in an arbitrary fashion, and how they so muddled up the transport arrangements that bed linen might be desperately needed in some places, while it was piled up in decaying heaps in others. In 1746 the medical administration was at last reduced to some kind of order. The *Protomedicus* was given authority over the employment of doctors and surgeons and the procurement of medicaments, while the *Commissariat* was ordered to confine itself to the role of economic supervision.

Van Swieten has been aptly described as 'one of those commanding, easygoing men with double chins, who combined unlimited intellectual vitality, natural authority, and great benevolence'.[21] He was a Catholic Dutchman, who had found it more rewarding to work and teach in the Austrian Netherlands than in his native land. He made a good impression on Kaunitz, who was employed in Brussels in 1744. and in the following year he was invited to Vienna and appointed as Maria Theresa's first personal physician. The Empress-Queen delivered the whole medical system of Austria into his hands and assured him of her full support.

In 1749 Van Swieten remade the medical faculty of the University of Vienna, and in 1750 he was able to persuade the *Hofkriegsrath* to admit to the army only such surgeons as had undergone a strict examination by the reformed university. The next year he established the principle that the orderlies (*Unter-Feldscher*) must submit to a test by the army medical authorities, and show that they were capable of working under only a modicum of supervision: 'nothing short of a proper knowledge of anatomy and physiology could recommend a man in the eyes of this great expert. It is thanks to him that the army has been rid of the former host of empirical quacks'.[22]

There were considerable murmurings in the army against the new system. Van Swieten explained that

> in the old days the officers used to repay their personal servants by having them made medical orderlies. At that time the medical faculty of the university was only too willing, in return for payment, to oblige any officer who asked for a certificate of competence. They never bothered to see or get to know the person concerned.[23]

Beneath the *Protomedicus* functioned the hand-picked *Stabs-Medici* and *Stabs-Chirurgen*, who were attached to headquarters and the main hospitals, and carried out complicated treatments or operations.

The post of regimental surgeon (*Feldscherer*; from 1752 *Regiments-Chirurg*) was first established in 1718. His was the chief responsibility for the care of the sick in the field and in garrison. He trained and supervised the company orderlies, he performed operations, and he dispensed medicaments from his medicine chest, which was carried on a pack horse.

Before the Brady and Van Swieten reforms the surgeons were very much a law unto themselves. They were in the habit of purloining medicines and selling them off, or at least using them in their private practice, and in 1749 the Field Service Regulations actually had to stipulate that they must remain with their regiments on campaign, since in former times 'very few of them stuck at their duties, but made off as it suited their whim, convenience or greed'.[24]

The orderlies were on an establishment of one per company. Van Swieten demanded that they 'must know how to draw blood, how to stick plasters, how to apply the ordinary bandages, and how to carry out easy operations like lancing abscesses, and other procedures of the kind'.[25]

In battle a fire of wood, straw, hay and leaves was kept up during the action, so that the column of smoke would indicate the position of the surgeons, orderlies, chaplains and transport carts in the rear. The lightly-wounded warriors were simply patched up and sent back to the fray. The more serious cases were helped to the dressing station by men who were specially told off for the purpose, and it was usually an offence for a soldier to step out of rank to help a wounded comrade. The stricken officers were carried by their servants or by the musicians.

The wounded and sick were piled with their muskets and cartridge pouches on to fodder or bread waggons, and transported to the rear in batches of about two hundred men at a time. The hospitals were divided into three categories, according to a regulation which dated back to 1738. The regimental reception centres were established by the surgeons in suitable buildings or improvised huts of logs and thatch. When the regimental hospitals could not cope, the overflow was distributed among the several *Filial-Spitäler*, or deposited in the large single *Feld-Spital*, which the *Protomedicus* sited in a secure town well to the rear. Every hospital normally stood under the command of a detached lieutenant or captain, and the regiments sent reliable old soldiers to work as orderlies.

Joseph II went into the question of hospitals in some detail, and complained in 1776 that they were all too often sited in old and ruinous buildings. 'In Prague, among other shortcomings, the rain and snow fall on the heads of the sick, and there is one of the houses which is about to collapse at any moment.'[26] All too often the surgeons had to draw the little curtain at the foot of the bed which signified that the occupant was about to die: 'Here is the battlefield where more men perish than in action'.[27]

With these reservations, the lot of the sick or wounded man was generally considered to be better in the Austrian service than in almost any other. Here at least there were responsible officers to look after his welfare, and his health was in the hands of surgeons and orderlies who were chosen with care.

The teachings of Austrian medical men were founded on good observations, even if the deductions and cures now seem somewhat odd.[28]

The cure of souls

In the Austrian service the chaplain (*Caplan* or *Regiments-Pater*) not only played a prominent part in regimental ceremonies, but exercised a considerable moral authority over officer and man alike.

All the Catholic members of the regiment heard mass on Sundays and the frequent feast days of eighteenth-century Austria, and the regulations laid down with great elaboration the ways in which due honour was to be paid to the Sacrament as it was carried in its monstrance through the ranks. As part of his day-to-day duties the chaplain visited the sick and wounded, and gave a basic education to the children of the regiment. Most of the chaplains were chosen from the religious orders, though once they arrived with the army they came under the authority of the field bishop (*Pater Superior*).

Protestants, devotees of the Greek Orthodox faith and other people of that kind were permitted the free exercise of their religion, provided they were not too noisy about it. The infantry regulations of 1769 sensibly remarked:

> Religion is something you should never speak about. Rather it is something you should strive to live by. Upon pain of severe and unfailing punishment we forbid any behaviour which may create ill-feeling between those of different faiths.[29]

Music

Nowadays it is difficult to appreciate that the rather splendidly apparelled regimental musicians of the eighteenth century performed one of the essential functions of the wireless operator of today – to transmit orders. Under the authority of the fearsome *Regiments-Tambour* every company of infantry owned two drummers and two fifers. In combat they were either arrayed behind the regiment or assigned in *Spiele* of one drummer and one fifer at a time to stand by the colours. Their counterparts in the cavalry were the trumpeters and kettle-drummers. Their instruments were hung about with tassels and embroidered cloths, and they themselves sported sumptuous coats with stripes and edges of gold. The cavalry musicians in general were renowned for their disorderly way of life, and the kettle-drummers in particular were virtually useless in battle, since they lost control of their horses as soon as they took up the drumsticks. It was probably for this reason that the kettle-drum was abolished some time after the Seven Years War.

Music of a softer and more beguiling kind emanated from the 'chapels' of woodwind which were maintained by *Inhabers* of wealth and good taste. There were mostly formed of civilian musicians, who played airs from the operas with the same expertise as military marches. It is recorded that the woodwind of the regiment of Daun became so popular in Vienna that when the troops marched off to war in 1756 the citizens petitioned for the *Hautboisten-Banda* to stay behind. The musicians of the Austrian artillery enjoyed a particularly high reputation, and the best performers of all probably hailed from the huge Orphanage in Vienna, which Father Ignaz Parhamer ran on military lines. Whole battles were represented by his hundreds of perfectly-drilled charges, and on at least one occasion Parhamer combed the district and put thousands of children on parade. Some contemporaries harboured reservations about the enterprise, and at the present time we find something peculiarly chilling about Parhamer's youthful army, with its colours, drums and patriotic enthusiasm.

Very rarely has the enjoyment of good music been so widespread as it was in the Theresian empire. In camp, when the *Tambours* and *Hautboisten* had fallen silent, the German and Bohemian troops would strike up their part songs and hold the listener spellbound for hours on end.

11

The Control of the Army

The army staff

The Austrians entered the Seven Years War splendidly equipped in every respect save for the means of managing their army. The French officer Montazet noted that the troops were good, especially the infantry,

> but there are hardly any proficient senior officers, there is no general staff and there is no kind of order. In other words the machine moves out of sheer habit . . . the execution of a combined plan becomes virtually impossible, since it is difficult to find functionaries who can carry it out.[1]

The work of what we would now call the chief of staff fell upon the oddly-named *Generalquartiermeister*, who had no direct concern with stores, but was mainly responsible for planning the movements of the army. General Peter Franz Guasco was the last man to hold this post in its unreformed state. He complained that the conditions of his job fell very far short of what was needed to 'inspire any ambition in the other officers to take it on, or to lend it the prestige which it enjoys in almost all foreign armies'.[2] In fact Guasco did little except fuss around camp sites, planting sticks to mark out the lines. The army still moved in a single mass down a single road, with the baggage strung out for miles behind.

The first campaigns of the Seven Years War displayed the defects of the system all too clearly. Daun accordingly gained Maria Theresa's consent to set up a proper general staff, and he chose as the head his gifted young protégé Franz Moritz Lacy. On 20 February 1758 Lacy was simultaneously promoted lieutenant-general and appointed *Generalquartiermeister*. Lacy got down to work immediately. He assembled the personnel for the new staff in little more than a month, and over the course of the year he trained the officers in their tasks and assembled contingents of 'staff' infantry, dragoons, *Jägers* and pioneers which stood at the immediate disposal of headquarters.

The *Generalquartiermeister* was now in a position to exercise a decisive influence on operations. Lacy demanded that every holder of this post must have a command of the details of the service, as well as a mastery of cartography, a ready eye for terrain and a facility for taking quick decisions. One or two major-generals functioned as the chief assistants of the *Generalquartiermeister*, and under their authority a staff of colonels, lieutenant-colonels, majors and captains helped the commander-in-chief and the other generals to run their commands, and more particularly to direct the marches and the planting of camps.

In peacetime the *Generalquartiermeister*'s staff was perpetuated in cadre form. The personnel were chiefly concerned with compiling maps and topographical and statistical surveys of the likely theatres of war. As happened in earlier times, the *Generalquartiermeister* was forced, whenever war approached, to collect the rest of his staff in some haste:

> The colonels are asked if they have any officers who know how to draw and have some command of geometry. The colonels take the opportunity to recommend the officers they want to get rid of, or the ones they wish to favour, boldly proclaiming that they own all the necessary qualifications. The first pistol shot of the war rings out, and the officers are reduced to confusion.[3]

The staff troops were an inspiration of Lacy's. They comprised two regiments of infantry (mostly composed of weedy recruits), one of dragoons, and a pioneer battalion with attached *Jägers*. The infantry and dragoons wore a Prussian-looking uniform of blue, while the pioneers and *Jägers* were clad in the inconspicuous and serviceable *Hechtgrau*.

These troops saw to a number of essential and specialised tasks, which up to now had been performed rather badly by men detached from the regiments of the line. Around headquarters the staff infantry provided guards for the generals, the staff and the places of detention. The dragoons helped in the same work, but also roamed afield and furnished escorts for convoys, reconnaissance parties and the like. The *Jägers* were fit and agile foresters and mountaineers, who were constantly up with the advance guard and threw out the screens behind which the pioneers could make their bridges and the staff could stake out their camps. The staff troops were disbanded after the Seven Years War, but revived for the War of the Bavarian Succession.

Most of the remaining personnel at headquarters were the counterparts of the regimental staff. The regimental chaplain here became the *Pater Superior*, the surgeon became the *Stabs-Medicus*, the *Auditor* became the *Auditor-General* and the *Wagenmeister* became the *Ober-Stabs-Wagenmeister*, while the *Profoss* was inflated into the *General-Gewaltiger* and kept the entire army in awe of his displeasure.

There was no regimental counterpart of the *Ober-Wegmeister* (or *Capitaine des Guides*). 'His responsibility is to keep up the recruiting of good and reliable guides, who have an accurate knowledge of the ground over which the war is being fought'.[4] It was seldom difficult for the *Ober-Wegmeister* or commanding general to gain passable information, for Maria Theresa retained many sympathisers among the townspeople and clergy of the lost province of Silesia, while the heavy-handed ways of Frederick won over most of the peasants to the milder manners of the Austrians. However, the Austrians had nothing to compare with the sinister network of informants, traitors and agents which Old Fritz habitually spun in the lands of his enemies.

The generals' staffs

Every general had a little military family to help him in the work of running his command. Once Lacy had expanded the army staff he was in a position to allot an establishment of senior *General-Adjutanten* and *Flügel-Adjutanten* to every commanding general. The *General-Adjutanten* were chosen from among the cleverer colonels or lieutenant-colonels. The first *General-Adjutant* was responsible for 'the detailed business of the whole army'.[5] He and his fellows kept up reports, tables, orders of battle, and a *Haupt-Protocoll* which enumerated all the orders and allocations of duties. No less importantly he acted as the main channel of communication between his commanding general and the adjutants of the subordinate generals. Much of the

less glamorous work was handed over to the lesser *Flügel-Adjutanten*. These were majors and captains who likewise hailed from the staff of the *Generalquartiermeister*.

Every general was surrounded by a bevy of chattering junior adjutants and ADCs. The *Generalsreglement* of 1769 sought to bring some order to the old custom by allocating just one captain to a full general, a first lieutenant to a lieutenant-general, and a second-lieutenant to a major-general. All the same, the rest of the army was still inclined to dismiss the young officers as members of a household rather than military functionaries.

Outside the hierarchy of adjutants the commander of the field army maintained a *Feld-Kriegs-Kanzlei* of a secretary and anything up to a dozen clerks, who lent him some assistance with the mass of incoming and outgoing paperwork. Unfortunately it seemed that every military reform and change of precedure involved more and more clerking. Early in the Seven Years War, for instance, it became the practice for the commander of the main field army to write frequent reports in person to their Imperial Majesties. In 1760 a captured Austrian officer informed his hosts that

> our Field-Marshal Daun is a great and brave commander, but the Prussian army benefits greatly from the fact that he spends so much time composing his official reports to Vienna and keeping up his field journal. He wakes up early, and his first task in the morning is usually to dictate from his bed or read over the descriptions of what happened the day before. We should prefer him to act like General Loudon. He is a lively kind of person, who prefers the saddle to the

writing desk, and it has never taken him long to plan and execute all sorts of fine schemes.[6]

Once an operational army embarked on campaign it established a *Feld-Post* to secure a reasonably rapid circulation of correspondence with Vienna. This normally comprised two or more postmasters and several couriers and postillions. Specially urgent messages were carried by hand of officer. The Prince de Ligne recalls how he was once detached by General O'Donnell for this purpose:

> The letter was for Emperor Francis Stephen, and I was so afraid of losing it that I sewed it up in my waistcoat. I arrived and addressed the Emperor. He asked me for the letter, but in return I had to ask him for a pair of scissors. 'What a commotion!' he remarked. When I told him why, he set to work on my pocket, he was so anxious to read the letter. He unpicked the document, but it had become heavily scented by an aromatic smudge and I think also a scrap of perfumed leather. He threw it away, picked it up like a dead cat, and dropped it once more. Thereupon he sent for some vinegar and fumigated the letter. He cursed me to the devil, but then forgave me'.[7]

Councils of war

The only good reason for calling together a council of war was the one attributed to Prince Eugene of Savoy, namely that he wanted somebody to back him up when he had already decided not to fight. The institution certainly favoured negative influences. In any given council the majority of the generals would usually oppose any decisive action, and so dampen the enthusiasm of a lively commander-in-chief. Conversely, on the few occasions when a council was in a bellicose mood, its intentions could still be overruled by a cautious leader, as Prince Charles of Lorraine proved before the battle of Prague in 1757.

Unfortunately the summoning of councils of war became only too fashionable in the Seven Years War, when Daun proved unwilling to shoulder personal responsibility. The habit was sanctified in the *Generalsreglement* of 1769, which required the commander to call his generals together when, for example, he got wind that the enemy were about to attack.

12

Military Operations

Camps

In the eighteenth century the armies committed themselves to open battle at the most on only three or four occasions in a given campaign. They spent the rest of the season in camp, or in progressing in elaborate fashion from one camp site to the next.

The choice of the ground was the responsibility of the *Generalquartiermeister*. He rode ahead of the army with a small escort, prospecting for a strong site which had good access to supplies of wood, water and straw. Lacy wrote:

> The best cover for the front of a camp is provided by rivers, marshes, ravines and sunken roads. Villages are also suitable, as long as they are furnished with tenable houses, churchyards, and other features of the kind. . . . Now we come to the security of the flanks. The best support is offered by ponds or streams, provided they are impassable on foot and horseback. There is also a lot to be said for treeless hills, which dominate the ground to the flanks and are broken up by ravines. There is also some advantage to be had from leaning the flank on a wood, but there are also many dangers to be considered, and unless you take certain precautions such a camp site is undesirable.[1]

In this comment about the woods, Lacy had in mind the difficulty of seeing enemy formations and movements through the trees, as happened at Kunersdorf and Torgau.

The camps were positioned if possible on high ground, which commanded a wide view without itself being overlooked by neighbouring heights. It was only common prudence to sound out fall-back positions, and 'you must take as much account of the rear of the camp, with respect to freedom of movement and the ability to retreat, as you do to guarding and obstructing the approaches. This is the fundamental rule for all positions'.[2]

Once they found a site that pleased them, the *Generalquartiermeister* and his staff did some quick measurements and sums, and staked out the positions of the army, regiment by regiment. As the army entered the camp, so the regimental quarter-masters led the units to their assigned places. The soldiers unloaded their linen ridge tents from the carts or mules, and pitched them in sets of double streets by companies or squadrons. The frontage of the regiment amounted to about 450 paces. The standards or colours were planted with escorts at the forward ends of the streets, and along the sides the muskets or carbines were stacked in prettily painted wooden racks (*Gewehrschranken*). This practice compelled the soldiers to carry the weapons to the shelter of their tents whenever rain threatened. Parties now streamed out from the regiments to draw water, cut wood, and collect fodder from the fields or the magazines. The command, administration and security of the camps were conducted on the same principles as in the contemporary Prussian army.[3]

When the time came to take up winter quarters the army was dispersed among villages and towns well to the rear. The *Cantonnirungs Quartieren* offered an intermediate stage between the field camps and winter quarters proper, and they were sited in localities close to the theatre of war.

Marches

Frederick became skilled in reading the signs that told him that the Austrians were about to bestir themselves from their inactivity:

> . . . at these times they cook more than usual. Such is their invariable habit, for they never march before the soldiers have eaten. It is easy to learn if they intend to take up a camp, for they reconnoitre the site well in advance and make no attempt at concealment. If, on the other hand, they feel energetic and want to attack you, you can divine their purpose from their habit of pulling back their light troops.[4]

On the day before the intended march the *Generalquartiermeister* worked out his *Marschzettel* – a document which specified the hour of departure, the routes to be followed, and the number and composition of the columns.

The advance was spearheaded by patrols of light cavalry. Then came the detachments which were told off to occupy the villages on the way, together with the *Generalquartiermeister* and the men who were going to stake out the next camp. An all-arms advance guard followed next, and last of all came the main army with the baggage, stragglers and women in the rear. Additional detachments guarded the flanks and rear if the enemy were anywhere in the neighbourhood. Generally speaking, in the earlier campaigns of the reign the army marched by lines in a compact block, very much in the formation in which it gave battle. A more flexible formation was preferred in later times, after the Austrians became more clever at moving masses of men. The *Generals-Reglement* of 1769 states that 'it greatly promotes the progress of the army if you can break it up and make it march in several columns'.[5] The artillery and baggage were assigned to the best road, but the rest of the army frequently marched across country in columns as wide as the terrain would permit.

Very early on the morning of the appointed day the drums beat *Vergatterung*, summoning the column commanders and the officers of the *Generalquartiermeister*'s department to a final conference. Half an hour was allowed for packing up the tents and forming the regiments into column,

> then the march must get under way immediately after morning prayers. You must always strive to make an early start from the old camp, so as to be able to enter the new one as soon as possible. This is especially important in the summer, in order to avoid the heat'.[6]

On the march the men were allowed to 'take off their stocks and tie them around their arms, and likewise they are permitted to hang their swords over their shoulders and undo some buttons of their waistcoats'.[7] On forced marches, however, the soldier had to 'put up with being directed through water and boggy patches, even when he could have passed dryshod by taking a path around the side. The progress of the army does not permit such conveniences. The only thing that matters is the speed of the march'.[8]

The soldiers were kept under close watch when they passed through woods or villages, lest anybody should take it into his head to slip away. For the same reason the filling of the water flasks was usually entrusted to corporals and a few reliable men.

The ordinary unforced march was a leisurely affair, which allowed the bakers to prepare their bread and the commanding general to collect his wits. This involved a complete rest on every third or fourth day of the march, and an average daily progress of something like six or eight miles. Troops were driven harder if they belonged to a corps which embarked on some particularly exciting enterprise. Hadik covered fifteen miles a day on his raid on Berlin 1757, while Lacy clocked up more than twenty on his 200-mile return trip to the same place in 1760.

Battle

Most Austrian commanders regarded open battle as a mighty and fearsome undertaking, which they embraced only after every rational alternative had failed. Even when they had steeled themselves to launch an offensive the Austrians still liked to take their time about things. Thus the elaborate preparations before the attacks at Soor and Hochkirch stand in marked contrast to the impetuous ways of Frederick, who was in the habit of hurling himself at the foe with the minimum of ceremony. Once they were on the move the Austrians groped forward with some circumspection – so circumspectly indeed, that some of the forces (and at Liegnitz an entire army) were liable to fall short of the objective altogether.

The Austrians were famous for their skill in defensive warfare. In the first place it was difficult to force them to fight a battle at all, as Frederick found out. He wrote in 1768:

> One must expect to be reduced to waging a war of outposts against the Austrians. This is because the superiority of our cavalry and the mobility of our infantry compels them to forsake the open plains. Moreover the terrain of Bohemia and Moravia and the Saxon and Silesian frontiers offers them favourable ground for taking up the defensive.[9]

Frederick claims that when the Austrians offered fight, they did so only after they had arranged their forces in depth behind zones of obstacles: 'The first rule of their commanders is never to be forced into giving battle. Such is the foundation of their system.'[10]

This analysis should not pass entirely unchallenged. Looking at the major battles in our period, we find that on at least five occasions (Chotusitz, Soor, Breslau, Hochkirch and Liegnitz) the Austrians were actually on the attack. Otherwise their artistry lay in an eye for ground, rather than in accumulating artificial obstacles. In their defensive actions the Austrians either received the attack in very lightly fortified positions, or were drawn or driven to give battle away from their lines, as at Leuthen. The one important exception is offered by the great battle of Torgau in 1760, and even there the Austrians merely occupied a position which had been left behind by Prince Henry of Prussia.

As regards the order of battle, the Austrians usually fought in a conventional way, with their infantry in the centre and the cavalry on either wing. The first line of battle was made of an almost continuous wall of regiments and guns. Between 300 and 500 paces to the rear was positioned the second line – a weaker formation in which the regiments were disposed at intervals. The job of the second line was to fill whatever gaps appeared in the first line, and to provide a support upon which the shattered regiments could rest. A small knot of regiments formed a third line, or *corps de réserve*, which stood still further to the rear.

In these circumstances 'Austrian' battlecraft was often a question of the skill with which the commander could counter enemy moves by shuffling regiments and divisions sideways, or wheeling or reversing whole lines at a time, as at Piacenza, Lobositz, Kolin and Torgau. At Leuthen the calculations went disastrously wrong.

Before an action the generals and officers were expected to put on a cheerful and confident manner, and make light of the coming ordeal, 'which will make all the greater impression . . . if the officers are already on good terms with their men'.[11] The Prince de Ligne writes that he had

> always noticed something very peculiar during the halt that is usually made to draw up the regiments, and afford them some rest and give them their final orders. This is the sight of men relieving themselves along the greater length of the two lines of battle. They are then given a general absolution, which is not calculated to fortify them against this weakness of nature.[12]

The light troops of the rival sides were usually the first elements to make contact, which gave rise to a hot but irregular fire of small arms. Then it was the turn of the heavy artillery. 'Nowadays the beginning of a battle gives the impression of a tennis court when a basket of balls is overturned – the ground is covered with leaping and bounding shot.'[13]

The army advanced or stood for some time with flying colours and sounding music, but the host fell silent as soon as fresh orders rang out or the range closed to a few hundred paces. When they were on the attack the infantry marched with shouldered muskets, and only when they came within good musket shot did the first one or two ranks lower their weapons and open fire, aiming at the middles of the enemy soldiers.

During this time the cavalry on the wings were often stranded powerless under the fire of the enemy guns. It was largely left to the initiative of the cavalry commanders when to put in their attack, 'but this must be carried out not just with a part, but with the entire two lines of the wing'.[14]

After the decision was gained, the infantry were expected to restore themselves to order, while the cavalry were to assemble one or two squadrons from every regiment and send them in pursuit. In the event of a reverse, the army was supposed to remove itself from the scene in a calm, orderly and silent fashion, though 'on such occasions the cannon, colours, standards, drums and ammunition carts must be defended to the uttermost, and every possible effort must be put up to save them'.[15]

Most of the continental powers were fortunate in that they could expect to encounter 'civilised' enemies who fought in much the same way as they did themselves. The Austrians, however, always had to reckon on the possibility of a war with the undisciplined but powerful hosts of the Turks. The Habsburg army was
 trained and equipped accordingly. The cavalrymen had to know how to shoot, as

well as how to use their swords, and the arsenals held all sorts of antique gear – the infantry *Schweinsfeder*, for instance, or the cavalry helmets and backplates – which saw the light of day only in the event of a Turkish war. The army as a whole was trained in special techniques like forming squares with thousands of troops at a time, which would have been suicidal in Western warfare, but were a basic means of survival amid the lava-like flow of the Turkish hordes.

The art of war

The admirably clear and straightforward Field Service Regulations (*Feld Dienst Regulament*) of 1749 were one of the most useful products of the first age of reform, defining as they did the responsibilities of the various ranks of generals, and explaining the principles of supply, camps, transport, marches, discipline, the arrangement and conduct of forces in battle, the tactics of the three arms and the treatment of the wounded.

The more inventive of the generals were in the habit of working out regulations and exhortations of their own. Thus in the Seven Years War Daun was able to explain his intentions in greater detail in documents like the *Lagerordnung*, *Ordre de Bataille* and *General-Schlachtordnung* of 24 May 1757, and the *Militär Feld-Regulament* of 12 March 1759.

After the war the essentials of the 1749 regulations were reworked and considerably expanded in the *Generals-Reglement* of 1769. The commander-in-chief was now given greater freedom in arranging his orders of battle, regardless of the seniority of the component regiments and generals, and a proper channel was established for transmitting orders through the army.

All these documents were concerned with the routine mechanisms of managing an army in war – affairs like arranging a camp, or shuffling the regiments into column of march. Nowhere do we find a strategic overview, or a reasoned discussion of the whys and wherefores of tactics. To the fundamentally unbookish Austrians the higher reaches of generalship appeared as a personal and arcane art – part of the style of naturally great commanders, rather than a body of knowledge accessible to any field officer of application and understanding.

This was one of the reasons why nobody bothered to subsume the vast corpus of experience and observation into anything which approached a doctrine of war. The opportunities were certainly there. Before the opening of the campaign of 1757 Emperor Francis Stephen sent his brother Prince Charles some remarkably perceptive analyses of the Prussian way of war. The Emperor pointed out that the Prussian army was a vulnerable organism, for the ranks were filled up with pressed troops, and the men were liable to be run into the ground by Frederick's feints and forced marches. Francis Stephen suggested a number of means by which these circumstances could be turned to good account. Proceeding to battle tactics, he mentioned that Frederick was fond of holding back one wing in reserve, while concentrating his best troops on the other wing in a striking force. The Emperor indicated that the most effective countermeasure would be to get in a blow against the 'refused' wing.[16] Unfortunately these documents remained a private communication from one royal brother to another, and they were never circulated in the army at large.

It was the same story with the evaluation of Frederick's *General Principia vom Kriege*, a copy of which was taken by the Austrians in February 1760. Daun read the essay with some care, and penned a memorandum for the enlightenment of the immediate Imperial circle.

Daun greatly approved of what Frederick had to say about discipline, and only wished that 'our own officers and generals showed greater application on this point'. He also admired the sections concerning subsistence, the knowledge of terrain, *coup d'oeil*, the choice of positions and camps, and the conduct of marches and battles. On strategy, Daun expressed full agreement with Frederick's principle of the concentration of force: 'you cannot defend everything at once,' wrote Daun, 'and it is better to bear with a small disadvantage than expose yourself to such a great danger [of dispersal], which is the particular consequence of making large detachments'. All the same, Daun found it incautious of Frederick to have 'communicated the most secret matters to so many generals'.[17]

With these considerations in mind, it is tempting to conclude that we ought to be talking about individual 'Austrian generals' rather than an identifiable 'Austrian generalship'. Maria Theresa certainly had some commanders who were up to the most daring and unpredictable enterprises – Browne in one of his aggressive moods, Lacy in his days as chief of staff, and Loudon throughout almost all of his career. However, the popular impression seems to be the correct one, namely that the Theresian generals seem to have been more interested in outlasting the enemy than outfighting him. On the whole the Austrian commanders tended to shine in the choice of good positions, in the management of logistics and staff work (at least after Lacy's reforms of 1758), and in closing off the sources of the enemy's subsistence. This preservative strategy stood Austria in good stead in the 1740s, but it failed to answer Maria Theresa's needs in the Seven Years War, when she was committed to the positive objective of destroying Prussia's power.

What was lacking in most commanders was the killer instinct. In such a cosmopolitan 'nation' it is curious to find commentators writing so consistently about 'something phlegmatic in the constitution of the inhabitants, physical and intellectual, which is adverse to strong emotions.[18] . . . The Austrians are equally skilful in the arts of war and peace, though they are more naturally inclined to the latter, thanks to their docile and easy-going temperament. Hence they find it difficult to remain angry for long'.[19] It was the Austrian in Daun which made him take issue with certain passages in Frederick's maxims on the art of war. He shrank from the cruelty involved in Frederick's methods of exacting information and fodder from the peasants, and he claimed that the king had

> often given battle without good reason. My opinion is that you should offer battle [only] when you find that the advantage you gain from a victory will be greater, in proportion, than the damage you will sustain if you retreat or are beaten.[20]

Nothing could be feebler than the section of the 1769 *Generals-Reglement* dealing with the conclusion of a successful battle, where the victorious commander is merely told to see the enemy out of sight, and then make sure that the plunder is divided in an orderly fashion. Altogether most Austrian officers would have been inclined to agree with the cavalryman who wrote in 1756 that in combat it was a question of 'driving away the unrighteous enemy, not of exterminating the human race'.[21]

13

Maria Theresa's Army and the Test of War

The state of the army in 1740

The Emperor Charles VI died on 20 October 1740, and his 23-year-old daughter Maria Theresa came into possession of the vast ramshackle Habsburg dominions. She inherited an army which bore less resemblance to a fighting force than to some horrid object that was preserved as a lesson in every ill capable of infecting a military organism.

As early as 1734 Prince Eugene of Savoy had complained to the Emperor concerning the damaging effects of a long peace, during which 'many disorders and abuses have crept in among the regiments, and many officers have forgotten part of their duties'.[1] Eugene's own powers were already sadly decayed, and he died in 1736, leaving the monarchy with no effective guidance in the series of disastrous wars which closed the old Emperor's reign. The Kingdom of the Two Sicilies was overrun by the Bourbon Spanish army in 1735, and four years later Serbia and the city of Belgrade were lost to the Turks. The 'disorders and abuses' remained as bad as ever.

The field-marshals Wallis, Neipperg and Seckendorff were disgraced and imprisoned, for their share in the débâcle, and the demoralisation of the officer corps was amply demonstrated in the first years of the new reign, when several generals took themselves off to foreign armies. The case of Carl zu Wied was typical. He deserted to the Prussians in 1742, and tried to justify his action to his brother in a lengthy apologia. He had already been stricken by a feverish melancholy in the war in Hungary, which was 'the graveyard of the Germans', and he went on to enumerate the ruin or miserable deaths of commanders like Caraffa, Wirich Daun, Seckendorff, Wurmbrand, Doxat, Wallis and Neipperg.

> [But] the worst of all is that promotion does not proceed according to merit. An extremely brave man will actually be at a disadvantage, if he has enemies, whereas a coward who has friends at court will be advanced over the head of a hero. It is just the same within the regiments.[2]

As for the Austrian private soldier, he returned from the Turkish wars in a battered state, and 'brought with him nothing but wounds, booty and laurels – things which do not appeal to well-mannered ladies'.[3] Instead of the full establishment of 160,000 troops the army had been reduced by its ordeals to about 108,000 effectives, and these survivors were dispersed in penny packets from the Netherlands to Transylvania, and from Silesia to Tuscany. In terms of units the army comprised 52 regiments of infantry, 18 of cuirassiers, 14 of dragoons and 8 of hussars.

Comradeship, discipline and training inevitably suffered, and there were no generally-accepted practices or regulations which might have helped to restore cohesion. In later years Maria Theresa made a famous declaration on the subject:

> You would scarcely believe it, but not the slightest attempt had been made to establish uniformity among our troops. Each regiment went about marching, drilling and taking alarm stations in its own fashion. One unit would close formation by a rapid movement, and the next by a slow one. The same words and orders were expressed by the regiments in quite different manners. Can you wonder that the Imperialists were invariably beaten in the ten years before my accession? As for the state in which I found the army, I cannot begin to describe it.[4]

The Prussian challenge

On 16 December 1740, in one of the truly decisive moments of history, the young king Frederick II of Prussia led his blue-coated army into the remote northern Habsburg province of Silesia. Nowadays we can appreciate that the Prussian invasion of 1740 began the process which was to swing the balance of armed strength away from western and southern Europe to Prussia, and ultimately to a Prussianised Germany. But, even in the shorter term, Habsburg Austria and other powers of Europe were compelled to put themselves into some kind of order and sharpen their teeth so as to be able to survive in this dangerous new world.

Nothing could have been more alien to Austrian habits than the strenuous mode of life of the Prussian squirearchy. This was a class of tough, small-time landowners, who were bred up on barren and windswept estates, and were penetrated with an instinct of unquestioning obedience to their Hohenzollern rulers. For almost three-quarters of a century, however, the Austrians had become accustomed to the support of these austere northern neighbours against hereditary enemies like the Swedes and the French, and (for all his grumblings) no sovereign of Germany had given more unselfish aid to the Emperor than the last king of Prussia, Frederick William I.

The old king's son, Crown Prince Frederick, came to the throne of Prussia on 31 May 1740. Here was a creature of quite different stamp. His humanity had been blighted by some appalling experiences in his earlier years, he was free from the constraints of religion, and he had seen the Austrian army in action in the 1730s and despised what he saw.

These circumstances conspired to present Frederick's aggression in a peculiarly shocking light. A Prussian officer testifies:

> The usual hate between belligerent nations attained an extraordinary pitch between the Austrians and the Prussians . . . And it was the Austrians, being so ignorant and still so far behind in enlightenment, who excelled in this national animosity. According to their political notions Frederick's war was a culpable rebellion against Emperor and Empire, and their religious delusions led them to believe that they were fighting heretics, who deserved to be stamped out.[5]

The Austrian military men were at first amused by the immaculate drill and turnout of the 'powdered army' of the Prussians, and they prided themselves on the fact that the Austrian soldier had been trained 'on the battlefield rather than the drill square'.[6] The Austrians had no inkling that all their manifold experience of war against the French, Spanish and Turks left them peculiarly unprepared for the coming encounter with the Prussians. 'What matters is not how long a nation has been at war, but *against whom* it has been fighting.'[7]

Silesia, the object of Frederick's ambitions, was stranded beyond the mountains of the Bohemian and Moravian borders, and both racially and strategically it belonged to northern Europe (it now forms part of Poland). The province was virtually untenable. The fortifications of the towns were in advanced decay, and the river Oder offered the Prussians a natural highway up the centre of the land. Frederick launched his 26,000 troops in a double-pronged offensive – one directly up the Oder, and another which curled to the south and rejoined the first prong at Neisse in Upper Silesia.

The Austrians had just 6,000 troops with which to meet the attack. The local commander, Lieutenant-General Browne, tried in vain to awaken the authorities in Vienna to the urgency of the situation, and by the end of the year his little force had been driven back to the snowy mountains of Moravia.

Only now did the Austrians bestir themselves into some kind of activity. Fifteen thousand troops were assembled in northern Moravia in the early spring of 1741, and the command of this improvised army was entrusted to the ill-fated Field-Marshal Neipperg. This gentleman enjoyed a certain reputation for his witty and biting repartee, but he had been heavily implicated in the military and political disasters of the last Turkish war, and he had only recently emerged from prison – an experience which was hardly calculated to bolster his confidence. There were those who alleged that he owed his command to the influence of his old pupil Francis Stephen of Lorraine, who wanted to give him a chance to rebuild his battered reputation.

The first appearance of Neipperg's little army in Silesia caught the Prussians off their guard, but the Austrian troops were so exhausted by their march that the field-marshal was content to establish contact with the fortress of Brieg, where there was an Austrian garrison, and he encamped his regiments around the village of Mollwitz. The trouble was that 'almost the entire infantry was made up of recruits, peasants and other poor material. On top of that most of them had reached their regiments only a matter of days before they took the field'.[8] Thus the Prussians were able to regain the initiative, and Frederick gathered 19,000 men to throw at the intruders.

The Austrians were still at their ease when, on the late morning of 10 April 1741, columns of Prussian troops were seen to be uncoiling over the snowy fields. Lieutenant-General Carl Römer appreciated at once what had to be done, and he deployed six regiments of cavalry so as to screen the rest of the army while it was sorting itself out. By this enterprising act he drew on himself the attention of the Prussian artillery. Nothing was more galling to cavalry than to stand inactive under fire, and Römer cut the misery short by hurling his command against the right wing of the Prussian cavalry. The enemy horsemen soon proved to be gratifyingly inferior:

> They fought at a stand, and so they got the worse of every clash. The extraordinary size of their horses did them no good at all – our cavalrymen always directed their first sword cut at the head of the enemy horse; the horse fell, throwing its rider to the ground, and he would then be attacked from behind. The Prussian troopers have iron crosses set inside their hats. These were splintered by our swords, which made the cuts more deadly still. I might add that we had been ordered to sharpen most of our swords before the action, and now their edges looked like saws.[9]

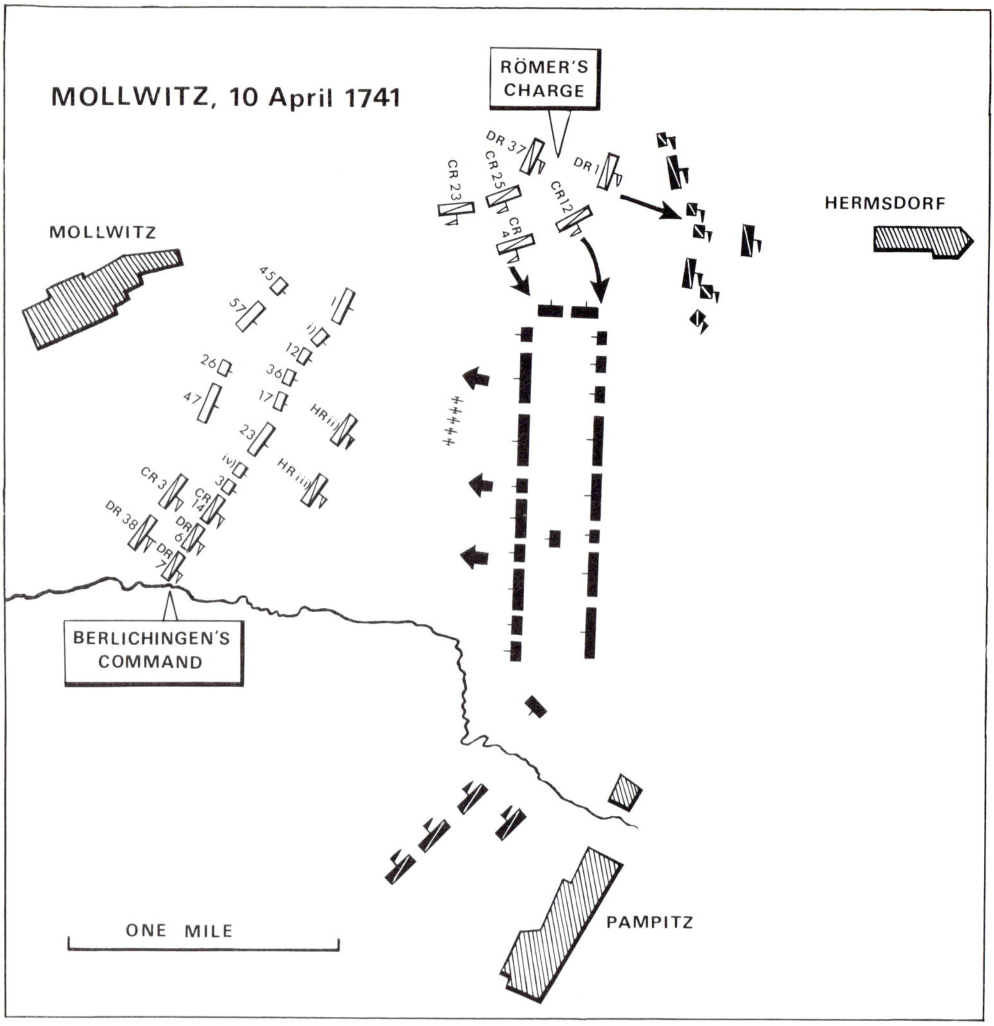

KEY TO THE BATTLE MAPS

AUSTRIAN INFANTRY REGIMENT
AUSTRIAN BATTALION
AUSTRIAN CAVALRY REGIMENT

AUSTRIAN REGIMENTS ARE IDENTIFIED BY NUMBER
(See list of Regiments in the appendix)

3 — 3 INFANTRY REGIMENT
CR 6 — 6 CUIRASSIER REGIMENT
DR 19 — 19 DRAGOON REGIMENT
HR 30 — 30 HUSSAR REGIMENT

ALLIED INFANTRY REGIMENT
ALLIED BATTALION
ALLIED CAVALRY REGIMENT

ENEMY INFANTRY REGIMENT
ENEMY BATTALION
ENEMY CAVALRY REGIMENT

Heights are given in metres

The Austrian cavalrymen now began to erode the exposed right flank of the Prussian infantry, which persuaded young King Frederick to remove himself from the field with some speed.

Unfortunately Römer was dropped by a pistol shot from a Prussian dragoon, and there was nobody to stop the Prussian infantry as it bore down on the main Austrian army with frightening composure and precision. Now it was the turn of the whitecoats to suffer. Neipperg admitted afterwards that

> the Prussian infantry kept up a really hellish fire. He had seen nothing like it in all his campaigns, for they got off five rounds before the Austrians fired so much as two. He therefore ordered the men to let the balls roll down the barrels without ramming. But this meant that the force of the shots was so feeble that after the battle the bullets were cut out of the Prussian wounded without any danger.[10]

In this respect it is worth recalling that the Austrian infantry were still equipped with beechwood ramrods, which snapped much more easily than the sturdy iron ramrods of the Prussians.

> The cavalry of the Austrian right at last began to move, but since the infantry refused to advance, our cavalry became so disheartened that it could in no way be persuaded to attack, even though General Berlichingen tried to inspire them through his personal example. He spurred to within twenty paces of the enemy, he exhorted, he threatened, all without any effect. He became so angry that he split the heads of two cavalrymen who were riding away, and he cut several others down from their horses. Things went from bad to worse. . . . Our infantry kept up a continuous fire, but could not be made to advance a step. The battalions sank into disorder, and it was pathetic to see how the poor recruits tried to hide behind one another, so that the battalions ended up thirty or forty men deep, and the intervals became so great that whole regiments of cavalry could have penetrated between, even though the whole of the second line had been brought forward into the first.[11]

In the evening Neipperg drew his army from the field, having lost more than 4,500 officers and men and most of his artillery.

It took something like fifteen years for the Austrian army to recover from the blow which the Prussians had dealt to its confidence at Mollwitz. In immediate strategic terms, however, the action decided very little, for the Austrians lingered throughout the summer in southern Silesia, and Frederick was not at all inclined to trust his luck to a second battle. Finally on 9 October 1741 Neipperg, as plenipotentiary, made a deal with Frederick at Klein-Schnellendorf by which that monarch annexed Lower Silesia and quartered his troops in Upper Silesia. In return Frederick gave his gracious consent for the Austrian army to march away undisturbed.

The crisis of the Austrian monarchy, 1741–2

The reason why the Austrians struck such a bad bargain at Klein-Schnellendorf was that developments in the west were threatening the monarchy with dissolution.

In the months following Maria Theresa's accession the kings of France and Spain and the electors of Bavaria, Saxony, Cologne and the Palatinate all lodged direct or indirect claims to Habsburg territory, thus denying the basis of the Pragmatic Sanction of 1713, the document by which the old Emperor had sought to preserve the unity of his family possessions. Hostilities broke out in September 1741, when 50,000 Bavarians and French moved into Upper Austria. The Saxon army and a further corps of French at the same time made ready to invade Bohemia.

Many of Maria Theresa's servants and nobles began to reckon on a transfer of power to one or more of the hostile sovereigns. The mood was one of calm acceptance – a far more dangerous state of mind than outright panic – and only a small knot of her more obstinate counsellors were at hand to lend Maria Theresa the support she craved. Prominent among these were the ministers Bartenstein and Starhemberg, the elderly Hungarian *Judex Curiae* Field-Marshal Johann Pálffy, and that splendid old war horse Field-Marshal Andreas Khevenhüller, who survived into the 1740s as a living embodiment of past glories. He was a grandson of the great Montecuccoli, and he had been born in 1683, the year when Vienna was saved from the Turks.

With Austria and Bohemia in imminent danger of being overrun, Maria Theresa used the political and moral authority of Johann Pálffy to make an approach to her Hungarian nobles, whom she met in a formal assembly at Pressburg. The Hungarians proceeded to drive some hard and realistic bargains, which secured for Hungary a privileged position in the new reign. All the same, the assembly was memorable for the emotion-laden session on 11 September, when Maria Theresa appealed to the loyalty of the magnates in the hall of the royal castle, whereupon those gallant gentlemen drew their sabres and the chamber rang to the cry of *Vitam nostram et sanguinem consecramus!*

> It was the supplication of a young and beautiful woman in distress, who, as her last refuge, threw herself on the affections of a nation, that had experienced from her ancestors, and even from her immediate predecessors, the severest treatment.[12]

In the first enthusiasm there were people who believed that the Hungarians would raise as many as 100,000 men. In the event the permanent Hungarian contribution consisted of three new regiments of regular hussars and six new regiments of infantry, which were raised over a long period of time. Otherwise the only Hungarians to reach the field were the thousands of irregular 'Insurgents' who swarmed in plundering bands through Vienna in the early months of 1742.

Meanwhile the fate of the monarchy was being decided on the Danube and in Bohemia. While Khevenhüller made ready to defend Vienna with whatever troops could be spared from the north, the Bavarians saved him the trouble by turning aside from the Danube valley and pushing northwards into Bohemia. Charles Albert, the elector of Bavaria, was less interested in crushing Khevenhüller than in making sure that none of his 'friends' grabbed Bohemia for themselves. By 23 November 1741 an unholy mass of more than 65,000 Bavarians, French and Saxons was crowding about the decayed walls of the Bohemian capital of Prague. The garrison consisted of three battalions, mostly untrained recruits, and these were taken completely by surprise when the allies stormed into the city on the night of 25/26 November.

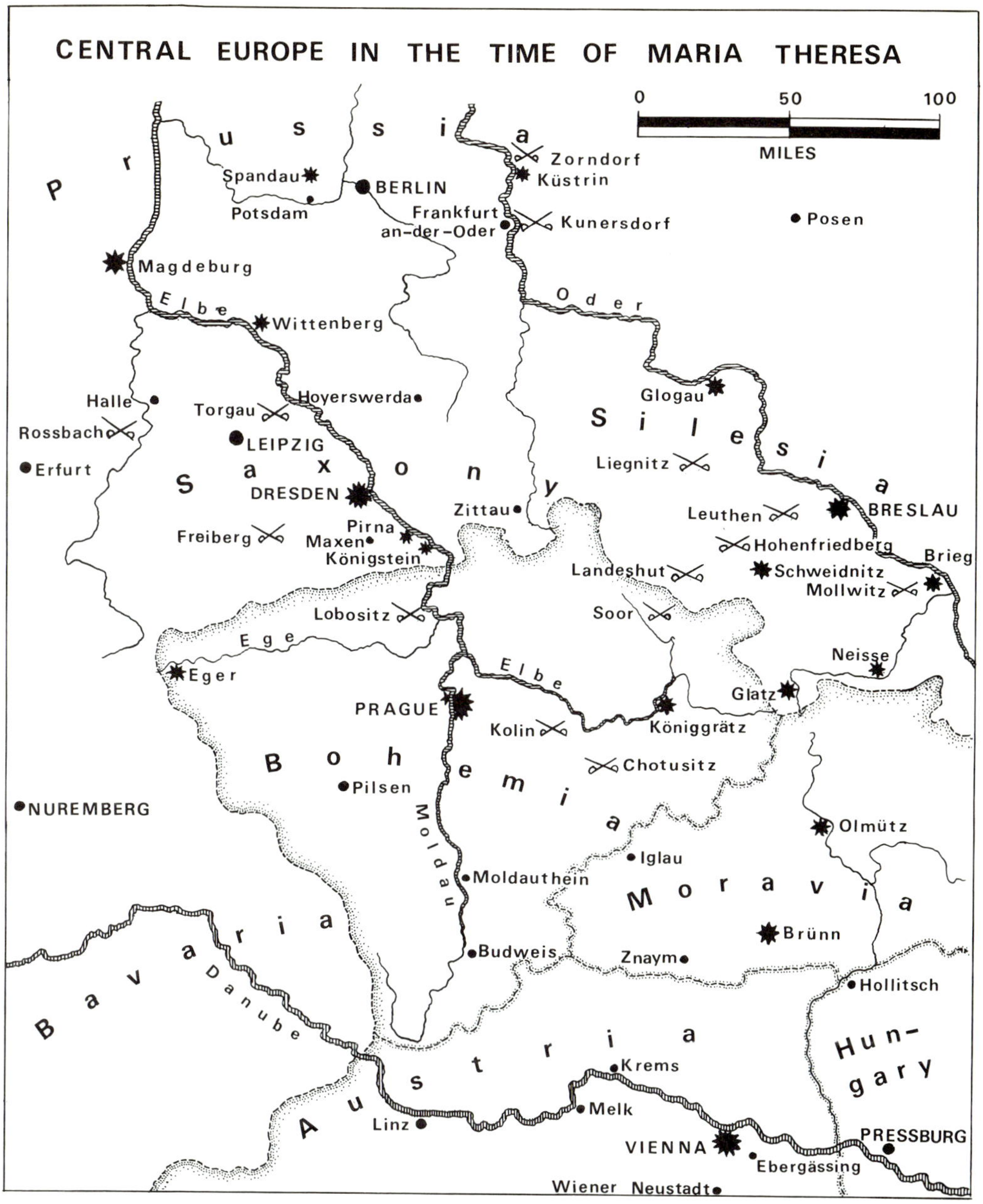

Maria Theresa conveyed her bitterness and determination in a celebrated letter to the Bohemian Chancellor, Philipp Kinsky:

> My mind is made up. We must put everything at stake in order to save Bohemia, and you must work and plan on this basis. Perhaps this will involve such destruction as will not be repaired in twenty years, but I must have land·and soil (*je veux avoir Grund und Boden*), and to this end I shall have all my armies, all my Hungarians killed off before I cede so much as an inch of ground.[13]

Revelling in his apparent good fortune, Chalres Albert had himself crowned King of Bohemia and elected Emperor of Germany. Maria Theresa, the heir of a huge empire, was now reduced to the authority of Archduchess of Austria and 'King' of Hungary.

Meanwhile Khevenhüller on the Danube was giving the first impetus to the counter-attack that was ultimately to take the Austrians far into western and southern Europe. The old field-marshal gathered together a scratch force, and on the last day of 1741 he took the offensive over the river Enns into Upper Austria. The Austrian hussars and free corps seemed to be unbeatable, and within less than two months Khevenhüller had cleared Upper Austria and conquered Bavaria up to the Isar.

The struggle for Bohemia, 1742

A long and singularly unpleasant chapter in Austrian military history opened towards the end of 1741, when Maria Theresa entrusted the gathering forces on the northern theatre to the command of her brother-in-law, Prince Charles of Lorraine. Charles had come to Vienna in 1736, on the occasion of the marriage of his elder brother Francis Stephen to Maria Theresa. He was reported to be 'an eminent, well built and handsome gentleman, almost a foot taller than his brother the Grand Duke'.[14] Charles further advanced his career when he married Marianne, the younger sister of Maria Theresa, thus making himself her brother-in-law twice over.

The heavy form and red face of Prince Charles came to be seen more and more in military circles, and he spoke loudly and convincingly on a wide range of subjects. It was only natural for Maria Theresa to entrust him with the high command, and take a sisterly interest in his progress. She advised him

> to send a report in German every second day for the benefit of the old men in our Court Chancellery. It's enough for you to sign some document telling of all the moves you are contemplating and something about the condition of the troops. I also urge you to report about insignificant things as well. This has created a favourable opinion of Khevenhüller here.[15]

No reasonable person could blame Prince Charles for the indecision he showed in the face of his first important and independent command. What was truly incomprehensible was the obstinacy with which he clung to power once his incapacity was revealed – a trait which compares unfavourably with the conduct of nineteenth-century incompetents like the Duke of Cambridge or the Union general Ambrose Burnside, who had the honesty to withdraw from field command as soon as they decently could. Charles remained impervious to every criticism.

> He was accused of spending a large part of every day at table, and of passing the evening in all kinds of excesses. There were some mornings when he was in no state to work, because he still had a heavy head from the debaucheries of the evening before. He put his trust in unworthy people, and in choosing his favourites he paid precious little attention to merit or military ability. He just wanted them to be 'lively lads' (a favourite expression of the prince), by which he understood gamblers, rogues, drunkards, debauchees, gluttons, buffoons and a fair ration of ponces.[16]

Charles embarked on his new career in the early winter of 1741, when he took over the former army of Field-Marshal Neipperg. The allies pounced on Prague

Prince Charles of Lorraine. Wearing field-marshal's uniform, and the cross of the Teutonic Order

before he could get to the scene, and early in December Charles marched his troops to winter quarters in southern Bohemia.

In spite of the unfavourable season the enemy began to show alarming signs of activity away on the eastern flank. First of all the Prussians planted winter quarters in northern Moravia, contrary to the terms of the Treaty of Klein-Schnellendorf. Then the Saxons and a corps of French moved into the area of the Bohemian-Moravian borders. Finally in February 1742 Frederick launched a full invasion of Moravia and reached out towards the Saxons and French. Having reached Znaym on the 19th, Frederick dispatched a small force of two battalions and 3,000 light cavalry which actually skirmished to within sight of the spires of Vienna. There were scenes of panic in the capital, for Prince Charles was away in Bohemia, and Khevenhüller was prosecuting his conquests on the upper Danube.

In fact the Prussian raid to the Danube was just an empty demonstration, for the allies were arguing among themselves, and their communications were endangered by the fortress of Brünn, where Maria Theresa's loyal Lutheran general Wilhelm Roth had a small but very active garrison. Frederick tamely pulled his main army out of Moravia and took up quarters in north-east Bohemia.

Despite all the urgings of Maria Theresa, Prince Charles did nothing positive until 17 May, when he tried to bring off a kind of 'Mollwitz' in reverse, by throwing his 29,000 men against the Prussians in their camp at Chotusitz. The affair began at eight in the morning. The left wing of the Austrian cavalry, after a first repulse, drove the opposing horse from the field and disappeared in enthusiastic pursuit. On the right flank the cavalry was still more successful, but the troopers gave themselves up to plundering the Prussian camp. The whole weight of the battle now rested upon the infantry and guns in the centre. The Austrians might still have carried the enemy position if Lieutenant-Colonel Livingstein had not had the bad idea of setting fire to Chotusitz village. The flames and smoke effectively disrupted the attack. Thus the Prussian left wing was able to hold its ground until Frederick brought the rest of the army to the scene. Now that his advantage was lost, Charles ordered his army to disengage at about noon.

This little battle (called 'Czaslau' by the Austrians, and 'Chotusitz' by the Prussians) cost Prince Charles over 6,000 men and one-third of his artillery. All the same, not a single colour or standard had fallen into the hands of the enemy. If the Austrians were wildly over-optimistic when they claimed the victory, they had at least put up a respectable performance, and certainly fought much better than at Mollwitz. It was here that Prince Liechtenstein conceived his ambition to remake the Austrian artillery, and that one of the lieutenant-generals, Leopold Daun, established a reputation for keeping his head under heavy fire.

It was plain that the Austrians could not cope with two such dangerous enemies as the Prussians and the French at the same time. On 11 June 1742 a new agreement, the Preliminaries of Breslau, bought off Frederick at the heavy price of allowing him to add most of Upper Silesia to the territory he had won the year before. This put an end to what is known as the 'First Silesian War'.

Now that they had their hands free, the Austrians could begin to think about turning the French from Bohemia. In the course of the summer Prince Charles slowly herded the French armies into Prague, then subjected the place to an appallingly mismanaged siege. He was forced to raise the siege in September, when a new French army irrupted into Bohemia from the west, and it became necessary to summon up Khevenhüller from the Danube with most of his troops.

The united army amounted to more than 50,000 men, and with this powerful force the Austrians were able to manoeuvre the new French army out of Bohemia and push down to the valley of the Danube, where they established winter quarters along the borders with Bavaria. Just 17,000 troops were left to keep up the blockade of the 'old' French army in Prague. The greater part of the French garrison broke out on the night of 16/17 December and made for Germany, where they arrived after appalling hardships. The rest capitulated on 26 December. Bohemia was now free of the French, except for some remnants in the Eger valley, and so the safety of the Austrian monarchy and its most important kingdom was assured.

The last campaigns against the Bourbons, 1743–8

GERMANY

Within the limits of our space, we can present only a summary treatment of the rest of the War of the Austrian Succession. This contrast represented the last episode in generations of strife between the houses of Habsburg and Bourbon, and it was fought according to the best rules of earlier eighteenth-century warfare.

The beginning of 1743 found Maria Theresa in a tigerish mood, resolved not just to punish the Bavarians, but to break the power of the French in Germany, reconquer Lorraine for the Empire and drive the Spaniards from Italy. There was a general resurgence of confidence, and the army sang:

> Vivat hoch die Kaiserinne
> Maria Theresia!
> Unser Feldzug so beginne,
> Dass sie hat Viktoria.

The cause of Maria Theresa had awakened sympathy in Britain, and in the early months of 1743 was set on foot the curious institution known as the Pragmatic Army, which was made up of British, Hanoverian and Austrian contingents and was intended to exclude French influence from the Empire. The mixed force scored a victory over a French army at Dettingen, on the river Main, on 27 June. The Pragmatic Army crossed to the west bank of the Rhine just below Mainz on 23 August, and advanced a short distance up-river before coming to a halt in front of some powerful French lines.

Meanwhile the main Austrian army had experienced little difficulty in clearing the enemy forces from Bavaria. When it came to moving into western Germany, however, Prince Charles was unwilling to subordinate himself to the command of the Pragmatic Army, and preferred to make a crossing of the Rhine further upstream. The attempt was made on 4 September, and ended in a muddled failure. A diarist put the blame on a certain general who 'dined with Prince Charles the day before. Having drunk too deeply he was unable to fulfil his duty in the passage of the river, which was fixed for later on the same night'.[17]

The Austrians remained in Germany for the next campaigning season, and finally effected their crossing of the Rhine at the beginning of July 1744. They began to make some progress on the far side, and after the fall of Lauterbourg Charles wrote exultantly to Francis Stephen: 'Now at last, my dear brother, we are in Alsace. I can scarcely convey to you how well our Hungarian regiments have behaved, both cavalry and infantry.'[18]

Then everything went wrong at once. The French began to move reinforcements down from the Netherlands, the natives proved disappointingly apathetic, and, worst of all, Frederick of Prussia made ready to renew the war in the east. News came on 20 August that the Prussians had actually invaded Bohemia, and four days later the Austrians had to recross the Rhine.

In the autumn and early winter all the available forces were concentrated against Prussia. The isolated Austrian enclave of Vorder-Österreich was abandoned to the French, and by the end of the year the enemy had reoccupied Bavaria.

In normal circumstances, however, it was not at all easy for the French to keep up a proper military presence in central Germany, and in March and April 1745 Field-Marshal Batthyány undertook a surprise offensive which conquered the unhappy land of Bavaria for the third time in the war. The Bavarians made a separate peace on 22 April, and since the last campaign against the Prussians had turned out unexpectedly well, the Austrians were able to take a sizeable contingent across Germany to join the Pragmatic Army on the Main. Francis Stephen arrived on 6 July to take up the nominal command, for the 'Bavarian' Emperor Charles Albert had died early in the year, and the Pragmatic alliance was inspired by the laudable ambition to set up Francis Stephen as Emperor in his place. The combined army of 50,000 troops forced the French to fall back to the west bank of the Rhine, and on 4 October 1745 Francis Stephen was enthroned as emperor in Frankfurt cathedral.

The event was fraught with all kinds of significance. The Habsburgs were able to invest themselves once more with all the trappings of the Imperial authority, while the army reclaimed its old heraldry and invested itself once more with the proud title of *kaiserlich-königlich* – the *kaiserlich* referring to the Imperial dignity and the *königlich* to the crowns of Hungary and Bohemia. In strategic terms, the French were now firmly excluded from the Empire.

THE NETHERLANDS

The same strategic 'sorting-out' process was in operation in the Austrian Netherlands, though in a fashion that was far more painful for the Austrians than in Germany. Stranded far outside any conceivable Austrian sphere of influence, the Netherlands had come to Charles VI in 1714 as his share of the realm of the defunct Spanish Habsburgs. Family sentiment apart, there was no good reason for the Austrians to be there. The communications with Austria were long and tenuous, the Dutch had garrisons annoyingly planted in the fortress towns, and the Netherlands overseas trade had been crippled in the interests of English and Dutch merchants.

The vulnerability of the Netherlands was brought home in a very evident manner in 1744, when the Marshal de Saxe drove back the forces of the Pragmatic alliance and wrested coastal Flanders from the nerveless garrisons. The year 1745 saw the loss of Tournai and Western Flanders, and as a result of the campaign of 1746 the allies were expelled from the Austrian Netherlands altogether and penned up on the lower Meuse around Maastricht.

The routine of sieges and manoeuvres was punctuated by a number of uniformly disastrous field battles. The Austrians did very little to influence the outcome. At Fontenoy (11 May 1745) their presence was represented by just eight squadrons of dragoons and hussars. In 1746 and the following campaigns the Austrians certainly maintained a sizeable contingent in the theatre, but in both the big battles (Rocoux, 11 October 1746; Laffeldt, 2 July 1747) their regiments were stranded on the far right of the positions and took little part in the combat.

ITALY

It was entirely in keeping with the contradictions of Austrian policy in the 1740s that while Maria Theresa was fighting to maintain her authority in the Netherlands, she also had armies heavily engaged in southern Europe. With the help of the aggressive little state of Piedmont–Sardinia, the Austrians were able to preserve their foothold in northern Italy against some concerted attacks by the Bourbon powers of France and Spain.

Here at least the Austrians took a proper share of the fighting. Much of the credit for the survival of Austrian Lombardy was due to Field-Marshal Otto Traun, who was *Statthalter* at the beginning of the war, and who repulsed a Spanish army at Camposanto on 8 February 1743. Traun was one of the oldest and certainly the gentlest of Maria Theresa's generals. His military career stretched as far back as 1695, when, after graduating from the high school at Halle, he served as a volunteer in the Brandenburg army at the siege of Namur. In the 1700s Traun entered the service of his native Austria, and in 1708 and the following years he completed his military education as an adjutant to Field-Marshal Guido Starhemberg in Italy.

> From this experience he learnt how to conduct marches and plant camps with foresight, and acquired the art of holding the defensive with inferior forces. Defensive operations were in fact his forte, and he had few rivals in this respect, as may be testified by all men who understand war. The soldiers were very fond of him, because he cared for their welfare, and they invariably called him their 'father'. He was really too good-hearted towards the officers, especially in matters of military economy. Indeed he had nothing left for his own servants, with the result that in later years he had almost nothing to live on, and was virtually compelled to contract his second marriage . . . so as to obtain a housekeeper and nurse.[19]

Austria's standing in Italy was further improved as a consequence of the Treaty of Worms of 14 September 1743, by which Maria Theresa gained an English subsidy and a formal undertaking of support from Piedmont–Sardinia. In the following year the new commander of the army, the vile-tempered Field-Marshal Lobkowitz, actually embarked on an offensive down the Italian peninsula in the direction of Naples. The move ended in a comic-opera campaign around Velletri, in the hills south of Rome, but this otherwise disappointing episode confirmed the reputation of Lieutenant-General Maximilian Browne, who was the one man in the Austrian camp who was willing to stand up to the dictatorial Lobkowitz.

One of the army's Irishmen, Browne was a tallish, active man with a beaky nose and bushy eyebrows. He drove his men hard, but himself harder still, and he showed a characteristic panache and proficiency in a variety of military operations – from bold *coups de main* to 'glorious' retreats and cunning defensive battles. Browne proved very useful to the Pragmatic alliance because he got on so well with the British, and whenever possible he liked to communicate with his acquaintances in his own heavily-accented brand of the English language (we note with interest spellings like 'overtorned' and 'cornel'). Among his suite was his protégé and kinsman Franz Moritz Lacy, the future field-marshal and remaker of the Austrian army.

In 1745 the war in the northern theatres had to take first priority for Maria Theresa, and so the Spanish and their French allies were able to take the initiative along the whole length of northern Italy. The demoralised Austrian army ended the year hemmed in around Novara, 'almost naked, without shirts, shoes, or stockings, and sadly clothed'.[20]

Peace was signed with Prussia on Christmas Day 1745, and Browne was immediately ordered to take off with some 20,000 men from northern Europe to redress the balance in Italy. Moving at an average rate of thirteen miles a day, Browne came across the Brenner Pass early in 1746 and proceeded to roll up the positions of the startled Spaniards from their eastern flank. The two Austrian armies joined forces on 11 April, which gave the overall commander, Prince Liechtenstein, a total of 56,000 men. With this force Liechtenstein and Browne were able to defeat the Bourbon armies at Piacenza on 15 June and hound them into France by way of the mountain passes and the Ligurian coastlands.

Tired but exhilarated, an army of 30,000 Austrians and Piedmontese was committed at the close of 1746 to no less an enterprise than the invasion of Provence. The object of launching the new campaign at such an unfavourable time of year was to provide some kind of diversion in favour of the Pragmatic Army, which was doing so badly in the Netherlands. Browne stormed across the border river of the Var into French territory, and by the middle of December the heads of columns had fanned out in a wide arc extending to Castellane, Draguignan and Fréjus. Unfortunately Browne had no means of cracking open the fortress-port of Antibes, which would have offered him an entry for sea-borne supplies, and in any case a great quantity of stores was lost when the city of Genoa rebelled early in December.

In January 1747 the French marshal Belle-Isle assembled an overwhelming force of 50,000 men and began to drive forward. Browne pulled his troops out of their positions, and by 3 February 1747 he had extricated his army intact from under the noses of the French. This was the kind of operation that was greatly admired at the time, and a Frenchman testified that Browne managed the business 'with all the artistry of a great captain'.[21]

Thereafter almost all the Austrian effort in Italy was devoted to vain attempts to reduce the rebellious Genoese.

The Second Silesian War, 1744–5

There was something familiar, almost comforting, in the last bout of the old-style wars against the French and Spanish. Much more serious was the problem of fighting off Maria Theresa's new and deadly enemy Frederick of Prussia, who reopened hostilities in August 1744, at a time which could scarcely have proved less convenient for the Austrians.

The Prussians swarmed over the Bohemian border in three columns, and by early September they had united before Prague in a strength of 80,000 troops. The Austrian commander Major-General Harsch was thoroughly demoralised, and on the 16th he delivered the city up to the Prussians together with its garrison of 3,000 regulars and 9,000 militia. Encouraged by this very easy success, Frederick proceeded to overrun central Bohemia.

As we have seen, the irruption of the Prussians into the virtually undefended heart of the monarchy forced Prince Charles to abandon his campaign on the west bank of the Rhine. The army began to recross the river on 23 August, and by 2 October the troops had united in Bohemia with the scanty survivors of the original garrison.

Field-Marshal Traun, the commander general in Bohemia, was content to leave Prince Charles with the nominal command of the force. Charles affected to despise the old man, but Traun was in fact physically tougher and far more active than the self-indulgent prince – a circumstance which in no way deterred Charles from arrogating to himself the credit for every success. Against all likelihood, these successes proved to be very substantial indeed. The superiority of the Austrian hussars and light infantry was evident from the first encounters, and Frederick drew back to Beneschau amid swarms of skirmishers. Meanwhile Traun played a waiting game with the main Austrian army, and posed a constant threat to the Prussians while never allowing them to catch him at a disadvantage.

Thus the Austrians had already gained the initiative before they were joined on 21 October by an auxiliary corps of their new allies the Saxons, which gave them a combined force of 70,000 men. Frederick hoped to salvage something from the campaign by taking up winter quarters behind the line of the upper Elbe, but this sanctuary was violated when the Austrians forced a crossing at Telschitz on 19 November. Later in the month Frederick set about withdrawing his army out of harm's way into Silesia. There were terrible sufferings among the retreating Prussian columns, and all told the enterprise cost Frederick anything between 10,000 and 30,000 men through disease and desertion.

By any reckoning the campaign of 1744 represented a notable Austrian victory. Charles characteristically claimed all the glory for himself, and his friends in Vienna persuaded Maria Theresa that the prince would be in a position to perform more brilliantly still if he was installed in sole, untrammelled command.

Vienna felt its first forebodings when Charles proved to be uncommonly slow in getting his Austro-Saxon force of 90,000 men under way in the new campaign. Finally at the beginning of June 1745 the main army lumbered out of north-eastern Bohemia and entered Silesia by way of Landeshut. On the early morning of the 4th the allies were resting in their scattered positions near Hohenfriedberg when they were assailed by the entire Prussian army. The first weight of the attack fell away to the left on the Saxons, and these unfortunate folk were convincingly defeated before the Austrians put in an appearance.

The conduct of the Austrians was at once complacent and sluggish. 'The horses were tied to the picket pales, and the Austrians took their ease in a quite unjustifiable fashion, as if the Prussians were twenty leagues distance.'[22] The battle had lasted nearly two hours before the cavalry so much as received the order to saddle up. The horsemen arrived on the field only towards seven in the morning, and instead of pressing on against the Prussian left they halted by the swampy banks of the Striegauer Wasser in the belief that this little barrier was impassable. The Prussian cavalry promptly proved the contrary, and they chased the panicky Austrian horse from the field. The Austrian general Berlichingen was furious at being captured by one of the Zieten hussars: 'Do I really have to be taken by a mob like this? I saw the Prussian hussars at Mollwitz. They're a tatty crowd, and they ran for their lives at the sight of the first Hungarians.' He went on in this vein until the hussar silenced him with a punch to the head. The general's hat fell off, then

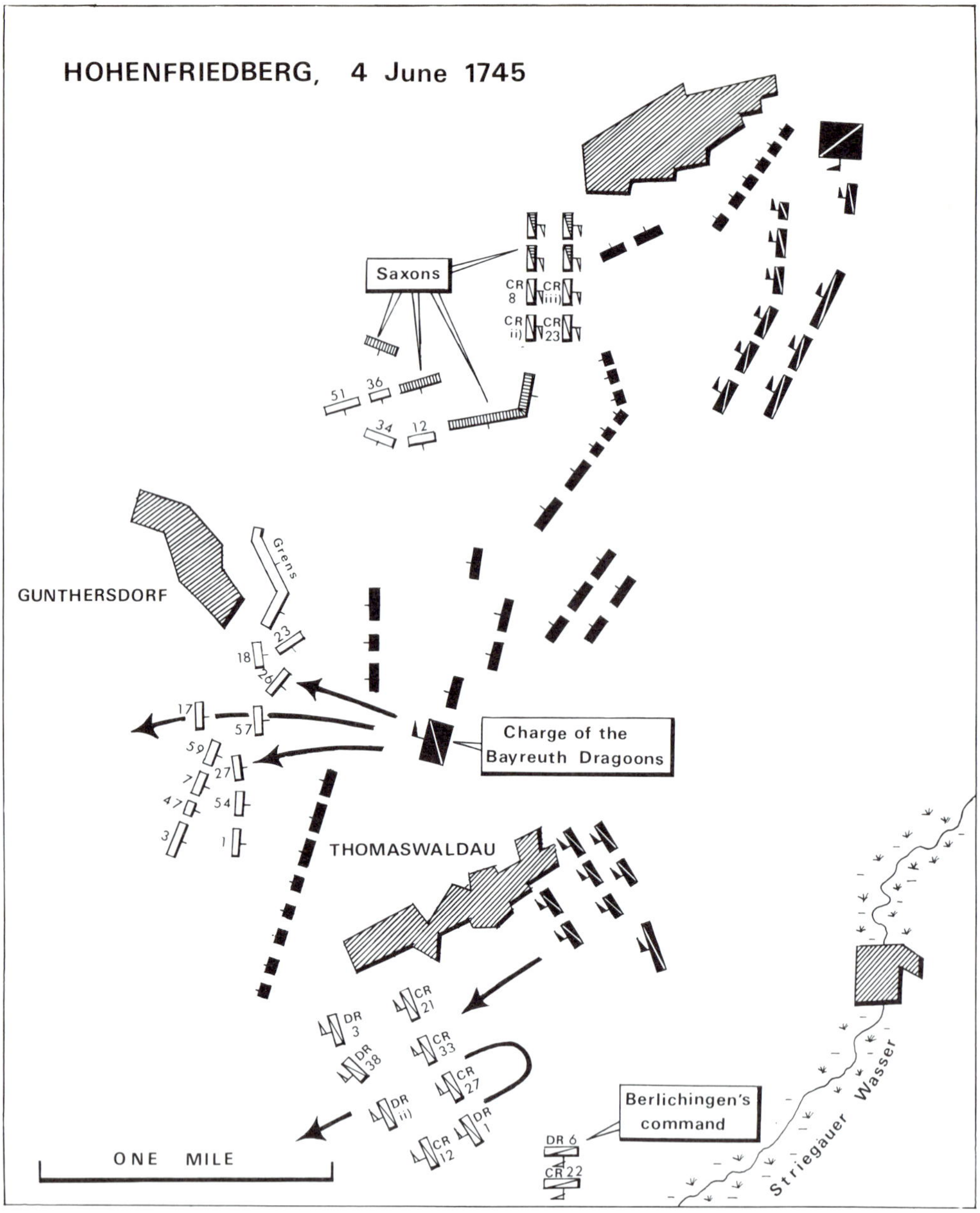

his wig, and finally his whole bulk toppled from the saddle on to the ground.[23]

Prince Charle's infantry was left totally unprotected, now that the cavalry had made itself scarce. For a time the foot soldiers put up a dogged resistance between two villages, but then the super-large Prussian dragoon regiment of Bayreuth launched a devastating charge which cleaved through the loose Austrian line and rode over the regiments of Marschall, Thüngen, Daun, Grünne and Kollowrat.

Prince Charles withdrew his battered army from the fight at nine in the morning. General Thüngen and three other commanders were dead, and about 10,000 men remained on the field or in the hands of the Prussians. Charles reported pathetically, 'we have suffered a total defeat in one of the finest positions you could imagine'.[24] The news of the little disaster at Hohenfriedberg reached Vienna on 6 June, and 'caused all the more consternation, since the great superiority of our army in no way led us to expect such a bitter reverse'.[25]

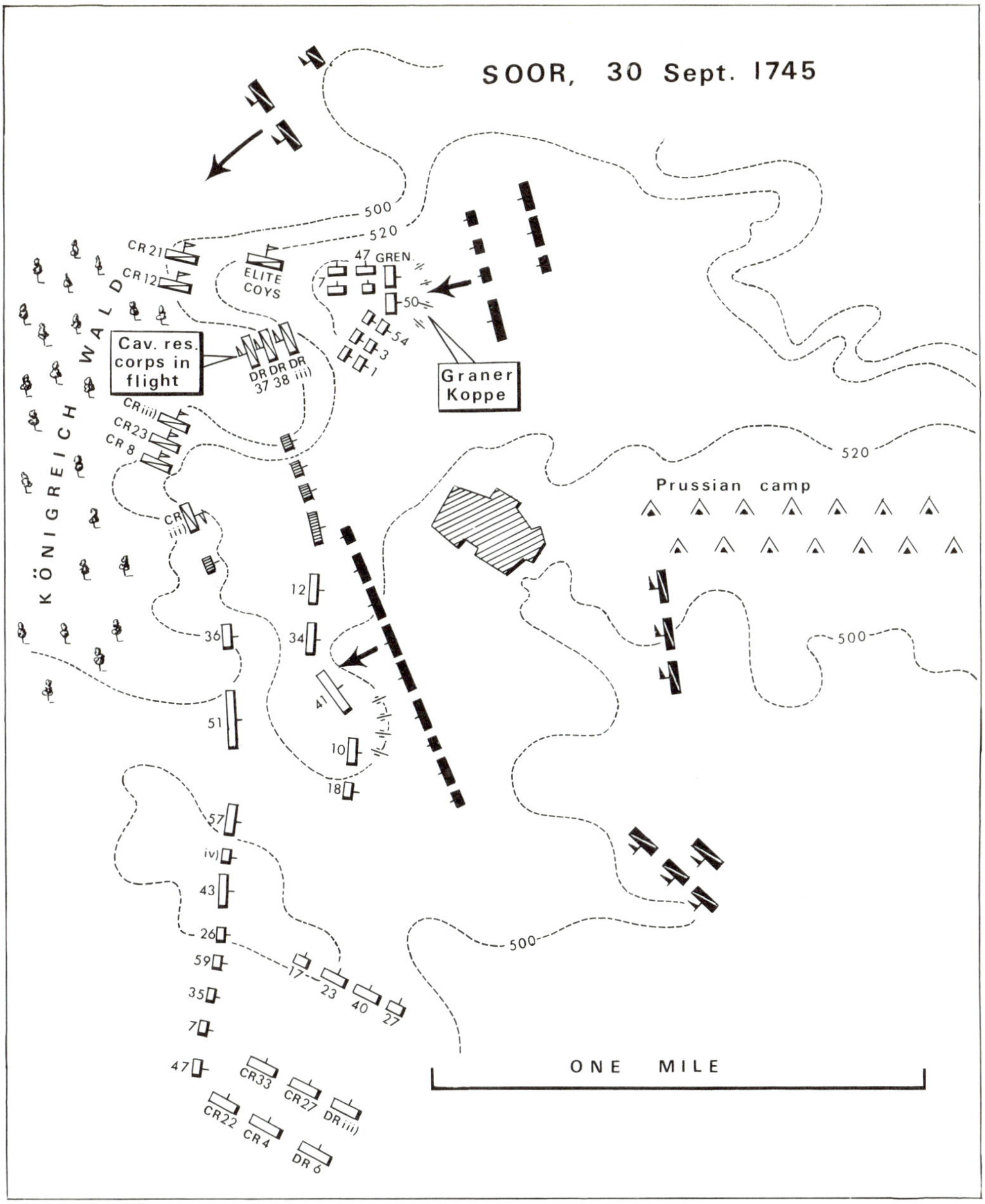

Prince Charles recoiled into Bohemia, and for more than three months he remained behind the river Adler, patching up his badly knocked-about army and incorporating the reinforcements. In the middle of September the Austrians began to grope forward again, and discovered that Frederick was encamped in an unconcerned fashion in broken country south of Trautenau. The active hussar general Nádasti sounded out the ground, and discovered that the extensive Königreich-Wald might give the Austrians an opportunity to make a concealed 'left-flanking' movement and roll up Frederick's position from the west. A good ten days passed in further reconnaissance, without Frederick showing any signs of life. The attack was finally determined for 29 September, but the column of the Duke of Arenberg got slightly lost and the other three moved so slowly that the army had to make camp overnight, with the rival outposts only 500 paces apart.

On the morning of the real 'surprise', 30 September 1745, the army arranged itself into a line of battle 6,000 paces long, extending along high ground from Burkersdorf to Neu-Soor – the place that was going to give its name to the action. At eight o'clock the mists in the valley beneath vomited forth a mass of Prussian cavalry, which climbed the slopes with powerful strides and overthrew the forty-eight squadrons of horse on the Austrian left. Frederick was clearly reacting with extraordinary speed. The right wing of the Prussian army was next to appear, and after two repulses it gained possession of the Graner Koppe, a key position on the Austrian left which was defended by no less than six battalions, fifteen companies of grenadiers and sixteen guns. Frederick now pushed his centre and left into the battle, and before the morning was out the Austrians had been cast back into the Königreich-Wald in some disorder.

The day of Soor cost Charles 7,444 out of his total command of some 41,000 men. Probably in no other battle of the 1740s was the slowness and muddled staff work of the Austrians so evident. Prince Charles talked about 'this disaster which is driving me mad',[26] and he was as quick as ever to cast the blame on others. He found some good words to say about the infantry, but he was unbridled in his strictures on the cavalry, which he described as being useless against the Prussians.

Charles was confident enough concerning his own standing in the eyes of the court, but the army was not to be won over so easily.

> One day Prince Charles was present at the Empress's table when General Spada turned the conversation to the battle of Soor. The general was careless enough to let slip the remark that he would bet a hundred to one that Her Majesty's troops would have beaten the Prussians if only they had been led by the King of Prussia. The prince became violently angry, and since he was unable to calm down he had to leave the table.[27]

Frederick remained in the neighbourhood until the middle of October, then stole away to quarters in Silesia. Charles began to wonder whether he ought to do something to re-establish contact with the Saxons, who had parted from him in August. In late November he showed his nose in Lusatia, but Frederick got to the road junction of Görlitz before him, and the Austrians prudently ducked back into Bohemia. Still seeking to effect the junction, Charles continued his march westward as far as the Elbe, then crossed to the west bank and marched down to the neighbourhood of Dresden, the Saxon capital. Without waiting for Charles to arrive, the Saxons inadvisedly accepted battle with a Prussian corps at Kesselsdorf on 16 December. They were soundly defeated, and Charles withdrew with his Austrians and the remnants of the Saxons into Bohemia.

With this sad episode we come to the end of the tale of the wars of the 1740s. In every way the price that Maria Theresa had to pay was a heavy one. On 25 December 1745 the Austrians signed over to Frederick the whole of Silesia with the county of Glatz, thereby renouncing an industrious population of 1,200,000 souls. The Netherlands were lost just as convincingly, in military terms, and when the French returned the land in 1748 it was largely at the expense of Austrian territory in Italy, where Maria Theresa had to make over the duchies of Parma, Piacenza and Guastalla to the Bourbon Infant Don Philip.

Chancellor Wenzel Anton Kaunitz (Steiner)

The end of the War of the Austrian Succession found Maria Theresa's troops exhausted and demoralised, and yet six years later she was able to put into the field 'an army that was full of strength and life'.[28] The difference in the two conditions was the effect of one of the most creative periods in the history of the Habsburg monarchy.

Put in the simplest terms, the aim of Maria Theresa and her ministers was to rebuild the army and state in such a way as to enable them to survive in competition with the Prussia of Frederick the Great. Significantly enough, the initiator of the most important administrative and financial reforms was a refugee from Silesia, Count Haugwitz. He got the *Stände* to vote monies for terms of several years at a time, and in compensation the government waived its rights to demand billets for the troops and supplies in kind. This arrangement had a double advantage: it reduced the intervention of the *Stände*, and it provided the basis for a more 'military' system of supply.

Foreign relations and many other branches of state activity were the concern of Count (later Prince) Wenzel Anton Kaunitz, who became chancellor in 1753. A man of notorious phobias and eccentricities, he nevertheless had a unique contribution to make to the monarchy. In the late 1740s, when the old advisers were at their least persuasive, Kaunitz came forward as the one man who seemed to know what he was about and who could present his ideas in a cogent form. Alone among Maria Theresa's assistants he knew how to stand clear of mechanical details and build up an argument step by step to what seemed afterwards to be a simple, obvious and irresistible conclusion.

We have already seen how Kaunitz came to exercise a sometimes decisive influence over strategy, and how very well he knew the capabilities of the Austrian military machine. In the sphere of foreign policy his first and most spectacular achievement was to guide the 'Diplomatic Revolution' – the complicated process by which the Austrians and French set aside their ancient enmity, and joined forces against Frederick of Prussia.

The initial agreement between Austria and France became known as the First Treaty of Versailles, of 1 May 1756, and it was a purely defensive deal. The Russians and Swedes were already showing an interest in the possibilities of the new arrangement when, at the end of August 1756, Frederick sent his armies into Saxony as a first blow against what he considered to be a hostile coalition. This drastic action furnished Kaunitz with the one argument which might persuade his foreign friends to commit themselves to a series of offensive agreements. The Russians signed themselves up on 2 February 1757, and so did the French in the Second Treaty of Versailles on 1 May. All but a small part of Frederick's dominions were doomed to dismemberment, with Silesia and Glatz returning to Austria, and other portions going to Saxony and Sweden.

It is not at all easy to assess the positive military value of this network of alliances. The French certainly sent over some useful 'volunteers' and technicians, while the Russians generously dispatched a battery of their strange new artillery (even if the Austrians did not particularly want it). When we look at operations, however, it is difficult to detect any effective working-together of the allied armies.

As early as 27 July 1757 Kaunitz ruled out any direct co-operation between the Austrian and French armies in that year's campaign. The chance did not come again, for in later years the French had their hands more than full in coping with the British-paid 'Army of Observation' in western Germany – something which had not entered Kaunitz's calculations. Moreover, the discipline of the French armies had undergone a sad decline since the great days of the Marshal de Saxe in the 1740s, which further detracted from the value of the French alliance. The Swedish army, too, was but a shadow of former times, and its commanders made only the most tentative forays from Swedish Pomerania.

The Russians put into the field some powerful armies which they had fashioned out of excellent human material. Unfortunately the system of Russian supply was rudimentary, and when the Austrian general Plunkett saw the army in 1760 he was taken aback by the clumsiness of the artillery and the quantity of the baggage waggons, which made him appreciate for the first time all the implications of the term *impedimenta exercitus*. Of the prominent Russian commanders, Saltykov was a comfortable Russian of the old school, while Fermor was a spiky Baltic Lutheran. All of them were inclined to hedge their bets, lest by prosecuting the war against Prussia too energetically they fell into disfavour with any new régime which might take power in St Petersburg.

Kaunitz believed that the only way of making the Russians useful was to prevail upon them to send an auxiliary corps of 30,000 or so men to fight alongside the Austrians, a doctrine which helps to explain why the campaigns of the main Austrian and Russian armies were so badly-co-ordinated. The Austrians seriously entertained the idea of uniting the two armies on just one occasion – after the battle of Kunersdorf in 1759 – and this solitary initiative was ruined by the caution of Daun and the obstinacy of the Russian generals.

It is difficult to escape the conclusion that, once having created his alliance, Kaunitz was not quite sure what to do with it. Unlike the British, who were experienced at this kind of thing, Kaunitz and Maria Theresa had no money to disburse as paymasters, and their concern remained with their own troops, who were directly and inextricably committed to major military operations. The winning or losing of the war therefore hung upon the Austrian army. How fit was it to stand the test?

The work of initiating and co-ordinating military reform was entrusted to a high-powered commission which first met on 8 February 1748, and held altogether twenty sessions. Prince Charles of Lorraine was appointed president, and the detailed work fell to the field-marshals Liechtenstein, Harrach and Cordua and the generals Wenzel Wallis, Daun and Schulenburg. Specialised knowledge was contributed by the *General-Kriegskommissär* Count Franz Ludwig Salburg, and by the war counsellor Augustin Wöber, who had a talent for soothing tempers and reconciling arguments.

The details of the reforms have been turned over in earlier chapters. Uniforms and weapons were improved and systematised, and the conduct of the service was regulated by an important series of instructions – the infantry and commissariat regulations of 1749, the cavalry and hussar regulations of 1751 and the artillery regulations of 1757. The artillery in particular grew in power and prestige, and the troops of the military borders became a versatile and effective force. All this implied a more pronounced professional commitment on the part of the officer. The Field Service Regulations of 1749 set out to educate the higher commanders, while the founding of the Wiener Neustadt military academy in 1752 began to give the officer corps as a whole an element of uniformity in its basic training.

In earlier times military manoeuvres had been fairly dismal affairs, carried out under the eyes of a major-general or a bored commissary. Now the field days became much more exciting and instructive, being designed at once to accustom the troops to some of the rigours of warfare and to give the commanders experience in moving large formations of men. Not a few heads were accidentally parted from their bodies at Prince Liechtenstein's artillery camps at Moldauthein, and Lieutenant-General Browne, as commanding general in Bohemia from 1752, introduced some alarmingly realistic contested exercises between rival army corps. A veteran recalled how two brigadiers got drunk and brought about a confrontation between Hungarian and German regiments on the heights of Skalka at Kuttenberg in 1752:

> Nobody believed that he could give way without losing face. Both sides became excited. . . The Hungarians began to shoot off their buttons, which were shaped like bullets, while the Germans answered by discharging their ramrods. I can still picture that major of the regiment of Haller who was skewered by a ramrod before my eyes.[29]

Browne put on a still more ambitious – but rather better disciplined – performance for the benefit of their Imperial Majesties when they visited the camp of Kolin between 17 and 23 August 1754.

The beneficial effects of these affairs were soon felt:

> They improved our marching both in line and column. They taught us how to deploy, how to traverse, and countless other technicalities, which were unknown in our old way of doing things. They gave the generals the oppor-

tunity they wanted to try out principles of tactics on a large scale, and manoeuvre their forces according to the nature of various kinds of terrain.[30]

As early as January 1747 the Prussian ambassador Podewils had foreseen powerful opposition to the reforms on the part of the vested interests which profited from the many abuses:

> I know that one day, while Maria Theresa watched a regiment parading, she expressed her general approval, but added that the coats were too long. She thought that these garments must be inconvenient to the soldiers on the march, whether in great heat or in the rain, and was of the opinion that they ought to be changed to the Prussian style. But the others objected that the long coats were necessary to protect the troops at night time, whereas the soldiers of Your Majesty [ie Frederick] did not need long coats, because every one of their tents had a cover. Well then, she said, her troops ought to have tents of the same kind. The next day they submitted to her the estimate of the cost. They grossly exaggerated the expense of the covers, of the pack horses to carry them, and of the men to look after the horses, so that the total bill reached an enormous sum and it was easy for them to persuade the Empress to give up her idea.[31]

Only the poorer or the more professionally-minded officers positively welcomed the changes, and many of the others left the service in disgust. Maria Theresa was not to be deflected: 'The new system has reduced the military men to order and contained them within reasonable bounds. They at once set up a great outcry, since the officers were thereby denied all opportunity of winning themselves some nice little benefits at the expense of the country . . . for that very reason I resolved to proceed with all the greater severity'.[32]

If the army was not inclined to take every last rubric of the regulations *au pied de la lettre*, a distinct tightening-up, almost a Prussianisation, became evident in military affairs:

> Now they all set about drilling, and everybody wanted to learn to load and fire smartly. Coats and waistcoats were cut closer to the body, and the hair was curled and powdered[33] . . . No more did we hear the old Gothick orders *Schlagt an! Gebet Feuer!* Instead the young officer gave vent to a clear, short and penetrating *An!* then exploded in a full-throated *Feuer!*, like Homer's Stentor. Now we saw the generals return smiling and inwardly satisfied from their peaceful battlefields . . . where they had gazed at their troops with a martial eye and timed them with watches in their hands, observing to their own great astonishment just how many rounds these new Austrians could fire in a minute.[34]

For all the finely-spun filaments of his intelligence network, Frederick of Prussia remained in almost wilful ignorance of the new-found power of his neighbours. He took no notice of the ex-Austrian general Schmettau, who was aware of what the Austrians were doing with their artillery. The king preferred to listen to the comforting words of Field-Marshal Schwerin (so soon to die before an Austrian cannon), who told him that the Prussians need have no anxiety concerning the outcome of a battle with Maria Theresa's army: 'I myself harbour no fear of their artillery. It had very little effect in all the battles in which I fought. This arm caused

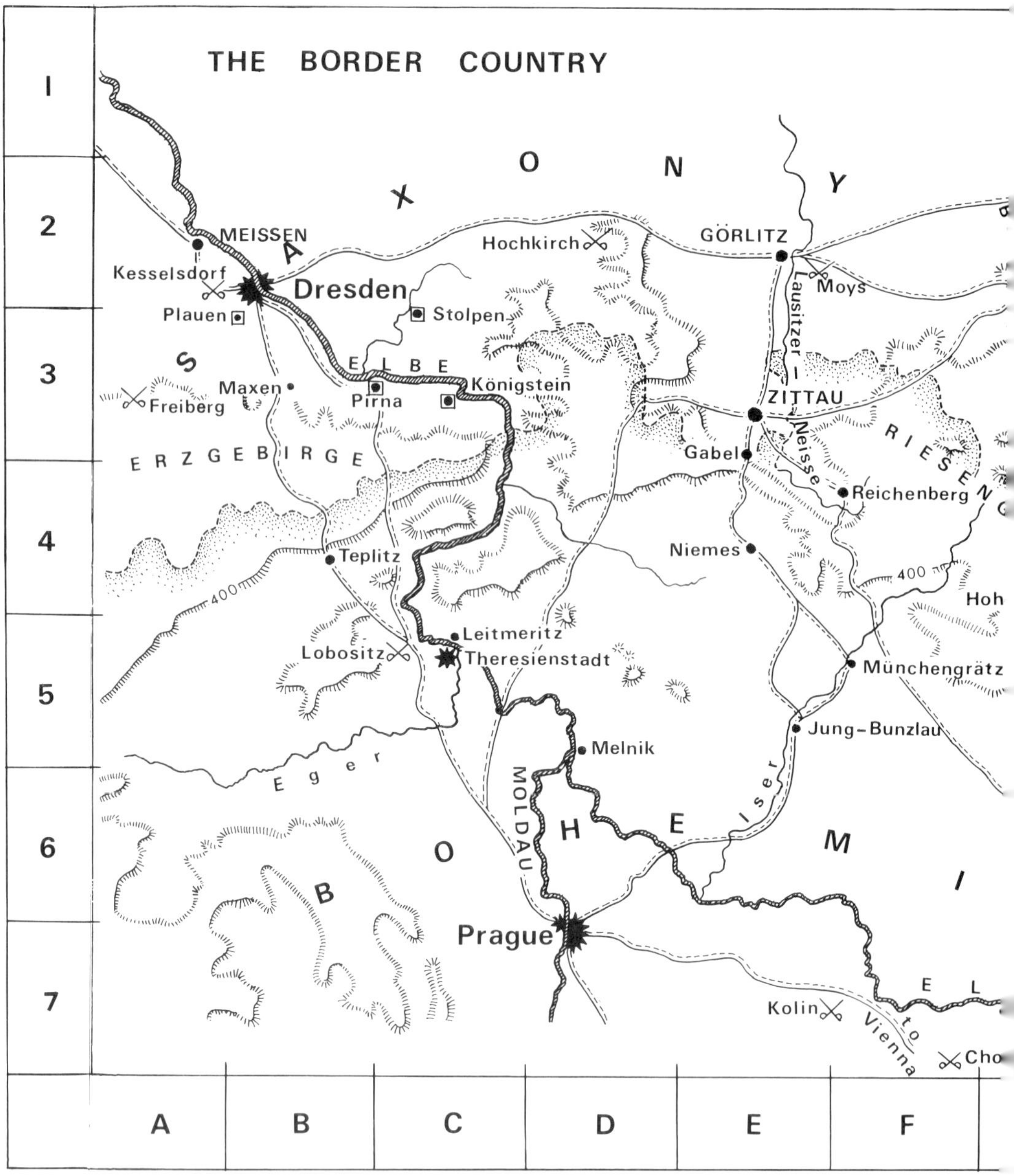

Areas of Strategic Interest (indicated by numbered co-ordinates in the margin).

1–2 A The plain of the lower Elbe. This region was the stamping ground of the *Reichsarmee* from the middle of the Seven Years War. The skilful Prince Henry of Prussia was able to find a number of good defensive positions at Torgau and other places, even though the country offered few obvious barriers to progress.

3 B–C The hill country south of Dresden. Then dense pinewoods and sandstone outcrops extended on both banks of the Elbe, and this tangled region was the scene of much camping and manoeuvring in the second half of the Seven Years War.

3–4 B–C The Erzgebirge passes. The most obvious invasion route of Bohemia for an enemy who had possession of Saxony (Prussian main army 1744, 1756 and 1757). The fortress of Theresienstadt was eventually built so as to counter the threat. The Elbe was navigable for barges as far up as Melnik.

5–6 A–B The Eger valley. A back door to Bohemia from western Germany (French armies 1742).

3–4 D The passes east of the Elbe gorge. These were difficult tracks which traversed broken country, and were chosen only by commanders who wished to bring off a strategic surprise (Browne 1756, Prince Henry 1778).

3–4 E The Lusatian passage. A goodish road passing through reasonably fertile country. It gave the Austrians the alternatives of turning against Dresden or into Silesia (Bevern 1757, Charles of Lorraine after Kolin 1757, Daun 1758).

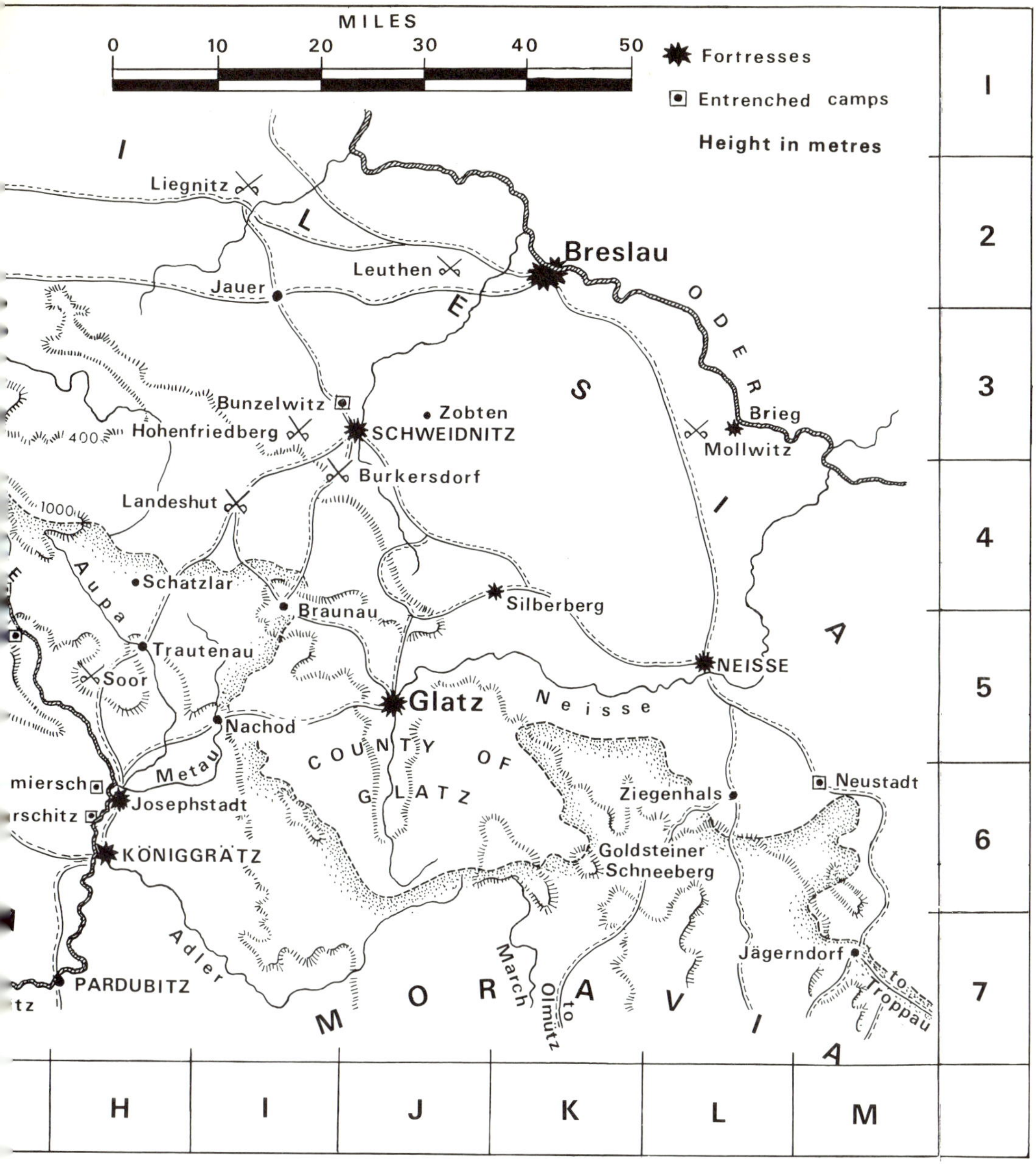

2 F–I The transverse routes north of the Riesengebirge. Most important for Frederick's lateral communications. The mountains were impassable.
5 H–I The Trautenau, Braunau and Nachod valleys. A vital series of avenues, which brought the Austrians into the heart of Silesia, and the Prussians deep into Bohemia. The camp of Jaroměř (and later the fortresses of Josephstadt and Königgrätz) secured the southern exit (Schwerin 1744, Charles of Lorrain 1745, Frederick 1745, Schwerin 1757, Loudon 1760 and 1761, Frederick 1778).
3 J Schweidnitz. Frederick fortified the place before the Seven Years War, and the stronghold and its associated camps became of the first importance for the possession of Silesia (captured by the Austrians 1757, the Prussians 1758, the Austrians 1761 and the Prussians 1762).
5–6 I–K The County of Glatz. An annoying strategic appendix, which the Austrians had to clear before they could feel safe in eastern Silesia. The best roads led from the north and west (captured by Loudon 1760).
7 M The Jägerndorf avenue. From here a network of roads led through wooded but not very difficult country to Olmütz, about forty-five miles to the south-south-west, and therefore offered the Prussians an opening into Moravia and the means of threatening Vienna itself (1758). Frederick secured himself against a counter-stroke by his camp of Neustadt and the fortress of Neisse. The difficult route northwards by way of Ziegenhals was taken by Neipperg early in 1741.

more noise than actual execution, and was capable of inspiring fear only among cowards, recruits and born poltroons.'[35]

The Seven Years War, 1756–63

MOBILISATION

Thanks to the work of military reform, the Austrian army of 1756 knew what it was supposed to do in wartime. The problem that remained was a physical one – how to bring together the manpower, animals and equipment to place the army on a war footing in a time of rising international tension. Whereas Frederick always kept considerable forces in Silesia, ready to spring, the Austrians did not have the money to hold large bodies of troops together for any length of time. Moreover, the statesmen knew that if they brought their forces together too quickly they would merely furnish Frederick with an excuse to blame Austria as the instigator of the war.

The Austrian army began to assemble for the deadly work in January 1756, when the first cavalry regiments slowly undertook the march west from Hungary. Over the following months the army was gradually brought up to a full peace establishment of 177,444 troops, and then, from 8 July, an intensification of the recruiting filled out the host to the war strength. On 20 September 1756 the Austrians had some 200,000 troops under arms. These consisted of:

55 infantry regiments	118,148 men
108 grenadier companies	10,800 men
30 regiments of German cavalry	24,000 men
10 hussar regiments	8,000 men
The infantry and hussars of the military borders	40,000 men

Some of the infantry regiments were actually over-strength, but the hussar's still needed time to reach their complement of horses, and for a short time there was an acute shortage of animals to move the artillery, ammunition and supplies to the armies which were forming in Bohemia and Moravia:

> Maria Theresa opened her stables and gave up her own horses in order to transport the cannon. The Austrian and Bohemian nobility thereupon vied with one another to imitate this great example. People came from all directions to make horses available, and so the movement was effected with completely unexpected speed.[36]

The morale and expectation of the troops was high. The Prince de Ligne records that, while his regiment was marching from the Netherlands to take part in the war, he

> brought an Irishman called Butler to dine with the Margravine of Bayreuth, through the territory of which our column was passing. 'What do you think of this war?' she asked. 'And what is going to become of the King of Prussia?'

'Madame,' said Butler, 'I believe he is all f . . . d up.' 'That would displease me somewhat', replied the Margravine, 'he's my brother.' 'In that case, madame, I am the one who is in that situation.'[37]

When hostilities broke out at the end of August 1756 the main army of 32,465 troops was assembled in Bohemia, with a supporting corps of 22,606 positioned to the east in Moravia. The respective commands went to the newly-promoted Field-Marshal Browne, who was approaching the culmination of his career, and the quiet and determined Field-Marshal Piccolomini.

The Lobositz–Pirna campaign, 1756

As is the way with small powers, the state of Saxony Poland clung to the delusion that an attitude of pious neutrality was the best guarantee of survival in a dangerous world. The innocence of the Saxons afforded them no protection at all when, late in August, 62,000 Prussians marched into their territory as the first move of a 'pre-emptive strike' directed against Austria and the other members of the gathering coalition.

The precise timing of the attack came as a surprise to Maria Theresa and Francis Stephen, who were on a hunting expedition at Hollitsch, on the Hungarian–Moravian borders. All the same, the Empress had accepted willingly the risk of being anticipated by the enemy, as the price of showing up Frederick as 'the undoubted aggressor'.[38] It was left to the army to face the military consequences.

The most important task that lay before Field-Marshal Browne was to do something to rescue the 15,000-strong Saxon army, which had contrived to strand itself in the camp of Pirna-Königstein, which crowned a sandstone plateau on the west bank of the Elbe above Dresden. Browne conceived the bold plan of sending a flying corps from Bohemia to Saxony by way of the wild border mountains on the right, or eastern, bank of the Elbe. The Saxons were then to cross the river, and escape with the Austrians into Bohemia.

Before Browne could put his scheme into effect he had to do something to check and hold the powerful forces which Frederick was beginning to feed up the west bank of the Elbe into northern Bohemia. This ambition brought the rival armies into contact at Lobositz on 1 October 1756.

Browne planted a force of Croats on the tangled slopes of the volcanic Lobosch hill in front of his right flank. There was an advance guard in close support of the Croats, but the main body of the army was cunningly disposed behind the ponds and marshy banks of the Morellen-Bach. Browne had about 34,000 men under his command, including the Croats, which was rather more than the Prussians, though he was inferior in guns and cavalry.

Frederick was at first under the impression that he was merely dealing with the rearguard of a retreating army, and the Prussian cavalry was very badly mauled when it carried out two charges across the plain towards the Morellen-Bach position. Meanwhile the Austrian artillery came into action against the enemy infantry, which was still packed in the valley beside the Lobosch hill. To the Prussian soldiers the cannon shot seemed to cleave the air above their heads, 'sometimes plunging into the earth behind us and throwing stones and clods high into the air, sometimes falling among us and snatching men out of the ranks as if they had been wisps of straw'.[39]

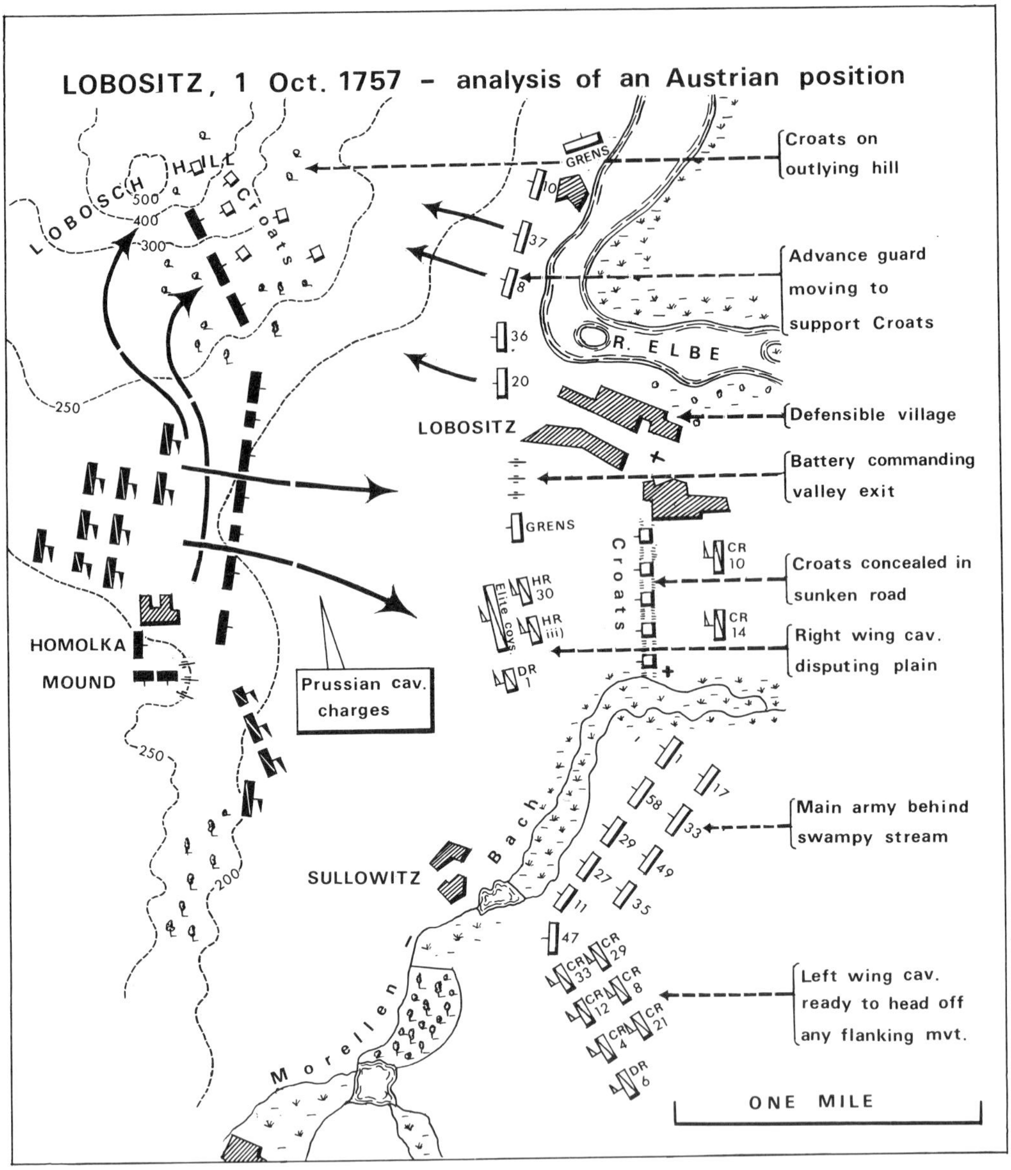

Frederick now saw fit to absent himself from the scene of action. However, the Prussian generals pushed more and more troops into the bitter fighting which had broken out on the Lobosch, and the decisive moment came when the Duke of Bevern charged down the hill, chasing the Croats before him and crashing into the Austrian advance guard. A Prussian wrote that 'the Austrian regiment of Jung-Colloredo fought well very on this occasion. It was formed, arranged and commanded on that day by Count Lacy. If the other regiments had done the same, the victory might have been with the Austrians'.[40]

As soon as the advance guard had abandoned the ground behind Lobositz village, Browne drew the main army across the plain to the Elbe, which placed a barrier athwart the Prussian pursuit and brought the action to an effective end.

The fighting had cost the Austrians 2,873 men and the Prussians rather more. The enemy troops began to mutter, 'these are no longer the old Austrians',[41] and one of Frederick's officers observed that the encounter had presented the king with a new experience:

On this occasion Frederick did not come up against the same kind of Austrians he had beaten in four battles in a row. He was not dealing with people like Neipperg or the blustering Prince Charles of Lorraine. He faced Field-Marshal Browne, who had grown grey in the service, and whose talent and experience had raised him to one of the heroes of his time. He faced an artillery which Prince Liechtenstein had brought to perfection at his own expense. He faced an army which during ten years of peace had attained a greater mastery of the arts of war, and had striven to adopt the methods of its former victors and shape itself according to their discipline'.[42]

The instructive little battle at Lobositz left Browne's strategy intact. While the Prussians remained inactive on the west bank of the Elbe, he took off with a picked band of 8,800 troops and made his way by forced marches through the wooded hills of the east bank, which were being lashed by freezing rain. Browne was already afflicted by tuberculosis, and this ordeal went far to contribute to the ruin of his health and judgement in the following year.

Browne's advance to the bank of the Elbe almost opposite the Saxon camp was 'a manoeuvre admired by all military men'.[43] However, the Saxons were too demoralised and too badly led to do anything about putting their side of the scheme into effect, and Browne was forced to retreat to Bohemia, leaving the Saxons to surrender to the enemy.

On his return to the main army Browne determined to 'dispute the terrain as far as the rules of war will permit'.[44] The Austrians effectively closed off the countryside to the enemy foraging parties, and the last week of October found the Prussians in full retreat into Saxony, leaving the roads littered with their dead horses.

THE CRISIS IN BOHEMIA, APRIL–MAY 1757

Now that he was committed to a major war, Frederick made up his mind to open the campaign of 1757 before the Austrians, which, as the Prince de Ligne ruefully admitted, was 'never particularly difficult'.[45]

A curious malaise and inactivity settled upon the Austrian counsels. Maria Theresa summoned Prince Charles of Lorraine from the Netherlands with the object of setting up a joint command with Browne, the hero of 1756. The field-marshal, however, dismissed the arrangement as unworkable, and loyally declared that he was willing to serve under Charles as second in command. This did not prevent the army and court from continuing to repose their chief trust in Browne, who persuaded himself that there was no likelihood of a new Prussian attack, and advised against bringing the army out of quarters too early and gobbling up the precious magazines.

On 18 April and the following days 113,000 Prussian troops broke across the Bohemian border in four sectors. Everything in Bohemia fell into chaos – 'regiments were looking for generals, generals were looking for regiments, and sometimes they failed to meet up'.[46] Browne for a time was sunk in physical and mental prostration, and his troops roamed in panic over the countryside.

Thus the Prussians were permitted to concentrate their forces deep inside Bohemia. The Duke of Bevern swept aside General Königsegg, who tried to arrest his progress at Reichenberg on 21 April, and he joined forces with Field-Marshal Schwerin, who had marched up through eastern Bohemia unmolested by the cold

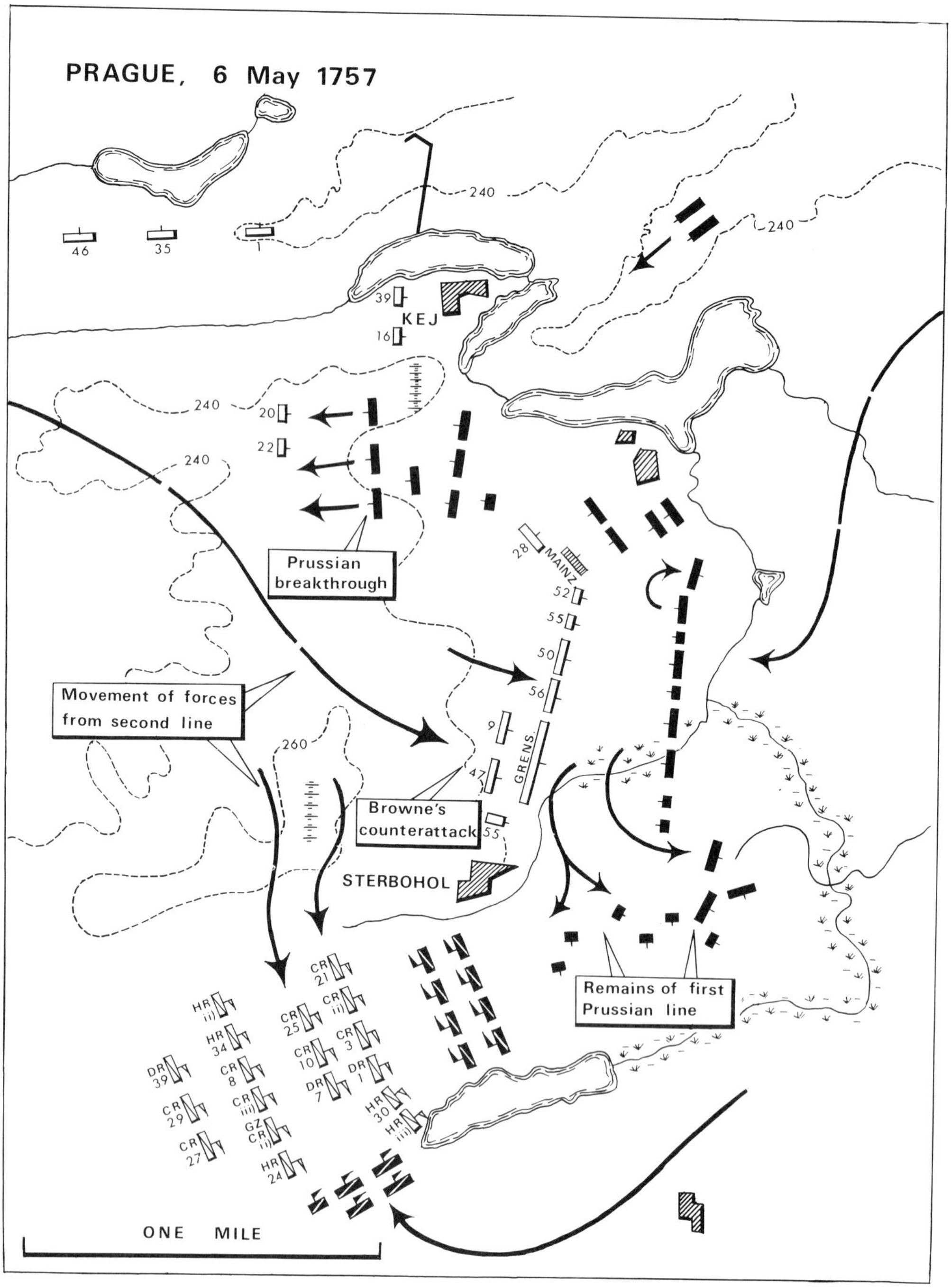

and slow-moving Serbelloni, who had taken command of the semi-independent corps in that part of the world.

Worst of all, the ill-feeling between Prince Charles and Browne permitted the king's main army to effect a junction with Schwerin's command on the early morning of 6 May, in the immediate presence of the Austrian army just outside Prague. Without halting the march Frederick directed the united army around the eastern, or right flank of the Austrian position.

The Austrian army of 62,000 troops was arrayed along the edge of a dusty plateau which extended for four miles to the east of Prague. Browne was the first

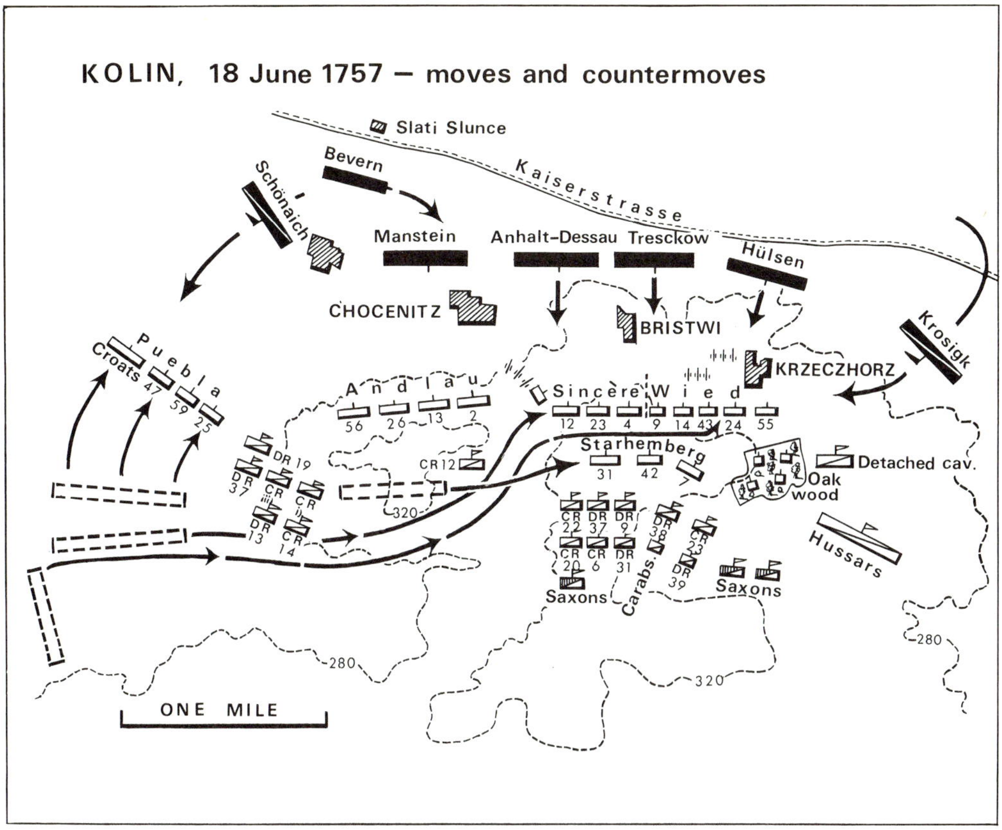

KOLIN, 18 June 1757 – moves and countermoves

to detect what the enemy were up to, and with all his old determination and speed he detached the second line of the army and threw it at the Prussians while they were floundering through a line of boggy ponds. The Austrian artillery was firing with speed and accuracy, and Browne might well have succeeded in turning the whole course of the battle if a cannon shot had not thrown him badly wounded to the ground (he died some weeks later).

Now the Austrians were overcome by one disaster after another. On the right wing of the new eastward-facing line the Austrian cavalry sank into confusion in the clouds of blinding dust and were worsted by the Prussian hussars. Away on the left flank the enemy infantry penetrated a gap which had opened in the angle between the new line and the old one, and in bitter fighting the Austrians were pushed back in disarray towards Prague.

The appalling day of 6 May ended with 3,000 troops scattered over the landscape of Bohemia, and all the rest milling about Prague in disorder. It was very small consolation that the Austrians had made the enemy pay very dearly for their success. The Prussians actually suffered 14,300 casualties as opposed to the 13,400 men (including over 4,500 prisoners) lost by the Austrians.

THE GOLDEN SUN OF KOLIN, 18 JUNE 1757

The disaster at Prague reduced the effective Austrian military force to the corps in eastern Bohemia, which Field-Marshal Daun had taken under his command two days before. Daun owed his position above all to his influential connections and to his part in the work of military reform. We shall become acquainted with his short-

 Field-Marshal Leopold Daun

comings later on, but in the crisis of May–June 1757 he was able to give the monarchy exactly what it most needed – someone who could restore shaken troops to order, and keep his composure on a day of battle.

Kaunitz, too, performed a signal service, by taking rapid stock of the situation and re-establishing contact between Vienna and the theatre of war. A message was accordingly got to Prince Charles, telling him to stay put in Prague with his shattered army, while Daun gathered the other fugitives from the battle and began to consider how he could save the city. On 7 June Daun was expressly ordered to give battle, if necessary, and armed with this authority he began the march on Prague five days later.

King Frederick left Prague under blockade, and in the crushing heat of mid-June he moved his army against Daun. In expectation of the coming shock Daun arrayed his 35,160 infantry, 18,630 cavalry and 154 guns along a low range of hills near Kolin, south of and parallel to the Prague–Vienna *Kaiserstrasse*. The Austrians were well acquainted with the ground, thanks to their prewar manoeuvres, and the expert knowledge of the military topographer Lieutenant-Colonel Veltetz.

The Austrians spent the night of 17/18 June under arms, and early the next morning they saw the dark columns of the Prussian army move into view on their left front. The day held the promise of being fine and hot, and the Prussians grounded their arms on the *Kaiserstrasse* to draw breath – 'never could you hope to see a more splendid day or a finer sight'.[47] Frederick was planning to repeat the manoeuvre of Prague and catch the Austrians in their right flank. He took his bearings from the attic of a wayside inn which, by a coincidence, bore the name of *Slati Slunce* (The Golden Sun).

Early in the afternoon there was a blinding flash from thousands of bayonets as the Prussians shouldered arms once more and resumed their tramp eastwards across the front of the waiting Austrian army. Daun had already taken the precaution of shifting his reserve corps under Lieutenant-General Wied to the right, and now that the danger to this flank declared itself more clearly with every minute that passed the field-marshal ordered the army to move over as a body.

Thus Frederick was frustrated in his hope of turning the Austrian flank, and from three in the afternoon the Prussian corps launched themselves one by one up the gradient against the front of Daun's position. They were set a suicidal task. The Austrians

> actually saw nothing of the Prussians save their brass caps which were gleaming through the thick growth of corn, and as soon as these brave but doomed men . . . had climbed one-third or a half of the steep slope with unspeakable difficulty, they were met and thrown back by the extremely regular vollies of the infantry, and a frightful rain of canister from the batteries which maintained a cross fire from every side.[48]

On the eastern flank of the field the command of the Prussian general Hülsen was the first to come into action. It surmounted the ridge but became entangled with a force of Croats and grenadiers who were holding an oak wood just south of the village of Krzeczhorz. Next in line to the west was Tresckow's corps, which was repelled in fine style by the regiments of Deutschmeister, Baden and Botta.

Some time after four in the afternoon the Austrian division of Starhemberg was directed into the fighting around the oak wood:

Four Sons of Erin:
Field-Marshal Maximilian Ulysses Browne (By courtesy of Kevin McGrath)

General Carl Claudius O'Donnell (By courtesy of Rupert Couglan)

Field-Marshal Franz Moritz Lacy

General Johann Sigismund Macquire von Inniskillin

The first grenadier company of the regiment of Gaisruck was on the right wing. Without firing a shot it pushed with great determination to within a short distance of the oak wood, then delivered a devastating platoon fire on the advance, just as if it had been on the drill square. All the time the veteran grenadiers reminded one another to keep aiming a little lower.[49]

The battle now became dangerously fluid. Starhemberg's success encouraged Wied and the reserve corps to make a counter-attack on their own account. Wied was taken between the enemy infantry and cavalry and badly mauled, and for a time the divisions to his left were caught up in the crisis as well. It was at this junction that the splendid Hungarian infantry regiment of Haller was crushed by the Prussian general Seydlitz and his two regiments of cavalry.

From half past four a blessed interval of one hour supervened before the enemy were again ready to renew the attack. The Prussian cavalry division of Penavaire put in a charge around the west of the village of Krzeczhorz, and there were renewed assaults on the part of the infantry of Manstein and Tresckow. The Austrians had long since been reduced along most sectors to a single line. Their artillery was firing with unprecedented effect, but the infantry were so low on ammunition that in at least one regiment the drummers cut open the tops of their drums and filled them with cartridges from the pouches of the dead and wounded.

Towards seven in the evening the Duke of Bevern with the First Battalion of the Prussian Garde and six other good battalions delivered a last assault against the Austrian centre in the area south of Bristwi. The bluecoats in turn came under a devastating counter-attack from six regiments of Austrian cavalry, which erupted from the direction of the oak wood with the Walloon dragoon regiment of de Ligne at the head. According to legend its beardless young troopers were on their mettle because Daun had just referred to them somewhat dismissively as *blancs becs*.

This blow precipitated a general collapse of most of the Prussian infantry, who were ridden down before they could form square. General Nádasti, the hussar commander, neither gave nor received any orders to carry out a prolonged pursuit, and Daun was content to let his army spend the night on the battlefield, surrounded by the more than 12,000 casualties of the Prussians.

This glorious day vindicated all the years of work of Daun and his fellow reformers, and, as a Prussian princess tartly commented, proved to the Austrians 'that after all they were only dealing with men, something which they might have doubted up to now'.[50] A captured Prussian lieutenant watched in fascination as the Austrians celebrated their good fortune in the village where he was being held prisoner:

There appeared an elegantly attired drummer and behind him two ranks of sounding trumpeters, who were likewise beautifully dressed. They rode into the village and progressed to the far end, all the time proclaiming their victory by beating on the drums and blaring with their trumpets. I had never yet seen anything to compare with the splendour of these instruments. The drums were hung about with red silk covers, richly interwoven with gold, while the trumpets were adorned with a multitude of costly tassels.[51]

 The court chamberlain bore the tidings to Maria Theresa at Schönbrunn on

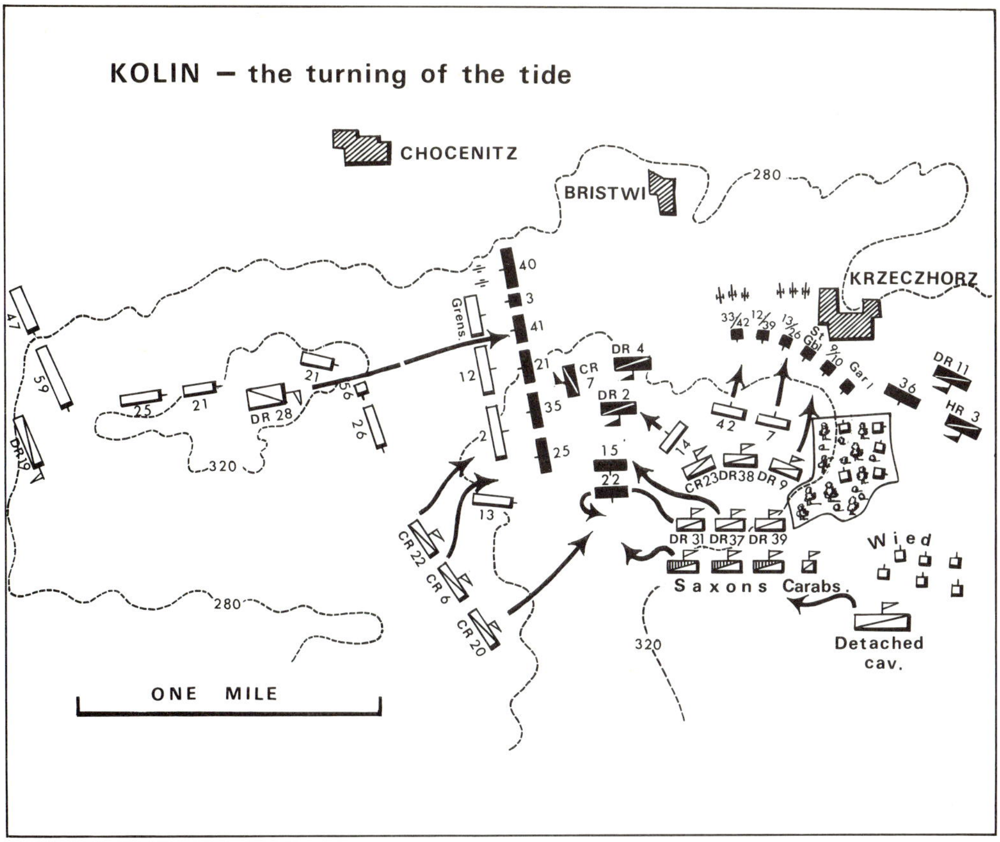

the early morning of 20 June. There could have been no more auspicious moment to proclaim the institution of the Military Order of Maria Theresa. The day of Kolin was designated as the birthday of the new order, and Daun was nominated Commander and awarded a Grand Cross in the first promotion. As a more personal testimony, Maria Theresa presented the field-marshal's little son with a map of Bohemia, on which the name of the battle was entered in gold lettering. The golden case bore the inscription in Maria Theresa's own hand:

> Toutes les fois que vous regarderez cette carte géographique, souvenez-vous de la journée, ou votre père a sauvé la Monarchie.

THE ARMY LOSES ITS WAY, JUNE–DECEMBER 1757

Already on 20 June the Prussians abandoned their lines before Prague, after they had submitted the place to weeks of blockade and intermittent bombardment. Daun reached the city on the 23rd, and on the next day the two Austrian armies united in a strength of 100,000 men.

Prince Charles resumed the overall command, and tamely permitted the Prussians to extricate themselves from Bohemia with the minimum of interference. The only encounter of any note was staged on 15 July, when the generals Macquire and Arenberg stormed the little town of Gabel:

> It was certain death to show yourself at the gate and try to enter. The lieutenant-colonel who planned the scheme . . . was standing against the wall and pushing

> the grenadiers inside. Finally a captain seized him by the scruff of the neck and threw him into the street, where he was killed in an instant.[52]

Two thousand Prussians were taken prisoner in this affair.

Moving into the mountains, the army reduced the Lusatian textile town of Zittau on 23 July, after a cruel bombardment which destroyed supplies that could have proved very useful to the Austrians. The troops spent the following weeks encamped in the Lusatian valleys, where they became subject to disease, demoralisation and desertion. Kaunitz declared that the only way to get things moving again would be to evict Prince Charles from the command, but the Emperor retorted that he would 'regard the recall of his brother as a personal dishonour'.[53]

The idle conduct of the victors of Kolin gave Frederick a precious opportunity to confront a danger which arose on his western flank, where the French and the states of southern and western Germany were gathering armies together in a hostile fashion. At the end of August he accordingly took himself off into Thuringia, leaving the Duke of Bevern with just 43,000 men at Bautzen to cover the approaches to Brandenburg and Silesia.

During the absence of Old Fritz the Austrians got in a number of blows which were gratifying in themselves, but offered little compensation for the greater opportunities which were being missed. On 7 September Nádasti led a little expedition against a detachment which Bevern had incautiously placed under General Winterfeldt at Moys, on the far side of the Lausitzer Neisse. The Austrian grenadiers were directed in column of division up the slopes of the dominating Jäckelsberg hill in broad daylight, and against all likelihood they brought off a complete surprise. These heroes then dispersed in search of plunder, leaving three battalions of fusiliers to bear the brunt of the counter-attack. The Prince de Ligne recalls:

> We are dealing with the regiments of Manteuffel and Tresckow. I have never seen anything so splendidly brave as the conduct of the Prussians on this occasion. Winterfeldt advanced against us like a madman, and got himself killed at their head. His command was climbing the hill from one side, while our battalion [of IR NO 38] came up the other. We reached the summit at the same time as the enemy, and for a moment we swayed back and forth like a crowd in the pit of an opera house. I tried to halt, consolidate and reassure our troops by forming a barrier with my partisan and the half-pikes of the NCOs. It was singularly unpleasant to find ourselves under fire from two directions. The Prussians were keeping up their heaviest fire of the war, while the Austrian regiment of Platz, instead of being on our right, was blazing off its cartridges behind us, so as to have an excuse to make off. The first ranks of the Prussians and my own men were so close that the muzzles were almost touching, and the circumstances of the action now became frightful. The hutments, field kitchens and tents had been set on fire by the discharges, and the enemy used them as a kind of parapet from where they fired into us at point blank range. Thus the wounds were so huge that you would have sworn that they had been inflicted by cannon shot.[54]

The Prussians were finally pushed down the hill and out of Moys, and when the action was over Winterfeldt was found lying dead on the slopes.

 Now that Winterfeldt was destroyed, Bevern was left with no alternative but to recoil into Silesia. He was followed by Prince Charles and the main body of the Austrians. The generals Marschall and Hadik were left with a small corps in Lusatia, and in order to give these folk something to do, Vienna decided that it would be a good idea for Hadik to embark on an expedition against Berlin, which was now virtually undefended.

Lieutenant-General Andreas Hadik combined a mild and genial demeanour with ruthless energy – traits which may have contributed to his original ambition to become a Jesuit – and on the present adventure he brought his command of 3,500 men from Hoyerswerda to the Prussian capital in just five days. Halting his troops outside Berlin, he demanded a contribution from the city fathers. 'After everything was agreed, General Hadik asked the magistracy for two dozen pairs of ladies' gloves, stamped with the city arms, for he wished to make a present of them to the Empress.'[55] Clutching his money and his gloves, he was off again on 17 October and threaded his way back to camp through the vengeful Prussian forces.

On the main theatre of war in Silesia the brand-new Prussian fortress of Schweidnitz had been under blockade since 30 September. The commander of the siege army was the hussar general Nádasti, the beloved *papa moustache*, who resolutely refused to show himself in the trenches. He had no time for the niceties of contemporary siege warfare, and on 12 November he cut the proceedings short by throwing an assault across open ground against Redoubt No 36 and the Bogenfort. As the columns closed in, 'General v. Rebentisch showed his cheerful and merry face through the palisades, and greeted his many acquaintances most courteously [he was an ex-Austrian officer]. But the smile was wiped off his countenance as soon as the troops were ordered to level their muskets'.[56] On the Austrian side the grenadier captain Rummel was making his way across the ditch and into the Bogenfort:

> He reached the top, and just as he had promised before he left, he announced his arrival to the generals and the princely volunteers who were looking on. It is said that the troops who were supposed to defend the fort were taken by surprise, and actually lent some aid to the escalading force. Looking at the dimensions of the fort and the immense belly of Herr Rummel, you would be tempted to conclude that they helped him with his ladder.[57]

The rest of the fortress yielded without further ado, which gave the Austrians 6,000 prisoners of war and the possession of the key to southern Silesia.

Meanwhile the rest of the army was pushing the Duke of Bevern back with agonising slowness towards the Silesian capital of Breslau. The French officer Montazet complained that 'this army is deficient in the vital things it needs to get it moving with any speed. There is almost nobody at hand to reconnoitre the terrain, mark out the camps or prepare the marches'.[58]

These stately motions did not correspond with the urgency of the situation. Not only was it imperative for the Austrians to gain possession of Breslau, if they were to stay in Silesia over the winter, but they had to reckon with the fact that Frederick had now settled accounts with the French and the German *Reichsarmee* (see below) and had his hands free.

At last on 22 November 1757 Charles threw his army at the outnumbered forces of the Duke of Bevern, who was holding an over-extended line of the villages, earthworks, hills, hedges and marshes in front of Breslau. The fighting proved unexpectedly tough, and the decisive push was finally made by the Austrian left wing, under General Macquire, who had been supposed to provide only a diversion.

The enemy abandoned the city of Breslau to the Austrians. As the Prussian columns were winding away a cuirassier consoled a weeping girl: 'Don't distress yourself, my dear. Give us fourteen days and we'll be back again.'[59] He was only slightly over-optimistic.

THE CATASTROPHE OF LEUTHEN, 5 DECEMBER 1757

It is significant that we have heard little so far about Austria's allies. In the high summer of 1757 an army of 55,000 Russians had moved heavily through East Prussia, and on 30 August the invaders beat the defending Prussian army at Gross-Jägersdorf. The cost, however, proved so high, and the supplies fell into such disorder, that the Russians withdrew once more into their own territory.

More dismal still was the performance of the other allies – the French and the princes of southern and western Germany. The start was deceptively encouraging. On 26 July the main French army had had the good fortune to defeat the Duke of Cumberland and his Army of Observation of Hanoverians and Protestant German auxiliaries at Hastenbeck, in the area of the lower Elbe. The Army of Observation was temporarily neutralised, as a consequence of a treaty in September, and the field was clear for a second French army under Marshal Soubise to unite with the *Reichsarmee* in Thuringia and meditate adventures further afield.

The French element in the combined force was very badly disciplined. The German contingents were, if anything, still less effective, for they were thrown together by greedy princes who were interested mainly in wresting concessions from Vienna and hiring out their subjects on the best terms.

The Austrian field-marshal Duke Joseph Friedrich of Sachsen-Hildburghausen was in direct command of the German regiments and exercised a small measure of control over the French as well. This intelligent but unlucky gentleman had won golden opinions from Prince Eugene, and in the 1740s he had undertaken the mighty work of reorganising the Croatian military borders. *Grosse Magnificence* was evident in his array of Croatian and Hungarian uniforms, and in the entertainments he staged in his garden in Vienna.

Plundering as it went, the Franco-German *Executions-Armee* advanced to its own execution at the hands of Frederick. Hildburghausen reported shortly before the clash that Soubise was 'the nicest man in the world', but inspired no respect in his army. The excesses of the troops had reached 'such awful proportions that it makes you shudder to talk about them. I cannot believe that such an unchristian and impious body of men can obtain God's blessing'.[60]

On 5 November 1757 the 42,000-strong host tried to turn the flank of Frederick's army at Rossbach. While they were still in column of march the allies came under devastating artillery fire, and were then overwhelmed by the torrential charges of the Prussian cavalry. In those dreadful minutes almost the only troops to acquit themselves with any credit were the two attached Austrian cuirassier regiments of Bretlach and Trautmannsdorf. Hildburghausen told the Emperor that by the end of the battle 'everything sank into confusion. It was quite impossible to rally a single unit, and even when you thought you had got a squadron or a battalion together it needed only a cannon shot to come whizzing down and they all ran like sheep'.[61]

With the French and Germans out of the reckoning, the term of grace of Prince Charles's army in Silesia had finally expired. Charles suffered Frederick to

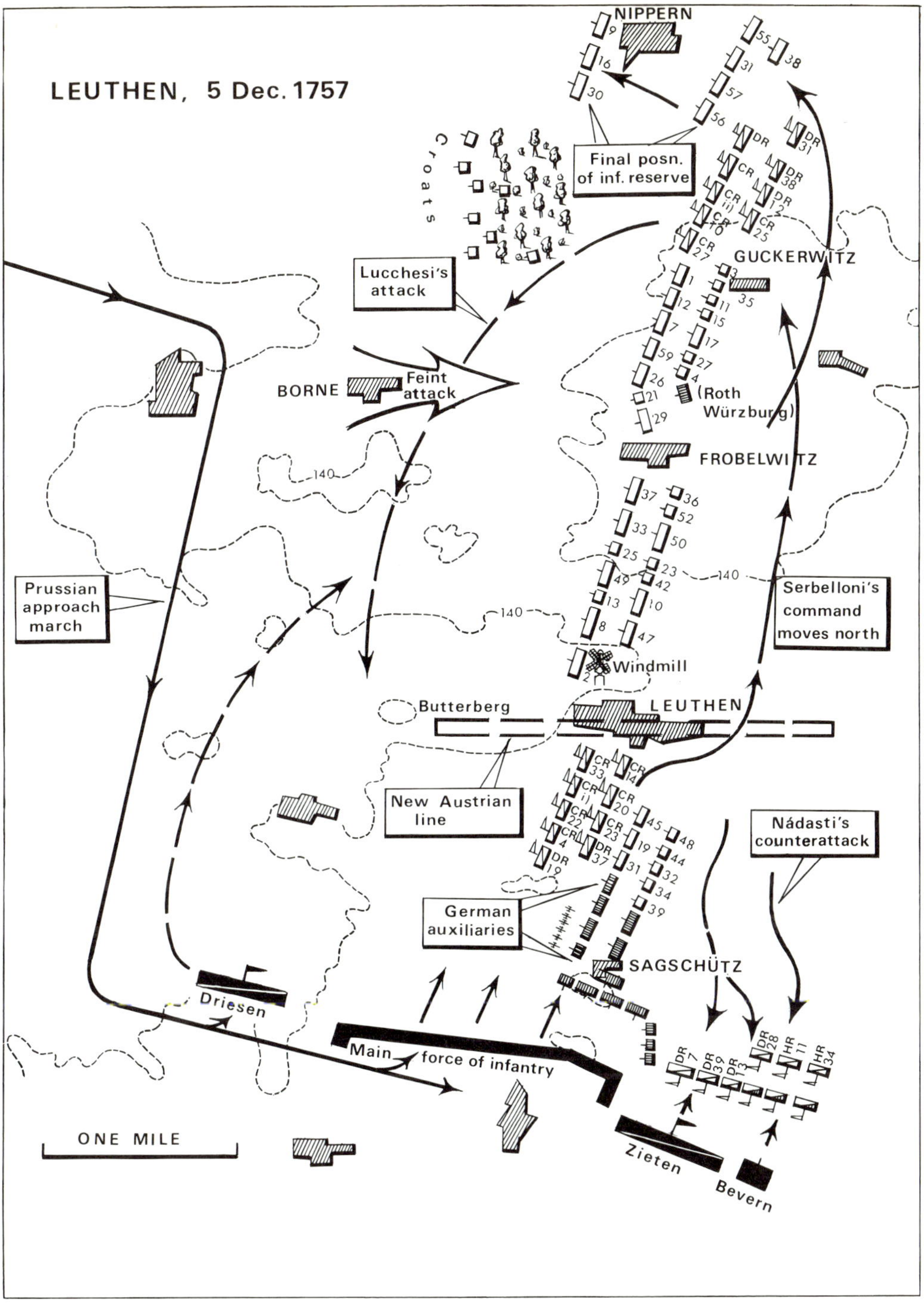

march his army eastwards into Silesia and gather up the remnants of Bevern's force. Then, when the Austrians could profitably have stayed put in the lines around Breslau, Charles took his troops out a few miles into the open country and arranged them along a not particularly strong front which faced to the west. The line extended for four and a half miles. The centre and the right were reasonably well posted, but the left flank stopped well short of the Schweidnitzer Wasser, which could otherwise have offered a useful support. Worse still, there was a misunderstanding which left some of the less-than-reliable Bavarian and Württemberg regiments holding the first line on this vulnerable sector.

With 65,000 troops at its disposal the Austrian high command was so confident, or so careless, that a good number of the heavy guns were left behind in Breslau, and the field bakery was actually positioned in front of the army.

> Many of the best-informed and most experienced officers were of the opinion that we could have avoided a major battle. But the faction of Prince Charles believed that his glory was at stake, and they were virtually certain of the victory.[62]

On the early morning of 5 December 1757 Frederick directed his army of 33,000 men over the snow-covered ground against the right centre of the Austrian position.

> The Austrians were standing in huge and apparently endless lines. This was the first time they had chosen to give battle in the open field, and they could hardly believe their eyes when they saw the small Prussian force advancing to attack them.[63]

Charles and the right-wing cavalry commander Lucchese assumed that the Prussians would continue to roll on in the same direction and hit the Austrian line somewhere near Frobelwitz. The infantry and much of the cavalry of the left were accordingly diverted to the north. The Austrians did not detect the change of direction when Frederick wheeled his army to his right and sent it south under cover of a fold in the ground. (Some time after the war, the Prussians out of curiosity ordered a horseman to ride with a flag along the line of Frederick's march, and they discovered that he remained completely invisible from the standpoint of the Austrian commanders.)

The danger appeared only too real to General Nádasti, commanding on the left flank, who sent messenger after messenger to warn Charles about the forces that were assembling to the south. He could evoke no response, and the Prussian army was given all the time it needed to dress its lines and bear down on the Austrian flank. At the first Prussian volleys the Württembergers took to their heels, and they were followed a few minutes later by the Bavarians, leaving the Austrian flank bereft of 11,000 or 12,000 men.

The troops from the Austrian right now came down at a run, only to pile up in disorder around the village of Leuthen. The officers strove to form the regiments into a new line facing south, but the Prussian infantry and heavy guns wrought frightful carnage, and by about half past three in the afternoon the Austrians had lost the village and were in retreat.

Only now did Lucchese commit the fine cavalry regiments of the right to the combat. Lucchese was killed in the mêlée, and his badly mauled command was repulsed, which brought about the final collapse of the Austrian infantry. A Prussian officer testified that 'the Austrian infantry fought magnificantly, but they were badly positioned. The cavalry could have won the victory on their own account, for they were stronger by themselves than the Prussians [this was a slight exaggeration], but in their usual fashion they did little or nothing of value'.[64]

The Prince de Ligne rode through the confusions of the following night to the quarters of Prince Charles and Daun at Grabischen. He found them 'sunk in the depths of despondency. The Prince seemed to be saying to himself "I can't believe it!", while Daun was evidently thinking "I told you so!".'[65]

Charles scarcely knew in what state he would find the army on the day after the carnage. We know now that he left behind no less than 6,000 or 7,000 wounded and 3,000 dead:

> The spectacle which presented itself was such as no language could well describe; great numbers of the men and horses which had fallen on the preceding day, being hard frozen, and their limbs fixed in the attitudes of pain or distortion in which they had expired.[66]

Entire regiments like the Durlach and Wallis infantry had been overwhelmed in the battle, which brought the number of prisoners to about 12,000, and another 17,600 men were lost when the demoralised fugitives in Breslau surrendered on 20 December. The survivors streamed over the wintry mountains to quarters in northern Bohemia, where cold and disease carried away many of those who had been spared in the last campaign.

Frederick himself was taken aback by the ease and magnitude of his victory, which delivered to him all the open country north of the border mountains. He asked the captured General Beck how the Austrians could have allowed themselves to be so completely beaten. Beck simply replied: 'We expected the main attack on our right wing, and we made our arrangements accordingly.' 'How was that possible?' rejoined Frederick, 'a single patrol against my left wing would have uncovered the truth almost at once.'[67]

On the Austrian side the débâcle gave rise to all kinds of sober reflections, but those astute critics the citizens of Vienna did not hesitate to lay the blame at the door of Prince Charles. Embarrassingly enough, it never crossed Charles's mind to give up the command. After two strong hints from the Emperor had failed, Maria Theresa drafted an unequivocal letter which was sent on 16 January 1758. Charles at last stepped down. The pity of it was that brave old Nádasti was sacrificed at the same time, to mollify the feelings of the Lorraine party. Never again was the 'Austrian Zieten' given active command.

THE TURNING OF THE TIDE – OLMÜTZ AND DOMSTADTL, MAY–JUNE 1758

The unfortunate outcome of the 1757 campaign left the initiative in Prussian hands. Frederick cleaned up some unfinished business from the last year and besieged the isolated fortress of Schweidnitz, which fell on 18 April. This eliminated the last Austrian foothold in Silesia, and added a further 8,000 prisoners to the bill which could be laid to the account of Leuthen.

With Silesia cleared, and Daun and the Austrian army ensconced in northern Bohemia, Frederick side-stepped to his left into Moravia and drove south against minimal resistance. There was much packing of bags in Vienna, for Frederick had 55,000 men under his command, and the only obstacle which stood between him and the capital was the lone Moravian fortress of Olmütz. 'At this juncture the Emperor happened to be passing his time *en joyeuse compagnie* at Hollitsch, but he was forced to curtail his recreation upon the repeated urgings of the Empress.'[68]

Considerably modernised of late, the fortress-town of Olmütz was well equipped with artillery and owned a garrison of 8,500 troops. The command lay in the hands of General Ernst Dietrich Marschall. His trembling voice and scarred face made him seem even older than his years, but he was counted as 'one of the most intelligent and courageous generals in the entire army'.[69]

Frederick laid Olmütz under preliminary blockade on 3 May, and stood by impatiently while a siege corps got on with the attack. The Austrians saw the Prussian generals and engineers ride out to reconnoitre the place on the 15th, and they were

> given a highly unpleasant greeting from our cannon at a range of 1,800 paces. The third shot was fortunate enough to bowl over an enemy hussar and his horse, and our guns continued to fire with such good effect that the party was soon driven behind the shelter of the summit of the Tafelberg.[70]

The Prussian batteries at last opened fire on 31 May, upon which Marschall issued the order to the townspeople and garrison that 'any talk of capitulation will be unfailingly punished by hanging'.[71] The garrison launched two destructive sorties, and the Austrian artillery commander Lieutenant-Colonel Alfson fired no less than 67,000 rounds from his cannon and mortars, which was more than enough to ensure superiority of the Austrian artillery throughout the defence. Thus Frederick's calculations were already going badly astray when some further misfortunes compelled him to abandon the siege in some haste.

It was Kaunitz who perhaps more than anyone else had kept alive Austria's will to continue the war through the gloomy winter of 1757–8. Heavy recruiting had gone ahead, especially in Bohemia, and the successive transports were incorporated by Field-Marshal Daun, the new commander, in his growing army. Fiery subordinates like Loudon were for doing something spectacular to stay Frederick's progress, but Daun thought it more important to train up the army in the strong and convenient camp of Skalitz. Amongst other things he combined his grenadier companies into powerful battalions of élite troops, and he taught his generals to place their regiments on the ground according to tactical necessity, instead of disposing them in long strings according to the order of battle. All the time General Lacy's new corps of staff officers was familiarising itself with its important work.

In May 1758 the army moved into the pleasant and fertile province of Moravia, which did a great deal by itself to raise the morale of the troops. Maria Theresa gave Daun complete freedom of action in the matter of relieving Olmütz, and on 22 June he was able to slip 1,200 troops into the fortress. Frederick exclaimed: 'I can hardly believe these are the Austrians! They must have learnt to march!'[72] Already the work of Lacy's staff was bearing fruit.

It was not long before the opportunity came for more decisive action. Word arrived that an important Prussian convoy of 4,000 ammunition and supply waggons had set out from Silesia for the force in front of Olmütz, which inspired Daun to commission the generals Loudon and Siskovics to intercept the transport in the wooded valleys. Loudon's detachment made an indecisive attack on the head of the column on 29 June, but on the next day he and Siskovics closed from opposite sides near Domstadtl and destroyed virtually the entire train. Meanwhile Lacy and his staff had reconnoitred the tracks through the hills, and the main army was bearing down on Olmütz in a clever arrangement of several columns.

All this was too much for Frederick, who raised the siege of Olmütz on 2 July.
 Old Fritz was never to be so dangerous again. The ghost of 1740–1 was at last

exorcised, and Austria was firmly set on the path of strategic and political counter-offensive.

MR BIGWIG TAKES HIS TIME, JULY–NOVEMBER 1758

If the new-found Austrian power was slow to assert itself, the explanation lies chiefly in the character of Field-Marshal Daun.

> He was famous for a number of high skills: the ability to keep his army supplied and to see to its security; the art of carrying out prudent marches; the knowledge of how to choose advantageous and happy positions; the secret of how to exhaust his enemies. But when we look for an aptitude for the offensive, or the determination required to exploit a victory, we find that these qualities were by no means present to the same extent.[73]

Frederick used to speak rudely about 'Mr Bigwig' or 'his fat excellency of Kolin', and one of the French officers at Daun's own headquarters lamented:

> If only the field-marshal was a little less timid: but this seems to be a vain hope. There is such a narrow margin between a timorousness of this kind, and the prudence you must always show when you are facing the King of Prussia, that a naturally cautious man is inclined to confuse the two.[74]

Daun was alive to the kind of thing that was being said about him. He once wrote to Maria Theresa:

> People talk about exterminating all and sundry, about attacking and fighting every day, about being everywhere at once, and anticipating the enemy. Nobody desires this more than I do . . . God knows that I am no coward, but I will never set my hands to anything which I judge to be impossible, or to the disadvantage of Your Majesty's service.[75]

In Daun's defence we should add that some of his generals gave him less than outstanding support, and that he had never desired to assume active field command itself. In one respect Daun's habits of mind actually placed Frederick in a quandary, for it was just when the field-marshal's slow uncoilings lulled Old Fritz into the deepest torpor that Daun was apt to listen to the bold counsel of someone like Lacy or Loudon. Against every expectation the Austrian army would therefore be committed to the attack, and the Prussians might find the whitecoats rampaging through their streets of tents.

At least Daun's superb professionalism was never in doubt. On 6 July 1757 a French officer admired the way he brought the army in eight columns from Benatek to Jung-Bunzlau: 'he is always the first on horseback, and he never returns to his quarters until he has examined the front and neighbourhood of his camps. To accompany him on his rides is therefore most instructive'.[76]

In 1758 it was unfortunate that the feeble 'exploitation' of the happy outcome of the campaign in Moravia gave the field-marshal's enemies so much ammunition. With Daun trailing a long way behind, Frederick executed a circuit into north-east Bohemia, then took himself back to Silesia and went in search of the Russians.

Daun gave up the chase, and in the late summer he moved over to Saxony, where he intended to act in concert with the Prince of Zweibrücken and the reconstituted *Reichsarmee.*

Daun and Zweibrücken hatched a mighty plan to encircle and crush the army of Prince Henry of Prussia, whom Frederick had left in charge of his forces in Saxony. However, Zweibrücken cooled towards the project, and Daun himself wasted a precious day holding a review in honour of Count Haugwitz. Thus the Austrians accomplished nothing of value before Frederick, having beaten the Russians at Zorndorf on 25 August, arrived in Saxony to resume his quarrel with Daun.

On 11 September news came that Frederick was in the offing, and Daun accordingly settled his army among the ponds, marshes, woods and ravines at Stolpen, in the tangled hill country east of Dresden. A French volunteer sighed: 'The junior officers and soldiers are unanimous in their desire to fight. Never has an army let slip such a magnificent opportunity of acquiring glory'.[77]

Frederick manoeuvred against the Austrian communications, and on the night of 5/6 October Daun began a march to a less exposed position at Kittlitz, where his 80,000 troops arrived on the 7th. Three days later Frederick came up with his own army about 30,000 men and disposed them in a notably ill-articulated fashion nearby at Hochkirch.

Frederick's carelessness enabled Lacy to overcome Daun's instinctive caution, and for several days in succession the field-marshal rode forward to sound out the ground for a full-scale attack on the Prussian camp. During one of the reconnaissances the little group of Austrian officers came under fire from the Prussian outposts. As the balls were buzzing around, General Serbelloni proclaimed 'They're only flies'. A moment later a bullet shattered his hand. Daun turned and quietly remarked, 'Yes, but they seem to bite.'[78]

The detailed working-out of the arrangements was left to Lacy, who devised a plan for seven main columns to converge on the Prussian camp. The principal focus of the assault was to be the exposed Prussian salient on the spur at Hochkirch, which was to be taken by forty-two battalions of line infantry with attached Croats and cavalry, and the attack was to go in when the clock in Hochkirch church struck five on the morning of 14 October.

Everything was done to leave Frederick's peace of mind undisturbed:

> The tents were left standing in the Austrian camp, and the usual watch fires were religiously maintained. A large number of workers spent the whole night felling trees for an *abatis*, and all the time they called out to each other and sang.[79]

At the appointed moment the Austrians burst through the enemy outposts in thick fog, then captured the heavy battery in front of Hochkirch and poured into the village behind. A Prussian describes how

> the air resounded with the whizzing and clattering of the cannon shot. The Hungarian battle cry *Hudry! Hudry!* penetrated through the shouts of the Prussian and Austrian grenadiers. The ear was filled with the noise of bullets and sword blades, as they found their mark, and with the cries of the wounded soldiers. The night had been as dark as pitch, but now it was illuminated as if

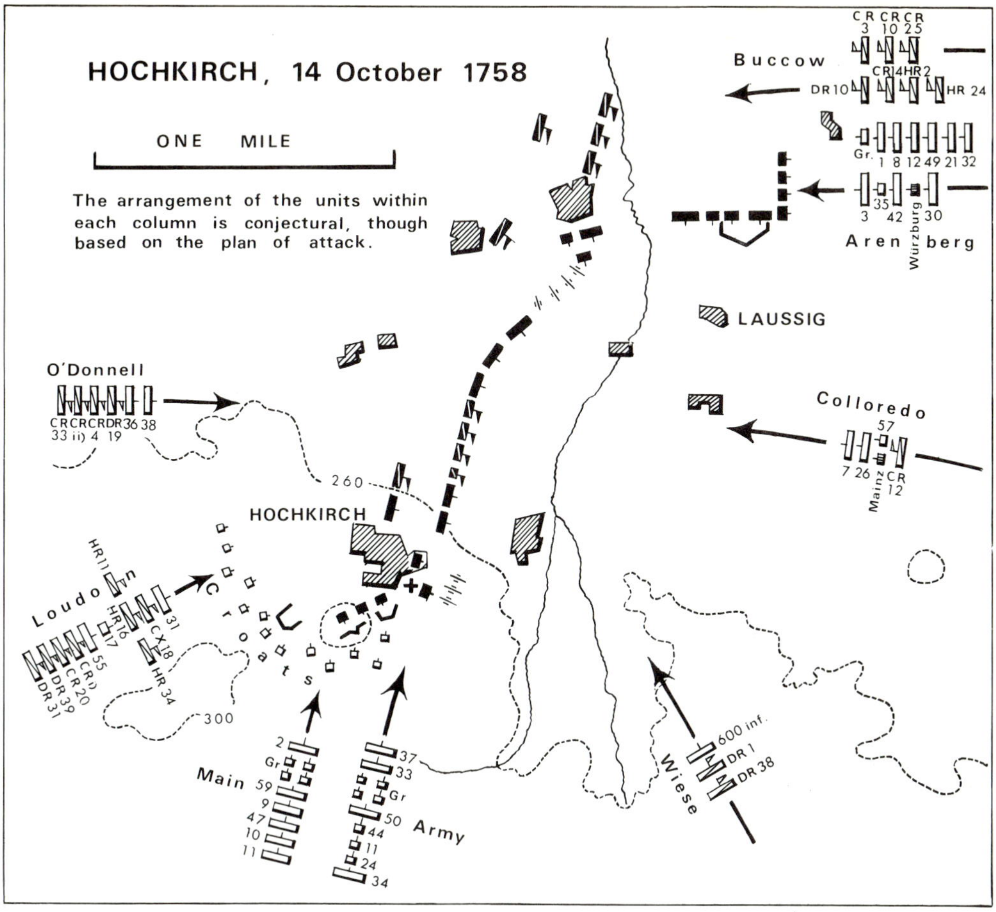

by continual lightning, enabling us to distinguish the white coats and bearskin caps of the enemy from the blue coats and brass grenadier caps of the battling Prussians.[80]

Frederick was still absent from the scene, but Field-Marshal Keith and other Prussian commanders organised a number of counter-attacks and threatened to recover the ground that had been lost. During these critical minutes General Lacy in person brought up three companies of mounted grenadiers and carabiniers and charged the Prussian flank. General Loudon too was in a fiery mood, and with his command he broke up a move by the Prussian cavalry under Zieten.

The Austrian right now entered the action, taking the villages of Koditz and Laussig in its first onrush, and battling its way into possession of the large battery on the Prussian left. Everywhere else, however, the Prussians made good their escape from the considerably superior Austrian forces. The officers were concerned only with gathering their men together again, and the generals Durlach, Arenberg and Löwenstein showed a distinct lack of energy.

At a cost to themselves of rather over 7,000 men the Austrians had inflicted a loss of more than 9,000 troops on Frederick's army in the bitterly-fought battle of Hochkirch. Field-Marshal Keith was numbered among the Prussian dead.

His body, after he fell, stripped and naked, was carried into the church in the village and laid upon a barrow, covered with a Croat's cloak. When all resistance on the part of the Prussians was completely at an end, and their army dispersed, Marshal Daun, accompanied by Lacy and several other officers entered the church. Seeing a dead body exposed on a barrow, and conceiving it to be a person of distinction, he enquired who it was. Lacy approached the corpse, and after attentively regarding it, exclaimed with great emotion 'Alas! 'tis my father's best friend, 'tis Keith!'. . . At so melancholy a piece of intelligence, Daun burst into tears, as did Lacy, and every person present. How affecting a moment, and how sublime, as well as touching a subject, for the pencil of an artist![81]

Drying his eyes, Daun took stock of what had been gained. The damage to Frederick was great, but the field-marshal was only too aware that the passivity of some of his generals had prevented his victory from being truly decisive.

Daun rejected a proposal from Lacy to launch a new attack on the 26th. Thus Frederick was allowed to break off contact and hasten eastwards into Silesia, where the fortress of Neisse had been invested by an Austrian corps under General Harsch. Daun abandoned all hope of catching up with Old Fritz – a tacit avowal of the superior marching qualities of the Prussians – and instead he turned back against the city of Dresden.

In his brisk fashion Frederick relieved Neisse and rushed back to Saxony before the Austrians had the opportunity to do anything of consequence against Dresden. This final disappointment deprived the Austrians of any hope of holding on in Saxony through the winter, and so in the second half of November the army crossed 'that furious chain of mountains'[82] into Bohemia.

THE AUSTRIAN ARMY IN THE MIDDLE OF THE SEVEN YEARS WAR

The inconclusive close of so many of Field-Marshal Daun's campaigns stood in unfortunate contrast to the very pronounced improvement in the battleworthiness of his army. Cognazzo had once known cases

> where the sight of a blue Prussian coat or the terrifying glint of their fusilier and grenadier caps had been enough to spread panic among our troops. But they failed to produce sufficient effect at Kolin and Breslau, and they had clearly lost most of their old power as the day dawned at Hochkirch.[83]

By the end of 1760 Lacy had become convinced that the Prussians had lost their edge:

> No troops could show more courage and steadfastness than ours have done on various occasions, especially in the battle of Breslau and just recently at Maxen. When it comes to a battle, both officers and men are brimming over with boldness and enthusiasm.[84]

At the higher level, Frederick of Prussia drew the attention of his generals to the proficiency which the Austrians were showing in their camps, in their marches and above all in the way they disposed their mighty artillery in defensive positions. General Fouqué replied to the king at the beginning of 1759 that he did not see how the Prussians could cope with this kind of warfare. He agreed with Frederick that it was a good idea to tempt the Austrians into fighting in the open plains, 'but when I reflect on the conduct of Field-Marshal Daun in the last campaign I almost doubt whether Your Majesty will be able to lure that old fox . . . from his earth'. In his circular Frederick had also raised the possibility of attacking the Austrians while they were on the move, but Fouqué had to point out that their marches were 'so well prepared, and masked by such a swarm of light troops, that we may scarcely hope to gain any real advantage on such occasions'. As for the guns, the Prussians simply could not compete: 'Your Majesty himself is willing to concede that the Austrian artillery is superior to ours, that their heavy guns are better served, and that they are more effective at long range – both from the quality of their powder and the weight of their charges.'[85]

Many of the older and less competent Austrian generals were withdrawn from active command in the course of the war. There was still a place for well-tried, or at least well-entrenched, senior warriors like Buccow, Arenberg, O'Donnell, Harsch, Sincère and Serbelloni, but the recent campaigns had thrown up a new generation of lively young commanders of the ilk of Lacy, Loudon, Beck, Brentano, Hadik and Macquire, who had been major-generals or simply colonels at the beginning of the war.

The tragedy was that Loudon and Lacy, the two most able of the younger gentlemen, were at dagger's drawn. Franz Moritz Lacy (1725–1801) was certainly the better connected of the pair. Brought up under the wing of Maximilian Browne, he had become the creator of Daun's staff corps in 1758 and consequently 'the field-marshal's right hand'. The official promotion to full general followed in February 1760. Lacy was just as good at inspiring bold attacks as at making the complicated arrangements for moving troops and supplies, and these qualities, together with his courtly ways, won him a secure place in the esteem of Daun and Maria Theresa.

Lacy's competitor in popular esteem was Gideon Ernst Loudon (1717–90), a man of very different stamp, and 'the King of Prussia's most dangerous and troublesome enemy'.[86] He was born in the Russian Baltic provinces in 1717, and spent his earlier career as a penniless soldier of fortune. In the early 1740s he had actually offered his sword to Frederick of Prussia, who spurned the approach, and after his rebuff he entered the Austrian service as a junior officer. He made his name very rapidly in the Seven Years War, and his devastating blow at Domstadtl in 1758 set him firmly on the path to high command. Kaunitz prized Loudon highly, but his rugged virtues won him precious few other friends in exalted places. He was 'a man of individualistic character, at once serious, modest and half melancholy . . . he spoke little, but what he had to say was accurate and true'.[87]

In comparing the two rivals, we find that Lacy's talents were considered 'more universal', Loudon's 'more concentrated'.

> One is greater in the theory of war, in the vast detail requisite for enabling an army to act with effect, and in combining or directing a variety of military operations. The other has no equal in rapid, decisive and successful execution. Lacy is more respected in Vienna: Loudon is more dreaded at Berlin.[88]

THE MOVE TO THE NORTHERN PLAIN, 1759

After the see-saw campaigning of the first three years of the war, the contest became a struggle of attrition. Frederick now raced desperately from one front to another, while the main Austrian army consolidated itself beyond the border mountains in southern Silesia and Saxony, and sent various corps to help out its friends on the two flanks – the Russians to the east, and the *Reichsarmee* on the Elbe to the west.

In 1759 it seemed for once that the allies were willing to make a significant contribution to the downfall of Old Fritz. The French concluded a secret treaty at the end of 1758, by which they promised new support to the German auxiliaries, while the Russians made ready to open up the Brandenburg-Prussian heartland from the east with an army of 70,000 men under the command of Field-Marshal Saltykov.

At the start of the campaigning season Daun had a total of almost 100,000 men at his disposal, of whom 53,000 remained with the main army, but it was only after some urgent prodding from Vienna that in late June he moved slowly from the border mountains into Upper Silesia. The Russians were left to fight their way towards the Oder without support, and the most that Daun consented to do for the moment was to detach Lieutenant-General Loudon with about 24,000 picked troops. This force reached the river Oder at Zilchendorf on 2 August.

The Russians had arrived on the east bank of the river opposite, but they quite reasonably demanded that Daun ought to bring up his main army before they could take the risk of crossing to the west bank. Loudon carried his corps to the far side to show his willingness to help, and he joined the Russians in their camp of Kunersdorf, which extended along a low sandy ridge opposite the town of Frankfurt-an-der-Oder. He had just persuaded the Russians to pass to the west bank after all, when the joint force was assailed by the enemy.

Frederick had disengaged all available troops and made his passage of the Oder unhindered by Daun, who was still fifty miles away at Triebel. The king had only 50,000 troops to pit against the 60,000 of the Russians and Austrians, but these odds were still very favourable indeed compared with the ones which would have obtained if Daun had put forward the extra effort needed to join hands with Saltykov.

On the night of 11/12 August Frederick sent his army on a wide clockwise circuit which was designed to take the camp of Kunersdorf in its north-eastern salient and rear. In the early morning a great cloud of dust arose from the woods as the Prussians marched to their start lines, then as the sun rose in the cloudless sky the Austro-Russian salient came under a devastating bombardment and a heavy attack by infantry. Loudon had sent twelve companies of Austrian grenadiers to help the Russians to hold this exposed position, but after three-quarters of an hour of fighting the survivors had to withdraw to the little Kuh-Grund valley which lay in front of the main position:

> We were looking into the sun, and the wind blew into our faces the smoke of the battle and the dense clouds of dust which were thrown up from this sandy soil. We could see no more than three paces, which greatly aided the enemy and acted to our severe disadvantage.[89]

Frederick brought into action the 'diversionary' corps of General Finck to support his attack from the north, and the allied line was bent into a hairpin shape with the open end facing towards the Oder. The Prussians battered in vain at the positions under the scorching afternoon sun, and 'the Austrians performed miracles',[90] although they were badly knocked about in the process.

In the late afternoon Loudon brought together the Russian and Austrian cavalry and threw it at the Prussian horse opposite the sandy height of the Grosser-Spitzberg. The Prussians were already exhausted by a night march and a day of strenuous combat, and they collapsed under this final ordeal. The Prussian cavalry fled, whereupon the left-wing infantry was ridden down by the allied troopers and the whole of the rest of the army dissolved in panic. By the end of the day Frederick was able to collect just 5,000 troops out of his original host.

The victorious day of Kunersdorf represented the only occasion on which the Russians and Austrians fought side by side in any numbers, and ironically enough the degree of co-operation was remarkable. The Austrian infantry and guns were employed wherever they were most needed, with no particular regard to the order of battle, and the Russians did not hesitate to commit their own cavalry regiments to the command of Loudon.

The Russian Empress Elizabeth sent Loudon a costly sword of honour as a token of her gratitude. Loudon, who dreaded compliments more than battles, forwarded the weapon to Daun, whom he over-generously held to be the author of his victory.

Although depleted by a quarter, the Russian army crossed to the west bank of the Oder in the middle of August, and parties of Cossacks began to present themselves to the astonished gaze of the Austrians. On one such occasion, 'after various grimaces and prostrations their chief made his report, while they proceeded to skewer several hares in the field-marshal's presence'.[91] Maria Theresa thought it would have been natural to combine the armies and exploit the victory by advancing on Berlin, which lay only fifty miles away. Saltykov, however, felt that he had done more than enough for the common cause, while Daun was obsessed with a desire to join with the *Reichsarmee* against Prince Henry of Prussia, who still commanded a reasonably intact army and was threatening to invade Bohemia.

The allied armies drew apart in the late summer. The Russians marched up the Oder, but in October they abandoned their half-hearted move against the fortress of Glogau when Frederick came up to see them off. Daun, after all these wasted months, took his army back to the south-west to do something to exploit a favourable opportunity which had suddenly opened up in Saxony, when the *Reichsarmee* and an Austrian corps under General Macquire had browbeaten the isolated garrison of Dresden into capitulating on 4 September. With Frederick still absent on the Oder, the responsibility of disputing Saxony devolved upon his brother Prince Henry of Prussia, a superb professional who rivalled the Austrians in the skill with which he chose his ground.

By retiring from one strong position to another Prince Henry preserved his army reasonably intact until Frederick appeared on the scene with reinforcements from Silesia. Daun drew back, and in the second half of November he began to settle his army for a long stay in the camp of Plauen in the hills south of Dresden.

Seeking to match Daun at his own game, Frederick dispatched Lieutenant-General Finck with about 15,000 troops to occupy the plateau of Maxen in the broken and heavily forested country in the Austrian rear. This tempting target induced Lacy to sound out the paths through the woods:

> There was great talk of difficulties. Lacy sought to allay them, engaging his honour and wagering his neck for the success of the enterprise. Debates went on until the last moment, and almost all the generals opposed the scheme. But

finally Lacy won over the field-Marshal, and on the spot he proceeded to make arrangements that were every bit as fine as the ones for Hochkirch.[92]

On the morning of 20 November 1759 the enemy came under concerted attacks from the Austrians and a detachment of the *Reichsarmee*. The wretched Finck discovered that the enemy were on all sides of him, and on the 21st he capitulated with 558 officers and some 13,000 men.

The *Finckenfang* at Maxen came too late to change the face of the war in Saxony, but it encouraged the flagging French and Russians to persevere in the alliance, and it gave Daun's reputation a new lease of life.

Now that Dresden was in his grasp, Daun was able to retain a useful foothold in southern Saxony for the winter. He sent his army into quarters in December, believing his duty was completed:

> Frederick's army was always reduced to less than half by the end of every campaign, but the Austrians invariably made the mistake of allowing him time to rebuild his forces. If they had ventured to make a single winter campaign they would have finished him off for good, for the Prussian army is not clothed to withstand a winter war.[93]

LOUDON'S YEAR, 1760

Even his brilliant coup at Maxen failed to rescue Lacy from a deepening depression. He was downcast when news came that his mother had died in the same month,

far away in Russia, and he was aware that the public and some of the military men held him responsible, however unjustly, for the delays and hesitations of the last campaign. The well-meaning Maria Theresa did him little good by advancing him to full general, for he was happier and more effective when planning for the army as a staff officer, than in exercising the heavy but localised responsibilities of the immediate commander of a wing.

Loudon and his ally at court, Chancellor Kaunitz, sensed that this was the time to take the initiative, and in the spring of 1760 they persuaded Maria Theresa to accept a plan of campaign that left the main army in Saxony with the obligation of holding down the main body of the Prussian forces, while Loudon took off with 50,000 troops into Silesia and joined an auxiliary corps of Russians. Lacy described the scheme as a 'carnival idea', engendered by the heady fumes of the *Fasching* season. The Russians failed to put in an appearance, but the Loudon–Kaunitz strategy was put into execution anyway.

While Daun and Frederick glowered at each other across their old stamping ground in southern Saxony, Loudon irrupted from Bohemia into Silesia. On the early morning of 23 June he swept the 12,000 troops of the Prussian commander Fouqué from the long ridge outside the road junction at Landeshut. Fouqué was one of those tigerish lieutenant-generals whom the Prussian service bred in such profusion, and he was badly cut up by the Austrian cavalry while he was holding out with the last of his men. He was saved from further dismemberment by Colonel Voit of the Löwenstein dragoons. With all the courtesy of eighteenth-century Austria, Voit brought up his own parade horse and begged the bleeding Fouqué to mount.

> He declined, commenting 'The blood would spoil your fine saddlery'. Voit replied 'It will become far more precious, when it is stained with the blood of a hero'. There was one officer who was vulgar enough to taunt the captured commander for his misfortune to his very face. But all the officers who were present condemned his bad manners. Fouqué interrupted, and merely said 'Let him speak, gentlemen! You know how it goes in war: it's my turn today, and to-morrow it's yours'.[94]

The news of these exciting events drew both Frederick and Daun towards Silesia. Upon reflection, however, Frederick found the idea of having to deal with the combined armies of Loudon and Daun somewhat unattractive, and before Daun could prevent him he doubled back and laid Dresden under siege on 13 July. This was an appalling risk. Frederick had thereby interposed himself between the active garrison of Dresden under General Macquire, and the main Austrian army which by itself was twice the size of his own.

Against all the instincts of the soldiers, the Austrian army remained motionless while Frederick subjected Dresden to a barbaric bombardment:

> We were chatting and regaling ourselves in our camp, while in the distance one of the finest capitals in the world was going up in flames . . . Field-Marshal Daun witnessed the sight from his headquarters at Schönfeld, as did the Prince of Zweibrücken from his fine castle of Gross-Sedlitz. Fragments of cloth and charred paper were carried as far as our camp.[95]

Frederick raised his siege of Dresden on 29 July, not on account of any pressure from Daun, but because he had heard that Loudon had stormed into the fortress of Glatz in brilliant style three days earlier. The king set off in some haste for Silesia, escorted by the Austrian army in its usual fashion.

Thus the stage was set for a concentration of all the combatants. Frederick dragged his exhausted 30,000 troops to the east and established communication with the corps of Prince Henry, who was holding off an army of Russians. Daun on his side joined forces with Loudon, which produced a combined army of 90,000, and the Russians even agreed to feed General Chernyshev with 25,000 troops into the mass of humanity that was trampling around central Silesia.

During these interesting proceedings Lacy happened to lose his baggage to the Prussians. King Frederick courteously sent back the personal effects, but Lacy asked him to be so kind as to return the maps as well – the ones he had made as chief of staff to Daun. He declared that he would rather have lost the maps to Frederick, than any one else, but added that he would be glad to have them back all the same. Old Fritz replied that it was his ambition to

> introduce more urbanity and politeness to a trade which is inherently hard and cruel. As soon as the pace of the campaign begins to slacken, my topographical engineers will set to work to copy your maps, and I shall be delighted to send them back to you as soon as they have finished.[96]

The Austrians steeled themselves to carry out a monster converging attack against Frederick's position – a kind of Maxen writ large. The scheme was for Loudon to creep with his 24,000 men across the Katzbach below Liegnitz and come at the enemy from the eastern flank, while Daun brought the main army across the little river in a frontal assault. The attack was due to go in on the early morning of 15 August 1760. During the night, however, Frederick shifted his ground to the plateau near Liegnitz, which was enough by itself to upset the Austrian calculations. Worse still, the column commanders of the main army ignored their orders, and the host was slow to get under way.

These delays left Loudon to face the enemy alone. He carried out his instructions to the letter, in ignorance of what had happened to the main army, and from before dawn until five in the morning he was engaged in a hopeless fight with the Prussians, who deluged his grenadiers with canister and launched a vicious counter-attack.

Loudon finally withdrew his battered command over the Katzbach in excellent order. As Frederick looked on he is said to have commended the example to his officers: 'Except for the bodies lying about you'd think they were marching off parade!'.[97] The main Austrian army scarcely got into action at all, but Loudon had lost more than 8,000 men of his corps.

In his first bitterness Loudon complained that the Austrian high command had deliberately left him in the lurch. Wherever the blame resided, the Austrian officers were full of recriminations over the fumblings which had lost them a unique opportunity of crushing Frederick's 30,000 men with 90,000 of their own.

Daun still owned a convincing superiority over Frederick, but the Russians had understandably lost interest in joining forces, and he felt that he could not justify the risk of giving another battle. In this time of frustration he seized with alacrity on a suggestion from the Russians that each of the allied armies should send a raiding corps against Berlin. On 28 September Lacy was accordingly dispatched from Langenwaltersdorf with a lightly laden force of about 15,000 troops. The Russians in their turn sent 20,000 men under the generals Tottleben, Chernyshev and Panin.

Lacy entered Berlin on 9 October 1760 – a matter of hours after the place had been taken over by the Russians. Vienna had ceded the Arsenal and the immense magazines to the Russians in advance, but the greencoats merely roamed through the stores like destructive children, and the citizens were able to retrieve most of the weapons and equipment for their king.

Lacy took under his care various trophies which had been captured from the Austrians in earlier campaigns and raised 50,000 in 'contributions' from Berlin and 31,000 from Potsdam and other towns. However, the Austrian commanders were very careful to leave private property intact. Major-General Emerich Esterházy placed the regiment of Kaiser on guard over the palaces of Potsdam and, according to the Prince de Ligne, 'he appropriated nothing more than a table for himself, a writing desk for the general [Lacy], a flute for O'Donnell, and a pen for me'.[98] Frustrated at Potsdam, the marauding Cossacks betook themselves to the palace of Charlottenburg and wrecked it in concert with the Austrian hussars and the Saxons: 'They marched knee-deep in shattered porcelain and crystal'.[99]

Lacy would have liked to have seized the opportunity to wreak really serious damage on the Prussian military machine, but the Swedes showed no inclination to venture from Pomerania, while General Tottleben was making a suspiciously incomplete job of wrecking the Prussian war establishments. Frederick in person was now moving on Berlin, and since it was dangerous to tarry any longer, the Austrians and Russians went their separate ways on 12 October.

THE TORGAU CAMPAIGN, OCTOBER–NOVEMBER 1760

Those dreadful weeks of marching and countermarching on the open Silesian plains under the late summer sun had worked as much destruction on Daun's main army as a major battle. The infantry and cavalry were almost on their knees, while the artillery horses were so depleted that many of the cannon were being dragged by oxen. Daun saw that it would be more profitable to transfer the theatre of war back to Saxony, where the *Reichsarmee* had been making good progress down the Elbe. Marching westwards, Daun was rejoined by Lacy's corps on 23 October, and the united army crossed to the left bank of the Elbe. Loudon was left behind in Silesia with 30,000 men, which was a severe diminution in itself, yet Daun took no measures to supply the deficiency by linking up with the *Reichsarmee* or even recalling the 11,000 Austrians who were serving with that noble body. Thus the Prussians and Austrians were evenly matched at about 56,000 troops each when Frederick marched to the attack on 3 November 1760.

For several days now the Austrians had been making themselves comfortable in an old camp of Prince Henry's, which extended along a narrow ridge to the west of Torgau. The army was facing south. It had the fortified town of Torgau to its left, the wooded Dommitzscher Heide on its right, and in front there were vineyards which sloped down to a bottom of ponds and swampy channels. The corps of General Lacy was stationed on the far eastern, or left, flank, facing the large Torgau Pond.

The 3rd dawned cold and windy, and every now and then the lowering black clouds discharged blinding showers of hail and sleet. The Prussians made their appearance from the south-east early in the morning, and as far as could be made out through the murk a large corps of bluecoats (actually Zieten with 18,000 troops) was making ready to attack the left of the Austrian line head-on. Daun therefore ordered Lacy to keep a watch on events in this part of the world, a commission which effectively tied up Lacy's corps and the neighbouring regiments of the main army – 26,000 men altogether.

Meanwhile Frederick and the rest of the Prussians took themselves on a wide westerly circuit through the woods, intending to come at the Austrians from their rear. Daun was at his best in this kind of situation. Responding calmly and efficiently to the enemy ploy, he rearranged his command so as to form a westward-facing flank and a new, northward-facing front. Many of the regiments simply had to reverse their fronts.

The purgatory of the Prussian army began towards two in the afternoon, when Frederick hurled his best troops – ten battalions of grenadiers – against the western sector of the new Austrian front. The Austrian artillery commander, Major-General Walther Waldenau, had assembled a total of 275 pieces in the position, and as the grenadiers emerged from the trees 'Daun received the Prussians with a cannonade such as has never been experienced since the invention of gunpowder'.[100] The grenadiers were massacred.

Three of the Austrian infantry regiments now made an ill-timed counter-attack, which helped to provoke the Prussians into throwing altogether sixteen battalions into a new assault. This, too, was convincingly repulsed, though in the process Daun received a painful musket wound in the left foot. He kept his injury a secret for two hours, until the blood was dripping from his boot.

The front of the main Austrian army actually grew stronger as the battle progressed, for General Sincère incorporated the flanking regiments in the new line, and General Ried brought up the reserve corps in time to catch the right flank of the third of the suicidal attacks of the Prussian infantry, which was launched by eleven battalions. Further to the east the Prussian left-wing cavalry under the Prince of Holstein carried out a dangerous two-pronged attack and made some progress into the Austrian position before it was finally repulsed by General Carl O'Donnell with the cavalry of the right. With these efforts the resources of the main Prussian army seemed to have been exhausted.

Now that the battle was going so gratifyingly well, Daun warned Lacy to give adequate support to the western flank at Süptitz, where some firing had broken out. He then left the command of the main army in the hands of O'Donnell and had himself borne away at half past six in the evening to have his wound dressed at Torgau.

We left Zieten and his corps of Prussians confronting Lacy away to the south-east. After several hours of fruitless cannonading, Zieten began to follow in Frederick's tracks with the ambition of rejoining his royal master on the far side of the field. He thereby set in train a chapter of accidents which turned the battle in favour of the Prussians. Seeking to cover his march against disturbance from the Austrian army, Zieten detached two brigades against the western end of the enemy position. Some of these battalions attacked the village of Süptitz (which gave rise to the noise which carried to the ears of Daun), while the others managed to pick their way across an unguarded causeway and up the slopes leading to the dominating slopes behind Süptitz. The Austrian response was muddled and slow, and Lacy had taken no effective counter-measures before the ragged remnants of the main Prussian army surged up from the other side and finally wrested the heights of Süptitz from the whitecoats.

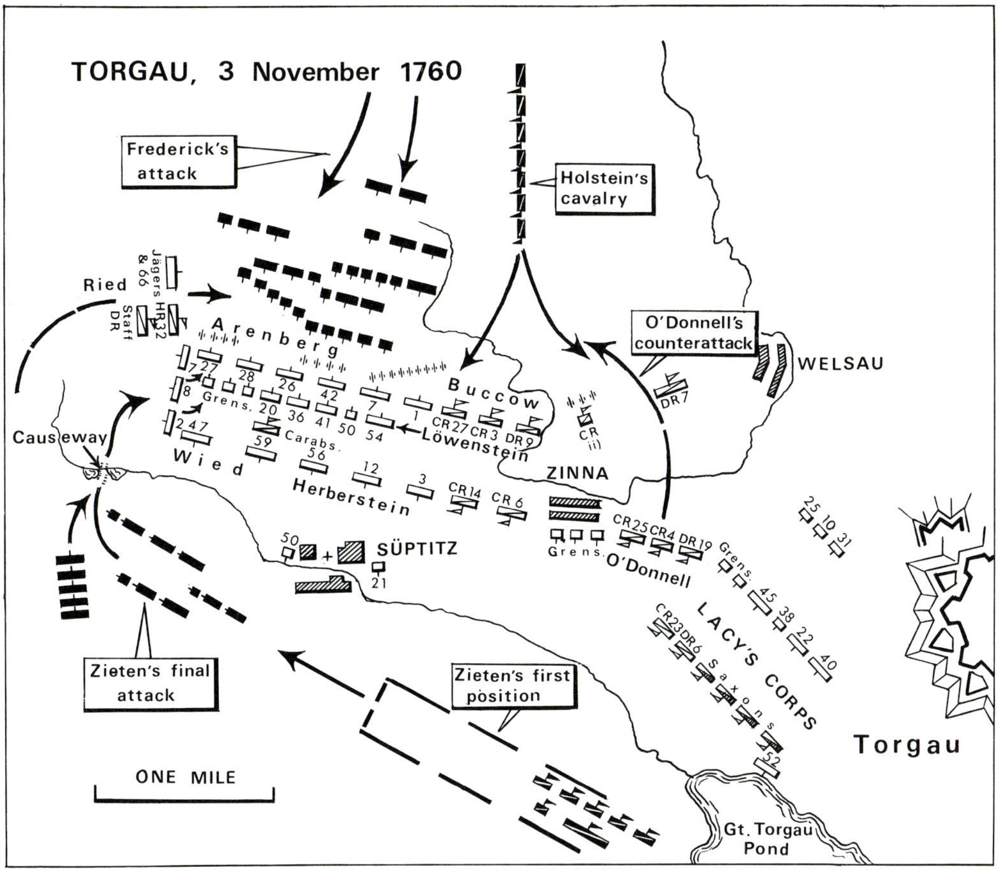

Amid all the uncertainties, it was only too clear that the vital heights were in the hands of the enemy, and that the rest of the position was untenable. Daun had already sent off a messenger to report his victory to Vienna, and he was thunderstruck when Lacy and O'Donnell came to him at Torgau with the dreadful news.

Whole regiments wandered about in confusion in the fourteen-hour night, and the casualties lay on the freezing field in their thousands.

> Weltering in their blood and deprived of all help, these unfortunates desired nothing but a speedy death. And yet many hundreds of them had to undergo still greater agonies before their wish was fulfilled. A host of degenerate humanity – soldiers, drivers and women – swarmed over the battlefield on that bloody night, robbing the living and the dead. The helpless wounded were not permitted to retain so much as their shirts. They uplifted their voices in loud complaint, but their cries were lost in the frightful sound of the general uproar which rose from thousands of throats towards the clouds. Many of the wounded were murdered by those monsters out of fear of discovery.[101]

Now that they had been turned out of their position with a loss of more than 15,000 men, the Austrians were left with no alternative but to try to dodge round the Prussian army and make for the safety of Dresden and the mountains. Over the following days Lacy managed this perilous operation with something like his old skill.

Thus the campaign in Saxony ended very much in the same state as it had begun. The Austrians seemed to be unbeatable as long as they held on in Dresden and the nest of nearby camps, but their luck ran out as soon as they ventured any distance into the northern plain.

The question of command was earnestly debated. Daun refused to institute a 'witch hunt' against his protégé Lacy, but that gentleman had effectively disqualified himself for field command through his apparent inactivity in the great battle. Lacy in his turn was unwilling to serve under Loudon. Daun therefore found himself once more the chief of the main field army, though with severely curtailed moral authority. This was surely the least desirable outcome of all.

1761, THE VANISHING OPPORTUNITY

The diminution of Daun's prestige was only too evident when the plans were being shaped for the next campaign. Maria Theresa and Kaunitz now hoped for great things of Loudon, who was to advance with about 70,000 men into Silesia and act in concert with the Russians. Lacy urged in vain that all the resources should be concentrated under Daun's command for a decisive blow in Saxony. Understandably, perhaps, Maria Theresa and her chancellor doubted whether on his past record Daun would be up to carrying out such a dramatic scheme. He was accordingly left to hold his positions in Saxony.

For most of the campaigning season Loudon seemed to be having no better luck with his war in Silesia. The Russians were certainly in a compliant mood, and sent Field-Marshal Buturlin into Silesia with an army which joined forces with Loudon's command on 17 August. Frederick, however, bid defiance to the allies from his famous camp of Bunzelwitz, and on 11 September Buturlin began to march most of his men back to Poland.

Late in September Frederick emerged from his shell and began a half-hearted move against Loudon's communications with Bohemia. Now that the war was mobile again, Loudon responded in devastating style. Learning that the vital fortress of Schweidnitz was held by just five battalions, he stole up on the place and on the early morning of 1 October he threw in an assault with eight companies of Russian grenadiers and twenty battalions of his own Austrians.

The 800 Russians were fired by drink, and upon the command of their officers the leading troops hurled themselves into the ditch of the Bogenfort, so creating a causeway of green-coated corpses for their surviving comrades. On the Austrian sector Count Wallis and the regiment of Loudon had the task of assaulting the Galgenfort:

> Twice the Austrians were repulsed. But then Wallis cried out to them 'We'll take the fortress, or I'll die in the attempt! I've promised it to our chief, and our regiment bears his name. Victory or death!' This little speech worked a miracle. The officers carried up the ladders in person, and the fort was stormed in the general warlike fervour.[102]

All the remaining outworks had fallen by five in the morning, whereupon the allies completed the conquest by storming over the town wall.

At a cost of 1,767 men, Loudon in a matter of three hours had reduced the most modern fortress of Central Europe and captured 3,700 troops, 221 cannon
 and great stores of all kinds. It is no exaggeration to say that there was probably

no other man of the century who could have carried it off so well.

Loudon's capture of Schweidnitz enabled the Austrians to plant their winter quarters in Silesia, for the first time in the war, and it was in Silesia that the Austrians were going to place more than half their forces in the coming campaign. The pity of it was that Maria Theresa's army was in no state to put forth the little extra energy which would have turned the war finally and decisively in her favour. The statistics confirm the impression that the material effort of the monarchy had reached its peak in 1759 and 1760. Now, when Austria needed to strain every nerve to overturn Frederick's battered army, the Vienna government embarked on a series of economies which eliminated the cadres of 20,000 men from the strength of the army and weakened some of the supporting services.

Then there was the issue of command. Loudon appears to have been embarrassed by the publicity that he had attracted in his campaign, and he was only too ready to hand over control in Silesia to Daun, who was hardly the man for desperate enterprises.

Lastly, Maria Theresa's loyal ally Empress Elizabeth of Russia died on 5 January 1762, and her successor Peter III not only withdrew his support from the alliance but went on to place his corps in Silesia at the disposal of Frederick. If the Austrians had been able to make little use of the Russians, while they were still friends, the defection of Russia nevertheless came as a painful and astonishing blow. 'Even the Austrian officers who were held prisoner in Breslau, and so could bear testimony with their own eyes and ears, were inclined to dismiss the happening as a false rumour, designed to demoralise the troops.'[103]

1762, THE YEAR OF DECISION

On the Saxon theatre the war went badly almost from the start. The command of the *Reichsarmee* and the 45,000 troops was united in the person of General Serbelloni, who proved to be no match for Prince Henry of Prussia. Henry took the offensive in May, and drove the Austrian corps back on Dresden and away from the *Reichsarmee*, which had to make a wide circuit by way of Franconia in order to escape.

Serbelloni was recalled to Vienna, and early in September the *Reichsarmee* and the Austrians combined under the command of Andreas Hadik. The new chief represented a great improvement, but even he was caught off his guard when Prince Henry attacked and beat the *Reichsarmee* and an Austrian detachment at Freiberg on 29 October. The open country of Saxony was once more delivered up to the enemy.

Meanwhile the issue of the Seven Years War was being resolved in Silesia, and more particularly around the fortress of Schweidnitz, which was at once the Austrian foothold in the Silesian lowlands and the symbol of Maria Theresa's claim to the whole duchy. Daun's strategy was dominated by the defensive. He placed Lieutenant-General Guasco with 12,000 picked troops in Schweidnitz, and for the rest he was content to manoeuvre with his army in the hills to the south.

Frederick was granted all the time he required to restore his army and await the arrival of the promised corps of 20,000 Russians, which reached him on 30 June 1762, and gave him a superiority of as many troops over the Austrians.

Perpetually anxious for his communications, Daun had already shifted his camp twice before the Prussians came at him on 21 July and overran the entrenchments on his right flank at Burkersdorf. To the dismay of Vienna, Daun recoiled to

the position of Wüste-Waltersdorf and gave up his communications with Schweidnitz. On 16 August Daun returned for the last time to the plain and carried out a feeble attack on a Prussian camp at Reichenbach, but two days later he was back in the mountains and the Austrians were burying themselves more deeply than ever. Out of all the stupendous armies which Austria had put into the field, only the forces in Saxony and the garrison of Schweidnitz were left to carry on the fight.

Schweidnitz came under complete investment at the beginning of August, and under regular siege from the 8th. The place contrived to hold out for sixty-three days, and this epic defence was proof enough that the strength of the Theresian army lay not in the high command but in the devotion and expertise of the officers and soldiers.

With the support of the sappers and the Bohemian miner captain Pabliczek, General Gribeauval brilliantly disputed every yard of the glacis and the mine galleries, and drove the Prussian engineer Lefebvre into a state of nervous collapse. The demoralised and starving Prussian infantry were driven to pick the grains from amid the horse dung, and they were apt to burst into tears when the Austrians attacked them in their trenches. The most famous single sortie was undertaken by the elegant Lieutenant Waldhütter ('pretty Miss Waldhütter'), who dashed forward with just thirty-three Hungarians on the night of 26/27 September and captured the third of Lefebvre's mine galleries.

The counter-attacks as a whole were inspired by the 28-year-old Colonel Tom Caldwell, a gallant gentleman who ultimately lost his life in one of the sorties. One

 of Caldwell's Irish compatriots, Captain James Bernard MacBrady, was holding the unrevetted Jauernicker Flèche when the Prussians tried to storm the work on the night of 18/19 August:

> He thereupon ordered the cannon to be fired, which created a dreadful slaughter among the storming parties, and completely filled the embrasures with their bodies. MacBracy himself took up a scythe, of which there were four planted on the breastwork. Lieutenant Heydecker and his sergeant followed the example. All the Prussians who appeared on the breastwork were hacked down and fell to the foot of the rampart.[104]

Daun sent a coded message to Guasco, authorising him to surrender. The garrison fought bravely on, but the artillery was badly knocked about and running short of cannon shot, and on 7 October the magazine of the main Jauernicker Fort blew up, killing more than two hundred officers and men. Guasco finally yielded his fortress two days later.

The Austrian armies spent a wretched winter amid the snows, frosts and fogs of the border mountains. The French and Swedes had already reached their own accommodations with the enemy, and on 15 February 1763 the Peace of Hubertusburg restored the boundaries of Prussia, Austria and Saxony to the lines they had followed before the war.

THE COST OF THE WAR

The six years of campaigning had cost the Austrians 303,595 men, of whom 32,622 were killed in action and 93,404 died of wounds or disease. The loss in horses amounted to 82,483, and the enemy had taken 89 colours, 23 standards, 397 cannon, 46 howitzers, 31 mortars and 554 ammunition carts.

Was the Austrian monarchy in any way compensated for the huge effort it had put forth? In terms of territory, obviously not, for Frederick was confirmed as master of Silesia. Yet everything was not pure loss. The troops had taken on – and frequently beaten – an army which had been reckoned the finest in the world, and Austria was now clearly an initiator of international politics, and no longer its passive victim. To Prince Albert of Saxony it seemed in 1764 that Austria had attained a new pinnacle of prestige: the land was ruled by a popular and admired monarch, her succession was safe, and 'her armies, in which the first princes of Germany reckoned it was an honour to serve, returned to her lands after seven years of warfare in a stronger and finer state than they had been before the outbreak of hostilities'.[105]

The army of the later years of the reign

For two months in the spring of 1763 the roads of Central Europe were full of traffic as the Austrian regiments made their way back to their scattered garrisons, and the horses were sent to market or restored to their original owners. The operation was directed by General Lacy with his characteristic efficiency, and only after it was complete did he appreciate that all the excitements and concerns of the last seven years were over. He wrote to a friend about the strangeness of peacetime life in Vienna:

> It is an invariable round. I get up when the sun already stands high over the city. I yawn, get dressed in a leisurely fashion, make a few visits, eat somewhere or other, attend the theatre, go for a stroll, dine and lastly find myself totally exhausted in bed, having really done nothing all day long. We occasionally go out hunting, and come back just as tired and pleased with ourselves as we once did when we returned from campaign.[106]

The direction of the peacetime machine remained in the hands of Field-Marshal Daun, as president of the *Hofkriegsrath*. His wife died on 19 January 1764, and two years later Daun himself fell dangerously ill. Maria Theresa wrote to him anxiously: 'This would be one of the greatest losses I could imagine. It is to you alone that I owe the existence of my army and the honour of my weapons.'[107] The field-marshal died on 5 February 1766.

THE NEW MEN

The army was carried into the later part of the century by youngish generals who had made their name in the Seven Years War, and who now acted under the authority of Maria Theresa and her eldest son Joseph II, who became co-regent after Francis Stephen died in 1765.

Joseph's traits of character were already evident to foreign observers. As long ago as 1747 the Prussian ambassador had noted:

> He is obstinate and wilful. He prefers to be locked up or made to go without food, rather than beg anyone's pardon. The Emperor and Empress are excessively fond of him, which prevents them from weaning him from his faults, and which will have only too great an influence on the formation of his character.[108]

Joseph grew up secretive, vain and impulsive. He dominated conversations, jingling the coins in his pocket as he talked, and seeking to anticipate the answers of the person he was addressing. Only among military men did he feel really at ease, for he was fascinated by the example of Frederick of Prussia, and longed to try conclusions with him on a field of battle. All of this boded ill for the peace of Europe.

Joseph's closest helpmate was the same Franz Lacy who had attracted the detestation of the public in the last campaigns of the Seven Years War. Connoisseurs of the military art like Frederick and Daun continued to hold him in high regard, and it was probably on the express recommendation of the dying field-marshal that Lacy followed him as president of the *Hofkriegsrath* in February 1766. The promotion to field-marshal came at the same time. For Maria Theresa, this was the one man in the monarchy who was capable of shouldering the burden of work ahead. Lacy's peculiar authority remained unshaken, even after ill-health forced him to resign the presidency in 1774, and he therefore exercised a predominant influence over the Theresian army for more than one-third of its existence. His achievement was summed up many years later by the Archduke Charles, who testified that 'Field-Marshal Lacy was the first man who brought the essential branches of military administration into a coherent system, designed both for war and peace.'[109]

Lacy the public personage was 'a man of detail and precision, ingenious, resolute and indefatigable'.[110] He customarily worked fourteen hours a day, and

The Emperor Joseph II

founded a reputation as the classic exponent of conventional eighteenth-century warfare. Maria Theresa once jokingly threatened to bring his bachelor existence to an end by marrying him herself, but Lacy valued the precious freedom of his off-duty hours, when he could chat within the select circle of 'the Princesses', relish his fine collection of Burgundy, or walk with his dogs through his estate in the Vienna Woods. Altogether, the range of Lacy's talents earned him the title of 'one of the greatest men of genius in our century'.[111]

The popular image credited Lacy with harbouring a deep antagonism towards his comrade in arms, the matchless soldier Loudon. Joseph at least behaved towards Loudon with respect and gratitude, even if the veteran's talents were not of a kind to shine in peacetime:

> Naturally modest, taciturn and shy, he scarcely ever obtrudes his opinions on any subject. . . . Neither his education, his manners, nor his habits qualify him . . . for the great world. In a mixed company he is lost, unless the discourse turns to war. . . . He presents to common eyes, a lank and bony figure, destitute of animation or address'.[112]

THE REFORMS

If the reforms of the 1740s and 1750s established an army that was run on professional, regular and humane principles, the objects in the Josephine period were 'to maintain a larger army than before, though at the minimum expense, and keep it constantly ready for action'.[113]

On 28 December 1766 Maria Theresa received from Joseph a memorandum which must be counted one of the most important documents of her reign. Joseph began: '*Si vis pacem, para bellum.* This is an obligation which lies upon us, and we must make ready accordingly. But consider how far short we are of this objective! Out of 100,000 men we have no arrangements to mobilise so much as 6,000.'[114] He desired both to increase the number of troops, and to make the army capable of springing to arms whenever hostilities threatened. He believed that something like the Prussian system of cantonal conscription would serve Austria very well.

Maria Theresa passed Joseph's paper to Kaunitz. The Chancellor argued in reply that the strength and welfare of the state hung upon three closely-interrelated considerations – sound finances, a well-managed army, and a wise and far-sighted foreign policy. He pointed out that no state could hope to keep on foot an army capable of meeting every conceivable enemy, and that in peacetime at least the number of troops must remain in correspondence with the available money. He feared that an increase in the military establishment would destroy the monarchy's financial credit.

Maria Theresa made no immediate decision in favour of either party, but it was soon evident that Joseph's militaristic enthusiasms were gaining the upper hand.

In earlier chapters we have seen the immense scope of the transformation that was effected by Joseph and Lacy: how they set up the machinery to raise the majority of the manpower of the army through the radically new principle of conscription, how they extended the military borders, how they worked out a code for the instruction of the generals, how they enhanced the power of the artillery and restored the proficiency of the cavalry.

 As for his own military qualities, Joseph was determined to harden his body and pack his mind with useful information. With these objects in view he liked to take off in the summertime with a few chosen companions on wide-ranging tours of inspection and military rides. Again and again he was drawn to the hilly northern borders, where the old heroes had died, and where he too might have to do battle with Frederick of Prussia, his enemy and his idol. One day in July 1768 he climbed the summit of the Goldsteiner Schneeberg to gain a distant prospect of the fortress of Neisse, in Prussian Silesia. As he reported to Maria Theresa, 'like Moses we viewed the Promised Land without being able to enter it'.[115]

The autumn was the season to go to the exercise camps and see the corps go through their paces. On such occasions Lacy dashed about shouting and putting people in order, while Joseph assiduously noted down the conduct of units and individuals.

In 1770 Old Fritz actually invited Joseph and a party of generals across the border of the 'Promised Land' to a review at Neisse, where he exposed the Prussian army to their fascinated gaze. The next year the Austrians returned the compliment at their camp at Neustadt. The weather on 4 September was blessedly fine, which displayed the troops to the best advantage, and 'the king could not refrain from showing his particular admiration for a battalion of Hungarian grenadiers, and said that they seemed to be like so many sons of Mars'. On the following day, however, a phenomenal cloudburst swept part of the camp down the hillside, ruining the baggage and uniforms, 'and the great Frederick, who had not brought along clothes suitable for this unexpected happening, had the inconvenience of wrapping himself up in his cloak and spending several hours by the side of a kitchen fire, over which he dried his breeches and his only coat'.[116]

What was the capability of the new army? In round numbers, Joseph and Maria Theresa could put almost 200,000 men into the field at the turn of the 1760s and 1770s. These were distributed among 59 regiments of line infantry, 17 of Croats, 15 of cuirassiers, 2 of carabiniers, 11 of dragoons, 2 of chevaulégers, 15 of hussars, and the units of gunners, sappers and the like.

By 1766 Frederick had already begun to notice the improvement in the strength and proficiency of the whitecoats: 'The work has begun well. God knows how far it will go.'[117] The Venetian ambassador claimed that the power of the army in Austria was at an unprecedented height. 'Taking everything into account, I think we can say that the military machine has become this people's favourite object of attention. I pity the powers which may feel its impact.'[118]

A great deal was lost in the process. Harsh and censorious, Joseph rated generals entirely in what he could see of their present efficiency, and Maria Theresa began to fear that he harboured an unfavourable view of mankind in general. If many old anomalies and abuses were rooted out, so was the gunners' Mayday and all sorts of customs and survivals which used to ameliorate the bleakness of military life. The tendency was to replace names by numbers, as in the nomenclature of regiments, and the population as a whole was forced to accept a large measure of direct state control. In striving to measure up to Frederick's Prussia, Austria had herself become to some degree Prussianised.

THE FIRST PARTITION OF POLAND, 1772

The monarchs of Central and Eastern Europe had long found something untidy and reprehensible about the chaos which sometimes overtook Polish politics, and in

1770, on the initiative of Joseph, Austrian troops were sent to occupy the small territory of Zips in southern Poland. Joseph asserted that he was merely exercising some ancient rights, but the precedent proved so attractive that on 17 February 1772 Frederick and the Empress Catherine of Russia agreed to help themselves to large chunks of Poland. Frederick hinted to Catherine that a considerable slice ought to be presented to the Austrians as well, lest they should take umbrage, and Kaunitz argued that Austria might as well join in the feast, since the others were going to carve up Poland anyway. All Maria Theresa's protests were overruled. The treaty of partition was concluded on 5 August 1772, and General Hadik directed a bloodless occupation of a large part of Galicia.

The gain was of extremely questionable worth. There was little additional security for the Hungarian borders in the open country and backward people of Galicia, and it was certainly unwise of the statesmen to have increased the wild diversity of the Habsburg empire. The dubious morality of the whole deal was tacitly admitted by Lacy, when he argued against the idea of raising specifically 'national' regiments in Galicia. He stressed that

> a national spirit is taking a general hold, especially among the common people. We may therefore expect the Poles to be as attached to their fatherland as the Silesians, and take just as long as that people to be weaned from their prejudice.[119]

THE IMPOSSIBLE WAR – THE AFFAIR OF THE BAVARIAN SUCCESSION, 1778–9

The next major initiative of Kaunitz and Joseph concerned nothing less than the annexation of Bavaria, where the elector died at the end of 1777 without leaving direct descendants. Frederick got wind of the scheme, and since Austria refused to consider a compromise he opened hostilities in July 1778.

For several months now Austria had been preparing for war. In March 1778 an Englishman described how Vienna was

> now transformed into an arsenal. The streets, as well as the public places, are crowded with cannon, ammunition, baggage, and all the apparatus of an approaching campaign. Every day, new regiments arrive, which, after being reviewed, continue their march towards Bohemia or Moravia. Nothing can convey a more striking idea of the greatness of the House of Austria, the magnitude of its resources, the extent of its dominion, and the number of provinces subject to Maria Theresa, than the scene to which I am daily a witness. From the shore of the Adriatic, and from the foot of the Apennines, to the frontiers of Moldavia and Wallachia, troops are constantly pouring in to maintain her quarrel. Albanians, Croats, Hungarians, and Italians successively arrive under the walls of Vienna. So many different nations, united in one cause, remind me of the fabulous ages of the earth, when all Greece, or the lesser Asia, flocked to a common standard, and fought under the same leader.[120]

While Maria Theresa herself dreaded the prospect of war, the Habsburg dominions were seized by an access of patriotic zeal:

> Recruiting went ahead extraordinarily well in all the Hereditary Lands.

Hungarians, Széklers and Wallachians came forward in swarms, and the young nobility joined in with enthusiasm. Parents proffered their own sons, and many villages, which were supposed to present a couple of men, provided ten or fifteen who volunteered of their own free will, and were very upset when they were not accepted . . . in short, the patriotic feeling was general, and no monarchs of the world could boast that they had better subjects, or were more loved, than Joseph and Maria Theresa.[121]

Where was all the enthusiasm going to be directed? Lacy had long been meditating how to defend Bohemia, and early in 1778 he clarified his ideas during a strenuous ride which he took along the Bohemian Elbe in the company of Joseph, Archduke Maximilian and Loudon. By April Lacy was in a position to draw up a definitive *Defensionsplan für das Königreich Böhmen*. The essential principle was to concentrate the Austrian forces just behind the northern border in a central position from which they could block or outflank any Prussian move across the mountains. The whole formed a rough triangle, which had an open rear, and two 45-mile-long sides meeting in an angle amid the border mountains.

The left-hand, or western, branch covered the ground in front of the Iser, and was occupied shortly after the outbreak of hostilities by Field-Marshal Loudon with his *Iser-Armee* of 80,000 troops and 250 guns. The right-hand branch ran along the right bank of the upper Elbe as it curled down from the primeval woods and massive outcrops of the Riesengebirge. Field works were dug at likely crossing-points, with larger groups of entrenched camps at Hohenelbe, Arnau, Jaromiersch and Smierschitz. The job of the upper Elbe line was to bar the access from Silesia, and it was here that Joseph and Lacy posted their *Elbe-Armee* of 100,000 men and 436 pieces.

Thanks to an alliance he had made with the Saxons, Frederick for once in his career enjoyed an actual superiority of force over the Austrians. The figure was something like 40,000 troops. He planned to exploit his advantage by undertaking a giant pincer movement – the main Prussian army was to assemble in Silesia and pour into north-eastern Bohemia by way of the passes of Trautenau, Nachod and Braunau, while Prince Henry with the Second Army and the Saxons took the direct route from Saxony on Prague.

Frederick crossed the border on 5 July 1778 and began to grope his way forward, whereupon Joseph ordered his armies to occupy their positions. The government of Europe waited in fearful anticipation for the impending collision of the massive armies, and Joseph's own enthusiasm began to abate in the presence of the realities of war. He wrote to his brother Leopold:

War is a frightful thing, what with the destruction of the fields and villages, the lamentation of the poor peasants, the ruin of so many innocent people and, for myself, the disturbances I experience for days and nights on end. This is how my time goes. I have to get up and be outside before daybreak, for that is the critical moment. In this season of the year this means that I must be in the saddle by three in the morning. I then endure the heat of the day, and I go to bed before eight in the cool of the evening. While I am abed I am awakened two or three times to hear the various reports which have arrived. As you can imagine, if I fall asleep again it is only out of exhaustion.[122]

Frederick was more than a little taken aback at the sight of the bristling Austrian entrenchments in the Jaromiersch sector, and in the middle of August he set off to try his luck further upstream. The Austrians found that the village near the abandoned Prussian camp were in an indescribable state, and that the whole area was pervaded by a stench of dead horses.

On the morning of 26 August Frederick emerged with considerable forces opposite the position of General Siskovics at Hohenelbe. The Austrians believed that a big battle was imminent, but Old Fritz recoiled once more in frustration. For almost three weeks the armies glowered at each other through the fine cold rain, and the first dusting of snow appeared on the crests of the mountains to the north. The Prussians suffered terribly in terrain which Frederick variously likened to the Alps or Siberia, but the Austrian troops were as well clad and fed as they usually were when Lacy was in charge of military economy.

> The campaign of 1778 was a masterpiece in this respect. No army has ever known such admirable arrangements, and everything was available in superfluity. Although the large and powerful army in Bohemia grew from day to day, the price of all kinds of provisions had fallen by the end of the campaign, and actually stood lower in Bohemia than in the provinces which were distant from the theatre of war.[123]

If tempers tended to fray in the Austrian camps, it was only because the troops were not allowed to get to grips with the enemy.

Frustrated on the upper Elbe, Frederick looked to the west and urged Prince Henry to get under way with his Prussians and Saxons. Henry masked his intentions by making some clever diversions, and at the end of July he led his main forces across the passes of the Lausitzer Gebirge against the Austrian *Iser-Armee*. The confused and disheartened Loudon consolidated on Münchengrätz, on the Iser, and expressed his doubts as to whether he would be able to make a stand even here. Joseph arrived at Münchengrätz on the night of 10 August, expecting the worst, but he found that Loudon's alarm was unnecessary.

There was in fact little more that Prince Henry could do in this direction. After crossing to the left bank of the Elbe, his forces fell back on Saxony in the last week of September. Away to the east Frederick withdrew first on Schatzlar, and then in the second half of October he retreated into Silesia. Joseph wrote to Lacy: 'We owe everything to you, uniquely and exclusively – to your knowledge of the ground, and to your gift for devising schemes that were capable of frustrating everything the enemy could undertake.'[124]

In the winter of 1778–9 the Austrians got the better of most of the clashes in the border mountains, but the Habsburg finances were near collapse and Maria Theresa was exerting all her influence in favour of peace. Russia offered to mediate between the two powers, and in May 1779 the respective deputies reached terms at Teschen. This time Austria was content merely to take over the corner of north-east Bavaria which lay between the Danube, the Inn and the Salza.

The War of the Bavarian Succession has always placed historians in some embarrassment. The students of statecraft dismiss the military trial of strength as of no importance, and prefer to stress the political outcome, which enhanced the position of Prussia in Germany. The military men, however, talk of the Austrians' strategy in terms of a 'Lacy cordon system', and emphasise the probably baleful influence of these experiences on the younger generation of Imperial commanders.

Few, if any, commentators are willing to acknowledge the upsurge of Austrian patriotism (for in their eyes people were not supposed to become enthusiastic about their governments before the coming of the French Revolution), or to concede that the course of the campaign represented a defensive victory that is directly comparable with Wellington's success in turning the French back from the lines of Torres Vedras in 1810. With inferior forces at their disposal, Lacy and Emperor Joseph had dictated the terms of the confrontation and sent Frederick and Prince Henry home with the disheartened and shivering remnants of their forces. If the war was a static one, this was simply the way in which the Austrians now preferred to fight. As Frederick had already observed in 1770, the Austrians were making the art of war more complicated, difficult and dangerous: 'we now have to battle not simply with men, but against powerful positions and strong artillery'.[125]

The last days of Maria Theresa

It was to Maria Theresa's bitter regret that she saw her state being run on lines which accorded less and less with her own moderate instincts. At home the inflated military establishment bore heavily on the welfare and liberties of the subject. Abroad, Joseph and Kaunitz embarked on an opportunistic foreign policy which aimed to carry Habsburg rule well beyond the historic boundaries. She was forced to give her consent to the First Partition of Poland 'because so many great and learned men will have it so. But long after I am dead you will experience the evil effects of this violation of everything we used to account holy and just'. Likewise, the approach of the War of the Bavarian Succession filled her with horror, and she ran to shut her apartment windows whenever regiments passed outside – something which would have appeared inconceivable to people who knew the Empress in the 1750s.

It was only when the war was over that Maria Theresa could bear to see her troops again. The army and the sovereign met for almost the last time on 12 May 1780, when Maria Theresa came to visit a corps of 32,000 men drawn up in line at Minkendorf:

> She arrived . . . in a gilded three-tiered phaeton, drawn by eight horses in costly trappings and driven by coachmen in Spanish court dress. She sat alone on the highest seat . . . A field-marshal rode at either door of the vehicle, namely Lacy and Loudon. Behind the carriage followed the higher diplomats and all the generals who were not on duty that day. You could scarcely imagine the richness of the saddle cloths and harness, all embroidered with gold and studded with diamonds. Add a peerless summer day, with not a cloud to be seen, and you might have thought that some goddess was staging her descent to earth . . . The Empress drove slowly along the whole front, fixing every man with her gaze . . . The officers, who were otherwise accustomed to reinforcing their orders with the stick, now treated their men as gently as if they had been delicate young girls. It was only now and then you could hear them muttering between their teeth, 'You people just wait till we get back to barracks!'[126]

The beloved Empress-Queen died on 29 November 1780, trusting in her God but apprehensive of the fate of her children in the new world.

In the short term Lacy and Joseph achieved their immediate ambition, namely to establish an army which stood on at least an equality with that of Frederick of Prussia. However, the Austrian armies, trained up in the received techniques of eighteenth-century warfare, fared badly against the springy and aggressive forces of the French Revolution and the earlier Napoleonic empire. The battle of Austerlitz in 1805 raged across the fields of the estate of the long-dead Prince Kaunitz, a circumstance which made a deep impression on the superstitious Viennese. In 1809 after the further Austrian defeat at Wagram, Napoleon stood before the pompous tomb of Field-Marshal Daun in the Augustinerkirche in Vienna and proclaimed: 'There he lies! Everything is vain, everything passes away like smoke!'[127]

The honour of the Austrian army was restored only when Archduke Charles rebuilt the structure on the more solid of the foundations which had been planted by Lacy. There was no need to re-examine the relationship between the military, the state and society, as was the case in contemporary Prussia. Maria Theresa had done her work too well for that. It was actually one of Lacy's old adjutants, Johann Joseph Radetzky, who was going to lead the Habsburg army to its last great victories in 1849, thus spanning a century of warfare in a living continuity of two generations.

When, however, the veterans looked back on the eighteenth century, they forgot about the reformers and the regulations and heartened themselves with the thought that they had once belonged to the army of Maria Theresa. Major-General Johann Heldensfeld recalled how as a child cadet he had seen the Empress-Queen on her last visit to Wiener Neustadt:

> The Empress inspected the pupils. She then admitted the children to her tent, took most of us in turn on to her lap, kissed us like a mother and repeatedly sighed, 'My dear children. This is the last time I see you!' There were tears in her eyes. During her stay at Wiener Neustadt she gave us a wonderful time. We were admitted to the programme of illuminations in the Cistercian Garden, and allowed to run about the garden and later on in her apartments. We enjoyed it just as if she had been our mother and we had been her children. I can still picture the motherly anxiety of our adored monarch, when one of the little ones fell into the Kehrbach, which flowed through the garden. . .
>
> Already in late November the sad prophecy of that great sovereign was fulfilled, to the loss of humanity and the Austrian state. I have never forgotten her in all the years that have passed. I have always called her to mind with gratitude, and remembered her in my prayers. I have never seen her portrait without a sense of consolation and thanks stealing over my heart. She has been accepted by the Almighty, and we must declare that she has been so. She was as good, and as complete as any human being can be.[128]

The concluding words are with another old warrior, Prince Charles Joseph de Ligne, who has been our companion through so much of our story. He died in the Vienna of 1814, when the capital was the scene of a famous diplomatic congress and crowded with a glittering international society. He shared in something of the excitement, even in his final days, but it was the recollection of an earlier age which roused him to his last cry:

En Avant! Marie Thérèse Vivat!

Notes

1 The Theresian State

1 Ligne, *Mêlanges*, xxviii, 57–8
2 Dutens, 152
3 Ligne, *Mêlanges*, I, 159
4 Ibid, I, 159
5 Cognazzo, *Beytrag*, 18
6 Ligne, *Mêlanges*, II, 202, 203
7 Cognazzo, *Beytrag*, 75
8 Ligne, *Mêlanges*, II, 203
9 Ligne, *Fragments*, II, 2
10 Cognazzo, *Geständnisse*, IV, 158
11 G. A. Guibert, II, 284
12 Cognazzo, *Beytrag*, 13
13 Loudon to *Hofrat* Hochstätter, Buchberger, 386
14 Ligne, *Mêlanges*, II, 11
15 KA (*Kriegsarchiv*), anonymous relation FA (*Feld-Acten*), 1756, X 7½
16 'Ueber die Liebe des Vaterlandes', 1771, in *Gesammelte Schriften*, VII, 5
17 Ligne, *Mêlanges*, II, 164
18 Teuber, *Österreichische Armee*, I, 79
19 Ligne, *Mêlanges*, I, 156

2 The Supreme Direction of the Armed Forces

1 To Tarouca, February 1766, Kretschmayr, 271
2 Podewils, 48
3 Archenholtz, II, 116
4 St Paul, 189
5 Küntzel, 55
6 Wraxall, II, 352
7 Gisors, 101
8 Cognazzo, *Geständnisse*, I, 25
9 KA, Field-Marshal Wallis, *Geschichte des Hofkriegsraths*, 1792, Nostitz-Rieneck F II
10 KA, *Denkschrift . . . über die Verbesserung des Militär-Systems*, 1792, Nostitz-Rieneck FV 10
11 Khevenhüller-Metsch, IV, 142
12 Arneth, XI, 829

3 The Officers

1 Ligne, *Mêlanges*, xxviii, 59
2 Lehmann, 11
3 Teuber, *Österreichische Armee*, I, 80.
4 Esterházy, 410
5 Cognazzo, *Beytrag*, 110
6 Cognazzo, *Geständnisse*, IV, 216
7 Ligne, *Fragments*, I, 246
8 Cognazzo, *Geständnisse*, II, 210
9 Arneth, VIII, 250
10 Ligne, *Mêlanges*, X, 83
11 M. Kelly, *Reminiscences*, London, 1826, I, 266–7
12 Khevenhüller-Metsch, V, 88
13 Esterházy, 312
14 Khevenhüller-Metsch, III, 50
15 Guglia, II, 22
16 Khevenhüller-Metsch, III, 213
17 Anon, 'Charakterzüge', 103
18 Esterházy, 395
19 *Betrachtungen*, II, 146–7
20 Duffy, *Army of Frederick the Great*, 24
21 Teuber, *Österreichische Armee*, I, 98
22 Esterházy, 259
23 Ibid, 334–5
24 Ligne, *Mêlanges*, I, 131
25 *Generals-Reglement*, 1769, 68
26 KA, *Oesterreichischer Erbfolge-Krieg*, I, 418
27 KA, *Gedanken über das Kauffen und Verkaufen der Chargen in der Armee*, Nostitz-Rieneck F II, no. 8
28 KA, *Normale über die Invaliden-Versorgung* 2 April 1772, Nostitz-Rieneck F III 9
29 Ibid
30 Esterházy, 400
31 G. A. Guibert, II, 114, 256
32 Lemcke, 31
33 *Reglement für die . . . Infanterie*, 1769, 55
34 St Paul, lxiv
35 Thadden, 235, 239
36 Ligne, *Fragments*, I, 208
37 Ibid, I, 220–1
38 Schwerin, 381
39 Lehndorff, 375
40 Khevenhüller-Metsch, V, 17–18

41 F. S. Sack, *Briefe über den Krieg*, Berlin, 1778, 56
42 Prittwitz, 182
43 Archenholtz, II, 132
44 *Erbfolge-Krieg*, I, 416
45 To Valentin Esterházy, Thürheim *Von den Sevennen*, 169
46 KA, J. Passel, *Betrachtungen*, 26 July 1790, Nostitz-Rieneck F VII, 6
47 Ligne, *Fragments*, I, 61
48 J. P. Pezzl, *Skizze von Wien*, Vienna, 1789, 694
49 Kotasek, 220
50 *Feld Dienst Regulament*, 1749
51 Wraxall, II, 354–7
52 Khevenhüller-Metsch, II, 32
53 *Reglement für die . . . Infanterie*, 1769, 103
54 Anon, 'Aus dem Letzten Lebensjahre', 123
55 Podewils, 48
56 Allmayer-Beck, 19
57 Teuber, *Österreichische Armee*, I, 82
58 Allmayer-Beck, 20
59 Hirtenfeld, 6
60 Walter, *Zentralverwaltung*, II, 347
61 Ligne, *Mêlanges*, II, 197
62 Warnery, 327
63 Thadden, 365–6
64 Waddington, I, 334
65 KA, *Schreiben eines Officiers der Cavallerie an seinen Freund*, Königgrätz, 28 December 1756, Kriegswissenschaftliche Mémoires II, 24
66 Cognazzo, *Geständnisse*, II, 199
67 Conference of 18 May 1757, in Khevenhüller-Metsch, IV, 340
68 KA, *Idé qui mest venue pour trouver avec les fonts destine pour le militaire*, Nostitz-Rieneck F III 1

4 The Men

1 Kotasek, 22
2 Nitsche, 77
3 KA, Passel, *Betrachtungen*, Nostitz-Rieneck F VII, 6
4 Ligne, *Mêlanges*, II, 196
5 Ligne, *Fragments*, I, 44
6 Esterházy, 311
7 Stephanie, I, 50
8 Ligne, *Mêlanges*, I, 205
9 Cognazzo, *Beytrag*, 90
10 Ibid, 91
11 Dikreiter, 23–4
12 KA, *Prot. in Publicis*, 8 January 1758
13 KA, *Puncten*, 29 February 1768, Nostitz-Rieneck F III 5
14 Anon, *Unterricht und Heilungsart*, 4
15 KA, *Einige Gedancken zum Dienst Eurer Kayserlichen Majestät*, undated, Nostitz-Rieneck F IV 3
16 *Urlaubs-Normale*, 1777
17 Berenhorst, II, 111
18 KA, Field-Marshal Wallis, *Geschichte des Hofkriegsraths*, 1792, Nostitz-Rieneck F II
19 Kotasek, 122
20 Richter, 83–4
21 Esterházy, 177
22 *Reglement für die . . . Infanterie*, 1769, 18
23 *Feld Dienst Regulament*, 1749
24 KA, Passel, *Betrachtungen*, Nostitz-Rieneck F VII 6
25 J. A. Guibert, *Observations sur la Constitution Militaire et Politique de Sa Majesté Prussienne*, Amsterdam, 1778, 132
26 KA, 10 October 1776, Nostitz-Rieneck F IV 5
27 *Reglement für die . . . Infanterie*, 1769, 236
28 Cognazzo, *Geständnisse*, III, 60–1
29 Kann, 152
30 Burgoyne, 74
31 *Magister F. Ch. Laukhards Leben*, 13th ed, 2 vols, Stuttgart, 1930, II, 34
32 *Feld Dienst Regulament*, 1749
33 Berenhorst, II, 107
34 KA, *Beschreibung der auf den 3ten August 1780 . . . angeordneten öffentlichen Prüfung*, Nostitz-Rieneck F IX 4
35 KA, undated note, 1780, Nostitz-Rieneck F IX 4
36 KA, *Normale über die Invaliden-Versorgung*, Nostitz-Rieneck F III 9
37 Esterházy, 425
38 KA, *Puncten*, Nostitz-Rieneck F III 5
39 Esterházy, 353
40 *Reglement für die . . . Infanterie*, 1769, 105
41 *Feld Dienst Regulament*, 1749
42 'Der Mann ohne Vorurtheil' in *Gesammelte Schriften*, III, 86
43 Esterházy, 443
44 'Reflections on the General Principles of War', *Annual Register*, London, 1766, 175

5 The Infantry of the Line

1 Ligne, *Mêlanges*, II, 123

2 Cognazzo, *Beytrag*, 106
3 KA, *Prot in Publicis*, 22 March 1758
4 KA, *Historische Nachrichten über den im Jahre 1778 . . . ausgebrochenen . . . Krieg*, Manuscripte 64
5 Anon, *Denckwürdiges Leben und Thaten*, 91
6 Alexich, 171
7 KA, Passel, *Betrachtungen*, Nostitz-Rieneck F VII 6
8 Teuber, *Österreichische Armee*, I, 83
9 Ibid
10 G. A. Guibert, 3
11 Teuber, *Österreichische Armee*, I, 124
12 Esterházy, 262
13 Cognazzo, *Geständnisse*, I, 18
14 Richter, 140–1
15 Teuber, *Österreichische Armee*, I, 123–4
16 Khevenhüller-Metsch, IV, 236
17 Anon, *Beschreibung und Heilungsart*, 5
18 KA, note 5 December 1765, Nostitz-Rieneck F XV 2
19 Moore, II, 403–4
20 Berenhorst, II, 317
21 Cognazzo, *Beytrag*, 141–2
22 Anon, *Denckwürdiges Leben und Thaten*, 8
23 Esterházy, 439–40
24 Cognazzo, *Beytrag*, 143–4
25 *Khevenhüller-Metsch*, II, 224–5
26 Introduction to the *Regulament und Ordnung*, 1749, I, 1
27 Podewils, 141
28 *Regulament und Ordnung*, 1749, I, 2
29 Richter, 41
30 Ligne, *Mêlanges*, I, 17
31 *Regulament und Ordnung*, 1749, I, 122
32 Esterházy, 113–14
33 *Regulament und Ordnung*, 1749, I, 191
34 Ibid, I, 209
35 *Feld Dienst Regulament*, 1749
36 *Erbfolge-Krieg*, I, 704
37 Cognazzo, *Geständnisse*, II, 354
38 Cognazzo, *Beytrag*, 31
39 D. Thiébault, *Mes Souvenirs de Vingt Ans de Séjour à Berlin*, 3rd ed, 4 vols, Paris, 1813, III, 221–2
40 Mirabeau, 226
41 *Regulament und Ordnung*, 1749, II, 138
42 Cognazzo, *Geständnisse*, III, 5

6 The 'Croats'

1 Mirabeau, 17
2 R. Fester (ed), *Die Instruction Friedrichs des Grossen für seine Generale von 1747*, Berlin, 1936, 70
3 Teuber, *Österreichische Armee*, I, 142
4 Bertling, 22
5 Teuber, *Österreichische Armee*, I, 144
6 Conference of 22 March 1755, Khevenhüller-Metsch, III, 231
7 Note of 7 November 1756, Ibid, IV, 251
8 Cognazzo, *Geständnisse*, III, 257
9 Bertling, 24
10 F. E. Boysen, *Eigene Lebensbeschreibung*, Quedlinburg, 1795, 254–5
11 G. A. Guibert, II, 89
12 Ibid, II, 70–2
13 Cognazzo, *Geständnisse*, III, 128
14 Military conference of 28 November 1756, Khevenhüller-Metsch, IV, 276
15 Bertling, 107
16 *Geschichte des Siebenjährigen Krieges*, II, 226–7
17 Ligne, *Mêlanges*, I, 159

7 The Cavalry

1 Mirabeau, 25
2 Alexich, 140
3 Khevenhüller-Metsch, I, 163
4 Anon, *Denckwürdiges Leben und Thaten*, 134
5 Anon, *Neues und sehr Curiöses Gespräch*, 28
6 18 May 1757, Khevenhüller-Metsch, IV, 342
7 Anon, *Zuverlässige Nachrichten*, 7
8 'Anhang' to the *Regulament und Ordnung, für . . . Husaren-Regimenter*, 1751
9 *Feld Dienst Regulament*, 1749
10 Ibid
11 *Regulament und Ordnung für . . . Cuirassier und Dragoner Regimenter*, II, 320–2
12 Schwerin, 260
13 Teuber, *Österreichische Armee*, I, 98
14 KA, *Schreiben eines Officiers der Cavallerie an seinen Freund*, Königgrätz, 28 December 1756, Kriegswissenschaftliche Mémoires, Kriege gegen Preussen, II, 24
15 Warnery, 127–8
16 Ibid, 13
17 Kotasek, 100
18 KA, Field-Marshal Nostitz, *Betrachtungen über die Oesterreichische Cavallerie . . . 1735 bis . . . 1792*, Nostitz-Rieneck FV 13

19 KA, *Allerunthänigstes Protocoll und Gutachten*, Nostitz-Rieneck F X 46
20 Burgoyne, 75

8 The Artillery

1 KA, *Artillerie Systeme ab Anno 1753*
2 Warnery, 126
3 Cognazzo, *Geständnisse*, II, 187
4 KA, *Das öst. Artillerie-System vom J. 1772*
5 KA, *Artillerie Systeme ab Anno 1753*
6 *Reglement für das . . . Feld-Artilleriecorps*, 1757, 8–9
7 Dirrheimer and Fritz, 70
8 KA, *Artillerie Systeme ab Anno 1753*
9 Ibid
10 Gribeauval, in Hennebert, 41
11 Ibid, 40
12 KA, Lieutenant-General Rouvroy, 28 December 1778, Nostitz-Rieneck F XI 3
13 *Reglement für das . . . Feld-Artilleriecorps*, 1757, 124
14 Gribeauval, in Hennebert, 38
15 *Feld Dienst Regulament*, 1749
16 KA, *Artillerie Systeme ab Anno 1753*

9 The Technicians

1 Teuber, *Österreichische Armee*, I, 167
2 *Erbfolge-Krieg*, I, 443
3 Cornet, 10
4 'Testament Politique' (1768), in *Die Politischen Testamente Friedrichs des Grossen*, supplement to *Politische Correspondenz Friedrichs des Grossen*, Berlin, 1920, 150

10 Financiers, Commissaries, Doctors and Priests

1 KA, Field-Marshal Nostitz, *Betrachtungen*, Nostitz-Rieneck F V 13
2 G. A. Guibert, II, 323
3 *Instruction für die Kriegs-Commissariatische Beamte*, 1749, 3
4 Cognazzo, *Beytrag*, 86
5 Anon, *Zuverlässige Nachrichten*, 19–20
6 *Instruction für die Kriegs-Commissariatische Beamte*, 1749, 231
7 Khevenhüller-Metsch, IV, 142
8 *Militär-Contributions und Cameral System*, 22 October 1748
9 KA, *Punkte welche bey Bilancirung des neuen Montirungs-Sistems gegen das vom Jahre 1749 zu beantworten kommen*, 1793, Nostitz-Rieneck F XV 14
10 *Militär-Contributions und Cameral System*, 22 October 1748
11 KA, A. M. Bohn *Patriotische Gedanken über das Kaiserl. König. Militaire Verpflegswesen*, 1793, Nostitz-Rieneck F XIII 20
12 KA, *Armee Verpflegungswesen 1793*, Nostitz-Rieneck F XIV
13 KA, *Militär Commissions Protocoll das Monturs Oeconomie Systeme betreffend*, 1794–5, Nostitz-Rieneck F XVI
14 Riesebeck, I, 238
15 *Regulament und Ordnung*, 1749, II, 77
16 *Feld Dienst Regulament*, 1749
17 KA, Anon, *Allerunterthänigste Prothocoll*, 1794, Nostitz-Rieneck F XII 36
18 KA, Anon, memorandum FA 1758 XIII cl27
19 See KA, Nostitz-Rieneck F XI 23 and F XII 36
20 *Generals-Reglement*, 1769, 80
21 Crankshaw, 221
22 Cognazzo, *Beytrag*, 151–2
23 Anon, 'Ein Schreiben van Swietens', 152
24 *Feld Dienst Regulament*, 1749
25 Anon, 'Ein Schreiben van Swietens', 151
26 KA, 10 October 1776, Nostitz-Rieneck F IV 5
27 Ligne, *Mêlanges*, I, 183
28 Anon, *Kurze Beschreibung und Heilungsart der Krankheiten, welche am öftesten in dem Feldlager beobachtet werden*, Vienna, 1758; A. F. Störck, *Medicinisch-Praktischer Unterricht fur die Feld und Landwundärzte der österreichischen Staaten*, 2 parts, Vienna, 1776
29 *Reglement für die . . . Infanterie*, 1769, 60

11 The Control of the Army

1 Waddington, I, 560–1
2 Peball, 125
3 Ligne, *Mêlanges*, II, 131
4 *Generals-Reglement*, 1769, 7
5 Ibid, 63
6 C. D. Küster, *Characterzüge das preussischen General-Lieutenants von Saldern*, Berlin, 1793, xi-xii
7 Ligne, *Fragments*, I, 274

12 Military Operations

1 *Generals-Reglement*, 1769, 25
2 Ibid, 23
3 See Duffy, *The Army of Frederick the Great*, 150–1
4 *Die Instruction Friedrichs des Grossen . . . von 1747*, 60–2
5 *Generals-Reglement*, pt II, 30
6 Ibid, pt II, 138
7 *Reglement für die . . . Infanterie*, 1769, 173
8 Ibid, 10
9 'Testament Politique' (1768), in *Die Politischen Testamente Friedrichs des Grossen*, 162
10 'Betrachtungen über die Taktik', 1758, in Frederick's *Militärische Schriften*, vol. VI of *Die Werke Friedrichs des Grossen*, Berlin, 1913, 119
11 *Feld Dienst Regulament*, 1749
12 Ligne, *Mêlanges*, I, 234–5
13 Ibid, II, 121
14 *Generals-Reglement*, 1769, 124
15 *Feld Dienst Regulament*, 1749
16 Arneth, V, 171–2
17 In KA, Kriegswissenschaftliche Mémoires, Kriege gegen Preussen II, 27
18 N. Wraxall, *Memoirs*, new ed, 2 vols, London, 1806, II, 255
19 Anon, *Beiträge zur Schilderung Wiens*, 2 vols, Vienna, 1781–3, I, 174
20 Kriegswissenschaftliche Mémoires, II, 27
21 KA, *Schreiben eines Officiers der Cavallerie*, Kriegswissenschaftliche Mémoires, Kriege gegen Preussen, II, 24

13 Maria Theresa's Army and the Test of War

1 M. Braubach, *Prinz Eugen*, V, Vienna, 1965, 217
2 F. v. dr. Wengen, *Karl Graf zu Wied*, Gotha, 1890, 32
3 Cognazzo, *Beytrag*, 50
4 Arneth, IV, 87
5 Archenholtz, II, 130
6 Cognazzo, *Geständnisse*, II, 21
7 Ibid, II, 2
8 Neipperg's relation, in Duncker, 'Militärische und politische Actenstücke zur Geschichte des ersten Schlesischen Krieges 1741', in *Mittheilungen*, 1887, 1888
9 Duncker, 'Actenstücke', *Mittheilungen*, 1887, 207
10 Anon, *Denckwürdiges Leben und Thaten*, 80
11 Duncker, 'Actenstücke', *Mittheilungen*, 1887, 205
12 Wraxall, II, 300
13 Arneth, I, 414
14 Ibid, II, 30
15 *Erbfolge-Krieg*, III, 256
16 Podewils, 74
17 Khevenhüller-Metsch, I, 175
18 Arneth, II, 549
19 Khevenhüller-Metsch, II, 211
20 Villettes, 29 January 1746, Public Record Office, London, SP 92/51 Sardinia 1746
21 R***, *Mémoires d'un Militaire*, Wesel, 1759, 135
22 General Stille, in Naumann, *Sammlungen ungedruckter Nachrichten*, 4 vols, Dresden 1782–3, I, 353–4
23 Hildebrandt, III, 122
24 KA, 4 June 1745, FA Krieg in Schlesien und Böhmen 1745 VI 13
25 Khevenhüller-Metsch II, 62
26 KA, to Francis Stephen, 30 September 1745, FA Krieg in Schlesien und Böhmen 1745 IX
27 Podewils, 74–5
28 Cognazzo, *Geständnisse*, II, 182
29 Cognazzo, *Beytrag*, 24
30 Ibid, 25
31 Podewils, 47–8
32 Arneth, IV, 34
33 Berenhorst, II, 70
34 Cognazzo, *Beytrag*, 21–2
35 Schwerin, 255
36 Archenholtz, I, 15
37 Ligne, *Fragments*, I, 88
38 Arneth, IV, 485
39 U. Braeker, *Lebensgeschichte*, Zürich, 1789, 152
40 Warnery, 57
41 Archenholtz, I, 20
42 J. A. Retzow, *Charakteristik der wichtigsten Ereignisse des Siebenjährigen Krieges*, 2 vols, Berlin, 1802, I, 61
43 Lehndorff, 306
44 KA, to Francis Stephen, 23 October 1756, CA X 15
45 Ligne, *Mêlanges*, XIV, 7
46 Ibid, XIV, 7
47 Ibid, XIV, 19
48 Cognazzo, *Geständnisse*, II, 355
49 Hoen, 'Kolin', 64
50 Princess Wilhelmine, 25 June 1757, in E. Berner and G. Volz, 'Aus

der Zeit des Siebenjährigen Krieges', in *Quellen und Untersuchungen*, IX, Berlin, 1908, 381
51 Prittwitz, 160
52 Ligne, *Mêlanges*, XIV, 28–9
53 Waddington, I, 599
54 Ligne, *Mêlanges*, XIV, 45–6
55 Archenholtz, I, 93
56 Letter of an eyewitness, in Khevenhüller-Metsch, IV, 398
57 Ligne, *Mêlanges*, XIV, 63–4
58 Waddington, I, 567
59 C. Grünhagen, *Die Oesterreicher in Breslau 1757*, undated, 57
60 KA, Zehentner's history of the Seven Years War, in Manuscripte 55
61 C. v. dr. Goltz, *Von Rossbach bis Jena und Auerstedt*, 2nd ed, Berlin, 1906, 21
62 Khevenhüller-Metsch, IV, 412–13
63 Archenholtz, I, 135
64 Warnery, 251
65 Ligne, *Mêlanges*, XIV, 90
66 Wraxall, I, 177–8
67 Archenholtz, I, 141
68 Khevenhüller-Metsch, V, 32
69 Cognazzo, *Geständnisse*, III, 3
70 Hirtenfeld, *Vor Hundert Jahren*, 55–6
71 Ibid, 40
72 Archenholtz, I, 153
73 Cognazzo, *Geständnisse*, II, 209
74 Champeaux, in Waddington, I, 334
75 Thadden, 374
76 Boisgelin, in Waddington, I, 254
77 Thadden, 374
78 Wraxall, I, 169
79 Archenholtz, I, 181
80 C. D. Küster, *Bruchstück seines Campagnelebens im Siebenjährigen Kriege*, Berlin, 1791, 36
81 Wraxall, I, 182
82 Ligne, *Mêlanges*, XIV, 194
83 Cognazzo, *Beytrag*, 139
84 Arneth, VI, 99
85 Büttner, *Fouqué*, I, 77, 79–80, 81
86 Berenhorst, I, 301
87 Professor Gellert, in *Münchener Intelligenzblätter*, 1790, no 25, 198
88 Wraxall, I, 346
89 KA, Anonymous relation, FA Corps Loudon 1759 VIII 13
90 KA, Chevalier de Mesnager-Belle-Isle, 12 August 1759, FA Corps Loudon XIII 47
91 Ligne, *Mêlanges*, XV, 34
92 Ibid, XV, 88
93 Warnery, 353
94 Archenholtz, II, 42–3
95 Ligne, *Mêlanges*, XV, 170–1
96 Arneth, VI, 446
97 Hildebrandt, III, 36
98 Ligne, *Mêlanges*, XVI, 49
99 Ibid, XVI, 50
100 Archenholtz, II, 106–7
101 Ibid, II, 113
102 Ibid, II, 179
103 Ibid, II, 218
104 Cognazzo, *Geständnisse*, IV, 189
105 Arneth, VII, 250
106 Kotasek, 219
107 Arneth, VII, 186
108 Podewils, 68–9
109 Kotasek, 253
110 Burgoyne, 72
111 Riesebeck, I, 236–7
112 Wraxall, I, 339–40
113 Cognazzo, *Geständnisse*, IV, 299
114 Arneth, VII, 530
115 Ibid, VII, 529
116 Ibid, VIII, 577, 577–8
117 Ibid, VIII, 556
118 Kotasek, 110
119 Ibid, 123
120 Wraxall, I, 348–9
121 Anon, *Oesterreichischer Kriegs-Almanach*, II, 153–4
122 Arneth, X, 498
123 Richter, 136
124 Kotasek, 163
125 *Eléments de Castramétie et de Tactique*
126 J. B. Fuchs, *Erinnerungen aus dem Leben eines Kölner Juristen*, Cologne, 1912, 161
127 Thadden, 471
128 Anon, 'Charakterzüge', 104

Appendix: List of Regiments

Infantry regiments

The numbers are those awarded to the regiments in 1769. Before this date the regiments were known by the names of their current *Inhabers*. Except where stated, the coat, waistcoat and breeches were white. The word 'facings' is here understood to relate to the distinctive colours of the cuffs, lapels and (in the 1740s) the turn-backs of the coat. The *Egalisierung* (colour scheme) of 1767 applies to the colour of the collar, cuffs and turn-backs of the new style of uniform.

In the older uniform the tricorn hat was worn with a pom-pom at the left side and a small bob at each of the two rearward corners: the order given for their colours is from the outside inwards.

IR NO I

Inhaber or designation 1740 Lothringen, 1745 Kaiser.
Uniforms (i) earlier part of reign – red or scarlet facings, with shoulder strap edged with red, yellow buttons; mixed red, black and yellow pom-pom, yellow and black bobs; (ii) *Egalisierung* 1767 – dark red with yellow buttons.
Record Recruited in Moravia and the Empire. The regiment of the male head of the Habsburg state. Decided the action at Simbach (Bavaria) 1743. Distinguished at Breslau and Leuthen, almost annihilated at Torgau.

IR NO 2

Inhaber or designation 1741 Ujváry, 1749 Erzherzog Carl, 1761 Erzherzog Ferdinand.
Uniforms (i) earlier part of reign – 1741 blue pelisse and pants; 1743 green facings; Seven Years War – yellow cuffs, yellow turn-backs, yellow tasselled *Litzen*, white shoulder strap, yellow buttons, dark blue waistcoat with yellow lace, dark blue pants, blue sabretache with yellow devices; (ii) *Egalisierung* 1767 – yellow with yellow buttons.
Record A Hungarian regiment, raised in western Hungary 1741. Very distinguished at Kolin, heavy casualties at Torgau.

IR NO 3

Inhaber or designation 1740 Lothringen (ie Prince Charles of Lorraine).
Uniforms (i) earlier part of reign – red facings, yellow shoulder strap edged with red, single-breasted waistcoat, yellow buttons; scalloped hat border, red, yellow, blue pom-pom, red bobs; (ii) *Egalisierung* 1767 – sky blue with white buttons.
Record Recruited in the Empire. Heavy casualties at Hohenfriedberg. Put up gallant last-ditch stands at Soor, Leuthen and Torgau.

IR NO 4

Inhaber or designation 1740 Deutschmeister.
Uniforms (i) earlier part of reign – dark blue facings, dark blue shoulder strap edged with white, yellow buttons; no pom-pom, blue (?) and yellow bobs; (ii) *Egalisierung* 1767 – sky blue with yellow buttons.

Record Recruited in the Empire, and especially the lands of the Teutonic Order. The *Inhaber* was the current head of the Order. A very famous regiment, distinguished at Camposanto, Rottofreno (1746), Kolin and Landeshut.

IR NO 7

Inhaber or designation 1740 Neipperg, 1774 Harrach.
Uniforms (i) earlier part of reign – blue facings, white shoulder strap, yellow buttons; red and yellow pom-pom, yellow and black bobs (?); (ii) *Egalisierung* 1767 – dark brown with white buttons.
Record Recruited in the Empire. Distinguished with heavy casualties at Hohenfriedberg and Soor. Almost destroyed at Torgau, restored 1761.

IR NO 8

Inhaber or designation 1740 Hildburghausen.
Uniforms (i) earlier part of reign – red facings, white shoulder strap, yellow buttons; no pom-pom, single red bob on right-hand corner of hat; (ii) *Egalisierung* 1767 – poppy red with yellow buttons.
Record Recruited in the Empire. Distinguished in the retreat from Leuthen, and at Meissen and Maxen.

IR NO 9

Inhaber or designation 1740 Los Rios, 1775 Clerfayt.
Uniforms (i) earlier part of reign – green facings, white shoulder strap, yellow buttons; no pom-pom, red and yellow bobs; (ii) *Egalisierung* 1767 – apple green with yellow buttons.
Record A Netherlandish regiment which first saw action at Dettingen. Distinguished at defence of Maastricht (1748), and at Prague, Kolin, Breslau, Leuthen and Kunersdorf.

IR NO 10

Inhaber or designation 1740 Jung-Wolfenbüttel.
Uniforms (i) earlier part of reign – red facings, white shoulder strap edged with red, single-breasted waistcoat, yellow buttons; blue, yellow and blue pom-pom, blue and red bobs; (ii) *Egalisierung* 1767 – parrot green with white buttons.
Record Recruited in SW Germany. Distinguished at Dettingen, and at Spechtshausen (Saxony, 1762).

IR NO 11

Inhaber or designation 1740 Wallis (Franz Wenzel).
Uniforms (i) earlier part of reign – red or scarlet facings, white shoulder strap, white buttons; no pom-pom, yellow and red bobs; (ii) *Egalisierung* 1767 – rose red with white buttons.
Record Recruited in the Empire. Raised by Wallenstein 1621. An old and fine regiment which kept its reputation through Maria Theresa's reign. Distinguished at Rottofreno (1746). Distinguished, with heavy casualties, at Prague and Leuthen.

IR NO 12

Inhaber or designation 1740 Botta, 1775 Khevenhüller-Metsch.
Uniforms (i) earlier part of reign – dark blue facings, black shoulder strap, yellow buttons; blue, white and blue pom-pom, yellow and red bobs; (ii) *Egalisierung* 1767 – dark brown with yellow buttons.

Record Recruited in the Empire. Heavy casualties at Hohenfriedberg and Soor. Very distinguished at Kolin.

IR NO 13

Inhaber or designation 1740 Moltke.
Uniforms (i) earlier part of reign – light blue facings, light blue shoulder strap edged with white, yellow buttons; no pom-pom, red and yellow bobs; (ii) *Egalisierung* 1767 – grass green with yellow buttons.
Record Recruited in the Alpine regions of Austria. In Transylvania on garrison duty late 1743–8. Two battalions captured in garrison 1758. Heavy casualties at Liegnitz.

IR NO 14

Inhaber or designation 1740 Salm-Salm, 1770 Ferraris, 1775 Tillier.
Uniforms (i) earlier part of reign – black facings, black shoulder strap edged with yellow, yellow buttons; no pom-pom, red and blue bobs; (ii) *Egalisierung* 1767 – black with yellow buttons. The very distinctive black facings survived into the twentieth century.
Record Recruited in the Empire. Distinguished at Dettingen, captured at Maastricht (1748). Distinguished at Kolin and Freiberg.

IR NO 15

Inhaber or designation 1740 Pallavicini, 1773 Fabris.
Uniforms (i) earlier part of reign – red facings, red shoulder strap edged with yellow, yellow buttons; red, white, red, white pom-pom, yellow and black bobs; (ii) *Egalisierung* 1767 – red with yellow buttons.
Record Recruited in the Empire. Distinguished at Velletri (1744), distinguished at Prague and defence of Dresden (1760). Distinguished in attack on Habelschwerdt (1779).

IR NO 16

Inhaber or designation 1740 Livingstein, 1741 Königsegg, 1778 Terzy.
Uniforms (i) earlier part of reign – dark blue or violet facings, black shoulder strap, narrow black collar, yellow buttons; no pom-pom, red and yellow bobs; (ii) *Egalisierung* 1767 – violet with yellow buttons.
Record Recruited in the Empire. Distinguished at Piacenza (1746). Heavy losses at the Sebastiansberg (1759).

IR NO 17

Inhaber or designation 1740 Kollowrat, 1773 Koch.
Uniforms (i) earlier part of reign – red facings, red shoulder strap edged with white, yellow buttons; yellow, red, yellow pom-pom, red and yellow bobs; (ii) *Egalisierung* 1767 – sulphur yellow with white buttons, changed *c* 1770 to light brown with white buttons.
Record Recruited in the Empire. Distinguished at Mollwitz, distinguished with heavy casualties at Hohenfriedberg and Soor.

IR NO 18

Inhaber or designation 1740 Seckendorff, 1742 Marschall, 1773 Brincken.
Uniforms (i) earlier part of reign – red facings, red shoulder strap, yellow buttons; no pom-pom, red and yellow bobs; (ii) *Egalisierung* 1767 – red with white buttons.
Record Recruited in the Empire. Third battalion captured at Prague 1741 and again at Freiburg 1744. Very distinguished at Meissen (1759).

IR NO 19

Inhaber or designation 1740 Pálffy (Leopold), 1773 D'Alton.

Uniforms (i) earlier part of reign – Hungarian-style facings in light blue, dark red barrel sash and dark red lace on blue waistcoat; (ii) *Egalisierung* 1767 – sky blue with white buttons.

Record A Hungarian regiment. A battalion destroyed by the mob in Genoa (1746). Distinguished at the storming of Schweidnitz in 1757 and again in 1761. Heavy losses at Liegnitz.

IR NO 20

Inhaber or designation 1740 Diesbach, 1744 Alt-Colloredo.

Uniforms (i) earlier part of reign – dark blue facings, dark blue shoulder strap, yellow buttons; dark blue or black with device of 'A' superimposed on 'C' in yellow beneath pom-pom, red and blue bobs; (ii) *Egalisierung* 1767 – red with white buttons.

Record Recruited in the Empire. Distinguished at Sarzana (1745). Very distinguished under Colonel Lacy at Lobositz. Captured at Breslau 1757, but restored and distinguished at Hochkirch.

IR NO 21

Inhaber or designation 1740 Schulenburg, 1754 Arenberg, 1778 Gemmingen.

Uniforms (i) earlier part of reign – light blue facings, white shoulder strap with blue central zig-zag, yellow buttons; light green and white pom-pom, black (?) and white bobs; (ii) *Egalisierung* 1767 – sea green with yellow buttons.

Record Recruited in the Empire. A battalion captured at Prague 1744. Distinguished in defence of Süptitz village at Torgau.

IR NO 22

Inhaber or designation 1740 Suckow, 1741 Roth, 1748 Hagenbach, 1757 Sprecher, 1758 Lacy.

Uniforms (i) earlier part of reign – red facings, red shoulder strap, single-breasted waistcoat, yellow buttons; yellow, red and white pom-pom, red and yellow bobs; (ii) *Egalisierung* 1767 – yellow with white buttons. Yellow was Lacy's favourite colour.

Record Recruited in the Empire. Distinguished at Hirschfeld (1757). Captured at Breslau 1757, reorganised 1758.

IR NO 23

Inhaber or designation 1740 Baden-Baden, 1771 Ried.

Uniforms (i) earlier part of reign – dark blue facings, white shoulder strap edged with dark blue, white buttons; (ii) *Egalisierung* 1767 – poppy red with white buttons.

Record Recruited in Baden. Heavy casualties at Kunersdorf.

IR NO 24

Inhaber or designation 1740 Starhemberg, 1771 Preiss.

Uniforms (i) earlier part of reign – dark blue facings, dark blue shoulder strap, yellow buttons; no pom-pom, blue and white bobs; (ii) *Egalisierung* 1767 – dark blue with white buttons.

Record Recruited in Inner Austria. Distinguished at Chotusitz, distinguished at Guastalla (1746). Heavy losses at Kolin, distinguished (after joined by 2nd bn) at Glatz (1760), severe casualties at Liegnitz.

IR NO 25

Inhaber or designation 1740 Wachtendonck, 1741 Piccolomini, 1757 Thürheim.
Uniforms (i) earlier part of reign – red facings, red shoulder strap, yellow buttons; no pom-pom, red and yellow bobs; (ii) *Egalisierung* 1767 – sea green.
Record Recruited in the Empire. Distinguished at Camposanto and Hochkirch. Very distinguished at Meissen (1759). Performed well in the 1762 campaign in Saxony.

IR NO 26

Inhaber or designation 1740 Grünne, 1751 Puebla, 1776 Riese.
Uniforms (i) earlier part of reign – red facings (and red turn-backs even in 1762), white shoulder strap edged with red, yellow buttons; scalloped hat edge, no pom-pom, red and yellow bobs; (ii) *Egalisierung* 1767 – parrot green with yellow buttons.
Record Recruited in the Rhine-Hessian Circle. Ridden down by the Bayreuth dragoons at Hohenfriedberg. Distinguished at Hochkirch, and again with heavy casualties at Torgau.

IR NO 27

Inhaber or designation 1740 Hessen-Cassel, 1753 Baden-Durlach.
Uniforms (i) earlier part of reign – light blue facings, light blue shoulder strap, white buttons; no pom-pom, red bobs; (ii) *Egalisierung* 1767 – yellow with yellow buttons. (NB. There is some uncertainty regarding the facings in the 1740s.)
Record Recruited in the Empire. One battalion suffered heavy losses at Hohenfriedberg. Distinguished and captured at Leuthen. Restored, and distinguished at storm of Schweidnitz 1761.

IR NO 28

Inhaber or designation 1740 Arenberg, 1754 Scherzer, 1754 Wied, 1779 Wartensleben.
Uniforms (i) earlier part of reign – green facings, yellow shoulder strap with central green zig-zag, single-breasted waistcoat, yellow buttons; scalloped hat edge, green, white and red pom-pom, yellow and black bobs; (ii) *Egalisierung* 1767 – grass green with white buttons.
Record Recruited in the Empire. Distinguished at Dettingen. Distinguished at Prague, captured at Breslau 1757. Distinguished at Maxen. Very heavy losses at Torgau, and a battalion captured at Freiberg.

IR NO 29

Inhaber or designation 1740 Alt-Wolfenbüttel, 1760 Loudon.
Uniforms (i) earlier part of reign – blue facings, white shoulder strap edged with blue, yellow buttons; scalloped hat edge; (ii) *Egalisierung* 1767 – light blue with white buttons.
Record Heavy losses at Leuthen. Very distinguished at Landeshut.

IR NO 30

Inhaber or designation 1740 Prié, 1753 Sachsen-Gotha, 1771 Ligne (Charles Joseph).
Uniforms (i) earlier part of reign – dark blue or violet facings, white shoulder strap, flecked with blue and red, yellow buttons; red pom-pom, red bobs; (ii) *Egalisierung* 1767 – pike grey with yellow buttons.
Record A Netherlandish regiment. In 1757 a battalion was attached to the French army. Very distinguished in the storm of Schweidnitz 1761. A battalion distinguished in the attack on Ober-Schwedeldorf (1779).

IR NO 31

Inhaber or designation 1741 Haller, 1777 Esterházy.

Uniforms (i) earlier part of reign – originally blue pelisse and pants, then white coat with light blue Hungarian-style decoration, white cuffs, white shoulder strap, light blue waistcoat with red lace, light blue pants, red and blue barrel sash; (ii) *Egalisierung* 1767 – yellow, yellow pants, white buttons.

Record A Hungarian regiment raised in 1741. Saw little action in the War of the Austrian Succession, but acquired a high reputation from its conduct at Kolin.

IR NO 32

Inhaber or designation 1741 Forgách, 1773 Gyulai.

Uniforms (i) earlier part of reign – originally blue pelisse and pants, then white coat with white tasselled *Litzen*, light blue cuffs and turn-backs, two light blue shoulder straps, light blue waistcoat with red lace, light blue pants, red and blue barrel sash, blue pom-pom, blue bobs; (ii) *Egalisierung* 1767 – sky blue, sky-blue pants, yellow buttons.

Record A Hungarian regiment raised in 1741. Recruited chiefly in Slovakia. Distinguished on the Rhine 1744, at Piacenza (1746) and in the defence of the Col de l'Assiette (1747). Suffered heavily at Torgau. Later became the popular Budapest *Hausregiment.*

IR NO 33

Inhaber or designation 1741 Andrássy, 1753 Esterházy (Nikolaus).

Uniforms (i) earlier part of reign – originally blue pelisse, then white coat with dark blue tasselled *Litzen*, dark blue cuffs, two dark blue shoulder straps, dark blue waistcoat with yellow lace, dark blue pants, yellow buttons, yellow and black barrel sash, yellow and blue pom-pom, blue and yellow bobs; (ii) *Egalisierung* 1767 – dark blue, dark blue pants.

Record A Hungarian regiment raised in 1741. Recruited chiefly in western Hungary. Distinguished in the storm of Monte Artemisio at Velletri (1744). Distinguished at Prague, Breslau, Leuthen and Hochkirch.

IR NO 34

Inhaber or designation 1740 Vettes, 1756 Batthyány.

Uniforms (i) earlier part of reign – white coat with yellow facings until about the middle of the Seven Years War, then with dark blue cuffs, turn-backs, shoulder strap, waistcoat and pants; (ii) *Egalisierung* 1767 – red, red pants, white buttons.

Record An older Hungarian regiment, raised in 1733. Suffered heavy casualties at Hochkirch and Liegnitz.

IR NO 35

Inhaber or designation 1740 Waldeck, 1763 Macquire, 1767 Hessen-Darmstadt, 1774 Wallis.

Uniforms (i) earlier part of reign – red facings, white shoulder strap, yellow buttons; no pom-pom, white and red bobs; (ii) *Egalisierung* 1767 – brownish red, yellow buttons.

Record Recruited in Franconia and Swabia. Lost at Leuthen, then reorganised. Distinguished at Hochkirch and Kunersdorf.

IR NO 36

Inhaber or designation 1740 Browne, 1759 Tillier, 1761 Kinsky.

Uniforms (i) earlier part of reign – light blue facings, white shoulder strap with blue edging and central blue zig-zag, white buttons; white scalloped hat edging, red and yellow pom-pom, red and blue bobs; (ii) *Egalisierung* 1767 – pale red with white buttons.

Record Helped to cover the retreat at Leuthen. Distinguished at Hochkirch and Maxen. Nearly wiped out at Torgau. Heavy losses when attacked by superior forces at Brüx (1778).

IR NO 37

Inhaber or designation 1741 Szirmay, 1744 Esterházy, 1747 Esterházy (Joseph), 1762 Siskovics.

Uniforms (i) earlier part of reign – originally blue pelisse and pants, then white coat with red *Litzen*, red cuffs, two red shoulder straps, red turn-backs, red waistcoat with blue lace, red pants, yellow buttons, red and blue barrel sash; yellow and red pom-pom, blue and red bobs; (ii) *Egalisierung* 1767 – red with yellow buttons, red pants.

Record A Hungarian regiment raised in 1741. Recruited chiefly in Slovakia. Distinguished at Hochkirch. Helped to cover the retreat at Liegnitz.

IR NO 38

Inhaber or designation 1740 Ligne (Claudius), 1766 Merode, 1774 Kaunitz.

Uniforms (i) earlier part of reign – rose red facings (the de Ligne house colours), two rose red shoulder straps, silver buttons; no pom-pom, light green bobs; (ii) *Egalisierung* 1767 – rose red with yellow buttons.

Record A Netherlandish regiment, made famous by the memoirs of Prince Charles Joseph de Ligne who served in it in the Seven Years War. Individual battalions distinguished at Dettingen, Kolin, Breslau, Leuthen and Hochkirch.

IR NO 39

Inhaber or designation 1756 Pálffy, 1758 Preysach.

Uniforms (i) earlier part of reign – originally with blue dolman, then white coat with white *Litzen*, red cuffs and turn-backs, two white shoulder straps edged with red, red waistcoat with white lace and white buttons, red pants, white and red barrel sash; no pom-pom, yellow and black (blue?) bobs; (ii) *Egalisierung* 1767 – dark red with white buttons.

Record A Hungarian regiment raised in 1756 at the cost of Count Johann Pálffy. Recruited chiefly in the area of Buda. Distinguished at Olmütz and Landeshut.

IR NO 40

Inhaber or designation 1740 Damnitz, 1754 Jung-Colloredo.

Uniforms (i) earlier part of reign: blue facings, white shoulder strap edged with grey (?), yellow buttons; white and blue pom-pom, blue and white bobs; (ii) *Egalisierung* 1767 – carmine red with white buttons.

Record Recruited in the Hereditary Lands. Heavy casualties at Soor and Torgau.

IR NO 41

Inhaber or designation 1740 Bayreuth, 1767 Plunquet, 1770 Fürstenberg, 1777 Belgiojoso, 1778 Bender.

Uniforms (i) earlier part of reign – red facings, red shoulder strap, white buttons; scalloped hat edge, green, yellow and white pom-pom, red and yellow bobs; (ii) *Egalisierung* 1767 – light brown with yellow buttons, replaced at the request of Prince Fürstenberg in 1770 by yellow with yellow buttons.

Record Recruited from Bavaria and Franconia. There was a significant Irish element among the officers. Capitulated at Freiburg (1744) but exchanged in 1745. Heavy losses at Moys and Torgau.

IR NO 42

Inhaber or designation 1740 O'Nelly, 1743 Gaisruck, 1769 Gemmingen, 1775 Mathesen.
Uniforms (i) earlier part of reign – blue facings, blue shoulder strap with white edge and central white zig-zag, yellow buttons; yellow and blue pom-pom, red and blue (black?) bobs; (ii) *Egalisierung* 1767 – orange red with white buttons.
Record Recruited in Franconia. Very distinguished under heavy fire at Kolin. Suffered heavily at Breslau, and fought as a single battalion at Leuthen. Distinguished at Hochkirch, almost annihilated at Torgau. A hard-fighting regiment which became still more famous in the nineteenth century.

IR NO 43

Inhaber or designation 1740 Platz, 1768 Buttler, 1775 Thurn.
Uniforms (i) earlier part of reign – red or orange-red facings, yellow buttons; (ii) *Egalisierung* 1767 – sulphur yellow with yellow buttons.
Record Fought at Soor, then went to the Netherlands theatre. Heavy casualties at Kolin, distinguished at Landeshut and Liegnitz.

IR NO 44

Inhaber or designation 1744 Clerici, 1769 Gaisruck, 1778 Belgiojoso.
Uniforms (i) earlier part of reign – red with yellow buttons; (ii) *Egalisierung* 1767 – red with yellow buttons.
Record An Italian regiment, raised in the Milanese in 1744 at the cost of Marquis Giorgio Clerici. Distinguished at Cuneo (1744). Asked for, and received, the honour to be the first regiment to storm the churchyard at Hochkirch. One battalion surrendered in disgraceful circumstances near Gabel in 1778.

IR NO 45

Inhaber or designation 1740 Daun, 1761 O'Kelly, 1767 Bülow.
Uniforms (i) earlier part of reign – red facings, red shoulder strap edged with white, yellow buttons; yellow and red pom-pom; (ii) *Egalisierung* 1767 – carmine red with yellow buttons.
Record Recruited in Moravia and Silesia. In the Italian campaigns 1744–7. Present at Breslau, Leuthen, Hochkirch and Torgau.

IR NO 46

Inhaber or designation The *Tiroler Land-und Feld Regiment;* 1748 O'Gilvy, 1751 Sincère, 1752 Macquire, 1764 Migazzi.
Uniforms (i) earlier part of reign – red facings, red shoulder strap, yellow buttons; green pom-pom, red bobs; (ii) *Egalisierung* 1767 – dark blue with yellow buttons.
Record Recruited in the Tyrol and SW Germany. Raised 1745, and placed on the footing of a German regiment in 1745. Distinguished at the storm of Schweidnitz (1757), Breslau and Leuthen.

IR NO 47

Inhaber or designation 1740 Harrach, 1764 Brandenburg-Bayreuth, 1769 Elrichshausen, 1779 Kinsky.
Uniforms (i) earlier part of reign – blue or violet facings, blue shoulder strap, yellow buttons; yellow pom-pom, blue and yellow bobs; (ii) *Egalisierung* 1767 – steel green with white buttons.
 Record Recruited in Austrian Silesia. Distinguished at Mollwitz, Prague and Torgau.

IR NO 48

Inhaber or designation 1740 Vasquez, 1755 Luzan, 1765 Ried, 1773 Caprara.

Uniforms (i) earlier part of reign – green facings, white shoulder strap, yellow buttons; no pom-pom or bobs; (ii) *Egalisierung* 1767 – light brown with yellow buttons.

Record An Italian regiment, recruited in the Milanese. Distinguished at the storm of Schweidnitz (1757).

IR NO 49

Inhaber or designation 1740 Walsegg, 1743 Bärnklau, 1747 Kheul, 1758 Angern, 1767 Pellegrini.

Uniforms (i) earlier part of reign – red facings, white shoulder strap, white buttons; no pom-pom, yellow and blue bobs; (ii) *Egalisierung* 1767 – pike grey with white buttons.

Record Recruited in SW Germany. Very distinguished at Prague, distinguished at Liegnitz.

IR NO 50

Inhaber or designation 1740 Wurmbrand, 1749 Harsch, 1773 Poniatowski, 1776 Stain.

Uniforms (i) earlier part of reign – red facings, red shoulder strap and red turn-backs, with unique white *Litzen* – one on the shoulder strap, seven down the side of each lapel, and three on each cuff; white buttons; no pom-pom, blue and red bobs. The hat and the cut of the uniform were made the norm for the rest of the infantry before the Seven Years War. (ii) *Egalisierung* 1767 – violet with white buttons.

Record A smart regiment, recruited in Bohemia. A battalion suffered heavily at Hohenfriedberg. Fought at Lobositz, Kolin, Breslau, Leuthen, Hochkirch, Maxen and Torgau.

IR NO 51

Inhaber or designation 1740 Gyulai. For a time known as the *siebenbürgisches National-Regiment.*

Uniforms (i) earlier part of reign – dark blue cuffs, shoulder strap and turn-backs, red tasselled *Litzen;* dark blue waistcoat with red lace and yellow buttons, dark blue pants, red and blue barrel sash; yellow and black pom-pom, yellow and black bobs; (ii) *Egalisierung* 1767 – dark blue with yellow buttons.

Record An old-established Hungarian regiment. Helped to cover the retreat at Hohenfriedberg. Decided the action at Teplitz (1762).

IR NO 52

Inhaber or designation 1741 Bethlen, 1763 Károlyi.

Uniforms (i) earlier part of reign – originally blue dolman and red pants, then 1743 red facings, 1748 blue facings, 1757 light green cuffs and turn-backs, white tasselled *Litzen*, white shoulder strap, light green waistcoat with yellow buttons, light green pants, red and yellow barrel sash; (ii) *Egalisierung* 1767 – dark red with yellow buttons.

Record A Hungarian regiment raised in 1741. Distinguished at Breslau.

IR NO 53

Inhaber or designation 1741 *Panduren-Corps von der Trenck*, 1748 *Slavonisches Panduren-Bataillon*, 1756 Simbschen, 1763 Beck, 1768 Pálffy.

Uniforms (i) earlier part of reign – 1741 Turkish-style dress with high black shako, red cloak and red dolman; Seven Years War – Hungarian style uniform with red cuffs, dark lilac tasselled *Litzen*, red waistcoat with yellow lace, red pants, black and yellow barrel sash, scalloped hat edging; (ii) *Egalisierung* 1767 – red with white buttons.

Record Recruited in the areas of Slavonia outside the military border. Enjoyed an exciting and disreputable career in the War of the Austrian Succession. Reorganised 1756. Distinguished at Olmütz and Liegnitz.

IR NO 54

Inhaber or designation 1740 Königsegg, 1751 Sincere, 1769 Callenberg.
Uniforms (i) earlier part of reign – red facings, red shoulder strap with red edging and central zig-zag, yellow buttons; scalloped hat border, yellow pom-pom, yellow and red bobs; (ii) *Egalisierung* 1767 – apple green with white buttons.
Record Recruited in Lower Austria and Moravia. Distinguished at the crossing of the Rhine (1744). Heavy casualties at Torgau. Captain James MacBrady and a detachment of 270 distinguished in the defence of Schweidnitz (1762).

IR NO 55

Inhaber or designation 1742 Chanclos, or *Erstes niederländisches National-Regiment*, . 1746 D'Arberg, 1768 Murray.
Uniforms (i) earlier part of reign – red or orange-red facings, white shoulder strap with red edging, yellow buttons; black pom-pom, red and yellow bobs; (ii) *Egalisierung* 1767 – blue with yellow buttons.
Record A Netherlandish regiment, raised in 1742. Fought at Dettingen. Distinguished at the storm of Schweidnitz (1761).

IR NO 56

Inhaber or designation 1740 Daun, 1741 Mercy, 1767 Nugent.
Uniforms (i) earlier part of reign – blue or violet facings and shoulder strap, yellow buttons, blue and white pom-pom, blue and white bobs; (ii) *Egalisierung* 1767 – steel green with yellow buttons.
Record Suffered heavily at Prague. Distinguished at Breslau, but fled at Leuthen. Heavy casualties at Torgau.

IR NO 57

Inhaber or designation 1740 Thüngen, 1745 Andlau, 1769 Colloredo.
Uniforms (i) earlier part of reign – red facings, white shoulder strap edged with red, yellow buttons; no pom-pom, red and yellow bobs; (ii) *Egalisierung* 1767 – pale red with yellow buttons.
Record Recruited in the Empire. Crushed at Hohenfriedberg. Until 1759 only one battalion was present in the Seven Years War – it suffered heavily at Leuthen, and was captured at the Pass-Berg in 1759. After reorganisation the whole regiment fought at Liegnitz.

IR NO 58

Inhaber or designation 1763 Vierset.
Uniforms (i) 1763 – blue facings, yellow buttons; (ii) *Egalisierung* 1767 – black with white buttons.
Record Raised by the French in Liège, and taken into Austrian service 1763. A battalion took part in the attack on Ober-Schwedeldorf (1779).

IR NO 59

Inhaber or designation 1740 Daun (Leopold), 1766 Daun (Franz), 1771 Langlois.
 Uniforms (i) earlier part of reign – red facings, red shoulder strap, yellow buttons; green

pom-pom with monogram 'ℝ' below, red and blue bobs; (ii) *Egalisierung* 1767 – orange yellow with yellow buttons.

Record Recruited in Upper and Lower Austria. Distinguished at Chotusitz, Simbach (1743), and (with heavy losses) at Hohenfriedberg. Helped to decide the battle of Breslau. Distinguished at Zuckmantel (1779).

Disbanded infantry regiments

Numbered according to the sequence of their dissolution

IR NO (i)

Inhaber 1740 Schmettau.
Uniform Red facings.
Record Disbanded in 1741 after its *Inhaber* deserted to the Prussians.

IR NO (ii)

Inhaber 1740 Heister.
Uniform Red facings.
Record On garrison duty in the Netherlands. Disbanded 1747.

IR NO (iii)

Inhaber 1740 Göldlin, 1741 Kheul.
Uniform Red facings.
Record Heavy losses in the siege of Genoa 1746–7. Disbanded 1747.

IR NO (iv)

Inhaber 1740 O'Gilvy.
Uniform Blue facings.
Record Recruited in Bohemia. Distinguished at Mollwitz. Took little part in the war after one battalion captured in Prague (1744). Disbanded 1748.

IR NO (v)

Inhaber 1740 Wallis, 1746 Hagenbach.
Uniform Rose red facings.
Record Mainly on the Italian theatre. Distinguished at Camposanto (1743). 1748 incorporated in IR NO 22.

IR NO (vi)

Inhaber 1740 Traun.
Uniform Red or blue facings.
Record Mainly on the Italian theatre. Disbanded 1748.

IR NO (vii)

Inhaber 1743 Arenberg.
Uniform Red facings.
Record Raised by Prince Arenberg in 1743 as *Zweites niederländisches National-Regiment.* Fought at Dettingen, Rocoux, Laffeldt, and in the defence of Maastricht (1748). Disbanded 1748.

IR NO (viii)

Inhaber 1743 Sprecher.
Uniform Red facings.
Record Raised in the Grisons by Colonel Salomon Sprecher 1743. Heavy losses when surprised at Codogno (1746). Disbanded 1749.

IR NO (ix)

Inhaber 1740. Marulli.
Uniform Blue facings.
Record An Italian regiment which saw little action, except at Velletri (1744). Disbanded 1751.

Grenzer ('*Croat*') *infantry regiments*

Numbered according to the scheme of 1769

GZ IR NO 60 CARLSTÄDTER LICCANER

Uniforms (i) Seven Years War – red jacket with pointed green cuffs and yellow lace; sea green waistcoat with yellow lace; red pants, red and green barrel sash; black or red cap; sword with iron furniture; (ii) 1769 – white coat with violet *Egalisierung*, yellow buttons, white pants.
Record First saw action 1742. Distinguished at Tetschen (1756), and the storm of Glatz (1760).

GZ IR NO 61 CARLSTÄDTER OTTOCANER

Uniforms (i) Seven Years War – red jacket with pointed blue cuffs and yellow lace; light blue waistcoat with yellow lace; red pants; red and blue barrel sash; black or red cap; sword with iron furniture; (ii) 1769 – white coat with violet *Egalisierung*, white buttons, white pants.
Record Raised 1746. Captured a Prussian battalion at Liebau (1758). Distinguished at Reichenstein (1759), the storm of Glatz (1760), and Meissen (1762).

GZ IR NO 62 CARLSTÄDTER OGULINER

Uniforms (i) Seven Years War – blue jacket with pointed yellow cuffs and yellow lace; blue waistcoat with yellow lace; red pants; red and yellow barrel sash; red cloak; black or red cap; sword with iron furniture; (ii) 1769 – white coat, orange-yellow *Egalisierung*, yellow buttons, white pants.
Record Formed in 1746. Saw action in Provence 1747. Heavy losses at Troppau (1759), distinguished at Landeshut.

GZ IR NO 63 CARLSTÄDTER SZLUINER

Uniforms (i) Seven Years War – blue jacket with pointed red cuffs and yellow lace; red waistcoat with yellow criss-cross embroidery; blue pants; blue and yellow barrel sash; black or red cap; red cloak; sword with brass furniture; (ii) 1769 – white coat, orange-yellow *Egalisierung*, white buttons, white pants.
Record Raised 1746. Distinguished near Maastricht (1747). On the 1757 Berlin raid, and distinguished at Pretschendorf (1762). Distinguished at Niklasberg (1778).

GZ IR NO 64 WARASDINER CREUTZER

 Uniforms (i) Seven Years War – short white coat, with light green round cuffs, collar, turn-backs, and tasselled *Litzen*; light green waistcoat with white lace and yellow buttons; white pants; white and yellow barrel sash; black cap, sword with iron furniture; (ii) 1769 – white coat, red *Egalisierung*, yellow buttons, white pants.

Record Raised 1745. One of the battalions distinguished at Brandeis (1757) and Kolin, but both captured at Breslau (1757). Reorganised and fought in later actions with success.

GZ IR NO 65 WARASDINER ST GEORGER

Uniforms (i) Seven Years War – short white coat with round green cuffs, green collar, turn-backs and tasselled *Litzen*; green waistcoat with white lace, white pants; white and yellow barrel sash; black hat; sword with iron furniture; (ii) 1769 – white coat, red *Egalisierung*, white buttons, white pants.

Record Raised 1745. A battalion distinguished at Görlitz (1757) and Breslau.

GZ IR NO 66 SLAVONISCH BRODER

Uniforms (i) Seven Years War – short dark blue or dark brown jacket with round yellow cuffs and yellow collar; dark blue waistcoat with yellow lace; blue pants, yellow and blue barrel sash; black cap, sword with brass furniture; (ii) 1769 – white coat, pale red *Egalisierung*, yellow buttons, white pants.

Record Raised 1747. Various battalions distinguished at Brandeis (1757), Friedland (1759) and Torgau.

GZ IR NO 67 GRADISCANER

Uniforms (i) Seven Years War – dark blue or red jacket, with pointed blue cuffs and collar; blue waistcoat; red pants; yellow or red barrel sash with blue knots; (ii) 1769 – white coat, pale red (?) *Egalisierung*, white buttons, white pants.

Record Raised 1747. Distinguished at the Pass-Berg (1759) and in the storm of Schweidnitz (1762).

GZ IR NO 68 SLAVONISCH-PETERWARDEINER

Uniforms (i) Seven Years War – brown or light blue jacket with red cuffs and collar; blue waistcoat with red lace; blue pants; red and yellow barrel sash; black cap, sword with brass furniture; (ii) 1769 – white coat, pike grey *Egalisierung*, yellow buttons, white pants.

Record Raised 1747. Distinguished in many small actions in the Seven Years War.

GZ IR NO 69 ERSTES BANAL-GZ-IR

Uniforms (i) Seven Years War – dark blue jacket with pointed red cuffs and yellow lace; red waistcoat with yellow frogging; red pants; blue and red barrel sash; black cap; sword with iron furniture; (ii) 1769 – white coat, carmine red *Egalisierung*, yellow buttons, white pants.

Record Raised 1750. Its name derived not from the Banát region, but from the Banus of Croatia, who was its *Inhaber*. Distinguished at the storm of Schweidnitz (1757), at Reinerz (1757) and in the retreat from Leipzig (1760).

GZ IR NO 70 ZWEITES BANAL-GZ-IR

Uniforms (i) Seven Years War – Blue jacket with pointed red cuffs and elaborate red and yellow *Litzen*; red waistcoat with yellow lace; red pants; red and blue barrel sash; black cap; sword with iron furniture; (ii) 1769 – white coat, violet *Egalisierung*, white pants.

Record Raised 1750. Fought at Lobositz, Prague, Meissen and Torgau.

GZ IR NO 71 TEMESVÁRER ANSIEDLUNGS-CORPS (OR REGIMENT)

Uniform White coat, dark brown *Egalisierung*, white buttons, white pants.
Record Formed in the Banát from German veterans 1765.

GZ IR NO 72 ILLYRISCHES-GZ-IR

Uniform White coat, pike grey *Egalisierung*, white buttons, white pants.
Record Formed 1766. United 1775 with the Walachisch-Banater Gz-I-Bn to form the Walachisch-Illyrisches Gz-I-R.

GZ IR NO 73 SIEBENBÜRGISCHES I SZÉKLER GZ-R

Uniform Originally national dress, then white coat, rose-red *Egalisierung*, white buttons.
Record Formed in Transylvania in 1762. Distinguished at Levin (1778).

GZ IR NO 74 SIEBENBÜRGISCHES 2 SZÉKLER GZ-R

Uniform Originally national dress, then as in the first regiment.
Record Formed in Transylvania in 1762. Distinguished at Olbersdorf-Mössnik (1778).

GZ IR NO 75 ERSTES SIEBENBÜRGISCHES WALACHEN-GZ-R

Uniform Originally national dress, then white coat, parrot green *Egalisierung*, yellow buttons.
Record Formed in Transylvania 1762. Joined with the second regiment in Moravia in 1779.

GZ IR NO 76 ZWEITES SIEBENBÜRGISCHES WALACHEN-GZ-R

Uniform Originally national dress, then white coat, parrot green *Egalisierung*, white buttons.

Other infantry units

STABS-INFANTERIE-REGIMENT

Uniforms (i) Seven Years War – blue coat with red collar and cuffs, white turn-backs, no lapels, blue waistcoat, white breeches; red pom-pom and bobs; (ii) War of Bavarian Succession – blue coat with red *Egalisierung*, yellow buttons; tricorn hat.
Record Raised for specialised duties 1758–63, and again 1778–9. Its unique uniform looked rather 'Prussian', and enabled the regiment to evade capture at Torgau.

DEUTSCHES FELD-JÄGER CORPS

Uniform Pike grey coat, waistcoat and breeches, green cuffs and collar, leather *casquet*.
Record Raised on a small basis 1758. Distinguished at Torgau. Made an independent united 1761, but disbanded 1763. Reconstituted in the War of the Bavarian Succession.

OESTERREICHISCHES GARNISONS-REGIMENT

Record Existed 1760–3 in garrison posts in Austria.

ERSTES GARNISONS-REGIMENT (IR NO 5)

 Uniform White coat and collar, dark blue cuffs, white buttons.

Record Formed from the half-invalids of the Prague house, 1766. Stationed on the eastern borders.

ZWEITES GARNISONS-REGIMENT (IR NO 6)

Uniform White coat and collar, black cuffs, yellow buttons.
Record Formed 1767.

DRITTES GARNISONS-REGIMENT

Uniform White coat and cuffs, black collar, white buttons.
Record Formed as a battalion in 1772, and converted to a regiment in 1776. Did garrison duty in the Netherlands.

Free corps, battalions, companies and legions

These were formed to the number of about sixty in the various wars of Maria Theresa. The grand titles had less to do with the size or organisation than with the enthusiasm of the founders. Only four of the units seem to have been of any great significance:

BATAILLON BECK

Uniform Green coat with buff cuffs and lapels, green waistcoat and breeches, white buttons, tricorn edged with buff.
Record Raised by Lieutenant-General Beck 1759. Distinguished in the defence of Neider-Arnsdorf (1760). Disbanded 1763.

BATAILLON LOUDON

Uniform Green coat with red cuffs and lapels, green waistcoat and breeches, yellow buttons, tricorn edged with white.
Record Raised by Loudon in 1758. Distinguished at Kunersdorf, Landeshut and Liegnitz. Disbanded 1763.

CORPS OTTO

Uniform Green coat, black cuffs, yellow buttons, yellow breeches.
Record A company of sharpshooters, with accompanying *chevaulégers* and hussars, raised by Captain Otto in Saxony in 1759. Joined the *Reichsarmee* and distinguished in many small actions. Disbanded 1763.

CORPS VON DER TRENCK

See IR NO 53.

Cuirassier regiments

Numbered according to the scheme of 1769, which assigned numbers throughout the cavalry regardless of subdivision into cuirassiers, dragoons, etc. Thereafter numbers were endlessly changing, according to the relative seniority of the *Inhabers*.

All cuirassier coats were white. They had two shoulder straps, but no lapels. The cuirassier and dragoon hats were plain black tricorns, without pom-poms, bobs or edging. A single button was worn on the left-hand side of the hat, just below the cockade.

CR NO 3

Inhaber 1740 Hohenzollern-Hechingen, 1750 Erzherzog Leopold.
Uniforms (i) earlier part of reign – red cuffs, turn-backs and shoulder straps, white waistcoat, white buttons – one row on coat, one row on waistcoat, red breeches, sword with iron furniture; (ii) 1765 – poppy red *Egalisierung*, yellow buttons, white breeches.
Record Recruited in the Empire. Distinguished at Sahay (1742). Heavy casualties at Torgau. Converted to dragoons 1775.

CR NO 4

Inhaber 1740 Hohenembs, 1756 Erzherzog Ferdinand, 1761 Erzherzog Maximilian.
Uniforms (i) earlier part of reign – red cuffs and turn-backs, white shoulder straps, white waistcoat, yellow buttons – one row on coat, one row on waistcoat, red breeches, sword with brass furniture; (ii) 1765 – poppy red *Egalisierung*, white buttons, white breeches.
Record Recruited in the Hereditary Lands. Entered the Habsburg service as a force of Florentine cavalry in 1619, and enjoyed many privileges in the Hofburg as a reward for having saved Ferdinand II from Protestant rebels in the same year. Heavy casualties at Mollwitz and Prague. Helped to cover the retreat at Leuthen, distinguished at Hochkirch.

CR NO 6

Inhaber 1740 Portugal, 1766 Berlichingen.
Uniforms (i) earlier part of reign – red cuffs, turn-backs and shoulder straps, red waistcoat white buttons – one row on coat, one row on waistcoat, red breeches, sword with brass furniture; (ii) 1765 – carmine red *Egalisierung*, white buttons, white breeches.
Record Recruited in Bohemia. Distinguished at Kolin and Torgau. Converted to dragoons 1779.

CR NO 8

Inhaber 1740 Pálffy, 1774 Rothschütz.
Uniforms (i) earlier part of reign – red cuffs and turn-backs, white shoulder straps, white waistcoat, white buttons – one row on coat, one row on waistcoat, red breeches, sword with brass furniture; (ii) 1765 – sea green *Egalisierung*, white buttons, white breeches.
Record Recruited in the Empire. Saw action at Chotusitz, Hohenfriedberg, Soor, Lobositz, Kolin, Landeshut, Liegnitz and Freiberg.

CR NO 10

Inhaber 1740 Lobkowitz, 1753 Stampach, 1768 Modena.
Uniforms (i) earlier part of reign – red cuffs, turn-backs and shoulder straps, red waistcoat, yellow buttons – one row on coat, double row on waistcoat, straw breeches, sword with brass furniture; (ii) 1765 – dark green *Egalisierung*, yellow buttons, white breeches.
Record Distinguished at Lopositz and Torgau.

CR NO 12

Inhaber 1740 Seherr, 1743 St Ignon, 1745 Serbelloni, 1778 Mecklenburg-Strelitz.
Uniforms (i) earlier part of reign – red cuffs and turn backs, white shoulder straps, red waistcoat, white buttons – two rows on coat and waistcoat, red breeches, sword with brass furniture; (ii) 1765 – dark green *Egalisierung*, white buttons, white breeches.
Record Recruited in the Empire. Distinguished at Sahay (1742), heavy casualties at Hohenfriedberg and Soor, distinguished at Kolin and Torgau.

CR NO 14

Inhaber 1740 Cordua, 1756 O'Donnel, 1773 Brockhausen, 1779 Haag.
Uniforms (i) earlier part of reign – red cuffs, turn-backs and shoulder straps, white waistcoat, yellow buttons – single rows on coat and waistcoat – red breeches, sword with brass furniture; (ii) 1765 – blue *Egalisierung*, white buttons, white breeches.
Record Recruited in the Empire and the Netherlands. Saw little action in the 1740s after Sahay (1742). Its *Inhaber* in the Seven Years War was Carl O'Donnell, one of the best heavy cavalrymen in the army. Very distinguished at Lobositz. Distinguished at Kolin, Breslau Leuthen and Hochkirch.

CR NO 20

Inhaber 1740 Miglio, 1745 Schmerzing, 1762 D'Ayasasa, 1779 Jacquemin.
Uniforms (i) earlier part of reign – red cuffs, turn-backs and shoulder straps, white waistcoat, yellow buttons – two rows on coat, two rows on waistcoat – red breeches, sword with brass furniture; (ii) 1765 – red *Egalisierung*, yellow buttons, white breeches.
Record Recruited in Bohemia. Distinguished at Piacenza, Meissen (1759) and Maxen.

CR NO 21

Inhaber 1740 Bernes, 1751 Trautmannsdorff.
Uniforms (i) earlier part of reign – red cuffs, turn-backs and shoulder straps, white waistcoat, white buttons – one row on coat, one row on waistcoat – red breeches, sword with brass furniture; (ii) 1765 – dark blue *Egalisierung*, white buttons, white breeches.
Record Very distinguished at Rossbach, Landeshut and Liegnitz.

CR NO 22

Inhaber 1740 St Ignon, 1750 Kalckreuth, 1760 Prinz Albert (of Saxony), 1768 Kleinholdt, 1773 Thurn.
Uniforms (i) earlier part of reign – red cuffs, turn-backs and shoulder straps, red waistcoat, white buttons – one row on coat, one row on waistcoat – straw breeches, sword with brass furniture; (ii) 1765 – light blue *Egalisierung*, yellow buttons, white breeches.
Record Recruited from the Empire. Distinguished at Landeshut and Liegnitz. Disbanded 1775.

CR NO 23

Inhaber 1740 Birkenfeld, 1761 Stampa, 1773 Jacquemin.
Uniforms (i) earlier part of reign; red cuffs, turn-backs and shoulder straps, white waistcoat, yellow buttons – single row on coat, double row on waistcoat – red breeches, sword with brass furniture; (ii) 1765 – parrot green *Egalisierung*, yellow buttons, white breeches.
Record Recruited in the Empire, and one of the oldest regiments in the army. Very distinguished at Kolin. Distinguished at Kunersdorf. Disbanded 1775.

CR NO 25

Inhaber 1740 Lanthieri, 1745 Bentheim, 1751 Stampach, 1753 Anhalt-Zerbst, 1767 Podstatzky.
Uniforms (i) earlier part of reign – red cuffs, turn-backs and shoulder straps, straw waistcoat edged with red at bottom, yellow buttons – one row on coat, concealed row on waistcoat – straw breeches, sword with brass furniture. (NB. In the Seven Years War the regiment is known to have worn a kind of jerkin). (ii) 1765 – sea green *Egalisierung*, yellow buttons, white breeches.

Record Recruited in Bohemia. Very distinguished at Hochkirch. Distinguished at Maxen. Disbanded 1775.

CR NO 27

Inhaber 1740 Pálffy (Johann), 1751 Radicati, 1756 Löwenstein, 1758 Daun (Benedict), 1766 Voghera.
Uniforms (i) earlier part of reign – red cuffs and turn-backs, white shoulder straps, white waistcoat, yellow buttons – single row on coat, double row on waistcoat – red breeches, sword with brass furniture; (ii) 1765 – carmine red *Egalisierung*, yellow buttons, white breeches.
Record Recruited in the Empire and Bohemia. A smart and well-maintained regiment, whose uniform was made the pattern for the others before the Seven Years War. Distinguished at Meissen and Torgau.

CR NO 29

Inhaber 1740 Lubomirski, 1745 Bretlach, 1767 Caramelli.
Uniforms (i) earlier part of reign – red cuffs, turn-backs and collar, straw waistcoat, white buttons – one row on coat, one row on waistcoat – straw breeches, sword with iron furniture; (ii) 1765 – black *Egalisierung*, white buttons, white breeches.
Record Recruited in the Empire. Lost heavily at Chotusitz. Distinguished at Lobositz, Rossbach and Freiberg.

CR NO 33

Inhaber 1740 Diemar, 1751 Anspach.
Uniforms (i) earlier part of reign – red cuffs and turn-backs, white shoulder straps, white waistcoat, white buttons – one row on coat, double row on waistcoat, red breeches, sword with brass furniture; (ii) 1765 – parrot green *Egalisierung*, white buttons, white breeches.
Record Very distinguished at Lobositz. Heavy casualties at Liegnitz.

Disbanded cuirassier regiments

Numbered according to the sequence of their dissolution

CR NO (i)

Inhaber 1740 Berlichingen, 1751 Gelhay, 1759 Ville.
Uniforms (i) earlier part of reign – red cuffs, turn-backs and shoulder straps, white waistcoat, yellow buttons – one row on coat, double row on waistcoat – red breeches, sword with brass furniture; (ii) 1765 – black *Egalisierung*, yellow buttons, white breeches.
Record Recruited in Bohemia. In Italy in the War of the Austrian Succession. Distinguished at Hochkirch. Disbanded 1768.

CR NO (ii)

Inhaber 1740 Caraffa, 1743 Lucchesi, 1758 Buccow, 1764 Kleinholdt.
Uniforms (i) earlier part of reign – red cuffs, turn-backs and shoulder straps, red waistcoat white buttons – one row on coat, double row on waistcoat – red breeches, sword with brass furniture; (ii) 1765 – red *Egalisierung*, white buttons, white breeches.
 Record Recruited from Westphalia. Distinguished at Torgau. Disbanded 1768.

CR NO (iii)

Inhaber 1740 Podstatzky, 1743 Czernin, 1755 Alt-Modena.
Uniforms (i) earlier part of reign – dark blue cuffs and turn-backs, white shoulder straps, white waistcoat, white buttons – one row on coat, one row on waistcoat – dark blue breeches, sword with brass furniture. NB. These blue facings were unique in the cuirassiers. (ii) 1765 – dark blue *Egalisierung*, yellow buttons, white breeches.
Record Recruited in Lombardy. In 1755 Maria Theresa described the burdens imposed on the men as 'exorbitant'. Very distinguished at Meissen and Maxen. Disbanded 1768.

Dragoon regiments

By 'earlier part of reign' is to be understood the uniform known to have been worn in the Seven Years War, regardless of the dark blue uniform that was decreed in 1757. A white coat with coloured *Egalisierung* was introduced in 1767. The shoulder strap was always worn on the left shoulder, and the aiglets on the right.

DR NO I

Inhaber 1740 Althann, 1748 Erzherzog Joseph, 1765 Kaiser (Joseph).
Uniforms (i) earlier part of reign – green coat with red cuffs, lapels, turn-backs, shoulder strap and aiglets, green waistcoat, yellow buttons – two rows on coat, double row on waistcoat – straw breeches, sword with brass furniture; (ii) as *chevaulégers* 1766 – grass green coat with poppy red *Egalisierung*, yellow buttons, white breeches. Emperor Joseph II was frequently depicted in this uniform.
Record Recruited in the Empire. Distinguished at Hohenfriedberg, Soor, Lobositz, Breslau, Leuthen, and Königgrätz (1758). Converted to *chevaulégers* in 1765.

DR NO 6

Inhaber 1740 Liechtenstein (Joseph Wenzel, the gunner).
Uniforms (i) earlier part of reign – dark blue or violet coat with red cuffs, lapels, turn-backs and aiglets, dark blue or violet shoulder strap, red waistcoat, yellow buttons – two rows on coat, double row on waistcoat – red breeches, sword with brass furniture; (ii) 1767 – light blue *Egalisierung*, yellow buttons, white breeches.
Record Recruited in the Empire. Distinguished at Lobositz, and at the Sebastiansberg (1758). Disbanded 1775.

DR NO 7

Inhaber 1740 Batthyány, 1773 Kinsky.
Uniforms (i) earlier part of reign – dark blue or purple coat with red cuffs, lapels, turn-backs and aiglets, dark blue or purple shoulder strap, dark blue or purple waistcoat, yellow buttons – two rows on coat, double row on waistcoat – dark blue or purple breeches, sword with brass furniture. This scheme was chosen in 1757 as the model for the rest of the dragoons (see above). (ii) 1767 – light blue *Egalisierung*, yellow buttons, white breeches.
Record Recruited in the Empire. Distinguished at Pfaffenhofen (1745). Heavy losses at Prague and Leuthen. Distinguished at Hochkirch. Very distinguished at Torgau. Converted to *chevaulégers* in 1775.

DR NO 9 ('SAVOYEN')

Inhaber 1740 Aspremont-Linden, 1773 Richecourt.
Uniforms (i) earlier part of reign – red coat with black cuffs, lapels, turn-backs and aiglets, red shoulder strap, red waistcoat, yellow buttons – two rows on coat, double row on

waistcoat – red breeches, sword with black furniture; (ii) 1767 – black *Egalisierung*, yellow buttons, white breeches.

Record Recruited in the Empire. Distinguished at Piacenza and Kolin. Suffered heavy casualties in 1759 when surprised by the Prussian Black Hussars when hearing Mass at Tanne. Further heavy losses at Torgau.

DR NO 13

Inhaber 1740 Khevenhüller, 1744 Holly, 1756 Jung-Modena.

Uniforms (i) earlier part of reign – red coat with light blue cuffs, lapels and turn-backs, red shoulder strap, white aiglets, light blue waistcoat, white buttons – two rows on coat, double row on waistcoat – light blue breeches, sword with brass furniture; (ii) 1767 – dark blue *Egalisierung*, white buttons, white breeches.

Record Recruited from Bohemia and the Empire. Ludwig Andreas Khevenhüller, the *Inhaber* from 1726 to 1744, was famous for his knowledge of the dragoon service and rose to field-marshal. Distinguished at Piacenza and Rottofreno (1746), captured many colours and standards at Maxen. Converted to *chevaulégers* in 1773, with no change of uniform.

DR NO 19

Inhaber 1740 D'Ollone, 1746 Hessen-Darmstadt.

Uniforms (i) earlier part of reign – light red coat with green cuffs, turn-backs and shoulder strap, yellow aiglets, no lapels, white waistcoat with green lower border, yellow buttons – single row on coat, single row on waistcoat – white breeches, sword with brass furniture; (ii) 1767 – dark green *Egalisierung*, yellow buttons, white breeches.

Record Recruited in the Empire. Distinguished at Kolin, Hochkirch, Torgau, and Zuckmantel (1779). Converted to *chevaulégers* 1773.

DR NO 28

Inhaber 1740 Sachsen-Gotha, 1767 Bettoni, 1773 Lobkowitz.

Uniforms (ii) earlier part of reign – red coat with blue cuffs, lapels, turn-backs and shoulder strap, yellow aiglets, blue waistcoat, yellow buttons – two rows on coat, double row on waistcoat – straw breeches, sword with brass furniture; (ii) 1767 – light blue *Egalisierung*, white buttons, white breeches.

Record Recruited in southern Germany. Very distinguished at Kolin under its commandant, Colonel Carl O'Donnell. Further distinguished at Moys and Landeshut. Temporarily converted to *chevaulégers* 1760 with no change in uniform. Permanently converted 1779.

DR NO 31

Inhaber 1740 Ligne, 1757 Daun (Benedict), 1758 Löwenstein, 1759 St Ignon, 1779 D'Arberg.

Uniforms (i) earlier part of reign – green coat with red cuffs, lapels, turn-backs, shoulder strap and aiglets, red waistcoat, yellow buttons – two rows on coat, double row on waistcoat – yellow breeches, sword with brass furniture; (ii) 1767 – red *Egalisierung*, yellow buttons, white breeches.

Record Possibly the most celebrated dragoon regiment of the army. Recruited in the Netherlands. Distinguished at Ramillies (1746). Its famous charge helped to decide the battle of Kolin, after which Maria Theresa presented the regiment with four standards. Distinguished at Hochkirch. Captured in considerable part at Torgau, but later escaped *en masse*. Converted to *chevaulégers* 1760, but reconverted 1765.

DR NO 37

Inhaber 1740 Römer, 1741 Philibert, 1753 Kollowrat, 1769 Sachsen-Gotha.
Uniforms (i) earlier part of reign – dark blue coat with poppy red cuffs, lapels, turn-backs, shoulder strap and aiglets, red waistcoat, white buttons – two rows on coat, double row on waistcoat – red breeches, sword with iron furniture; (ii) 1767 – poppy red *Egalisierung*, white buttons, white breeches.
Record Recruited in Lower Austria and Bohemia. Took part in the fatal charge of its *Inhaber* Römer at Mollwitz. Distinguished at Lobositz, Kolin, Hochkirch (where it captured the silver kettle-drums of the Jung-Platen dragoons), Landeshut and Liegnitz.

DR NO 38

Inhaber 1740 Württemberg.
Uniforms (i) earlier part of reign – red coat with black cuffs, lapels, turn-backs and aiglets, red shoulder strap, straw breeches, yellow buttons – two rows on coat, single row on waistcoat – straw breeches, sword with brass furniture; (ii) 1767 – black *Egalisierung*, white buttons, white breeches.
Record Recruited in SW Germany. Distinguished at Mollwitz, Laffeldt, Kolin, Domstadtl, Kunersdorf and at the defence of Schweidnitz (1762).

STAFF DR

Uniform Dark blue coat with red cuffs and shoulder strap, white turn-backs and aiglets, no lapels, dark blue waistcoat, yellow buttons – single row on coat, single row on waistcoat – red breeches, sword with brass furniture.
Record Set up in 1758 to see to special duties. Detachments distinguished at Maxen. Disbanded at the end of the war, but reconstituted in 1769.

Disbanded dragoon regiments

Numbered according to their order of dissolution

DR NO (i)

Inhaber 1740 Limburg-Styrum.
Uniform Red coat with green facings.
Record Distinguished at Dettingen. Disbanded 1748.

DR NO (ii)

Inhaber 1740 Preysing.
Uniform Red coat with blue cuffs.
Record Fought at Hohenfriedberg but placed in reserve at Soor. Disbanded 1750.

DR NO (iii)

Inhaber 1740 Koháry, 1758 Althann.
Uniforms (i) earlier part of reign – white coat with red cuffs, lapels, turn-backs and shoulder strap, yellow aiglets, white waistcoat, yellow buttons – two rows on coat, single row on waistcoat – white breeches, sword with brass furniture; (ii) 1767 – poppy red *Egalisierung*, white buttons, white breeches. NB. This was the only dragoon regiment to wear the white uniform in the earlier part of the reign.
Record Recruited in the Empire. Raised in 1733 at the cost of Count Andreas Koháry. Distinguished at Piacenza. Heavy losses at Liegnitz. Disbanded 1768.

CL R NO 18 (CHEVAULÉGERS REGIMENT)

Inhaber 1759 Jung Löwenstein.
Uniforms (i) 1759 – grass green coat with red cuffs, lapels, turn-backs, shoulder strap and aiglets, red waistcoat, yellow buttons – two rows on coat, double row on waistcoat – red breeches, sword with brass furniture; (ii) 1767 – grass green coat, poppy red *Egalisierung*, yellow buttons.
Record Recruited in Moravia. Formed before the campaign of 1759 from part of DR NO 31. Distinguished at Kunersdorf, Landeshut and Liegnitz.

CB R NO 5 (ERSTES CARABINIER-REGIMENT)

Inhaber 1768 Sachsen-Teschen.
Uniform White coat with dark red *Egalisierung*, yellow buttons, white breeches.
Record Founded 1768.

CB R NO 15 (ZWEITES CARABINIER-REGIMENT)

Inhaber 1768 Althann, 1770 Erzherzog Franz.
Uniform White coat with dark red *Egalisierung*, white buttons, white breeches.

Hussar regiments

Unless otherwise stated, the uniform is that of the Seven Years War. The fur of the pelisse was always black. In the later 1760s the fur *kalpak* was replaced by a felt shako. Except in the case of HR NO 2, all *kalpaks* seem to have been brown.

HR NO 2 (KAISER-HUSAREN)

Inhaber 1756 the Emperor.
Uniform Yellow *kalpak* with dark blue or purple bag. Dark blue or purple pelisse, dolman, pants and sabretache with yellow lace, yellow and blue barrel sash, black boots, sabre with brass furniture. (Black shako 1767.)
Record Raised by Emperor Francis Stephen at his own expense in Slovakia in 1756. Saw its first action at Kolin.

HR NO 11

Inhaber 1740 Csáky, 1741 Nádasti.
Uniform *Kalpak* with light green bag, Light green pelisse and dolman with yellow lace, yellow and green barrel sash, dark blue or purple pants, black boots, sabre with brass furniture. (Black shako 1767.)
Record An old-established and excellent regiment, raised in 1688. Distinguished at Pisek (1742), Simbach (1743), Soor, Görlitz (1757), Landeshut, Liegnitz, Hartmannsdorf (1761) and Nonnenbusch (1761).

HR NO 16

Inhaber 1740 Károlyi, 1759 Pálffy (Rudolph), 1758 Hadik.
Uniform *Kalpak* with red bag. Blue pelisse, dolman and pants with red lace and white buttons, red sabretache with blue double eagle, red and blue barrel sash, black boots, sabre with brass furniture. (Black shako 1767.)
Record Recruited in NW Hungary. Raised by Alexander Károlyi 1734. Distinguished at Landeshut, and at Neustadt (1761).

HR NO 17 (SIEBENBÜRGISCHES HUSAREN-REGIMENT)

Inhaber 1749 Kálnoky.
Uniform *Kalpak* with red bag. Light blue pelisse and dolman with yellow lace, yellow and blue barrel sash, red pants, red sabretache with yellow 'K' monogram, black boots, sabre with brass furniture. (Poppy red shako 1767.)
Record Raised by the Transylvanian Stände 1742. Distinguished at Nachod (1758), Kunersdorf, Lindewiese (1760).

HR NO 24

Inhaber 1742 Esterházy (Paul Anton), 1762 Lusinsky, 1773 Wurmser.
Uniform *Kalpak* with red bag. Light blue pelisse and dolman with yellow lace, yellow and blue barrel sash, red pants, red sabretache with yellow 'E' monogram, yellow boots, sabre with brass furniture. (Green (?) shako 1767.)
Record Raised in western Hungary at the cost of Prince Esterházy in 1742. Saw action at Chotusitz, Hohenfriedberg, Soor, Prague, Leuthen, Hochkirch and Torgau.

HR NO 30

Inhaber 1740 Baranyay, 1766 Nauendorf, 1775 Wurmser.
Uniform *Kalpak* with red bag. Green pelisse and dolman with red lace and yellow buttons, red and yellow barrel sash, light blue pants, green sabretache with black double eagle, black boots, sabre with brass furniture. (Black shako 1767.)
Record Raised in 1696. Distinguished in Upper Austria 1742, at Piacenza, and with the *Reichsarmee* from 1758.

HR NO 32

Inhaber 1740 Dessewffy, 1742 Festetics, 1757 Széchényi, 1767 Ujhazy, 1768 Esterházy (Emerich).
Uniform Dark blue pelisse, dolman and pants with red lace. Dark blue sabretache. (Grey shako 1767.)
Record Raised in 1702. Distinguished in Silesia 1741, Bohemia 1742 and at Maxen.

HR NO 34

Inhaber 1740 Hávor, 1744 Dessewffy, 1768 Ujházy, 1773 Graeven.
Uniform Blue pelisse and dolman with carmine red lace. Carmine red pants. (1767 parrot green pelisse and dolman, red pants, light blue shako.)
Record Raised in 1733. Distinguished at Piacenza, Hochkirch, Losdorf (1760) and Libochowitz (1778).

HR NO 35

Inhaber 1741 Beleznay, 1754 Morocz, 1759 Bethlen, 1773 Barcó.
Uniform *Kalpak* with red bag. Light blue dolman and pelisse with red lace and yellow buttons, red and blue barrel sash, light blue pants, black boots, sabre with brass furniture. (Green shako 1767.)
Record Raised in 1741. Distinguished at Neisse (1741), Nordheim (1745), Grünberg (1759) and Oppeln (1761). In 1778 it carried out a brilliant charge against superior cavalry at Trautenau.

HR NO 36 (JAZYGIER UND KUMANIER, OR THE PALATINAL-HUSAREN-REGIMENT)

Inhaber 1756 the Palatine Count Ludwig Batthyány, 1765 Török.
Uniform *Kalpak* with red bag. Light blue dolman and pelisse with white lace, red and

white barrel sash, red pants, yellow boots, sabre with iron furniture. (Grey shako 1767.)

Record Raised in 1756. Distinguished at Maxen and served generally well in the Seven Years War. Disbanded 1775.

HR NO 47 (SIEBENBÜRGISCHES SZÉKLER)

Uniform Dark blue pelisse and dolman, red pants. (Black shako, dark blue pants 1767.)

Record Raised in Transylvania in 1762 without an *Inhaber*.

Disbanded hussar regiments

Numbered according to the order of their dissolution

HR NO (i)

Inhaber 1740 Pestvármegyey, 1743 Trips.

Record Raised in 1743. Distinguished at Nordheim (1744). Disbanded 1748. No details of uniform are preserved.

HR NO (ii)

Inhaber 1740 Splenyi, 1762 Esterházy (Emerich).

Uniform *Kalpak* with red bag. Dark green pelisse and dolman with red and white lace, red and white (?) barrel sash, red pants, green sabretache with black double eagle.

Record Raised 1733. Distinguished at Prague, Maxen and Kirchhain (1762). Disbanded 1768.

HR NO (iii)

Inhaber 1740 Ghilányi, 1753 Hadik.

Uniform *Kalpak* with red bag. Dark blue pelisse and dolman with red lace, red and yellow barrel sash, red pants, black boots, red sabretache with a bear device in black, sabre with brass furniture.

Record Raised 1734, and recuited in Transylvania. Distinguished at Nachod (1758) and Kunersdorf. Disbanded 1768.

Grenz *cavalry regiments*

GZ DR NO (i) (WALACHISCHES GRENZ-DRAGONER-REGIMENT)

Uniforms (i) 1763 – casquet, dark blue coat with carmine red facings and sabretache, yellow buttons, white pants; (ii) 1767 – white coat with red *Egalisierung*, yellow buttons.

Record Raised in Transylvania 1763. Disbanded 1771.

GZ HR NO (ii) (CARLSTÄDTER GRENZ-HUSAREN-REGIMENT)

Uniforms (i) Seven Years War – *kalpak* with red bag, dark blue pelisse, dolman and pants with yellow lace, dark blue sabretache with yellow double eagle, yellow and white barrel sash, black boots, sabre with brass furniture; (ii) 1769 – black shako, grass green pelisse and dolman with yellow lace, yellow barrel sash, red pants.

Record Raised in Croatia 1746. Saw a good deal of action in the Seven Years War. Distinguished in Bohemia in 1778. Disbanded 1780.

 GZ HR R NO (iii) (WARASDINER GRENZ-HUSAREN-REGIMENT)

Uniforms (i) Seven Years War – *kalpak* with red bag; red dolman and pelisse with white lace, red and white barrel sash, red pants, sabre with iron furniture; (ii) 1769 – black shako, grass green pelisse and dolman with yellow lace, red pants.
Record Raised in Croatia 1746. Distinguished at Landeshut. Disbanded 1780.

GZ HR NO (iv) (BANAL GRENZ-HUSAREN-REGIMENT)

Uniforms (i) Seven Years War – *kalpak* with red bag; dark blue dolman and red pelisse with yellow lace, red and yellow barrel sash, dark blue pants, red sabretache with black double eagle, sword with brass furniture; (ii) 1769 – black shako, grass green pelisse and dolman with yellow lace, yellow barrel sash, red pants.
Record Raised in Croatia by the Banus Count Carl Batthyány in 1750. In the Seven Years War it saw action mainly in Saxony. Disbanded 1780.

GZ HR NO (V) (SLAVONISCHES GRENZ-HUSAREN-REGIMENTS)

Uniforms (i) Seven Years War – red (or green) pelisse and dolman with yellow lace, red pants; (ii) 1769 – black shako, parrot green pelisse and dolman with yellow lace, yellow barrel belt, red pants.
Record Raised in Slavonia 1747. Distinguished at Strehlen (1760) and Döbeln (1762).

Mounted free corps

Of the various exotic units the most famous was that of Colonel Johann Daniel Menzel, which was raised in 1743. Colonel Bertolotti took over the command after Menzel was killed in 1744, and the corps fought in Germany and Italy until it was disbanded in 1746. The uniform was characterised by the red pelisse and dolman. A short-lived 'hussar free corps Csernoevich' served on the Main in 1745.

Three corps were raised in the War of the Bavarian Succession, and seem to have consisted mainly of lancers from Galicia. These were the O'Donnell free corps and two units of *Bosniaken*.

Bibliography

(a) Principal manuscript sources in the Kriegsarchiv, *Vienna*

Feld-Acten and *Cabinets-Acten* (reports from commanders in the field).
Hofkriegsräthliche-Acten (instructions from the *Hofkriegsrath*).
Prot Exp, *Prot Reg* and *Prot in Publicis* (summaries of the *Hofkriegsrath*'s correspondence).
Kriegswissenschaftliche Mémoires (occasional memoranda on various subjects).
Muster-Listen.
Papers of the *Nostitz-Rieneck Hofcommission.* (This committee was set up to investigate military reform, in virtue of an order of 28 December 1791; General F. Nostitz assumed the chairmanship in 1792. To support its work, the committee collected a large quantity of memoranda, illustrative documents and statistical abstracts relating to the army in the earlier part of the century. Historians have so far neglected this mass of material, which is a prime source of information as to how the Theresian army was run.)

(b) Contemporary official publications

Reglement für das Ingenieurs-Corpo, Vienna, 1748
Regulament und Ordnung des gesammten Kaiserlich-Königlichen Fuss-Volcks, Vienna, 1749 (reprinted Osnabrück, 1969)
Regulament und Ordnung für gesammte Kaiserl. Königl. Cuirassier und Dragoner Regimenter, 2 pts, Vienna, 1749 (fundamentally unaltered in the *Exercier-Reglements* of 1769 and 1772)
Artillerie Exercitia und Experimenten welche zu Moldau Thein Anno 1749 . . . bewürcket word, Vienna, 1749
Instruction für die Kriegs-Commissariatische Beamte, Vienna, 1749
Feld Dienst Regulament, Vienna, 1749
Regulament und Ordnung, für gesammte Kaiserl. Königl. Husaren-Regimenter, Vienna, 1751
Reglement für das Kaiserlich Königliche gesammte Feld-Artilleriecorps, Vienna, 1757
Kurze Beschreibung der Heilungsart der Krankheiten welche am öftesten in dem Feldlager beobachtet werden, Vienna, 1758
Exercitium fur die sämmentliche K.K. Infanterie, Vienna, 1769
Reglement für die sämmentliche K.K. Infanterie, Generals-Reglement, Vienna, 1769

(c) Other sources

ANON. 'Aus dem letzten Lebensjahre der grossen Kaiserin: Das Kloster als Correctionsmittel für Officiere', in *Mittheilungen des K.K. Kriegs-Archivs*, Vienna, 1881
ANON. *Beiträge zur Geschichte des österreichischen Heerwesens*, vol I, Vienna, 1872
ANON. 'Charakterzüge des Kaiserin Maria Theresia', in *Mittheilungen*, Vienna, 1877
ANON. *Denckwürdiges Leben und Thaten des berühmten Herrn Johann Daniels von Menzel*, Frankfurt and Leipzig, 1743
ANON. 'Die Ernährung und Leistungsfähigkeit der k.k. Truppen im Felde, von der Zeit des 30 jährigen Krieges bis zur Gegenwart', in *Mittheilungen*, 1885
ANON. 'Feldmarschall Prinz Joseph zu Sachsen-Hildburghausen', in *Mittheilungen*, 1881
ANON. 'Der hohe Adel im kaiserlichen Heere einst und jetzt', in *Mittheilungen*, 1884
ANON. *Neues und sher Curiöses Gespräch zwischen einen Franzosischen Deserteur und einigen Oester-*

reichischen Husaren, Frankfurt and Leipzig, 1742

ANON. *Oesterreichischer Kriegs-Almanach*, 2 vols, Vienna, 1779

ANON. 'Ein Schreiben van Swietens in Angelegenheit des Militär-Sanitätswesens', in *Mittheilungen*, 1885

ANON. *Zuverlässige Nachrichten von dem traurigen Schicksale der Stadt und Universität* Halle, Amsterdam, 1759 (the experiences of a Prussian city under Austrian and Imperial German occupation)

ALEXICH, K. 'Die freiwilligen Aufgebote aus den Ländern der ungarischen Krone im ersten schlesischen Krieg', in *Mittheilungen*, 1889

ALLMAYER-BECK, J. C. 'Wandlungen im Heerwesen zur Zeit Maria Theresias', in *Maria Theresia. Beiträge zur Geschichte des Heerwesens ihrer Zeit*, Graz, 1967 (this important volume is one of the series *Schriften des Heeresgeschichtlichen Museums in Wien*)

ARCHENHOLTZ, J. W. *Geschichte des Siebenjährigen Kriegs in Deutschland* (1790), 5th ed, 2 pts, Berlin, 1840

ARNETH, A. *Geschichte Maria Theresias*, 10 vols, Vienna, 1863–79 (the classic study of the reign)

BANGERT, D. E. *Die russisch-österreichische militärische Zusammenarbeit im Siebenjährigen Kriege in den Jahren 1758–1759*, Boppard, 1971

BENEDIKT, H. *Kaiseradler über dem Apennin*, Vienna, 1964

——. *Als Belgien Österreichisch war*, Vienna, 1965

BERENHORST, G. H. *Betrachtungen über die Kriegskunst*, 3 pts, Leipzig, 1798–99 (for some highly critical comments concerning the Austrian army)

BERTLING, M. *Die Kroaten und Panduren in der Mitte des xvii Jahrhunderts und ihre Verwendung in den Friderizianischen Kriegen*, Berlin, 1912

BLECKWENN, H. 'Die Regimenter der Kaiserin', in *Maria Theresia. Beiträge* (by the foremost expert on eighteenth-century uniforms)

——. 'Uniformen und Ausrüstung der österreichischen Grenztruppen 1740–1769', in *Die K.K. Militärgrenze. Beiträge zur ihrer Geschichte*, Vienna, 1973 (another important contribution to the series *Schriften des Heeresgeschichtlichen Museums in Wien*)

BODART, G. *Les Troupes Belges au Service de l'Austriche 1714–1801*, undated thesis in the *Kriegsarchiv*

BOLTEK, J. 'Das k.k. Cavallerie-Geschütz', in *Mittheilungen*, 1885

BRINNER, W. *Geschichte des k.k. Pionnier-Regiments*, 2 vols, Vienna, 1878–81

BUCHBERGER, K. 'Briefe Loudon's. Beiträge zur Charakteristik Loudon's und der Geschichte des Siebenjährigen Krieges', in *Archiv für österreichische Geschichte*, XLVIII, Vienna, 1872

BURGOYNE, J. 'Observations on the Present Military State of Prussia, Austria and France' (1767), in *Political and Military Episodes . . . from the Life and Correspondence of the Right Hon. John Burgoyne*, ed Fonblanque, E.B., London, 1876

BÜTTNER, G. A. *Denkwürdigkeiten aus dem Leben des Königl. Preuss. Generals von der Infanterie Freiherrn de la Motte Fouqué*, 2 pts, Berlin, 1788 (for Fouqué's memorandum on the Austrian conduct of war, 2 January 1759)

COGNAZZO, J. *Geständnisse eines Oestrichen Veterans*, 4 pts, Breslau, 1788–91

——. *Freymüthige Beytrag zur Geschichte des österreichischen Militairdienstes*, Frankfurt and Leipzig, 1789. (The identity of the author of these works has been debated for almost two centuries. 'Cognazzo' was evidently an Austrian officer from the Adriatic provinces who betook himself to Prussia under something of a cloud. I myself harbour no doubt that most of his observations on the Theresian army are well-considered and accurate.)

CORNET, H. (ed). *Siége de Prague (1742). Journal authentique d'un Lieutenant-Ingénieur dans l'Armée Autrichienne devant Prague*, Vienna, 1867

CRANKSHAW, E. *Maria Theresa*, London, 1969

CRISTE, O. *Kriege unter Kaiser Josef II*, Vienna, 1904

DIKREITER, H. G. (ed). *Altösterreichische Soldatengeschichten aus der Zeit Maria Theresias*, Breslau, 1925 (the all-too brief testimony of a haberdasher's apprentice who was forcibly recruited into the army in 1744)

DIRRHEIMER, G., and FRITZ, F. 'Einhörner und Schuwalowsche Haubitzen', in *Maria Theresia. Beiträge*

DOLLECZEK, A. *Geschichte der österreichischen Artillerie*, Vienna, 1887 (nicely written and very informative)
——. *Monographie der k.u.k. österr.-ung blanken und Handfeuer-Waffen*, Vienna, 1896
DUCHESNE, A. 'Le Souvenir que les Belges ont conservé de l'Impératrice Marie Thérèse', in *Maria Theresia. Beiträge*
DUFFY, C. J. *The Wild Goose and the Eagle. A Life of Marshal von Browne 1705–1757*, London, 1964. (For details concerning the campaigns in Silesia 1740–1, Bohemia 1741–2, Bavaria 1743 and 1745, west Germany 1743 and 1745, Italy 1744 and 1746–8, and Bohemia 1756–7. The augmented translation *Feldmarschall Browne*, Vienna and Munich, 1966, contains a list of Irish officers in the Imperial service).
——. *The Army of Frederick the Great*, Newton Abbot, 1974 (the companion volume of the present work)
DUNCKER, K. 'Die Invasion Schlesiens durch die könig. preussischen Truppen im Monate December 1740', in *Mittheilungen*, 1885
——. 'Militärische und politische Actenstücke zur Geschichte des ersten Schlesischen Krieges 1740' in *Mittheilungen*, 1887, 1888, 1891, 1892
DUTENS, M. L. *Intinéraire des Routes les plus frequentés*, London, 1793
ESTERHÁZY DE GALLANTHA, J. *Regulament und unumänderlich-gebräuchliche Observations-Puncten*, Gavi, 1747 (probably the last and most significant of the private regimental regulations)
GATTI, F. *Geschichte der k.k. Ingenieur- und k.k. Genieakademie 1717–1869*, vol I, Vienna, 1901
LE COMTE DE GISORS 1732–1758, ed. C. Rousset, Paris, 1868. (Gisors, a young French officer, visited the camp of Kolin in 1754.)
GROSSER GENERALSTAB (Prussian). *Die Kriege Friedrichs des Grossen*, 20 vols, Berlin, 1890–1913
GUGLIA, E. *Maria Theresia*, 2 vols, Munich, 1917
GUIBERT, G. A. *Journal d'un Voyage en Allemagne fait en 1773*, 2 vols, Paris, 1803 (especially for conditions on the military borders)
HAUSMANN, F. 'Die Feldzeichen der Truppen Maria Theresias', in *Maria Theresia. Beiträge*
HENNEBERT, LT-COL. *Gribeauval*, Paris, 1896 (for Gribeauval's detailed report on the Austrian artillery, 3 March 1762)
HENNING, F. *Und sitzet er zur linken Hand: Franz Stephan von Lothringen*, Vienna, 1961
HILDEBRANDT, C. *Anekdoten und Charakterzüge aus dem Leben Friedrichs des Grossen*, 6 vols, Halberstadt, 1829–55
HIRTENFELD, J. *Der Militär-Maria-Theresien-Orden und seine Mitglieder*, 4 vols, Vienna, 1857 (especially useful for biographical details)
——. *Vor Hundert Jahren! Erinnerung an Olmütz und seine ruhmvollen Vertheidiger*, Vienna, 1858
HOEN, M. *Die Schlacht bei Kolin am 18. Juni 1757*, Vienna, 1911
HOEN, R., and BREMEN. *Preussen-Deutschlands Kriege*, 2 vols, Berlin, 1907–12
JAHNS, M. *Geschichte der Kriegswissenschaften vornehmlich in Deutschland*, vol III, Munich and Leipzig, 1891
JIHN, F. 'Der Feldzug 1760 in Sachsen und Schlesien mit besonderer Berücksichtigung der Schlacht von Torgau', in *Mittheilungen*, 1882
——. 'Der Feldzug 1761 in Schlesien und Sachsen', in *Mittheilungen*, 1884
KAINDL, F. 'Die K.K. Militärgrenze – zur Einführung in ihrer Geschichte', in *Die K.K. Militärgrenze. Beiträge*
KHEVENHÜLLER-METSCH, J. J. *Aus der Zeit Maria Theresias. Tagebuch des Fürsten Johann Josef Khevenhüller-Metsch, Kaiserlichen Obersthofeisters 1742–1776*, 8 vols, Vienna, 1907–72. (The diary of the court master of ceremonies. This fund of information and gossip is all the more valuable since K-M described in disapproving detail many of the innovations in state affairs. The diary is supported by documents and the minutes of conferences. The publication of this work is a triumph of persistent scholarship over the assorted horrors of Central Europe in the twentieth century.)
KISZLING, R. *Die Kroaten*, Graz, 1956
KOPETZKY, F. *Josef und Franz von Sonnenfels*, Vienna, 1882
KORNAUTH, F. *Das Heer Maria Theresias. Faksimile-Ausgabe der Albertina-Handschrift 'Dessins des Uniformes des Troupes I.I. et R.R. de l'année 1762'*, Vienna, 1973. (A beautiful reproduction of a contemporary series of plates of uniforms. The introduction and commentary are also useful.)

KOTASEK, E. *Feldmarschall Graf Lacy. Ein Leben für Österreichs Herr*, Horn, 1956 (a work of the first importance for the history of the later Theresian army)
KRAJASOVICH, P. 'Die Militärgrenze in Kroatien', in *Die K.K. Militärgrenze. Beiträge*
KRETSCHMAYR, H. *Maria Theresia*, Leipzig, 1938
K.U.K. KRIEGS-ARCHIV. *Oesterreichischer Erbfolge-Krieg 1740–48*, 9 vols, Vienna, 1896–1914 (the uncompleted official history of the War of the Austrian Succession)
KRONES, F. *Ungarn unter Maria Theresia und Josef II*, Graz, 1871
KUNISCH, J. 'Der kleine Krieg', in *Frankfurter Historische Abhandlungen*, IV, Wiesbaden, 1973. Esp. on 'partisan' warfare as a path to promotion. NB at the time of writing, Prof. Kunisch is engaged on detailed studies of the career of Loudon.
KÜNTZEL, G. *Fürst Kaunitz-Rittberg als Staatsmann*, Frankfurt, 1923
LEHMANN, M. *Friederich der Grosse und der Ursprung des Siebenjährigen Krieges*, Leipzig, 1894 (on the Austrian mobilisation and the question of 'war blame')
LEHNDORFF, E. *Dreissig Jahre am Hofe Friedrichs des Grossen*, Gotha, 1907
LEITNER V. LEITNERTREU, T. G. *Ausführliche Geschichte der Wiener-Neustädter Militär-Akademie*, Hermannstadt, 1852
LEMCKE, J. F. 'Kriegs und Friedenbilder', in *Preussische Jahrbücher*, CXXXVIII, Berlin, 1909 (for the experiences of a Prussian subaltern in Austrian captivity)
LIGNE, C. J. *Mélanges militaires, littéraires et sentimentaires*, vols, I, II, IX, X, XIV–XXII, XXV, Dresden, 1795–1802
——. *Fragments de l'Histoire de ma Vie*, ed F. Leuridant, 2 vols, Paris, 1928. (Prince Charles Joseph de Ligne is our most valuable single source of information on the atmosphere of the Theresian army.)
LLOYD, GENERAL. 'Reflections on the General Principles of War', in *Annual Register*, London, 1766. (Lloyd served with the Austrian army in the later campaigns of the Seven Years War, but his 'Reflections', like his historical works, are disappointingly dry and uninformative.)
LOEHR, A. O. 'Die Finanzierung des siebenjährigen Krieges', in *Numismatische Zeitschrift*, LVIII, Vienna, 1925
MARCZALI, H. *Hungary in the Eighteenth Century*, Cambridge, 1910
MEYNERT, H. *Geschichte der k.k. österreichischen Armee*, 4 vols, Vienna, 1854
MIRABEAU, H. G. *Système Militaire de la Prusse*, London, 1788
MOORE, J. *A View of Society and Manners in France, Switzerland and Germany*, 2 vols, London, 1780
MÜLLER, W. *Gerhard van Swieten*, Vienna, 1883
NITSCHE, G. *Österreichisches Soldatenthum im Rahmen Deutscher Geschichte*, Berlin and Leipzig, 1937
NOSINICH, J., and WIENER, COLONEL. *Kaiser Joseph II als Staatsmann und Feldherr*, Vienna, 1885
OTRUBA, G. *Die Wirthschaftspolitik Maria Theresias*, Vienna, 1963
PATERA, H. V. *Unter Österreichs Fahnen*, Vienna and Cologne, 1960
PEBALL, K. 'Das Generalsreglement der Kaiserlich-Königlichen österreichischen Armee vom 1. September 1769. Versuch einer Quellenanalyse', in *Maria Theresia. Beiträge*
PETERS, CAPTAIN. 'Die österreichischen Befestigungen an der oberen Elbe', in *Mittheilungen*, 1902
PICK, R. *The Empress Maria Theresa*, New York, 1966, and London, 1968
PODEWILS, O. C. *Friedrich der Grosse und Maria Theresia. Diplomatische Berichte von Otto Christoph Graf von Podewils*, Berlin, 1937
PRERADOVICH, N. *Des Kaisers Grenzer. 300 Jahre Türkenabwehr*, Vienna, 1970
PRITTWITZ, C. W. *Unter der Fahne des Herzogs von Bevern. Jugenderinnerungen*, Berlin, 1935 (for the experiences of a young Prussian officer after his capture at Kolin)
REGELE, O. *Die österreichische Hofkriegsrat 1556–1848*, Vienna, 1949
——. *Generalstabschefs aus vier Jahrhunderten*, Vienna, 1966
RICHTER, A. F. *Historische Bemerkungen über den k.k. österreichischen Militärdienst*, Pressburg, 1845. (An interesting work. Despite the late date of publication, it is clearly drawn from direct experience of the Theresian army.)
RICHTER, H. M. *Oesterreichische Volksschriften und Volkslieder im siebenjährigen Kriege*, Vienna,

1869 (especially good on 'public opinion')
RIESEBECK, K. *Briefe eines reisenden Franzosen*, 2 vols, no place of publication, 1784
ROTHENBERG, G. E. *The Military Border in Croatia 1740–1881*, Chicago, 1966 (probably the best coverage of the subject in any language)
ST PAUL, H. *A Journal of the First Two Campaigns of the Seven Years War*, ed G. G. Butler, Cambridge, 1914 (the diary of an English 'volunteer')
SCHWERIN, D. *Feldmarschall Schwerin*, Berlin, 1928
SCHWICKER, J. H. *Geschichte der österreichischen Militärgrenze*, Vienna, 1883
SEEGER, K. *Marschallstab und Kesselpauke. Tradition und Brauchtum in der deutschen und österreichisch-ungarischen Armee*, Stuttgart, 1939
SODERSTERN, E. *Der Feldzug in Mähren oder die Belagerung und der Entsatz von Olmütz*, Frankfurt 1858
SONNENFELS, J. *Gesammte Schriften*, 10 vols, Vienna, 1783–7
SRBIK, H. R. *Deutsche Einheit*, vol I, Munich, 1935
STEPHANIE, G. *Stephanie des jüngern sämmtliche Lustspiele*, 6 vols, Vienna 1771–81 (with *Die Werber* (1763), *Die abgedankten Officiers* (1770) and *Die Kriegsgefangenen* (1771)
STORCK, A. F. *Medicinisch-praktischer Unterricht für die Feld-und Landwundärzte der österreichischen Staaten*, 2 pts, Vienna, 1776. (Anton Störck was van Swieten's pupil and successor.)
TEUBER, O. *Ehrentage Osterreichs*, Vienna, 1892
——. *Die Österreichische Armee von 1700 bis 1867*, 2 vols, Vienna 1895, reprinted Graz, 1971; with illustrations by R. Ottenfeld. (Luxurious and detailed, though somewhat patchy in its coverage. The fine illustrations have not entirely withstood the criticisms of modern experts. Hans Bleckwenn describes it as 'the coffee-table book of the Austrian army'.)
——. *Historische Legionen Habsburg*, Vienna, 1896
THADDEN, F. L. *Feldmarschall Daun*, Vienna, 1967
THÜRHEIM, A. *Feldmarschall Otto Ferdinand Graf von Abensberg und Traun 1677–1748*, Vienna, 1877 (contains very useful lists of Austrian generals and regiments from 1701 to 1748)
——. *Von den Sevennen bis zur Newa*, Vienna, 1879 (for the visit to Vienna of the French officer Count Valentin Esterházy)
VANIČEK, F. *Specialgeschichte der Militärgrenze*, 4 vols, Vienna, 1875
WADDINGTON, R. *La Guerre de Sept Ans. Histoire Diplomatique et Militaire*, 5 vols, Paris, 1899–1914 (especially for the reports of French officers serving with the Austrian army)
WALTER, F. *Die Geschichte der österreichischen Zentralverwaltung in der Zeit Maria Theresias (1740–1780)*, Vienna, 1938
——. *Männer um Maria Theresia*, Vienna, 1951
WANGERMANN, E. *The Austrian Achievement 1700–1800*, London, 1973
WARNERY, K. E. *Campagnes de Frédéric II, Roi de Prusse*, Amsterdam, 1788 (this Prussian hussar general makes some interesting comments on the Austrian cavalry.)
WRAXALL, N. *Memoirs of the Courts of Berlin, Dresden etc*, 2nd ed, 2 vols, London, 1799–1800
WREDE, A. *Die Geschichte der k.u.k. Wehrmacht*, 5 vols, Vienna, 1898–1905 (an indispensable source book, which contains especially useful lists of regiments)
ZIMMERMANN, J. 'Militärverwaltung und Heeresaufbringung in Österreich bis 1806', in *Handbuch der deutschen Militärgeschichte*, pt 3, Freiburg, 1965

Index

Albert of Saxony, Field-Marshal, 102, 205
Alfson, Nikolaus, Colonel, 106, 188
Althann, Michael Anton, General, 102
Arad, 122
Arenberg, Carl, Field-Marshal, 27, 45, 161, 181, 191, 193
army, Austrian:
artillery, 6, 105–17; evolution, 105–7; equipment and ammunition, 112–13; gunners, 108–9; horse artillery, 110–11; ordnance, 109–12; organisation, 107–9; proficiency, 192–3; regulations, 106, 166; transport, 113–15
battle formations and tactics, 141–3
camps, 139–40
cavalry, 91–103, 166; arms, equipment and uniforms, 93–5; organisation, 91–2; remounts, 103–4; tactics, 99–103, 142–3, 147; *Chevaulégers*, 91, 92, 95, 103; cuirassiers, 91–5; list of cuirassier regiments, 235–9; dragoons, 91–2, 95, 103; list of dragoon regiments, 239–42; hussars, 91, 95–9, 102, 103, 166; list of hussar regiments, 242–5
chaplains, 133–4
Croats, 14, 82–9; evolution, 82, 84–8; organisation, 88–90; tactics, 82, 85–6, 90; uniforms, 84–9
engineers, 118–20
fortresses, 122
generals, 33–4
Hofkriegsrath, 13, 19, 21–3, 35, 47, 56, 58, 86, 126, 206
infantry, 63–81; arms, equipment and uniforms, 17, 69–76; organisation, 63; tactics, 76–81, 146, 166–7; regulations, 166; foreign infantry, 68–9; free corps, 67–8; garrison regiments, 67; grenadiers 63–4; Hungarian infantry, 64–6, 190; *Jäger*, 67, 74; Netherlands infantry, 66; Tyrol infantry, 66–7; list of infantry regiments, 221–32
marches, 140–1
medical services, 131–3
men, 47–62; children, 57–8; conditions of life, 53–6; discipline and morale, 11, 12, 13, 16–17, 18, 56–7, 61–2, 145–7; invalids, 58–9; recruits, 9–14, 47–53
music, 134
NCOs, 59–60
officers, 29–46; careers and promotion, 28–33; 34; conditions of life, 38–9; 41–3; education (esp. Wiener Neustadt Academy), 24, 29–30, 35, 166, 214; morale and proficiency, 43–6; orphans, 35–6; pensions, 35; prisoners, 39–40; ranks, 30–3, 34; recruitment and origins, 24–8; uniforms and equipment, 36–7
orders and decorations (esp. Military Order of Maria Theresa), 11, 24, 25, 44, 45, 106, 120, 181
pioneers, 120–1
pontoniers, 121
regiments (if cited in text): Arenberg LR 21, 58; Baden-Durlach LR 27, 187; Botta IR 12, 177; Brettlach CR 29, 39, 184; Erherzog Carl IR 2, 80; Clerici IR 44, 66; Jung-Colloredo IR 40, 80, 172; Hessen-Darmstadt IR 35, 58; Deutschmeister IR 4, 177; Erherzog Ferdinand IR 2, 65; Fürstenberg IR 41, 48; Grünne LR 26, 160; Gyulai, IR 51, 61; Haller IR 31, 66, 166, 180; Kaiser IR 1, 199; Kollowrath IR 17, 76, 160; Kreutzer Warasdiner GZ IR 64, 84; Lacy IR 22, 72; *Leibgarde* (German), 68; *Leibgarde* (Hungarian), 68; Ligne (Walloon Dragoons) DR 31, 12, 180; Löwenstein DR 31, 92; Los Rios IR 9, 51; Marschall IR 18, 50, 51, 160; Mainz (hired), 69; Mercy IR 56, 68; Modena CR iii), 93; Pallavicini IR 15, 68; Platz, IR 43, 182; St Georger Warasdiner GZ IR 65, 84; Thüngen IR 57, 160; *Trabanten-Garde*, 68; Trautmannsdorf CR 21, 184; *Panduren Corps von der Trenck* IR 53, 68; Tuscan (hired), 69; Tuscan Swiss Guard, 68; *Tyroler Land-und-Feld Regiment* (Macquire) IR 46, 50, 66–7; Waldeck IR 35, 65; Wallis IR 11, 187; Wurmbrand IR 50, 65; Blau-Würzburg (hired), 69; Roth-Würzburg (hired), 69
regimental system, 32–3, 60–1, 68
sappers, 120
size of army, 145, 170
staff system, 135–8, 140, 143, 183, 188
strategy, 143–4, 213
supply system, 125–31; commissariat, 21, 125–7; bread, 128–9; contractors,

127–8; fodder, 129–30; transport, 130–1
army, Prussian, 17, 146
army, Russian, 165, 195
army, Swedish, 165
Arond, Lieutenant, 58
Auersperg, Wilhelmine, Princess, 21, 42
Auloch, F., Colonel, 76
d'Ayasasa, Joseph, Lt-Gen, 23
Ayrenhoff, Colonel, 45

Bánát of Temesvár, 8
Baranyay, Johann, Lt-Gen, 97
Bartenstein, Johann Christoph, 19
Batthyány, Carl, Field-Marshal, 84, 156
Bechard, Johann, Major, 120
Beck, Philipp, Lt-Gen, 23, 34, 39, 84, 86, 187, 193
Beecke, Ignaz, Major, 45
Berenklau, Johann Georg, Lt-Gen, 97
Berlichingen, Johann, General, 149, 159
Berlin, raid on (1757), 183; raid on (1760), 199
Bohemia, 8, 10–11
Bohn, Paul Ferdinand, Colonel, 118–19
Botta d'Adorno, Anton Otto, Maj-Gen, 26
Brady, Dr, 131–2
Bragança, Dom João, 28
Breslau, battle (1757), 38, 141, 183–4, 192, siege (1757), 26; Preliminaries of (1742), 154
Brettlach, Carl Ludwig, General, 26
Brieg, 147
Browne, Maximilian Ulysses, Field-Marshal, 45, 62, 147, 157–8, 171–5, 178
Brünn, 122
Buccow, Adolph Nikolaus, Lt-Gen, 26, 193
Bunzelwitz, camp (1761), 202
Burkersdorf, action (1762), 203

Caldwell, Tom, Colonel, 204
Camposanto, battle (1743), 157
Caraffa, Johann Carl, Field-Marshal, 145
Caramelli, Colonel, 26
Charles VI, Emperor, 9, 14, 34, 46, 58
Charles VII, Emperor (Elector Charles Albert of Bavaria), 11, 150, 151, 156
Charles, Archduke, 206, 214
Charles of Lorraine, Prince, character: 152, 206, 214; 44, 118, 122, 138, 143, 154, 155, 159, 160, 161, 166, 173, 181, 183–7
Chotek, Rudolph, 19
Chotusitz, battle (1742), 72, 101, 105, 109, 141, 154
Clerici, Giorgio, Lt-Gen, 26
Clerfayt, Francois-Sébastien, Lt-Gen, 27
Colloredo, Carl, Field-Marshal, 19
Colloredo, Joseph, Field-Marshal, 107
Cordua, Caspar, Field-Marshal, 166
Crespi, Giuseppe, 95
Creutz, Peter, General, 52

Damnitz, Wolfgang, General, 26
Daun, Leopold Joseph Maria, Field-Marshal, character: 154, 189; 16, 19, 21, 23, 38, 42, 43, 44, 45, 46, 50, 62, 110, 119–20, 121, 135, 137, 138, 143–4, 176, 177, 180–1, 187, 188, 190, 192, 193, 194, 197, 199, 200, 202, 203–5, 106, 214
Daun, Wirich, Field-Marshal, 145
Dettingen, battle (1743), 155
Domstadtl, action (1758), 64, 188, 193
Dresden, siege (1760); 197–8; 190, 195–6

Esseg, 122
Esterházy, Emerich, Maj-Gen, 199
Esterházy, Joseph, Maj-Gen, 25, 36, 62, 74, 76
Eugene of Savoy, Prince, 8, 138, 145, 184

Felbiger, Ignaz, Bishop, 57
Fermor, Wilhelm, General, 97
Fesztetics, Joseph, General, 97
Feuerstein, Andreas, 106
Feuerstein, Anton, Maj-Gen, 106, 109–10, 116
Finck, Friedrich, Lt-Gen, 40, 195–6
finances, 11, 123–5
Fontenoy, battle, (1745), 156
Fouqué, Heinrich, General, 197
Francis Stephen of Lorraine, Emperor, character: 20–1; 14–15, 44, 46, 124, 126, 138, 143, 155, 156, 171, 206
Frederick II (the Great), King of Prussia, 6, 15, 16, 39, 40, 140, 141, 144, 146, 172, 167, 177, 182, 187, 189, 209, 211
Freiberg, action (1762), 203
Fuchs, Charlotte, Countess, 21, 42

Gabel, action (1757), 181–2
Galicia, occupation (1772), 67, 131, 209–10
Genoa, 158
Ghilányi, Johann, Lt-Gen, 97
Giannini, Ernst, Lt-Gen, 118
Glatz, storm (1760), 44, 120, 198
Gradisca, 122
Grechtler, combine, 127–8
Gribeauval, Jean-Baptiste, Lt-Gen, 116, 120, 204
Gross-Jägersdorf, battle (1757), 184
Guasco, Peter Franz, General, 26, 135, 203, 205

Hadik, Andreas, Field-Marshal, 23, 42, 97, 102, 141, 171, 183, 193, 203, 210
Harrach, Johann Joseph, Field-Marshal, 19, 21, 22, 24, 166
Harsch, Ferdinand Philipp, General, 45, 118, 122, 158, 192, 193
Hasewander, J., Captain, 113
Haugwitz, Friedrich Wilhelm, 29, 164, 123, 124
Henry, Prince of Prussia, 39, 141, 195, 199, 203, 211, 212
(Sachsen-) Hildburghausen, Joseph Friedrich, Field-Marshal, 19, 46, 82–4, 184
Hochkirch, battle (1758), 6, 28, 45, 68, 86,

92, 102, 141, 190–2
Hohenfriedberg, battle (1745), 82, 109, 159–60
Hubertusburg, peace (1763), 205
Hungary, 8, 11–12, 13–14, 150

industry, 125
Irish officers, 6, 19, 23, 25, 27–8, 34, 41, 45, 46, 48, 52, 59, 67, 76, 77, 102, 121, 122, 124, 128, 131–2, 135–6, 138, 147, 157–8, 170–5, 178–9, 181, 184, 188, 189, 191, 192, 193, 195–6, 197, 198, 199–202, 204–6

Jahnus, Franz, Maj-Gen, 26, 86
Joseph II, Emperor, character: 206; 15, 28, 39, 44, 52, 92, 106, 110, 122, 133, 208–13
Josephstadt (Pless), 122
zum Jungen, Johann, Field-Marshal, 26

Kálnocky, Thomas, Colonel, 61
Karlsbad, 41
Kaunitz, Wenzel, Chancellor, character and achievement: 19–20, 164; 15, 52, 84, 85, 124, 132, 165, 166, 177, 182, 193, 202, 208, 210, 213–14
Keith, Jacob, Field-Marshal, 191–2
Kesselsdorf, battle (1745), 162
Khevenhüller, Ludwig Andreas, Field-Marshal, 17, 19, 21, 25, 46, 56, 62, 79, 150, 152, 154
Khevenhüller-Metsch, Johann Franz, Captain, 39
Kinsky, Franz Ulrich, General, 106, 107, 115
Kinsky, Franz Joseph, General, 30
Kinsky, Philip, 19, 51
Klein-Schnellendorf, treaty (1741), 149
Koch, Ignaz, cabinet secretary, 22
Kolin, battle (1757), 7, 12, 79, 80, 86, 91, 142, 177, 180–1
Königgrätz, 122
Königsegg, Christian, General, 173
Königsegg, Lothar, Field-Marshal, 43
Kunersdorf, battle (1759), 26, 91, 139, 165, 194–5

Lacy, Franz Moritz, Field-Marshal, character: 193, 196–7, 206–8; military reforms, 128, 131, 135, 188, 206, 208–9; 19, 23, 34, 41, 46, 48, 52, 59, 67, 77, 121, 122, 124, 139, 141, 144, 172, 179, 189, 190, 191, 192, 195–6, 198, 199–202, 205–6
Laffeldt, battle (1747), 157
Landeshut, battle (1760), 197
Leuthen, battle (1757), 39, 69, 126, 141, 142, 185–7
Liechtenstein, Joseph Wenzel, Field-Marshal, artillery reforms: 24, 105–6, 108, 109–10, 111–12, 113, 117, 154, 166, 167–8; 19, 158, 166
Liegnitz, battle (1760), 80, 141, 198
Ligne, Charles Joseph, 10, 17, 27, 33, 38, 41, 43, 44–5, 54, 63, 79, 80, 100, 138, 142, 170, 182, 214
Lobositz, battle (1756), 45, 80, 100, 142, 171–3
Lombardy, 9, 12, 26
Loudon, Gideon Ernst, Field-Marshal, character: 193, 208; 13, 16, 18, 34, 46, 62, 86, 188, 189, 191, 194, 195, 197, 198, 202–3, 211, 212
Löwenstein, Christian Philipp, General, 102, 191
Lucchese d'Averna, Joseph, General, 26, 186
(Aspremont-) Lynden, Ferdinand Carl, Field-Marshal, 102

MacBrady, James Bernard, Captain, 6, 204–5
Mack, Carl, General, 103
Macquire, Johann Sigismund, Lt-Gen, 179, 181, 184, 193, 195
Maria Theresa, Empress-Queen, character and achievement: 6, 9, 14–16, 18–20, 151, 214–15; Maria Theresa and the Army, 18–21; 22, 29, 31, 34, 38, 43, 46, 52, 56, 57, 58, 70, 71–2, 76, 84, 101, 105, 145–6, 167, 170; Maria Theresa in the War of the Austrian Succession, 145–6, 150–2, 154–5, 157, 162; Maria Theresa between the wars, 164, 166–7; Maria Theresa in the Seven Years War, 170, 171, 173, 180–1, 187, 195, 197, 202, 203; Maria Theresa after the Seven Years War, 206, 208–14
Marschall, Ernst Dietrich, General, 26, 183, 188
Maxen, capitulation (1759), 39–40, 86, 91, 110, 192, 195–6
Menzel, Johann Daniel, Major, 68
Mollwitz, battle (1741), 101, 109, 147–9
Moltke, Philipp, Field-Marshal, 50, 60
Montazet, Antoine, General, 28, 135
Moravia, 8, 10–11, 16–17
Moys, action (1757), 79, 86, 182

Nádasti, Franz Leopold, General, 25–6, 44, 62, 97, 161, 180, 183, 186, 187
Neipperg, Reinhard Wilhelm, Field-Marshal, 19, 21, 22–3, 76, 84, 145, 147, 149, 152
Netherlands, 12, 27, 156–7
Nugent, James, 41

O'Donnell, Carl, General, 102, 138, 178, 193, 200, 201
Olmütz, siege (1758), 122, 187–8
Österreicher, Lazar, 127
Otto, Michael, Colonel, 68

Pabliczek, Joseph, Captain, 204
Pálffy, Johann, Field-Marshal, 150
Pallavicini, Gian-Luca, Lt-Gen, 26
Panovsky, Andreas, General, 14
Parhamer, Ignaz, Father, 134
Penzeneter, Anton, 125
Petau, 35–6
Peterwardein, 122

Piacenza, battle (1746), 142, 158
Piccolomini, Octavio, Field-Marshal, 45, 171
Pirna, camp (1756), 171
Prague, siege (1741), 150; siege (1742), 118, 154–5; siege (1744), 158; battle (1757), 36, 57, 64, 79, 85, 102, 138, 174–5; siege (1757), 120, 181

Querlonde, Louis, General, 122

Radetzky, Joseph, Field-Marshal, 214
Reichenbach, action (1762), 14, 204
Reichenberg, action (1757), 100, 173
de la Reintrie, Lt-Gen, 104
Ried, Johann Heinrich, General, 86, 200
Rocoux, battle (1746), 157
Römer, Carl, Lt-Gen, 147
Rossbach, battle (1757), 39, 184
Roth, Wilhelm, Lt-Gen, 154
Rouvroy, Theodor, Lt-Gen, 110, 114

Sachsen-Hildburghausen, *see* Hildburghausen
Salburg, Franz Ludwig, 25, 126, 166
Schilling, Heinrich, Major-General, 58
Schmettau, Samuel, General, 32, 167
Schulenburg-Oyenhausen, Ludwig, General, 26
Schweidnitz, first siege (1757), 183; second siege (1757), 187; storm (1761), 86, 202; siege (1762), 6, 26, 120
Schwerin, Kurt Christoph, Field-Marshal, 39, 100, 167–8, 173
Seckendorff, Friedrich Heinrich, Field-Marshal, 45, 145
Serbelloni, Johann Baptist, Field-Marshal, 14, 26, 44–6, 190, 193, 203
Seydlitz, Friedrich Wilhelm, General, 101, 180
Silesia, 8, 146, 149, 162
Sincère, Claudius, Lt-Gen, 26, 191, 200
Siskovics, Joseph, General, 14, 34, 86, 188, 212
Slavonia, 8, 82
Sonnenfels, Joseph, 17, 55, 62
Soor, battle (1745), 141, 161–2
Spada, N, Maj-Gen, 162
Sprecher v. Bernegg, Salomon, Lt-Gen, 26, 67
Starhemberg, Guido, Field-Marshal, 157
Starhemberg, Winulph, Lt-Gen, 180
Stephanie, Gottlob, 48
Van Swieten, Gerhard, 131–3

Theresianum academy, 24
Theresienstadt (Kopist), 122
Thüngen, Adam Sigmund, General, 79
Thürheim, Franz Ludwig, General, 39
Torgau, battle (1760), 102, 139, 141, 142, 199–202
Transylvania, 8, 12, 86–7
(Abensperg und) Traun, Otto Ferdinand, Field-Marshal, 157, 159
Trenck, Franz, Colonel, 68
Trips, Adolph, Lt-Gen, 97

Valenziani, Colonel, 13
Veltetz, Colonel, 177
Versailles, treaty (1756), 164; treaty (1757), 164
Vienna, 8, 9, 16
Visconti, Hannibal, Field-Marshal, 26

Waldenau, Walter, Maj-Gen, 200
Waldhütter, Lieutenant, 204
Wallis, Franz Wenzel, Field-Marshal, 52, 202
Wallis, Georg Olivier, Field-Marshal, 145
Wied, Carl, Lt-Gen, 145, 177, 180
Wiener Neustadt academy, *see* officers, education
Winterfeldt, Hans, Lt-Gen, 45, 102, 182
Wöber, Augustin, 21, 23, 166
Worms, treaty (1743), 157

Zieten, Hans, General, 102, 191, 200
Zittau, bombardment (1757), 182
Zorndorf, battle (1758), 190
Zweibrücken, Friedrich Prince of, Field-Marshal, 190, 197